Few topics in Chinese politics are as significant as the nature, state and prospects of the political regime. While the topic had been unduly understudied for a long period of time, a new generation of scholarship has emerged on this subject. Among others, the book by Hongyi Lai stands out and provides a comprehensive and penetrating analysis on this topic ... . I am confident that his book will make a significant contribution to the study of Chinese politics and may well define the debate on China's political development, governance and model for years to come.

Yongnian Zheng, Director, East Asian Institute,
National University of Singapore

China's Governance Model

Many studies of government in China either simply describe the political institutions or else focus, critically, on the weaknesses of the system, such as corruption or the absence of Western-style democracy. Authors of these studies fail to appreciate the surprising ability of China's government to rapidly transform a once impoverished economy and to recover from numerous crises from 1978 to the present. This book, on the other hand, takes a more balanced, more positive view. This view is based on a study of changes in China's institutions for coping with critical crises in governance since 1978. These changes include better management of leadership succession, better crisis management, improved social welfare, the management of society through treating different social groups differently depending on their potential to rival the Party state, and a variety of limited, intra-party and grassroots democracy. This book applies to the Chinese model the term "pragmatic authoritarianism." It explains changes to and the likely future direction of China's governance model. It compares current risks in China's governance with threats that terminated dynasties and the republic in China over the past four thousand years and concludes that the regime can be expected to survive a considerable period despite its existing flaws.

Hongyi Lai is an Associate Professor in the School of Contemporary Chinese Studies and a Senior Fellow of the China Policy Institute at the University of Nottingham, UK.

China Policy Series

Series Editor
Zheng Yongnian, East Asian Institute, National University of Singapore

China's Governance Model

Flexibility and durability of
pragmatic authoritarianism

Hongyi Lai

Routledge
Taylor & Francis Group

LONDON AND NEW YORK

First published 2016
by Routledge
2 Park Square, Milton Park, Abingdon, Oxon OX14 4RN

and by Routledge
711 Third Avenue, New York, NY 10017

Routledge is an imprint of the Taylor & Francis Group, an informa business

British Library Cataloguing in Publication Data
A catalogue record for this book is available from the British Library

Library of Congress Cataloging in Publication Data
Names: Lai, Hongyi, 1965- author.
Title: China's governance model : flexibility and durability of pragmatic
    authoritarianism / Hongyi Lai.
Description: Abingdon, Oxon ; New York, NY : Routledge, 2016. | Series:
    China policy series ; 44 | Includes bibliographical references and index.
Identifiers: LCCN 2015032481| ISBN 9780415734196 (hardback) |
    ISBN 9780415734479 (pbk.) | ISBN 9781315832654 (ebook)
Subjects: LCSH: Political planning–China. | China–Politics and
    government–1976-2002. | China–Politics and government–2002- |
    Authoritarianism–China. | Political culture–China.
Classification: LCC JQ1509.5.P64 L35 2016 | DDC 320.60951–dc23
LC record available at http://lccn.loc.gov/2015032481

ISBN: 978-0-415-73419-6 (hbk)
ISBN: 978-0-415-73447-9 (pbk)
ISBN: 978-1-315-83265-4 (ebk)

Typeset in Times New Roman
by Taylor & Francis Books

In memory of Lai Jiuzhang (1936–2010)

Contents

PART 4
Conclusion 265

List of illustrations

Figures

Tables

Box

Acknowledgements

I would like to thank Yongnian Zheng for offering a constructive suggestion on the notion of authoritarian flexibility and for positive feedback on the proposal and ideas of my book. I also thank Peter Sowden for his support and patience for my completion of this monograph. I also thank staff at the Routledge for their help and service in the production and promotion of this book. They include Sabrina Lacey, Lucy McClune, Fliss Watts, Laura Brant, and Emily Newsome. I also express my thanks to colleagues in the field to whom I presented some of my ideas in this book, including scholars at the East Asian Institute (EAI) of National University of Singapore, as well as the School of Contemporary Chinese Studies (SCCS), University of Nottingham, UK. I also express my thanks to SCCS. It was in the research leave granted by the SCCS in Spring 2015 (albeit long overdue) that I finally completed this monograph. I also acknowledge the support from the SCCS for covering the indexing expenses via my personal research account. In addition, I would like to express my gratitude to the EAI where I collected some valuable materials and literature for the monograph. I also express thanks to my family members Lisa and Isabella who endured my intensive work on completing and revising the book.

I dedicate my book to my father, who passed away in 2010. Having received an above average education in southern China, he had strong reasoning, writing and speaking skills in his generation. However, his career was much frustrated by the political and social atmospheres of his times. He was entangled in the political taboos in Mao's time by two factors, a weak and formalistic family connection with an uncle who was an officer in the Nationalist army (though my father did not live with his uncle), and the fact that his wife's siblings were in Hong Kong. He was thus unable to advance in his career. Despite his talent and his record of military service, which was a glorious experience in Mao's era, he did a physically very demanding job in harsh conditions at a factory for two decades. Only years after the economic reform was he able to become one of the most able technicians in his manufacturing area in the nation.

I am also grateful that my father, a worker of a state-owned enterprise, arranged for me the best education available in the late Mao era and the early reform period in China. He made his best efforts to ensure that I would not repeat his unfortunate past. The roller-coaster ride in his career and my personal experience makes me appreciate the significance of a proper political and social environment and minimization of prejudices for the full utilization of talents and for social progress.

Foreword

Few topics in Chinese politics are as significant as the nature, state and prospects of the political regime. While the topic had been unduly understudied for a long period of time, a new generation of scholarship has emerged on this subject. Among others, the book by Hongyi Lai has stood out and provided a comprehensive and penetrating analysis on this topic.

The evolution and especially the fate of the Chinese political regime has captivated numerous scholars for decades. Their endeavor is made for both empirical and analytical reasons. Empirically, China has been the most important emerging economy. Since 2011 it has become the second largest economy in the world. In 2014 the International Monetary Fund even declared that China had become the largest economy in the purchasing power parity (PPP) terms. China has wielded enormous economic weight around the world. Combined with the largest population in the world and the second highest military expenditure on the globe, China has become an upcoming superpower whose influence the world has reckoned with in the recent years. Yet behind this facade of the seemingly unstoppable rise of China is the critical role of the Party state led by the ruling party, that is, the Chinese Communist Party (CCP). It is the Party state that holds together a Chinese nation that is stretched cross nearly a continent by size, and meanwhile is strained by social and political discontents, noticeable economic, cultural and linguistic diversities across regions, multiple ethnicities, and simmering ethnic tension in several areas. Should the Party state crumble as some pessimistic analysts have predicted due to various reasons such as infighting among its leaders, failure to democratize, and losses in external conflict, the devastation will certainly spill over its vast borders into the world economy and communities. The type, progress and prospects of the political regime (of which the CCP is the central force) may well hold the final clue for our understanding of China's continuous economic, political and even military rise in the world in the coming decades. Analytically, the fate of the one-party regime in China has challenged political scientists in general and China scholars in particular. Aged 66, the People's Republic of China founded and governed by the CCP is fast approaching the longest reign of a single-party regime, a record of 73 years held by the Communist Party of the Soviet Union. However, scholars are divided over whether the CCP regime has shown clear signs of decay and is heading toward inevitable disintegration soon.

Relatively speaking, the efforts to analyze the nature and evolution of the political regime in China in the reform have been scant when compared to studies of non-democratic regimes elsewhere in the world. The authoritarian regime in the former Soviet Union has been well examined. According to the line of argument by Zbigniew Brzezinski and Gordon H. Skilling, the Soviet political regime had undergone gradual transformation, from totalitarianism under Stalin, to quasi-pluralistic authoritarianism under Khrushchev, to consultative authoritarianism after him, to democratizing and pluralistic authoritarianism under Gorbachev. On the other hand, scholars, especially Guillermo O'Donnell in his 1973 book, had identified and well analyzed bureaucratic authoritarianism, a form of authoritarianism prevalent in Latin America in the 1960s and 1970s.

While in general China scholars in the West agree that Mao's China practiced totalitarianism, there have been few analytical attempts to explore the nature and evolution of authoritarianism in China since 1978. Of course, there have been efforts to characterize operational features of the Chinese bureaucracy. In 1992 Kenneth Lieberthal and David Lampton coined the multi-agency bargaining decision-making process as fragmented authoritarianism. Twelve years late Dali Yang shed a very positive limelight on public administration in China by detailing the progress in transparency, downsizing, accountability, governmental spending, auditing, and anti-corruption.

In the last decade there were several efforts to assess the state of the political regime in China. Three assessments of the regime came to my mind. Andrew Nathan argued for authoritarian resilience in his brief but insightful article in 2003. He pointed to the evolving norms in leadership succession and official promotion, specialization of critical state apparatus, and local elections and institutional channels for grievances. The other two studies were devoted to the institutional renewal and transformations of the CCP, partly out of the reason of the prominent role of the CCP in China's politics and development. David Shambaugh documented the CCP's adaptive efforts in organizational and ideological renewal in his book in 2009. Supplement these two studies was the book by Yongnian Zheng in 2010 on the CCP's transformation of the Chinese political culture of dominance by incorporating modern and democratic elements. With this transformation the CCP has emerged as an organizational emperor and is able to face tough challenges. The relative optimism over the fate of the CCP in the latter two of these three studies somehow responded to a damning but popular view on the regime in 2006 by Minxin Pei. Pei argued that the state was in rapid decay due to corruption, lack of democratization and rule of law, declining fiscal capacity, and insufficient social services.

While these studies, especially the last three studies on the state of the regime, have advanced our understanding on the topic, areas for further exploration are clear and present. First of all, other than Richard Baum's brief and non-systemic efforts in 2006 to characterize the regime as "consultative Leninism", there has been almost no systemic endeavor to survey the nature of the regime and provide a sound characterization and explanation. Second, the argument for or against the regime stability in China has not been held strictly against the empirical tests, namely, how the regime coped with potentially fatal crises or challenges in governance in the past decades. While it is laudable for scholars to pinpoint shortfalls in the regime, it is a far more demanding yet meaningful to assess how well the regime can manage stresses and crises and perform its basic tasks in governance, and how likely the regime can sustain itself. It is of course also challenging to yield an assessment and characterization that withstand the test of the development in the later years. Third, the discussion on the China model has been largely restricted to the developmental state in China. Insufficient attention has been paid to its model of governance.

I am pleased to see that Lai has written a book that well addresses these aforementioned three analytical issues. He has broken new ground in analytical terms by applying the term "pragmatic authoritarianism" to the political regime in China in the reform era, especially since the 1990s. In developing this characterization he is mindful of the existing literature on the variety of authoritarianism. He painstakingly shows the differences between pragmatic authoritarianism in China and other forms of authoritarianism that have been examined in the existing studies. By doing so his work illuminates to non-China scholars the nature of Chinese authoritarianism in a broad context of comparative politics.

Turning to Lai's analysis of the political regime in China, his notion pragmatic authoritarianism is an appealing and very useful concept to capture the evolving political regime in China. It conveys the following important meanings. The Party state that is less concerned with lofty political ideals than practical results of its political endeavors, is willing to adopt good practices and fruitful policies and implant effective institutions from other polities, is flexible in institutional building and is willing to innovate in a high degree. Indeed, the Chinese leaders have made various attempts to remake its ideological formulation (the latest attempt being Xi Jiping's China dream). These formulations have become increasingly practical and echo the Chinese traditional concerns with national strength, individual prosperity, and social harmony. Ideology has thus been much downplayed and has departed from Marxism and Leninism, pointing to the significance of pragmatism in authoritarianism in China. Of course, the ultimate objective of this political pragmatism and institutional flexibility is to ensure the leadership position of the CCP in Chinese politics. This goal can thus limit the type of institutions the CCP is willing to adopt. For example, upgrading the local elections to municipal, provincial and national levels has been out of the question due to the immediate and apparent threats the process may pose for the CCP's control of the local officials and its considerable leverage over local policies.

In explaining pragmatic authoritarianism Lai also examines in detail several major political institutions and a number of key aspects of the operation of the regime in China. Lai has done us a wonderful service by documenting progress in building of state institutions that are critical for the very survival of the regime, including leadership succession and crisis management. Until recently these institutions have not been examined in details, despite their rapid evolution in the recent decades. In doing so, he provides a rare, systemic and up-to-date glimpse on some of the most secretive but critical institutions within the Party state. Meanwhile, he informs us how well these institutions performed before and after the institutional overhaul he describes and how well they respond to critical events and major crises in governance. We can see this point very well in his chapters on leadership succession, crisis management, provision of social services, and pro-growth authoritarianism. Thus his analyses on the political regime are embedded in a conscious judgment of the effects and effectiveness of the institutional building he describes against the actual tests of governance. Through documenting the institutional flexibility of the Party state he thus provides a consistently developed analysis of the durability of the Party state, an issue that has preoccupied a large number of scholars on Chinese politics. In doing so he also relates to the book title cogently.

Throughout the book Lai's analysis is fresh, informative, and balanced. When institutions have been much discussed in the existing literature, he is still able to provide a new, broad-range yet insightful perspective. This point can be clearly seen in his explanation of the unusual mixture of high economic growth and frequent social protests, and his survey of intra-Party and grass-roots democratic initiatives in China. He can deliver such a refreshing examination of these much-studied topics by providing a new analytical angle and by presenting a carefully compiled yet comprehensive summary of the topic/issue.

On the life span of the current regime, arguably the most intriguing and interesting topic in the book, his analysis is no less informative and innovative. He uses political history of China as his data for analyses. By scrutinizing the pattern of longevity of unified regimes after long division and contrasting that of unified regimes after short division, and by examining the causes of collapse of the past unified dynasties and republic, he is able to find new meanings in all-to-familiar political history in China and draws meaningful insights on the life span of the current regime. Undoubtedly, the current regime is one that is unified (in the sense of China mainland) and was set up after a short period of division (that is, after the anti-Japanese war and the civil war). In this sense, some of the factors that benefited unified regimes after a short division may well benefit the current regime. Lai observes that the Party state has yet to confront any of the persistent threats that have caused the eventual downfall of the previous unified regimes, that is, large-scale domestic armed rebellions, devastation from a formidable invading foreign army, and China's severe defeats in major wars against a foreign power. This observation is illuminating as far as the implications of Chinese history for the longevity of the current Party state regime is concerned. It is also exciting to read some of his intelligent conjectures about possible ranges of life spans of the Party state.

I have had the chance to witness some of his endeavors reported in this book. Back in 2001, I was closely involved in an academic conference on social movements in China based on Boston University and hosted by Joseph Fewsmith. At this conference Lai presented an earlier yet much developed version of his chapter on religious policies in China. About a year later, in a conference discussion at the East Asian Institute of National University of Singapore, he offered the point about the life span of unified regimes after short division in the Chinese history. This was one of the key insights in his chapter on the life span of unified regimes and of the Party state in China. As far as I can see, this book is an accumulation of his persistent efforts to interpret China's political development for the past 15 years. I am confident that his book will make a significant contribution to the study of Chinese politics and may well define the debate on China's political development, governance and model for years to come.

Yongnian Zheng
Director, East Asian Institute
National University of Singapore
July 2015

Acronyms and Abbreviations

ACFLU	All-China Federation of Labor Unions
APDLSG	Aiding-the-Poor and Development Leading Small Group
BCCCC	Bishop's Conference of the Catholic Church in China
CBA	Chinese Buddhist Association
CCAC	China Catholic Administrative Committee
CCC	Chinese Christian Council
CCCCCP	Central Committee of the Chinese Communist Party
CCP	Chinese Communist Party
CCPA	Chinese Catholic Patriotic Association
CDA	Chinese Daoist Association
CDC	Center for Disease Control and Prevention
CDIC	Central Disciplinary Inspection Committee
CEC	China Enterprise Confederation (*Zhongguo Qiye Lianhehui*)
CIA	Chinese Islamic Association
CMC	Central Military Commission (an institution of top military command in China)
CPSU	Communist Party of the Soviet Union
CR	Cultural Revolution
DOO	Department of the Organization (of the CCP)
DVC	director of the village committee
FDI	foreign direct investment
FTZ	free trade zone
MCA	Ministry of Civil Affairs
MLA	minimum living allowances
MLSS	Ministry of Labor and Social Security
MULA	minimum urban living allowances
NAMs	nationally-administered municipalities
NCMS	new rural cooperative medical scheme
NCTPMPCC	National Committee of Three-self Patriotic Movement of the Protestant Churches in China (Three-self Church or TSC in short)
NDRC	National Development and Reform Commission
NESRC	National Economic Structure Reform Commission
NGOs	non-governmental organizations

NPC	National People's Congress (the national legislature in China)
NRSP	new rural social pensions
PRC	People's Republic of China
PSC	Politburo Standing Committee (a Party committee comprising of the most powerful leaders in China)
RC	residents committee
RMLA	rural minimum living allowances
SARS	Severe Acute Respiratory Syndrome
SCS	semi-competitive selection
SEZs	special economic zones
SOEs	state-owned enterprises
TC	township chief
TPA	transparency of public affairs
TSC	Three-self Church (see NCTPMPCC)
TSPM	Three-self Patriotic Movement
UEMI	urban employee medical insurance scheme
UEBMIS	urban employees basic medical insurance scheme
URBMIS	urban residents basic medical insurance scheme
USSR	Union of Soviet Socialist Republics (the Soviet Union)
WTO	World Trade Organization

Part 1

Introduction

1 Understanding China's model of governance and development
Improvement without democracy

China, long being the most populous country, has become the second largest economy and the second most influential country in the world. It is expected by some analysts that it may become the largest economy in a decade. Understandably, governance of China profoundly affects this upcoming superpower and the rest of the world. As widely known, the Chinese Communist Party (CCP) dominates the Chinese state (hence it is coined the Party state) and is the pivotal force of governance of China. Inside and especially outside China skepticism over the serious problems in China's governance and structural problems in the Party state abounds. A proper understanding of China's governance, the past trajectory of its evolution, and its likely development is of immense value for the international community as the latter's stake in the well-being of China has grown exponentially over the years.

This book aims to address the question where China is heading politically by examining the major institutional changes in governance in China in the recent decades. I will start with a related topic that has attracted tremendous attention from within and outside China, that is, the so-called China model of development. I will briefly review the debates on the China model that have been waged in Chinese and English among China scholars and observers. I will then move to discuss the debate on the political development and possibility of democratization in China in the Western literature, followed by an overview of the Chinese and English literature on governance in China. The last section is about the theme of the book and of each of the following chapters.

The China model: the Chinese and Western perspectives

By sustaining near double-digit annual economic growth for the past three decades, China has created an economic growth miracle unparalleled in world history in several aspects. First, no other countries have kept growing at an average around 10 percent a year for over three decades. Second, no country has witnessed such a rapid lift in the overall living standard within such a short time. In 2011 per capita disposable incomes of urban and rural houses were over ten times as much as that of 1978. Third, no country has experienced such a drastic decline in the population in poverty. The population with income less than US$2 a day at purchase power parity in China declined from 97.8 percent in 1981 in an early year of reform to merely 27.2 percent in 2009, an incredible decline by 70 percentage points within 28 years.[1] Understandably China's economic and social successes in the course of development have attracted worldwide attention, as well as scholarly analyses.[2] In the following paragraphs I will first sketch the brief history of the academic discussion on the China model of development in and outside China, and then proceed to outline and comment on these viewpoints.

The earliest efforts to popularize the concept regarding the Chinese approach to development were done by the Western analysts. In 2004 the United Kingdom's Foreign Policy Centre published a booklet by Joshua Cooper Ramo entitled *The Beijing Consensus*. Ramo, a former senior editor and foreign editor of *Time* magazine, regarded the Beijing Consensus as an alternative economic development model to the Washington Consensus, which is a pro-free-market policy program the IMF, World Bank and U.S. Treasury have been promoting in developing countries. He claimed that the Beijing Consensus followed three theorems, that is, innovation-driven development, sustainable and equitable economic development that goes beyond per capita GDP growth, and self-determination.[3]

Prompted by the international attention and discussion on the so-called Beijing Consensus Chinese scholars also launched their own discussion on the Chinese approach to development. One of the biggest and earliest efforts was an international academic conference on the Chinese developmental path in Tianjin in August 2005. Jointly sponsored by the Central Translation Bureau of the Central Committee of the CCP, the conference was attended by Joshua Ramo, noted Chinese scholars such as Yu Keping and Zhu Guanglei, accomplished China scholars from the West, such as Joseph Fewsmith and Arif Dirlik, and international scholars and intellectuals such as Samir Amin and David Schweickart. The papers and discussions at the conference were published as a book in Chinese in 2006 entitled *The China Model and the Beijing Consensus*. Clearly, Chinese scholars such as Yu Keping preferred to coin the Chinese path of development as the China Model, and refrained from using the Beijing Consensus largely because the concept was not properly specified.

In the following years the discourse on the topic resulted in three collections of essays in Chinese published in China. They included a book entitled *On the China Model* written by scholars from Renmin University and published by the People's Press in 2007, a book entitled *The China Model* edited by Pan Wei and published by the Central Translation Bureau in 2009, and a book entitled *The Debate on the China Model* published by the Chinese Social Science Press in 2013.

Outside China one of the best efforts to examine the topic were a number of articles published in the *Journal of Contemporary China* (JCC). They were authored by Suisheng Zhao, Barry Naughton, Scott Kennedy, Minglu Chen and David Goodman.[4]

An additional title in the English list of the publications on the topic included a book entitled *The Beijing Consensus* by Stefan Halper. He argued that China's state-directed capitalism and authoritarianism constituted an alternative model of development in the world away from the western model. However, Halper's book has a focus different from the main theme of my book. Instead of investigating in detail how the China model operated at home, which this book focuses on, Halper examined the global influence of China's model of development.[5] Indeed, as he rightly suggested, the Chinese model is seen by a growing number of countries as an alternative to the liberal democracy and free market that Western countries promote. Up to the present the Chinese state has intentionally avoided ostensibly promoting its model of development abroad despite its active initiatives to project its soft power in recent years. Its aim is not to arouse unnecessary hostility from the West that could in return hinder China's further development.[6]

In the following paragraphs I will first outline the Chinese discourse of the China model by examining primarily Chinese authors in the four aforementioned books in Chinese plus a few other commentaries. I will then turn to the English discourse by discussing the books by Ramo, Halper, non-Chinese authors in the aforementioned *The China Model and the Beijing Consensus* and especially the articles from the JCC.

Ramo's characterization of the Beijing Consensus has been criticized intensely by the China scholars within and outside China. Suffice it to say here that his conception of the Beijing Consensus was loose and that his analysis was not accepted by many mainstream scholars in China. As Scott Kennedy suggested, Ramo tried to use the Beijing Consensus to denote an alternative to the Washington Consensus, but the three so-called "theorems" of the Beijing Consensus did not substitute for those in the Washington Consensus. In addition, it is an exaggeration to claim that China has not adopted any contents from the Washington Consensus. Kennedy argued that "China essentially followed eight of the ten elements" of the Washington Consensus.[7]

The three "theorems" of the Beijing Consensus were problematic. The first "theorem" of the Beijing Consensus was largely questionable. China's rapid economic growth has not been based on technological innovation as much as on borrowing of readily available foreign technology. More importantly, China's high growth is possible largely because of its adoption of sound incentive structures and good economic institutions that promote competition among firms and reward hard-working individuals. The second theorem, namely, sustainable and equitable growth, was counter-factual. At the time of the publication of his booklet, China's officials were still mainly emphasizing a rapid growth in GDP often at the expense of the environment and a comfortable life of the public, and China was experiencing serious but still rising income inequality. The third "theorem," i.e, self determination, is a somewhat clumsy term used by Ramo to describe independence of diplomacy and avoidance of a major conflict with the U.S. While it captured an important feature in China's foreign policy, China and the US are closely linked economically, and such an economic interdependence is critical for stable and peaceful ties among these two giants. Importantly up to the present China's leaders realize that it should not mount any challenge to the US leadership in the world, and should not advocate a replacement of the US global agenda such as the Washington Consensus with China's own agenda such as the Beijing Consensus.[8]

In addition, the concept of the Beijing Consensus has simply left out many critical features in China's development. A non-exhaustive list of these elements should include incremental reform instead of shock therapy, national implementation of prior successful local experiments, progression of reform from a basic sector (such as agriculture) to a complex sector (such as manufacture and finance), utilization of China's comparative advantage through promoting labor-intensive manufactured exports, a linkage with the global economy, promotion of non-state enterprises, incremental reform of state-owned enterprises (SOEs), an emphasis on rapid economic growth, improvement of governance and cadre promotion, a stress on political stability, and slow political reform.[9]

Out of these reasons, it is not surprising that many China scholars, be they based in China or in the West, refuse to accept Ramo's concept of the Beijing Consensus. Put straightforwardly, there is no consensus among scholars on the Beijing Consensus. Rather, China scholars prefer to use the term "the China model" to describe the possible components and features in China's path of development. Yu Keping, for example, stated plainly that he did not agree with the use of the Beijing Consensus and that he preferred the concept of the China model, as a consensus implied a widely recognized and agreed program and remedy. Following his definition I use the concept of the China model, which refers to distinctive developmental strategy, institutions and ideas.[10]

Three discernible views emerge in the Chinese discourse on the China model. They can be regarded as three stances on a spectrum. At one end of the spectrum is one group of Chinese scholars who proudly proclaim that the model is substantive, very successful, and sustainable. I term this school the affirmative view. The advocates of the affirmative view include a number of leading scholars on Marxism, such as Cheng Enfu, the Director of the Marxism Research Institute of the Chinese Academy of Social Sciences, incumbent or retired senior officials on ideology such as Yang Huang, the chief editor of *Qiu Shi* (*Seek Truth*), the top Party theoretical journal, Zhu Muzhi, the former Director of the Press Office of the State Council, and Zhao Yao, the Honorary Head of the Chinese Scientific Socialism Society, as well as a few noted scholars of China's politics such as Pan Wei. Cheng proclaimed that the China model has matured and that China has established comprehensive and mature political, economic, social and cultural institutions. Yang, Zhu, Zhao, and Cheng regarded the CCP leadership as one of the core elements of the China model and argued that the success of the China model demonstrated the superiority of socialism to capitalism and the attraction of communism (or in Zhu's view, Chinese socialism) in the long run. They held that the success of the China model suggested that each nation could successfully find its path of development suitable to its national conditions.[11] Pan, a professor in international relations at Beijing University, though briefly admitting the serious errors in economic policies in Mao's era, argued with exuberant confidence and national pride that the China model is a theoretical summary of China's successful exploration for a path of development since 1949 and is based on the continuity of the Chinese civilization.[12] Yun-han Chu, a prominent scholar from Taiwan, also suggested that the China model offered a very useful alternative from the Western approach to development. He argued that China's government has been very effective in eliminating poverty, urban slums and rural land inequality and can be a very meaningful institutional arrangement in achieving substantive instead of procedural democracy that satisfies the need of the people.[13]

At the other end of the spectrum is the view that the China model is problematic and contains severe flaws. This view maintains that the China model faces daunting challenges and that it is too early to call the Chinese path the China model. I term this view the negation school. Advocates of this school include noted economists such as Wu Jianlian and Gao Shangquan, scholars from the Central Party School such as Li Junru, a former Vice President and Xin Ming, a professor at the School, political scientists such as Bao Xinjiang, scholars from leading universities such as Yan Jirong in public administration, as well as noted liberal public intellectuals Li Zehou, Gan Yang, and Yang Jisheng.

The primary reasons for the negation school to reject the concept of the China model are as follows. The model is still evolving and in transition, full of profound flaws and is not sustainable in its current form. Wu Jinglian, one of the advocates of this view, attributed the economic success in China to reform and opening. He criticized the advocates of the China model who claimed that China's economic success originates from the powerful state in the economy as it could mobilize resources to achieve economic growth and accomplish major projects. Wu identified a series of problems and practices in China, including the state's control of tremendous economic resources including land and funding, single-minded reliance on the state's fiscal stimulus to cope with crises, a lack of the rule of law, monopoly of state-owned enterprises in key sectors, official corruption and rent seeking, environmental degradation, inequalities, and problematic practice in maintaining social stability. He suggested that China could degrade into state capitalism, bureaucratic capitalism, or elite capitalism. Gao echoed some of Wu's concerns and called on the government to reduce its interference in the economy and reduce chances for rent seeking. Liberal intellectuals such as Li and Yang, as well as scholars such as Yan Jirong and Bao Xinjiang, agreed with Wu's criticisms that the government's excessive role in the economy had given rise to serious corruption and distortion of the economy such as unstoppable housing prices. These intellectuals and scholars also suggested that political reform, genuine rule of law and protection of human rights were much needed in China if these persistent problems were to be overcome.

Another reason for these scholars of the negation school to reject the concept of the China model is that talking about the model exaggerates China's achievements in the reform era, and would lead to a failure to recognize the need for profound structural and political reforms. For Li Junru, Bao Xinjiang, and Yan Jirong, praise for and hyped talk about the China model could lead to a wrong impression that the model has stabilized, has matured and has become perfect and that this could generate fears or antagonism toward China around the world. For this reason Li, Xin, and Gan prefer to use a more modest and prudent concept such as the China path of development, or in the case of Li, socialism with Chinese characteristics.[14]

In between these two stances is the middle view that the China model exists but is still undergoing adjustment, is in a state of flux and that it has both advantages and disadvantages. I call this stance the cautious view. Scholars under this school include Yu Keping, overseas China scholars Yongnian Zheng and Hongyi Lai, and a number of scholars in China such as Tian Chunsheng and Zhuang Junju. They suggest that the China model does contain distinctive features that differentiate itself from other models or paradigms of development and that it has experienced successes, especially economic ones. However, they also caution that the China model is neither a fixed nor mature one, that it confronts a set of problems, that as a result it needs further improvement, and that it may not be readily replicable elsewhere. Yu regarded the China model as a developmental strategy and the governance model China has adopted in order to further modernization and respond to globalization. He believed that China had paid a heavy price and had accumulated valuable lessons in choosing the strategy and the governance model and that these lessons were valuable for other developing nations.[15] Zheng, Director of the East Asian Institute, National University of Singapore, shared some of Yu's opinions by referring the China model to China's experience and lessons in development. Zheng believed the China model was very meaningful for the developing world. Nevertheless, similar to Pan he expanded the experience to the largely unsuccessful efforts to introduce the command economy in Mao's era. He also treated the China model as one that is still evolving in order to overcome many existing flaws.[16] Lai, who was a China scholar at the University of Nottingham in the UK, believed that rapid economic development, vast improvement of infrastructure, and the success of the Beijing Olympic Games should heighten the attraction of China's model of development as a useful reference for the developing nations. On the other hand, he believed that the China model faced a number of challenges, such as environmental degradation, weak protection of rights, ineffectual checks on official abuse of power, excessive economic power of officials, and preferential treatment of state-owned enterprises at the expense of non-state ones.[17]

Overall the English scholarly discourse on the China model tends to be more critical of the Chinese experience of development. Nevertheless, a consensus among the majority of these scholars is discernible, which is critical of the view that the China model can be an alternative to the Western model of development. For scholars or thinkers critical of capitalism in the Western world, the China model has yet to break out of the developmental paradigm the West has created, though the model offers glimpses of hope to modify the paradigm. Samir Amin, an Egyptian Marxist economist, regarded China's future as uncertain. He pointed to external and internal challenges for China's further development. On the global level the West led by the U.S. has maintained dominant armed forces in the world and exercises its influence through placing its European allies in subordinate positions and subjecting Russia, China, and the Third World countries to dependency. Inside China an alliance between power-holding groups was formed, excluding workers and peasants. In the course of urbanization peasants' entitlements and rights to land could be endangered and they could be marginalized.[18] David Schweickart, a U.S.-based philosopher and a proponent of economic democracy (a form of market socialism), believed that post-Mao China has made good strides toward economic democracy and that the ruling class in China was aware of the deadly consequences of improperly managing the grievances of workers and peasants. He also regarded the China model as an incomplete historical experiment. He argued that most of the developing nations could not achieve as rapid economic growth and poverty reduction as did China.[19]

For China scholars based in the West, China's success has much to do with the unique marriage of a strong state with the market-oriented and globalized economy that is not easily replicated elsewhere. Therefore, it is too ambitious to claim that the China model has offered a resounding alternative to the market-friendly and democratic model of development. The future of the China model is uncertain. The four articles on the topic published in the JCC that are authored by some of the leading China scholars in the West offer a very good sample of the views of China scholars outside China. In the following section I shall outline the political and economic components of the China model and their assessment of these components. I will also supplement their views with insights from the Chinese discourse on the issue and from the English literature on China's reforms (see Box 1.1). Limited space prevents me from systemically surveying the Chinese discourse on the components of the China model.

According to Naughton, Lin, Lai and Tian, the Chinese economy is a mixed one with a multitude of ownership forms. This is thanks to the gradual removal of the restrictions on non-state enterprises in the reform era. Nevertheless, the government is more concerned with creating competition than private ownership. A mixture of various forms of ownership helps stimulate competition, with state ownership dominating non-competitive sectors and private ownership concentrating in competitive sectors. The government also uses state ownership for the greater benefit of society. It does so by allowing SOEs to generate revenue for investment especially investment in infrastructure and public utilities. The government also compels the executives of the SOEs to improve the commercial value of the enterprises by linking their pay with their efforts to maximize the asset values of the enterprises.

High economic growth in China is enabled by heavy investment. In China massive investment is made in infrastructure even ahead of the demand in order to create capacity that can be used gradually. As a result, China has the best infrastructure, such as high-speed rail, expressways, and state-of-the-art airports, among the emerging economies. In addition, the government fully utilizes China's comparative advantage in abundant labor through opening up the economy and promoting labor-intensive exports.

Box 1.1 Components of the China model

Economic Aspects

Initial Conditions

1   Large potential internal market.
2   Relatively healthy and well-trained work force.

Economic Components

1   Mixture of various types of ownership with private ownership dominating the competitive sectors and government ownership non-competitive sectors.
2   Policies aim at promoting competition more than private ownership, though the entry to the market has been eased for non-state ownership after 1978.
3   Public ownership can be used to generate investment and to ensure provision of public goods.
4   Investment-led growth is essential in order to create capacity that can be used gradually later.
5   The government can offset costs for business operation and create business opportunities by investing in infrastructure.
6   Managers of SOEs can be incentivized by linking their pay with their maximization of the asset value of the enterprises.
7   China's comparative advantage is utilized by labor-intensive manufactured exports and through strong linkage with the world economy.
8   Incremental reform is pursued through initial local trials before being spread nationwide.
9   Reform started with a basic sector or aspect such as agriculture before moving to a complex one.
10 Critical pro-market institutions, such as household farming, township and village enterprises (TVEs), private businesses, dual track pricing, and incremental reform of SOEs, originated indigenously, instead of being forcefully transplanted from abroad.

Political Aspects

Initial Conditions

1   Diverse social-economic conditions across provinces.

Political Components

1   The rule of the CCP has been reformed and efforts are made to strengthen the Party's governance capacity.
2   The leadership system has been institutionalized and intra-Party democracy is introduced.
3   Cadre accountability has been improved in order to prevent official mishaps in governance, such as improper handling of epidemics and unrest.
4   National leaders use cadre appointment to jump-start reform in critical provinces (such as Guangdong and Shanghai) and to ensure national unity.
5   Decentralization permits localities and local officials to vie for bold but sound reform efforts and the best economic outcomes.
6   Ability to generate local economic growth has become a core element in the promotion of local cadres.
7   Constitutional reforms help to offer some protection of private property and ownership and the rule of law.
8   The CCP remains the sole ruling party, which values political stability and has so far rejected liberal democracy.

Notes: Under economic aspects, initial conditions, and components 1, 3, 4, 5, 6 and the first half of 2 come from Barry Naughton, "China's Distinctive System: Can It be a Model for Others?", *Journal of Contemporary China*, 2010, 19(65), June, 437–60. Component 7 came from Justin Lin *et al.*, *The China Miracle*. Components 8–9 came from Lai, *Reform and the Non-state Economy in China*. Economic component 10 came from Tian Chunsheng, "'Zhongguo Moshi': Ruhe Lijie – Cong Zhidu Zhuanxing de Shijiao" (How to Make Sense of the "China Model": Angle from Institutional Transition), in Yu Keping *et al.*, eds, *Zhongguo Moshi yu "Beijing Gongshi,"* 21–33. Under political aspects, Components 1, 2, and 3, and part of Component 7 came from Suisheng Zhao, "The China Model: Can It Replace the Western Model of Modernization?" *Journal of Contemporary China*, 2010, 19(65), June, 419–36. Components 4–5 came from Lai, *Reform and the Non-state Economy in China* and Yasheng Huang, *Inflation and Investment Control in China* (Cambridge: Cambridge University Press, 1999). Component 6 came from Susan Whiting, *Power and Wealth in Rural China* (Cambridge: Cambridge University Press, 2001). Component 8 is agreed by virtually all the aforementioned authors in the Chinese discourse on the China model.

As many analysts and scholars have commented, China has followed an incremental reform approach. Reform is usually tested out in selected localities and then is promoted nationwide if it is found successful. A number of important reform measures, such as dual track pricing and gradual reform of SOEs, were conceived indigenously; some reform measures such as household farming and TVEs were even created by the common Chinese. These indigenous reform schemes, which were not directly transplanted from the West, could suit the Chinese conditions well. Reform was also launched initially in a basic sector, such as household farming in agriculture in the late 1970s and the early 1980s. After the reform has proved successful (such as the success of rural reform by the mid-1980s), the state shifted the focus of the reform to a more complex issue (such as reform of urban-based sectors).

Naughton argued that the intermingling between the state and the market was a core component of the economic model of China. The China model may signify a worldwide trend to move away from market fundamentalism and the Washington Consensus and toward an activist and interventionist government in the economy. He was not so optimistic about the applicability of the economic model of China elsewhere. All the economic components that he listed, he argued, entailed important lessons for other developing countries, but none could be easily taken up by these countries.[20]

Turning to the political model of China in the reform era, the main features can be summed up as technical overhauls, instead of fundamental change of the CCP-led political system. The bottom line that China's leaders including Deng Xiaoping and his successors have maintained in the reform era is that the CCP remains the ruling party and that liberal democracy preached by the West should not be accepted. So far no national elections have been held in China to allow non-CCP parties to contest for power.

Within the confines of one party rule by the CCP, nevertheless, many institutional changes have taken place. The ideology and the policies of the CCP have been reformed. The CCP has shifted its focus away from ideological campaigns and class struggle to economic development. It has made efforts to improve its ability to govern the nation. The exercise of leadership (such as the decision making at the State Council) has been institutionalized. A certain degree of transparency and consultation has been introduced within the CCP. The constitution has been amended to advance the political goals of economic modernization and the rule of law. The Party stresses political stability which helps attract investment and economic growth.

Several institutional changes help improve China's governance. Administrative power has been decentralized to localities, encouraging leaders of localities to compete against each other for bold but sound reform schemes in order to attract investment, stimulate growth in the economy and revenue. Officials who are able to generate local economic growth have a much better chance to be promoted. National leaders also use cadre appointment to initiate economic reform in important provinces (such as Guangdong and Shanghai) and to ensure national unity. In the 2000s and especially under the Hu–Wen leadership a degree of cadre accountability has been institutionalized and officials will be punished for their mishaps in governance, such as improper handling of epidemics and unrest.

Suisheng Zhao pointed to the selective learning and ideological-doctrine-free pragmatism in China's approach to modernization. Echoing the observation by Naughton, Zhao saw the marriage of an authoritarian state and the market economy as a unique feature of the China model. Zhao argued that China offers a third way to political development in addition to the Western liberal model of competitive and multiparty election and to the shock-therapy-typed radical embrace of democracy. The Chinese approach is "non-ideological, pragmatic, and experimental." It can be appealing to the poor developing nations. However, the current China model, Zhao cautioned, is transitional, lacks moral appeal and is tainted by environmental degradation and political suppression. Hence he concluded: "[I]t is too early to assert that the China model will replace the Western model of modernization."[21]

Regardless of their agreement or disagreement with, or optimism, caution or pessimism over the China model, virtually all the aforementioned authors agree that a strong, authoritarian and developmental state plus a market economy have been the essence of the China model. There has been a strong global movement toward democracy toward the end of the Cold War. In this context the sustainability of the authoritarian state in China has been questioned by many analysts, especially those who are not China scholars. Despite the fact that the Chinese state has overseen rapid economic growth for over 35 years, as an autocracy it can be politically fragile. Once the political regime gives away, the so-called China model as we know it will go away. This political feature thus constitutes the most vulnerable aspect of the economic and political models of China.

In the view of advocates of democracy, the fragility of the Chinese authoritarian regime is underscored by breakdowns and transformations of numerous authoritarian regimes since the late 1980s. These events, which are often mentioned in relation to political change in China, include the sudden democratization of the former Communist bloc in the former Soviet Union and Eastern Europe as well as the democratic transformation of authoritarian regimes in East Asia and Southeast Asia in the 1980s and 1990s, especially South Korea, Taiwan, the Philippines, and Indonesia, and the dramatic events of the Arab Spring from December 2010 to May 2014. During these events a number of governments or ruling parties, after witnessing decades of impressive high economic growth, were swept away from power or confronted strong domestic opposition. This happened in a variety of ways, including mounting popular protests, creeping democratization, and/or rebellion from sub-national governments. As a result of these changes, these countries have entered years or even decades of political and economic upheavals. As a result, many political and business leaders, as well as the intellectual, journalist, and analyst circles were caught off-guard and were struggling to make sense and to cope with these sudden changes.

Given the gigantic demographic, economic, and political weight China carries in the world, it is imperative that we have a good understanding of political development in China in the recent decades and the likely direction of future political development. For example, if political instability erupts in China a massive exodus of Chinese immigrants who can afford to flee with their considerable wealth and with formal immigration status and refugees who escape with minimum income alone and need to seek external protection will put unbearable pressures on its neighbors as well as many advanced economies in the world.

There have been various views on where China's Party state will be heading, ranging from imminent collapse through smooth democratization to strong resilience. In the following section I would like to review and assess several outstanding perspectives. I will start with the social-economic conditions for democracy and the perspective on China's possible transition to democracy. Then I will review the main perspectives in the circle of China studies on China's political development.

Is China ready to transition to democracy?

Whether or not democratization will take place in China has been a major topic of interest for policymakers as well as China scholars. The literature on democratization has long emphasized social-economic causes for democracy. One set of theories postulates that economic development would lead to demand for and emergence and consolidation of democracy. Viewed in this light, economic and social conditions may be ripe for a transition to democracy in China.

In the past quarter of century, China's economy has undergone phenomenally rapid modernization. From 1978 to 2010 it chalked up 9.9 per cent of growth per year, the highest in the world, and its gross domestic product (GDP) grew by nearly 19 times. In 2010 China's GDP in current price surpassed Japan to become the world's second largest, only next to the U.S.

Concomitant with breakneck economic growth is a rapid surge in Chinese living standards. From 1978 to 2010 China's GDP per capita grew by 14.7 times.[22] In terms of per capita gross national income (GNI) China improved its worldwide rank from the 175th out of 188 economies in 1978 to the 112th out of 213 in 2012. In other words, China ascended miraculously from the 93rd percentile in 1978, the bottom of the league table of nations, to the 53rd percentile in 2012, an average level of per capita GNI.[23] In the period of 1978 to 2010, the Engel coefficient of rural households, which measured the share of food expenses in these households' expenditure, declined from 68 percent of total consumption to 41 percent; the Engel coefficient of urban households declined from 58 percent to 36 percent. The most beneficial outcome of China's rapid growth for the Chinese people is the reduction of poverty. In the countryside alone, the share of the population below the official poverty line decreased from 40 percent in 1980 to about 14 percent by the mid-1990s.[24] In 2009 only 11.8 percent of the Chinese lived below the international line of poverty of $1.25 a day.[25] Most Chinese have moved beyond a life of mere subsistence. In the cities, electronic appliances, computers, cell phones, internet, automobiles, and until recent years, even modern housing ownership have become accessible for average income earners.[26]

Rapid economic growth has also brought forth modernization of the society. The population is being urbanized. In 2010, for the first time in history 50 percent of the Chinese permanently resided in the cities, up from the 21 percent in 1982.[27] Back in 2002 46.9 percent of urban residents surveyed in China identified themselves as middle class. The CASS survey in 2001, on the other hand, suggested that 5.6 percent of the population belonged to the upper middle stratum, 14.3 percent the middle stratum, and 28.7 percent the lower middle stratum.[28]

Rapid economic growth has also greatly facilitated telecommunications. In 2010 on average each urban household had 1.4 color TV sets and each rural household had 1.1 color TV sets. The majority of the Chinese can thus obtain news about the nation and the outside world through television.[29] Moreover, the population of internet users in China has been expanding rapidly, from 0.62 million in 1997 to 410 million in 2010.[30] Nowadays urban Chinese have easy access to the internet either at home, at their office, or at internet shops at many corners of the cities.[31] Thus, an increasing number of urban and rural residents can obtain news and political information from the internet. They can even access views critical of the government or its policies, as many Chinese nowadays vent their political grievances on microblog and internet chatrooms. Furthermore, the common ownership of fixed line phones and mobile phones has greatly facilitated the spread of information on political events and especially inter-personal discussion on policies and political issues. In 2010 as high as 81 percent of the urban households in China had a fixed-line telephone, and each urban household had about two mobile phones (1.88 to be exact). Even in the countryside, communications have ceased to be a problem. As much as 61 percent of the rural households had access to a fixed line phone, and each rural household had at least one (1.4 to be exact) mobile phone.[32]

All these attributes of modern society, including a lower-middle level of income by international standards, urbanized population, high literacy, a sizable and expanding middle class, easy communication, convenient and affordable transportation, and a dynamic and commercialized modern media, seem to bode well for democracy in China. As Lipset argued, a society will naturally embrace democracy once the population attains a high literacy rate, reaches a certain level of affluence and becomes fairly urbanized. The rising economic standard and urbanization will produce an expanding middle class that is conscious about their economic interests and social rights and yearns for political participation. High literacy will give rise to a confident, discerning and informed constituency that can exercise its political rights and make prudent political choices.[33] In the case of China all these favorable factors are present. One can add that the popularization of mass media, such as newspapers, magazines, the internet and especially television, gives average Chinese immediate access to news and political information that in return enables them to make sound political judgments.

Indeed, when compared to India and Indonesia, the two largest and most populous democracies in the developing world, China fares very favorably in its level of social and economic development. According to the World Bank, China's per capita gross domestic product (GDP) reached $6,091 in 2012, about four times as much as that of India, and nearly twice that of Indonesia. In terms of purchasing power parity (PPP), China's per capita GDP reached US$9,233 in 2012.[34] Przeworski, Alvarezk, Cheibub and Limgongi asserted in their well-known elaborate and extensive study of democracy and development: "Above $6,000, democracies are impregnable and can be expected to live forever."[35] This seems to bode well for any prospective democracy in China. China also surpasses Indonesia and India in reducing mass poverty. During 2009–2010, merely 27.2 percent of the Chinese lived below the international poverty line of $2 a day, far lower than the 68.8 percent for India and slightly lower than the 46.1 percent of Indonesia.[36] In 2010 as high as 94 per cent of Chinese adults can read, 31 and 1 percentage points higher than that in India and Indonesia, respectively.[37]

A number of observers of China, even top leaders in the West, have also cherished the democratic prospects for a rapidly growing China. In engaging China and helping it to enter the World Trade Organization (WTO), President Bill Clinton believed that a rising living standard and integration with the world economy would propel China to walk down the path of democracy, just as Taiwan and South Korea have done in previous decades.[38] President Clinton confidently spoke of the inevitable democratization in China that was driven by social and economic changes inside China and by information from outside in the following terms: "I believe that the impulses of the society and the nature of the economic change will work together, along with the availability of information from the outside world, to increase the spirit of liberty over time ... I don't think that there's any way that anyone who disagrees with that in China can hold that back. I just think it's inevitable, just as inevitably the Berlin wall fell."[39] His successor President G.W. Bush was also convinced that further economic development and external trade of China would open the gateway for democracy there. In arguing for granting China normal trade relations (NTR) in May 2000, the first compelling reason he listed related to liberty in China. He proclaimed as follows: "Trade with China will promote freedom ... . Economic freedom creates habits of liberty. And habits of liberty create expectations of democracy."[40]

Among the China scholars, Bruce Gilley delivered the parallel argument. He suggested that the Chinese elites had seen the virtue of gradual transition toward democracy in order to avoid institutional collapse. He predicted that "regime-led extrication" would be the "most likely path from power for the CCP."[41]

Scholarly views on political development in China

In the last two decades there have been a number of published works on the institutional changes, the state of governance, and the direction of political development in China. China scholars disagree sharply over the state of the Chinese state, especially the state of political institutions in China and where China is heading. Five views have emerged. Their views relate to two dimensions: (1) the likelihood of democratization in China, and (2) the state of governance, especially whether China is experiencing improvement in governance. Accordingly four main views have emerged, depending on their view along these two dimensions (Table 1.1). They are (1) governance conducive to democratic transition, (2) an imminent transit to democracy, (3) authoritarian resilience, and (4) degeneration into malaise and even collapse. The fifth school of scholars, which is not listed in Table 1.1, take a cautious and mixed stance on both aforementioned dimensions. Each of these views will be discussed below.

In the upper left cell of the table is the most optimistic view on political development in China, which I term governance-conducive-to-democracy. This school of scholars holds that China has experienced impressive improvement in governance and has a bright prospect for democratization. Dali Yang, one of the two most vocal advocates of the view, argued that despite limits in democratization there had been a multitude of improvements in China's governance. This school delivers a very positive verdict on the improvements in governance in China. These improvements included enhancement of fiscal prowess and market order, crackdown and decrease in corruption, administrative downsizing, accountability of civil servants, greater transparency especially in administrative discretion and spending, and increased legislative oversight and government audit. Yang ended his study with a high note: "[T]he governance reform being undertaken to improve the efficiency, transparency, and accountability of the administrative state will prove indispensable for the fledging democratic polity if and when elite politics does make the democratic turn. … The reconstitution of the Chinese state thus has fundamental implications for the expansion of liberty and democracy."[42] Suzanne Ogden pushed this view even further. She claimed that driven by four forces China was making decent strides away from totalitarianism toward democracy. These four forces included the Chinese political culture, increasingly institutionalized pluralistic interests in the wake of economic development, China's yearning to gain international respect, and the leaders' belief in embracing an open and transparent society to curb the politically fatal corruption.[43]

In the upper right cell of Table 1.1 is the school of scholars who believe in China's democratic transition in the wake of a deepening crisis in governance, which has been discussed briefly. Bruce Gilley (2004), the most vocal advocate of the school, argued that many of the Chinese elites believed in the virtue of gradual transition in coping with the looming crisis in governance and that China will transition incrementally to democracy.

In the lower left cell are advocates of authoritarian resilience. They have a pessimistic view on democratization but an affirmative view on the

Table 1.1 Scholarly perspectives on political development in China

		State of Governance	
		Improved governance	*Deteriorating governance*
Likelihood of democracy	Democratization likely	Governance-conducive-to-democracy (Yang); Decent progress toward democratization (Ogden)	Democratic transit (Gilley)
	Democratization unlikely	Authoritarian resilience (Nathan; Shambaugh; Lieberthal)	Authoritarian degra- dation (Pei; Saich); autocratic collapse (Chang)

Note: The mixed stance on the state of China's governance is not shown. It is probably toward the center of the table.

adaptability of the autocratic regime in China. One of the earliest proponents of this view is Andrew Nathan. Nathan postulated that the Chinese author- itarian regime had consolidated itself since 1989 through at least four insti- tutional changes. These changes included the emergent norms in succession politics, an increasing emphasis on meritocracy in political promotion, and specialization of agencies within the regime into clusters in charge of ideology, economic affairs, legislative affairs, and the military. In addition, he observed that the local elections, especially village elections, and institutional channels for complaints by citizens (such as the court, the bureau of letters and visits and media) have served as institutions for people to have input into politics and policies. Nathan concludes that it was possible that "authoritarianism is a viable regime."[44] Shambaugh surveyed the major changes in the CCP in order not to be swept away in the democratization tidal waves like its counterpart in the former Soviet Union. These changes included a systemic analysis of causes for the collapse of the Soviet Union, adoption of effective policies of successful ruling parties elsewhere in the world, rebuilding the Party's ideology, ease of factional conflict within the leadership, training of cadres and enhancing their compe- tence, rebuilding the local Party organizations, strengthening Party discipline and stepping up the fight against corruption, expanding extra-Party consultation, and introducing intra-Party democracy. He concluded in a guardedly upbeat note on the CCP by stating: "[T]he CCP is adapting fairly (but not entirely) effectively to meet many of these challenges... thereby sustaining its political legitimacy and power. Whether the CCP can continue to make the necessary adaptations and enact the necessary reform is, of course, an open question. So far, so good – but this is no guarantee of continued success."[45] Other scholars who voiced a similar view included Richard Baum. Baum saw that the CCP resorted to "consultative Lenin- ism" in grappling with the pressure for democratization through "substituting paternalistic consultation for autonomous political participation, co-optation for representation, advice for empowerment, and consensus-building for the clash of conflicting interests."[46] However, Baum was far more pessimistic than Nathan and Shambaugh. Baum cited Bruce Bueno de Mequita and George W. Downs who found from a study of a large data set that by ensuring considerable economic growth, providing administrative services, but restricting coordination services such as freedom in media, authoritarian regimes could delay the start of democratization for a full decade or longer. Baum noted in 2006 that in this regard China's consultative Leninism might have already been "living on borrowed time."[47] Kenneth Lieberthal, whose view fell under the category of authoritarian resilience, will be discussed in a coming section on governance.

The lower right cell of Table 1.1 is the most critical view of China's state during reform. Minxin Pei has eloquently articulated the negative assessments of politics in China, which clashed directly with Yang's optimistic portrayal. Pei argued that with only partial economic reform but no political reform, China was trapped in a quandary of transition. As the CCP refused to democratize in order to maintain its grip on power, a host of problems and crises had emerged. They included rampant official corruption; eroding state capacity in terms of revenue extraction, insufficient provision of social services, and weak enforcement of laws and rules. They also included rising strains in societal-state relations revealed in rising inequality, escalating tension, loss of social values, emergence of an elitist coalition and marginalization of lower classes. He painted a very grim picture of the prospects of the Chinese state.[48] In a book published years ahead of Pei, Gordon Chang issued an apocalyptic prediction on China. His book offered a preview of malfeasance, broken institutions, disintegrating social order, and political suppression of China. He foresaw growing popular resentments against corruption, unemployment, economic decline in the wake of China's entry to the World Trade Organization, and especially mainland China's defeat in its war against Taiwan. He predicted that popular uprisings would eventually lead to the collapse of the Party state.[49]

Quite a number of scholars, on the other hand, take a cautious stance (the third view) in between the optimists and the pessimists. Zheng argued that the Chinese state had adapted to a large extent to globalization. It promoted the expansion of the entrepreneurial class, reformed and streamlined the state bureaucracy and SOEs, strengthened its fiscal capacity, and coordinated redistribution of social interests to ease social discontent. However, unlike Yang, Zheng cautioned that Chinese leaders' reluctance to implement the rule of law and democracy might limit the progress of the rebirth of the Chinese state.[50]

Among the above first two views, the democratic transition school seems too optimistic. All the paramount leaders in China in the reform era, including Deng Xiaoping, Jiang Zemin, Hu Jintao and now Xi Jinping, have categorically and vehemently rejected the idea of liberal democracy as well as open and multiparty elections. With this political conservatism prevailing in Chinese politics there is little chance that China would democratize even if it is plunged in a governance crisis.

The two other schools have the virtue of identifying the strengths and weaknesses in China's governance. The governance-conducive-to-democracy proposition by Yang highlighted China's impressive achievements in its efforts to

revamp political institutions and to adjust to an increasingly marketized economy and rising social demands. The authoritarian degradation argument made
by Pei, on the other hand, pointed to the severe limits of the authoritarian
regime. Nevertheless, it is clear that both only focus on one aspect, that is,
paralyses versus improvement in the institutions, and that they ignore the other
dimension. Therefore, their verdicts seem simplistic. Overall, pessimistic analysts like Pei tend to overlook improvement in governance and simply
ignore newly-built modern state institutions in China. In contrast, optimists
like Yang and Ogden like to shed light on the pleasant side of Chinese politics
and play down the grave potential risks in China's governance. Hence in their
analyses they seem to be unbalanced and lose sight of development in the
opposite direction.

Advocates of authoritarian resilience such as Nathan and Shambaugh have
chosen a prudent stance by examining areas of China's institutional progress
as well as deficiencies. Their approach is more balanced and their conclusion
more sensible. Nevertheless, their analyses can be more robust and substantial
through careful analyses of changes in institutions and provisions of programs
critical to the sustainability of the regime in China. Among institutions critical to the survival of the Party state, Nathan offered a helpful but sketchy
analysis only of leadership succession. However, he made no mention of other
institutions as well as social and economic governance. Shambaugh, on the
other hand, focused mainly on the interpretation by the CCP of the causes of
the collapse of communism in the European bloc and its renewal of ideology
and organization. He has largely left out institutions critical to the Party state,
such as leadership succession, management of the society and the provision of
public goods. Baum, while offering an insightful characterization of the Chinese
regime and a helpful global perspective of the longevity of authoritarian
regimes, also did not investigate the numerous changes in these institutions. Nor
did these authors explore the life span of the current political regime from a
perspective of China's history.

Views on governance in China

While China scholars based in the West acutely look for any signs of democratization in China in the last two decades, scholars in China, especially those
who have close contact with the policy makers and who shape the discourse on
political reform in China focus mainly on improvement in governance. Good
governance, as a concept, has gained worldwide attention among both policy-
making and analytical circles since the publication of the landmark book
entitled *Governance and Development* by the World Bank in 1992. In this
aforementioned book it was prescribed that the key to sustained economic
growth was good governance, i.e. comprised of official accountability (where
officials were held accountable for their actions), the rule of law (implying governance by law and "not by whims of men"), and transparency (whereby "economic actors have access to relevant, timely, and reliable information"). Since

then the World Bank has been trying to institute these principles for governance in its projects of aiding the developing countries. In the subsequent years the notion of good governance was also embraced by a number of Chinese scholars who shaped the thinking of Chinese leaders. For this reason it is useful to turn our attention first to the Chinese discourse on governance in China, followed by the English academic literature on China's governance.

There have been two noticeable effects of the World Bank-induced discourse on good governance in China since the 1990s. Chinese economists started to heed corporate governance, and Chinese political analysts were more interested in the applicability and the contents of good governance in politics. Yu Keping, the then Director of Contemporary Research Institute at the Central Translation Bureau of the Central Committee of the Chinese Communist Party (CCCCP), suggested during 1999–2002 that in the Chinese political context criteria for assessing good governance included legitimacy, transparency, accountability, the rule of law, responsiveness, effectiveness, public political participation, order and stability. The detailed list of criteria he supplied also included plurality, human rights and citizenship, supervision of the Party and government, intra-Party democracy and cooperation between the CCP and the "democratic parties" (or "satellite parties" coined in the West), and civil organizations. He has called on Chinese elites to make political progress and forge incremental political reform along these criteria, especially by heeding intra-Party democracy.[51]

According to Yu, a number of political reforms had helped move China toward incremental democracy. They included the separation of the Party from the administrative and executive branch and from enterprises, the rise of the civil society, the proposal of the rule of law as a political goal, and village and grass-roots elections. He also took note of the efforts toward good governance at the local level, including greater transparency in governmental affairs, improvement in the quality of public services, an improved process for selecting officials, the expansion of elections, and "improvement of administrative efficiency and the promotion of 'clean government'."[52] Yu's view resembled that of Ogden by declaring that China was progressing toward democracy incrementally. This is obviously too upbeat given the Chinese leaders' stress on the inapplicability of the Western liberal democracy for China. As an agent for change in governance in China, Yu also spearheaded the organization of the annual awards of Local Governmental Innovation Prize since 2000. The award aims to promote efforts toward good governance and democracy at the local level.

Since 1997 the CCP has gradually re-defined its role as a ruling party in a series of documents and speeches, abandoning its previous mission as a revolutionary party. In the report delivered to the Sixteenth Party Congress in 1997 the then General Secretary Jiang Zemin proclaimed that the CCP would have to improve its capacities to lead and govern the nation and to build itself into a strong party. After the Sixteenth Party Congress Zeng Qinghong, a member of the Standing Committee of the Politburo, spoke to a group of officials of the ministerial and provincial ranks upon their graduation of their training program at the Central Party School. He urged them to help the Party to strengthen its governing capacities. These endeavors culminated in a special resolution entitled the *Decision of the CCP Central Committee on Enhancing the Party's Ruling Capacity* passed by the Fourth Plenary Session of the Sixteenth Party Congress in September 1994. The document designated the improvement of governance and the Party's governing capacity as a major task in the rebuilding of the Party.[53]

As Shambaugh argued, these efforts by the CCP to improve governance reflected its painful soul-searching lessons after the ousters of the communist parties from power in the former Soviet Union and Eastern Europe in the early 1990s.[54] Viewed in this light promoting good governance without introducing full-fledged democracy has become a politically imperative but safe option for the CCP to avoid these failing precedents.

Governance in China has also attracted a growing stream of literature from China scholars who are based outside China, especially in the United States. Some of them aimed to provide an overview of governance and its evolution in the reform era and to enhance our understanding of governance in China. Under this category two of the monographs in English have arguably gained much more attention than others. In one of the earliest examinations of governance and mechanisms in China under reform published in 1995 and lightly updated in 2003, Kenneth Lieberthal provided an insightful view of the key organizational structure in the Party state in China, especially the horizontal and vertical clusters known as *kuai* and *tiao*, power structures at the national and local levels, and the Party's control of the government. In a survey of governance in China which was published later (first in 2001) and updated in 2004 and 2011, Tony Saich gave an overview of the governing apparatus at the national and local levels, the state's management of the society, political participation and protests, as well as economic, social and foreign policies.[55] Lieberthal and Saich differed in their opinions over the prospects of the Party-state. Lieberthal observed optimistically in 1995 that the CCP would adopt new policies regarding political succession and social welfare, which had been borne out. He suggested that the CCP might allow other parties to organize support and contest in elections without giving up its political dominance, which did not occur. He foresightedly observed: "China is unlikely to experience either national disintegration or the full development of democracy during the 1990s." Saich, however, is far more pessimistic and seems to side with Pei by highlighting largely insufficient adaptation of political institutions to make the state accountable. He declared: "Without further reform, it is hard to see such a system providing the kind of stability that will produce long-term economic growth," even though he claimed that the system has been most successful in generating high economic growth.[56] Indeed, the GDP growth in China decelerated from 14.2 percent in 2007 to a respectable 7.7 percent in 2012–13 and to 6.9 percent in 2015. The slower growth partially has to do with one of the reforms introduced by President Xi since 2013, namely, the ani-corruption drive which has dampened the official entreprenuerial urge to generate growth. Saich's concern thus has not fully materialized.[57]

Four other books in English are devoted specifically to examining and assessing the renewal of governance in China in the recent decade. The first book was mainly about public and fiscal administration, the second one was about economic governance, the third book was devoted to mostly social governance plus political governance at the grass-roots level, and the fourth book covered mainly political governance.

Bill Chou examined the trend in public administration in China in contrast to that in the OECD countries and was interested in governing capacities and policy making. He analyzed the following selected aspects of China's governance, that is, citizen participation in urban China, fiscal reform, reform of spending control, civil service reform, and implementation of administrative licensing law. He observed that while decentralization of authority for better meeting of the need of citizens was the dominant trend in the OECD countries, institutional reform in China had emphasized centralization of authority in order to cope with the problems of decentralization and had followed a top-down approach. The reform was flawed as the need of local constituencies was not fully respected, as spending control induced officials to bypass official regulations, and after fiscal reform less developed localities were cash strapped, payroll expenditure burdens remained, and fiscal transfer was not well institutionalized.[58]

The second and third of the four aforementioned books were volumes that surveyed various aspects of and changes in China's governance. A study by the OECD systematically documented improvement as well as limits in China's administrative, taxation, fiscal, corporate, and regulatory governance.[59] It acknowledged institutional improvements and pointed out deficiencies in these arenas. The other volume comprising studies by some of the leading China scholars examined China's progress and limits in modernizing its civil services, managing state-societal relations, introducing villages and township elections, and strengthening the rule of law.[60] It argued that reform of the political institutions had been diluted by the Party's tendency to maintain its grip on power and deeply webbed interests.[61] Nevertheless, the editor for the volume did not categorize the current state of the Chinese governance and was less certain about its prospects: "It is hard to speculate with any certainty upon the prospects for governance... However, if there is one certainty for China's future, it is that governance matters."[62]

In one of the latest available collections of papers published in 2008, leading China scholars surveyed political changes and prospects for democracy in China. Their views echoed some of the aforementioned five views. In particular, Cheng Li voiced a view similar to that by Ogden. In analyzing the careers and views of the fifth generation of leaders who would lead China from late 2012 onwards, Li suggested that they might pursue political reform that would lead to democratic elections in the next decade or so. Pei continued to express his dismay at the unconstrained corruption in China and foresaw that either the

CCP would allow the media, the civil society and the judiciary to check on corruption, or would collapse and permit a new oligarchy to form. Nathan, Shambaugh, Jacques deLisle and Dorothy Solinger delivered a verdict on China similar to authoritarian resilience. Nathan argued that China's leaders were interested in improving the Party's rule to make the authoritarian regime fairer and more effective. Shambaugh noticed the CCP's "eclectic borrowing" of useful practices and institutions from ruling parties of all types. DeLisle held that the Chinese leadership wanted to substitute the rule by law for democracy and restrain the reinforcing effects between the rule of law and democracy. Solinger argued that the regime had entered an alliance with the upper class while keeping those lower classes "minimally satisfied but still politically excluded."[63] Therefore, it followed from the analyses of the last four scholars that the Party state would aim to improve several aspects of its governance of the country but would not push forth democratization.

In addition, there are a number of studies on political or governmental institutions that had an effect on China's governance. The topics that were covered included elite politics, China's institutional setups, Party and administrative apparatus, local governance, civil-military relations, political economy, and state-intellectual interaction.[64] The institutional improvements that these scholars pointed out included emerging norms to reduce the damage in leadership conflict, decentralization, redefined central-local authority, formulating political procedures and laws, incremental enhancement of legislative power, village elections, regional representation within the national leadership, administrative rationalization and modernization, and divestiture of the military from business. The rise of over-lapping economic and political elites and the state's handling of relations with labor were also discussed.[65]

This body of literature on governance in China sheds light on a range of institutional changes that have taken place in China since 1978. The literature also offers an assessment of some of these institutional changes and evaluates the improvement in governance against the main criteria of good governance proposed by the World Bank. It thus significantly enriches our understanding of the topic.

Nevertheless, there are obvious limits in the literature on governance in China. First and foremost, the literature has made insufficient efforts to examine critical and complex changes up to the present in institutions that are very critical to the survival of the political regime in China. These institutions include leadership succession, crisis management, and to a lesser extent, management of organized social forces, and provision of social welfare programs. Second, despite the acknowledgement from scholars such as Shambaugh that the CCP has made considerable efforts to learn from the collapse of the Communist Party of the former Soviet Union, the existing literature has failed to reveal a number of formidable challenges the CCP has managed to avoid since 1978. These challenges included widespread grievances from inland peasants and urban unemployed in the 1990s and the early 2000s, the SARS epidemic and ineffective crisis management, a reviving society in the wake of economic reform, and to a lesser extent, the legitimacy crisis for the CCP in the late Mao era, and failed leadership succession until 1992 and its entanglement with the most dramatic and destructive crises for the CCP, such as the Cultural Revolution and the 1989 Tiananmen movement. Third, the bulk of the literature covers mainly the period up to 2002, and in the case of Shambaugh and Chou, up to 2007. Although Saich included an update by the late 2000s his book in 2011 was a sketchy overview, instead of in-depth study of governance in China. Fourth, most of these studies were empirically-minded. With the likely exception of Shambaugh and Nathan these studies failed to clarify the nature and direction of China's institutional changes. They also failed to suggest exactly where the Chinese regime is heading and into what form it is evolving. Fifth, very few studies provided a historical perspective of the durability of the current regime by examining the causes for the collapse of the other regimes or dynasties that ruled a unified mainland China. Sixth, many of these studies left the audience much to desire in understanding the dynamics behind major and important events and developments in Chinese politics. China experts often clash with each other over how to interpret the institutional changes they discuss. As we have noticed, the concept of the China model involves a wide range of issues and disciplines regarding contemporary China, including politics, the economy, society, culture, and laws. Therefore, it is necessary to select a suitable angle in order to pursue a fruitful and manageable enquiry into the operation and sustainability of China's current path of political and economic development.

Making sense of China's model of governance

As rightly noted by the aforementioned scholars on governance in China a key dimension for a productive scrutiny of the China model is governance. By governance I mean the state's management of the country and its efforts in promoting economic, political, and social development. Governance could involve the state's management of the economy (economic governance), of the society (social governance), and political issues (political governance). Good governance refers to effective, efficient, publicly acceptable, and sustainable management of the nation. As will be mentioned, good governance often entails the legitimacy of the state, official accountability, effective policy implementation, considerable political transparency, a low level of corruption, and a high degree of regime stability.

By examining governance, we can come to a good understanding of the way the Party state governs this rising superpower and the ability of the Party-state to sustain its role to lead the course of modernization and cope with various problems. In my view governance is a single aspect of the China model that is critical to the success of China in the past and future decades. Many of the serious problems analysts have identified in the China model, such as corruption, abuse of power, weak protection of rights, and environmental degradation, can be traced to governance, or specifically, flawed institutional arrangements in the state structure and ineffectual enforcement of the rules.

Crucial to our understanding of the China model and China's governance are a number of important yet unanswered questions: In what direction is China's political system likely to evolve? What has been the improvement in key institutions critical to the survival of the Party state? What has the Party state done socially and economically to defuse public grievances? What has been changed in the Party state's management of crises? What has the CCP done regarding the promotion of democracy? Has the Party state lived well beyond its borrowed time? Answers to these questions cannot only help us to understand Chinese politics, but also its future development. They can also help us to understand institutional forces that help to generate dramatic crises and responses in China. They can help us, hopefully, to reduce the "surprises" or "shocks" in our observations and establish a sounder expectation of Chinese politics. This would also mean fewer fatal errors in making decisions in policy, business decisions, and even academic and journalistic arguments regarding China.

The issue of the model of governance in China and its sustainability has great implications. China has become the world's second largest economy in 2010 and the second most influential nation. It is widely expected to be the largest economy in terms of nominal GDP within one decade. The state and prospects of governance and the sustainability of China's governance model have vast global implications, including tremendous effects on global investment, international trade, and economic growth in developed nations such as the United States, Japan and the European Union and in many developing countries. The events in the Middle East in 2011, however, exposed the fragility of autocracy. It is thus important to understand the durability and adaptability of the political regime in China.

In the following chapters the aforementioned questions regarding political development in China are addressed, the model of governance in China is investigated and major changes in the critical institutions are examined. The central argument in the book is that pragmatic authoritarianism is emerging in China. This type of authoritarianism is flexible and politically calculative. It is also pragmatic in its practical aim of sustaining one-party rule and averting major crises through attempting to overhaul governance without resort to democracy. Pragmatic authoritarianism involves pragmatic yet authoritarian forms of economic, social and political governance. Economically, pragmatic authoritarianism seeks to deliver robust economic growth through the state's mobilization of economic resources and its pursuit of economic reform. In addition, the state provides economic aid to disadvantaged segments of the population. The objective is to defuse popular discontents, ward off popular upheavals, and bolster legitimacy. Socially, pragmatic authoritarianism means tolerance of non-organized, non-political and non-disruptive social activities even if they involve tens of millions of people. Meanwhile, the state tries to coopt and regulate organized social activities and groups into officially sanctioned organizations. If these organized social groups show their defiance, they will be met with the state's restriction and crackdowns, as in the case of Falun Gong and the underground Catholic Church. Politically, pragmatic authoritarianism entails efforts in overhauling institutions critical to the survival of the regime, such as leader-ship succession and crisis management, ensuring that the regime will function smoothly in the case of major crises. In addition, the state allows limited channels of expression and political participation in order to divert pressures for democrati-zation. These channels include grass-root and intra-Party democracy as well as expression of grievances on the internet and occasionally through media reports.

Organization of the book

Part I, Introduction, consists of Chapters 1 and 2. Chapter 2 develops the analytical and theoretical framework of this study. It surveys the main variants of authoritarianism and assesses their relevance to contemporary China. It spells out the concept of pragmatic authoritarianism and marks its distinction from these existing concepts of authoritarianism. This is followed by an overview of some of the key components of pragmatic authoritarianism.

The subsequent chapters explore three aspects of China's governance model, namely, economic, social and political governance. Part II, consisting of Chapters 3, 4 and 5, is devoted to socio-economic governance. Chapter 3 analyzes pro-growth politics adopted by the Party state. It argues that the regime has achieved much in reforming China's planned economy, linking the economy with the world economy, coordinating reform in the localities, engineering high growth, and improving the living standard of the population. It also points to a major drawback and a puzzle in pro-growth authoritarianism, that is, collective protests grew faster than the GDP since the early 1990s. It suggests that a main cause is the rising popular consciousness of rights and reckless official abuse of power and infringement of rights in their push for economic growth. It also reviews several remedial measures that have been introduced by the Chinese leaders in recent years and discusses the necessary solution. Chapter 4 analyzes a core economic-social program the Party state has adopted since the late 1990s in defusing social grievances. It demonstrates the gravity of rural and urban discontents in the 1990s. It examines social wel-fare programs that were introduced since the 1990s and that aimed to help out rural residents, migrant workers, and the urban unemployed. It suggests that via these measures the Party state had eased the largest wave of popular discontents after 1989. Chapter 5 turns the analysis to social governance. Using religious policies as a case, this chapter probes the mode and the rationale of the state's management of social activities and groups. Religious activities have revived in the reform era, posing a potential challenge to the state. In response, the state differentiates a variety of religious groups and activities and treats them differently. It cracks down on organized religious groups that defy the state's authority. Nevertheless, it allows disorganized, apolitical yet popular religious activities to take place relatively freely.

Part III concerns political governance and consists of Chapters 6–8. Chapter 6 reviews the overhaul of China's crisis management. Improper crisis manage-ment has the significant potential to inflict severe damage on the legitimacy of the Party state. Triggered by the run-away SARS epidemic in early 2003, the Hu–Wen leadership overhauled epidemic and crisis management in the following years. These improvements are documented. The chapter concludes that the regime's crisis management capacity has considerably improved. Chapter 7 discusses the improvement in leadership succession. The most severe crises that the CCP has experienced since it came to power relate to failed leadership succession. Nevertheless, in the recent two decades the Party has largely evaded crises of this kind. The emerging norms for leadership succession and for resolving leadership conflict, as well as partial institutionalization of the process are described. Their effects are discussed. Chapter 8 examines an issue that has attracted considerable interests from the West, namely, democratization in China. The main schemes and initiatives in introducing democracy in the CCP and at the grass-roots levels are reviewed. In particular, it gives a quick update of intra-Party democracy, local consultative democratic experiments, village elections and urban community elections. It also discusses Xi Jinping's attitudes on this issue and the prospects for democratization.

Part IV is the conclusion of the book and consists of two chapters. Chapters 9–10 address an issue that interests business and policy circles, namely, the durability of the political regime in China. Chapter 9 provides a survey of the life span of unified regimes in the history of China and supplies an analysis of causes for their collapses. It is suggested that from the historical perspective the current regime may be blessed due to the absence of formidable external threats and that of credible organized internal opposition. Chapter 10, the concluding chapter, responds to a widely-discussed recent argument by Shambaugh about the coming crackup of the Party state. Building on the findings and insights from the previous chapters, this chapter points to the flexibility and durability of pragmatic authoritarianism in China in the foreseeable future.

Notes

1 Data on the change in disposable income of households came from China Statistical Bureau, *China Statistical Yearbook 2012*, Table 10–2 "Per Capita Annual Income and Engel's Coefficient of Urban and Rural Households"; data on poverty came from the World Bank, "Poverty headcount ratio at $2 a day (PPP) (% of population)," posted at: http://data.worldbank.org/indicator/SI.POV.2DAY?page= 6, accessed on August 18, 2013.

2 One of the best written economic explanations of China's economic success is Justin Yifu Lin, Fang Cai, and Zhou Li, *The China Miracle: Development Strategy and Economic Reform* (Hong Kong: Chinese University Press, 2003). For an example of the political-economic interpretations of China's successful reform, see Hongyi Lai, *Reform and the Non-State Economy in China: The Political Economy of Liberalization Strategies* (New York and London: Palgrave Macmillan, 2006).

3 Joshua Cooper Ramo, *The Beijing Consensus* (London: The Foreign Policy Center, 2004).

4 The information on these Chinese and English sources will be provided in the following discussion.

5 Stefan Halper, *Beijing Consensus: How China's Authoritarian Model Will Dominate the 21st Century* (New York: Basic Books, 2010).

6 For a recent study on China's soft power, see Hongyi Lai and Yiyi Lu, eds, *China's Soft Power and International Relations: Public Diplomacy, Aid, Perception and Strategy* (Abingdon and New York: Routledge, 2012). China's aversion to promote its model is in line with Deng Xiaoping's international strategy of keeping a low profile and biding the time (*taoguang yanghui*) for China's rise.

7 Scott Kennedy, "The Myth of the Beijing Consensus," *Journal of Contemporary China*, Vol. 19, No. 65, 2010, 461–77.

8 For criticisms of Ramo, refer to Kennedy, "The Myth of the Beijing Consensus"; Minglu Chen and David Goodman, "The China Model: One Country, Six Authors," *Journal of Contemporary China*, Vol. 73, No. 21, 2012, 172–73; Arif Dirlik, "Beijing Consensus/Beijing Gongshi: Who Recognizes Whom and to What End," in Yu Keping *et al.*, eds, *Zhongguo Moshi yu "Beijing Gongshi": Chaoyue "Huashengdun Gongshi"* (*The China Model and the Beijing Consensus: Beyond the Washington Consensus*). (Beijing: Shehui Kexue Wenxian Chubanshe, 2006), 99–112.

9 For an overview of the successful components in China's reform strategy, see Lai, *Reform and the Non-State Economy in China*, 2006.

10 Yu Keping, "Zhongguo Moshi: Jingyan yu Jianjie" ('The China Model': Experience and Lessons), in Yu Keping *et al.*, eds, *Zhongguo Moshi yu "Beijing Gongshi"* (*The China Model and the Beijing Consensus*) (Beijing: Shehui Kexue Wenxian Chubanshe, 2006), 11–20.

11 See Cheng Enfu *et al.*, "Ruhe Lijie 'Zhongguo Moshi'" (How to Make Sense of the 'China Model'); Chen Jinhua, "Zhongguo Moshi de Hexin Shi Zhongguo Zhidu" (The Core of the China Model is China's System); Cheng Enfu *et al.*, "Zhonguo Moshi Yanjiu de Ruogan Nandian" (Several Difficulties in Studying the China Model); Zhao Yao, "Zhengque Renshi he Pingjia Zhongguo Moshi" (Correctly Understand and Assess the China Model); Yang Huang, "Zhongguo Moshi yu Shehui Zhiyi" (The China Model and Socialism); Zhu Muzhi, "Guanyu Zhongguo Moshi Wenti" (On the Issue of the China Model), in Cheng Enfu and Li Jianguo, eds, *Zhongguo Moshi zhi Zheng* (*A Debate on the China Model*) (Beijing: Zhongguo Shehui Kexue Chubanshe, 2013), 3–9, 19–24, 25–37, 51–56, 69–75, 155–161.

12 Pan Wei, "Dangdai Zhonghua Tizhi" (Contemporary Chinese Institutions), in Pan Wei, ed., *Zhongguo Moshi* (*The China Model*) (Beijing: Zhongyang Bianyi Chubanshe, 2009), 3–85.

13 Yun-han Chu, "Zhongguo Moshi yu Quanqiu Chixu Chongzu" (The China Model and the Restructuring of the Global Order), in Pan Wei, ed., *Zhongguo Moshi* (*The China Model*), 603–30.

14 Wu Jinglian, "Zhongguo Moshi Huofu Weiding" (The Fortune and Setbacks of the China Model Are Still Far from Certain); Wu Jingling, "Zhongguo Moshi, Haishi Guodu xing Tizhi" (The China Model, or a Transitional Institution), Gao Shangquan, "Qiangdiao Zhongguo Moshi Keneng Hui Yudao Gaige" (Stressing the China Model Could Mislead Reform); Qin Xiao, Li Zehou, and Ma Guochuan, "Fadui Xianzai Ti Zhongguo Moshi" (Against Mentioning the China Model Now); Gan Yang, "Zhongguo Daolu Haishi Zhongguo Moshi" (The China Path or the China Model); Yang Jisheng, "Wokan Zhongguo Moshi" (My View on the China Model); Li Junru, "Shen Ti 'Zhongguo Moshi'" (Be Careful in Mentioning the China Model); Xin Ming, "Bu Zhuzhang Yong 'Zhongguo Moshi' Gaikuo Fazhan Shijian" (Propose Not to Use the China Model to Sum Up the Developmental Practice); Bao Xinjian, "'Zhongguo Moshi' Shi Yige Weimingti" (The 'China Model' is a False Proposition); Yan Jirong, "Zhongguo Moshi de Xueshu Fenxi" (An Academic Interpretation of the China Model), in Cheng Enfu and Li Jianguo, eds, *Zhongguo Moshi zhi Zheng* (*A Debate on the China Model*) (Beijing: Zhongguo Shehui Kexue Chubanshe, 2013), 225–7, 228–36, 237–41, 242–51, 252–9, 265–76, 171–73, 183–6, 196–206, 207–14.

15 Yu Keping, "Zhongguo Moshi: Jingyan yu Jianjie," 12–13.
16 Yongnian Zheng, "Guoji Fazhan Geju zhong de Zhongguo Moshi" (The China Model in the Order of International Development), in Cheng Enfu *et al.*, eds, *Zhongguo Moshi Zhi Zheng*, 146–54.
17 Hongyi Lai, "Beijing Aoyun yu Zhongguo Moshi" (The Beijing Olympic Games and the China Model), *Lianhe Zaobao* (*United Morning Post*), August 11, 2008, posted at: www.zaobao.com/yl/yl080811_501.shtml; Hongyi Lai, "Zaitan Beijing Aoyun yu Zhongguo Moshi" (Again On the Beijing Olympic Games and the China Model), *Lianhe Zaobao* (*United Morning Post*), August 20, 2008, posted at: www.zaobao.com/yl/yl080820_509.shtml on August 22, 2008.
18 Samir Amin, "Ouya: Zuoxiang Xin de Zhiyu" (Euro Asia: Towards a New Counter), in Yu Keping *et al.*, eds, *Zhongguo Moshi yu "Beijing Gongshi"*, 57–71.
19 David Schweickart, "Cong Zhe'er Ni Dao Buliao Naer: Dui 'Beijing Gongshi' de Sikao" (You Can't Get There from Here: Reflections on the 'Beijing Consensus'), ibid., 72–98.
20 Naughton, "China's Distinctive System: Can it be a Model for Others?"
21 Zhao, "The China Model: Can it Replace the Western Model of Modernization?" 419–36.
22 China Statistical Press, *Zhongguo Tongji Zaiyao* (*China Statistical Abstracts*) (Beijing: China Statistical Press, 2011), Table 2–5, "Indices of Gross Domestic Product."
23 China Statistical Press, *Zhongguo Tongji Zaiyao* (*China Statistical Abstracts*) (Beijing: China Statistical Press, 2006), 216; World Bank, "Gross National Income Per Capita 2012, Atlas Method and PPP," posted at: http://data.worldbank.org/data-catalog/GNI-per-capita-Atlas-and-PPP-table, accessed on August 9, 2013.
24 Data come from *China Statistical Yearbook*, 2003, 244.
25 See World Bank, "Poverty Headcount Ratio at $1.25 a Day (PPP) (% of Population)," posted at: http://data.worldbank.org/indicator/SI.POV.DDAY, accessed on August 9, 2013.
26 Personal observations from my numerous trips to Chinese cities along the coast and in the western region in recent years.
27 China Statistical Press, *Zhongguo Tongji Zaiyao* (*China Statistical Abstracts*) (Beijing: China Statistical Press, 2011), Table 3–1, "Population and Its Composition."
28 See Lu Xueyi, *Dangdai Zhongguo Shehui Liudong* (*Social Mobility in Contemporary China*) (Beijing: Shehui kexue wenxian chubanshe, 2004), 13.
29 China Statistical Press, *Zhongguo Tongji Zaiyao* (*China Statistical Abstracts*) 2006, 11, 107.
30 "Zhongguo Wangmin da 4.17 Yi" (Chinese Net Users Total 417 Millions), posted at: http://society.dwnews.com/news/2010-07-08/56182821.html, accessed on July 8, 2010.
31 Author's own experience and observation in ten coastal and interior cities in China in recent years.
32 China Statistical Press, *Zhongguo Tongji Zaiyao* (*China Statistical Abstracts*) (Beijing: China Statistical Press, 2011), Table 10–23, "Ownership of Durable Consumer Goods per 100 Rural Households at Year-end"; Table 10–10, "Ownership of Major Durable Consumer Goods per 100 Urban Households at Year-end"; Table 10–30, "Number of Durable Consumer Goods Owned."
33 Seymour Martin Lipset, "Some Social Requisites of Democracy: Economic Development and Political Legitimacy," *American Political Science Review*, 1959, No. 53, 69–105. For a classic argument on the role of the middle class in democracy, see Barrington Moor, Jr., *Social Origins of Dictatorship and Democracy* (Boston, MA: Beacon Press, 1966).
34 The data is based on World Bank, GDP per capita, "PPP (Current International $)," posted at: http://data.worldbank.org/indicator/NY.GDP.PCAP.PP.CD?order=

wbapi_data_value_2012+wbapi_data_value+wbapi_data_value-last&sort=desc, accessed on August 9, 2013.

35 Adam Przeworski, *et al.*, "What Makes Democracies Endure?" in Larry Diamond and Marc F. Plattner, eds, *The Global Divergence of Democracies* (Baltimore, MD: Johns Hopkins University Press, 2001), 169. See also their book, *Democracy and Development: Political Institutions and Well-being in the World, 1950–1990* (New York: Cambridge University Press, 2000).

36 See World Bank, "Poverty Headcount Ratio at $2 a Day (PPP) (% of Population)," posted at: http://data.worldbank.org/indicator/SI.POV.2DAY, accessed on August 9, 2013.

37 See World Bank, "Literacy Rate, Adult Total (% of People Ages 15 and Above)," posted at: http://data.worldbank.org/indicator/SE.ADT.LITR.ZS?page=1, accessed on August 9, 2013.

38 Interview with a former economic adviser to President Bill Clinton, August 2005.

39 R. W. Apple Jr, "Clinton Concedes China Policy Hasn't Helped Much on Rights," posted at: www.nytimes.com/1997/01/29/world/clinton-concedes-china-policy-hasn-t-helped-much-on-rights.html on January 29, 1997, accessed on August 12, 2013.

40 "George W. Bush on China," posted at www.ontheissues.org/George_W_Bush_China.htm, accessed on August 12, 2013.

41 See Bruce Gilley, *China's Democratic Future: How it Will Happen and Where it Will Lead* (New York: Columbia University Press, 2004), 118.

42 Dali Yang, *Remaking the Chinese Leviathan: Market Transition and Politics of Governance in China* (Stanford, CA: Stanford University Press, 2004), 314.

43 Suzanne Ogden, *Inklings of Democracy in China* (Harvard, MA and London: Harvard University Press, 2002), 3–7.

44 Andrew Nathan, "Authoritarian Resilience," *Journal of Democracy*, Vol. 14, No. 1, January 2003, 6–17.

45 David Shambaugh, *China's Communist Party: Atrophy and Adaptation* (Washington, DC: Woodrow Wilson Center Press and Berkeley, CA: University of California Press, 2009), 9. As to be stated in Chapter 10, he embraced the view of authoritarian decay in his news commentary in 2015.

46 The "consultative Leninism" framework mentioned by Baum was later taken up by Steve Tsang to characterize the post-Deng political changes in China. See Steve Tsang, "Consultative Leninism: China's New Political Framework," *Journal of Contemporary China*, Vol. 18, No. 62, November 2009, 865–880.

47 Richard Baum, "The Limits of Consultative Leninism," in Special Report of Asian Program, *China and Democracy: A Contradiction in Terms?* (Washington, DC: Woodrow Wilson International Center for Scholars, June 2006), 13–20.

48 Minxin Pei, *China's Trapped Transition: The Limits of Developmental Autocracy* (Cambridge, MA: Harvard University Press, 2006).

49 Gordon G. Chang, *The Coming Collapse of China* (New York: Random House, 2001), xv–xx, 256–85.

50 Yongnian Zheng, *Globalization and State Transformation in China* (Cambridge and New York: Cambridge University Press, 2004).

51 Yu Keping, "Toward an Incremental Democracy and Governance: Chinese Theories and Assessment Criteria," in Yu Keping, ed., *Democracy and the Rule of Law in China* (Leiden and Boston, MA: Brill, 2010), 3–34. The Chinese version of his book was published in 2003. See Yu Keping, "Zhengliang minzhu yu shanzhi," in Yu Keping, *Zhengliang Minzhu yu Shanzhi* (*Toward An Incremental Democracy and Governance*) (Beijing: Sheke Wenxian Chubanshe, 2003), 148–65.

52 Ye, ibid.

53 "Fully Push Ahead Construction of the Party" (Quanmian tuijin dang de jianshe), posted at: http://baike.baidu.com/view/3155407.htm; "Zeng Qinghong Stresses to Constantly Improve the Leading and Governing Capacity of the Chinese

Communist Party" (Zeng Qinghong qiandiao yao buduan tigao Zhonggong dang de lingdao he zhizheng shuiping), posted at: www.chinanews.com/2002-11-29/26/248615.html; "Sixteen Key Words in Party Construction" (Dangjian shiliuge guanjian ci), posted at: http://www1.dzu.edu.cn/bumen/dzxynxx/index/mcwnsy.php?fid=12&id=332. The above websites were all accessed on August 17, 2013.

54 See Shambaugh, *China's Communist Party*, 45–61.

55 Kenneth Lieberthal, *Governing China: From Revolution Through Reform* (New York and London: W. W. Norton & Company, 1995) (updated in 2003); Tony Saich, *Governance and Politics of China* (New York: Palgrave Macmillan, 2011) (first published in 2001 and updated in 2004 and in 2011).

56 Lieberthal, *Governing China*, 1995, 228–30; Saich, *Governance and Politics of China*, 2011, 7.

57 Data on China's economic growth were posted at: http://data.worldbank.org/indicator/NY.GDP.MKTP.KD.ZG, and multiple web sources, accessed May 9, 2015.

58 Bill K.P. Chou, *Government and Policy-Making Reform in China: The Implications of Governing Capacity* (London and New York: Routledge, 2009), xi–xiii, 1–15, 130–3.

59 OECD (Organization for Economic Cooperation and Development), *Governance in China* (Paris: OECD, 2005).

60 Jude Howell, ed., *Governance in China* (Lanham, MD: Roman & Littlefield, 2004).

61 Ibid., 17.

62 Howell, *Governance in China*, 17.

63 See Cheng Li, ed., *China's Changing Political Landscape: Prospects for Democracy* (Washington, DC: Brookings Institution Press, 2008).

64 Examples of these studies are too numerous to cite. Limited space allows me to only mention a few related to China's governance and institutional changes. David Finkelstein and Maryanne Kivleham, eds, *China's Leadership in the 21st Century* (Armonk, NY: M.E. Sharpe, 2003); Wang Gungwu and Yongnian Zheng, eds, *Damage Control: The Chinese Communist Party in the Jiang Zemin Era* (Singapore: Eastern Universities Press, 2003); Tun jen Cheng, Jacques deLisle and Deborah Brown, eds, *China under Hu Jintao: Opportunities, Dangers, and Dilemmas* (Singapore: World Scientific, 2006). Note that almost all these books were written prior to the 16th Congress of the CCP. The last volume was largely written shortly after the congress before China scholars gained a clear view about power succession and policies by Hu and Wen. A representative collection on China's elite politics is Jonathan Unger, *The Nature of Chinese Politics: From Mao to Jiang* (Armonk, NY: M.E. Sharpe, 2002). For a thorough study on state-intellectual relations, refer to Joseph Fewsmith, *China since Tiananmen: The Politics of Transition* (New York: Cambridge University Press, 2001).

65 See Chien-min Chao and Bruce Dickson, eds. *Remaking the Chinese State: Strategies, Society and Security* (London and New York: Routledge, 2001); Merle Goldman and Roderick MacFarquhar, eds, *The Paradox of China's Post-Mao Reforms* (Cambridge, MA and London: Harvard University Press, 1999).

2 Pragmatic authoritarianism in China

What type of political regime is emerging in China? This is an important, valuable yet very difficult question. As the preceding review of the studies on the China model and on political development and governance in China suggests, we have yet to have a satisfactory answer to this question. Nor do the existing studies on authoritarianism, which will be reviewed shortly afterwards, offer us a good and clear answer.

In the following sections I will start with a review of the existing typologies of authoritarianism proposed by comparative political scientists. I argue that the Party state is adopting pragmatic authoritarianism, which is practical, adaptive, and calculative in actual policies but ultimately aiming at prolonging the rule of the single party. I will then describe the main features of pragmatic authoritarianism by placing the institutional changes in China in a comparative political context. Pragmatic authoritarianism involves overhauls of institutions (especially those critical to the survival of the Party state), improvement of governance, efforts to deliver results of economic performance, defusing of public discontents through welfare provision, and ease of pressure for democratization through very limited opening of the political system. Through these efforts the state aims to keep the CCP as the only effective ruling party of the nation.

Typology of authoritarianism in the literature

A small number of studies do offer interpretations of the political regime in China in the post-Mao period. One declares that China has not yet moved out of totalitarianism.[1] This view is highly questionable, given the similarities between post-Mao China and post-Stalin USSR in the weakening of the state's totalitarian control of the society. Gordon Skilling and Juan Linz, who were among the best scholars on post-Stalin communist regimes and authoritarian regimes, respectively, regarded the post-Stalin USSR as an authoritarian regime.[2] Thus, the classification of post-Mao China as a totalitarian regime seems problematic. The other study, which was done by the author in 2006, used religions as a case to analyze the state's strategy of managing a reviving society in China. It suggested that post-Mao China entered the era of post-totalitarianism that was characterized by the weakening of the political ideology, the resurgence of religions, the state's reduced control of the society and its selective intervention into social activities to guard its core political sphere.[3] Despite the virtue of the argument the concept of a post-totalitarian regime remains vague. It literally meant authoritarianism after totalitarianism, which, to be explained later, can take on a variety of forms as in the post-Stalin Soviet Union. The type of political regime in China has yet to be clarified.

Naturally, the political regimes after Stalin and de-Stalinization in the Soviet Union and Eastern Europe have been referred to as post-totalitarian authoritarian regimes. Linz (2000) and Skilling (1970) distinguished the following categories of post-totalitarian authoritarianism, but neither places China under any of these categories.[4]

1   Consultative authoritarianism, the prime example being the Soviet Union after Khrushchev. Under the regime, group activities take place spontaneously and express fundamental opposition, yet broader social groups and creative intellectuals are strictly controlled and remain impotent. The top leadership remains dominant in politics. While professional groups such as economists and scientists can participate in decision-making, the Party apparatus continues to play the dominant role, and they are in charge of expressing the interests of broader groups.

As stated, several China scholars, chiefly Baum, placed China in this category. This concept is useful in describing the change in the relationship in post-Mao China between the state on one hand, and social groups including intellectuals and the public and satellite parties on the other. It indicates the state's willingness to incorporate voices from satellite parties, social groups, and the public. However, it does not denote other major aspects of governance, such as the provision of welfare, the state's subtle management of the society, the state's drive to deliver high economic growth through reforms and intervention, the overhauls of critical political institutions, as well as improved channels for the public to choose officials and have inputs in local policies.

2   Quasi-pluralistic authoritarianism, whose good examples are the Soviet Union under Khrushchev and Hungary and Poland during the thaw of 1953–56. This regime is marked by greater group initiatives and more group conflict, as well as dominance of the Party leadership. "Although bureaucratic groups, especially the party hierarchy, remain powerful, they cannot entirely exclude the intellectual and opinion groups in general from participation. Both types of group show a greater determination to express interests and values in opposition to the party line, advancing alternative policies, criticizing official decisions and actions, and in some cases challenging frontally a whole series of official policies. Ironically, these active groups continue to be for the most part noninstitutionalized, whereas organized groups such as the trade unions remain impotent."[5]

This form of authoritarianism seems to suggest greater room for social groups in policy deliberation. In terms of state-societal relations China in the last two decades may fall between consultative authoritarianism and quasi-pluralistic authoritarianism. In the light of the tight political control the state exercises over social groups, especially broader ones, the Chinese state currently resembles the former. Nevertheless, in terms of expression of interests and public discussion, China may come close to quasi-pluralistic authoritarianism. The media in China sometimes carries frank and critical coverage of serious social and economic problems and speaks for various strata and social groups. Nevertheless, very few China scholars apply this concept to contemporary China. In contrast, as stated, a few China scholars prefer to view China as consultative authoritarianism (or consultative Leninism). Again, like the concept consultative authoritarianism this concept fails to depict other major aspects of governance, such as the provision of welfare and a higher living standard to the public, pro-growth policies and institutions, and overhaul of key institutions.

3   Democratizing and pluralistic authoritarianism, the good examples being Czechoslovakia in the first half of 1968 and Yugoslavia after 1966. Under these regimes, "with the endorsement of the leadership, political groups were to a substantial degree institutionalized and they played a significant role in policy making."[6] Very few China scholars would equate contemporary China under a strong and determined authoritarian state to Czechoslovakia in the spring of 1968 where democratization was bubbling. Thus this concept is not applicable to China.

In addition, three other forms of authoritarianism have emerged in the literature of China politics or comparative politics. They are worth a quick review and assessment.

4   Fragmented authoritarianism. According to Lieberthal and Lampton, political authority in China was divided among multiple bureaucratic agencies. These agencies often bargained with each other over the final shape of the policy. If there were different opinions among them, a compromise or consensus was thus needed for adaptation of any policy and its effective implementation.[7] This view is more about the making and implementation of policies in China. It is not concerned with the institutional improvement, social or economic governance, and the issue of China's democratization.

5   Bureaucratic authoritarianism. This concept was developed and employed by Guillermo O'Donnell in the analysis of Latin American politics in the 1960s and early 1970s, and the best example was Argentina. Under this type of regime, a coalition of pro-development elite in the military, bureaucracy, and enterprises tried to exclude activated popular sectors, particularly urban working classes. This coalition also relied on its rich linkage with the elites in advanced countries.[8]

The Chinese authoritarian state shares a few features with bureaucratic authoritarianism: emphases on development, technocratic leadership and international economic linkages and aversion to public mobilization. Other than that, this model of authoritarianism differs from that in China in several marked areas. First, in China the Communist Party (though accepting capitalism), instead of the military, is dominant in politics. The military is subject to civilian leadership (including the Party's leadership). Second, the CCP pursued an open trade policy, whereas the Latin American state endorsed a protectionist trade policy. Third, the ruling party's ideology plays a more visible role in policy and politics in China than that in Latin America, though the ideology has been downplayed and has become far less utopian in China since 1978. Fourth, while the working class is discouraged from participating in politics, the Chinese leaders (under late Deng Xiaoping and Hu Jintao) openly claim their legitimacy on the basis of improving people's economic well-being and alleviating their economic hardship. Concurrent with this emphasis was the pro-people ideology announced by Hu Jintao. Meanwhile, in the last decade the state has permitted democratic experiments and greater transparency in discussion of public policies in a likely attempt to address the problems of popular participation.

6   Soft authoritarianism. This concept is employed to depict authoritarian governments in Singapore and Malaysia (and in Taiwan at the start of its democratization in the late 1980s). I will focus on Singapore and Malaysia as soft authoritarianism in these two countries has remained until today. Soft authoritarianism in Singapore and Malaysia is characterized by the dominance of a single party in politics and over media, and even the court, as well as limited press freedom and the presence of formalistic national elections. Gordon Means also suggested that persecution of dissidents took place through the legal system and was justified by the state as rule of law.[9]

This concept has been occasionally applied to China. Nevertheless, the scholarly use of this concept remains patchy and inconsistent. Back in 2000 Minxin Pei observed optimistically as follows: "Since the late 1970s, the political system has been evolving into soft authoritarianism with real potential for democratic transition, perhaps in the second decade of the twenty-first century." The evolution, he noted, was indicated in a marked decline in political prisoners, the rise in rudimentary form of separation of power and of the rule of law, public political participation through democratic schemes and civil society.[10] However, by 2006 Pei gave up his hope for democratic transition in China. Instead, he argued that due to the lack of democratization the Party state in China is trapped in an incomplete transition and faces political degradation.[11] Richard Baum, in his short essay in 2006, also observed that the Party state in China had adopted soft authoritarian measures in order to increase "political inclusion" and "consultation" without enhancing public "accountability" or "empowerment." These measures included expanding the role of the people's congress and the "united front," recruitment of entrepreneurs and members of the middle class into the Party, information dissemination and public feedback through the e-government website, open hearings over local policies, and greater use of "letters and visits" (*xinfang*) offices to help individuals to report official abuse of power. Nevertheless, shortly afterwards he maintained that the Chinese regime is still consultative Leninism. Thus, these measures, though seemingly soft authoritarian, did not amount to a fundamental change in consultative Leninism in China.[12] It thus appears that neither Pei nor Baum believed in their final assessment that the concept of soft authoritarianism best characterized China.

Therefore, none of the aforementioned concepts of authoritarianism seems to capture the changes in contemporary China and depict the Party state in China. Linz, for example, rightly noted that bureaucratic authoritarianism tended to "underestimate the possibility of political engineering."[13] These categories emphasize heavily the relations between the state and social groups and ignore other vital aspects of state institutions and state policies. The latter include institutionalization of leadership succession, official accountability, shrewd management of social-economic interests of the population, and democratization. Therefore, the discussion in this book emphasizes these ignored aspects, instead of concentrating on the state-social groups relations.

Pragmatic authoritarianism: the concept

We thus need to search for a new concept to describe political development in China. I argue that the Party state in China in the reform era, especially since 1992, is evolving into pragmatic authoritarianism. The core elements of pragmatic authoritarianism are the following two. First, as Shambaugh's study of the CCP reveals, the Party state is flexible, practical, and adaptive. It "eccentrically borrows" effective policies and practices from a variety of sources and countries, including social welfare from Western countries and authoritarian developmentalism from the East Asian neighbors. It has made considerable efforts to improve its institutions and governance. Second, the various endeavors of the state in China have one final goal, that is, the maintenance of the leadership of the CCP. For this goal it can be highly strategic. In 1978, after suffering from Mao's disruptive policies and exhausting campaigns between 1958 and 1976, the CCP decisively shifted its focus away from ideological campaigns and class struggle to economic modernization. It has maintained its focus since then.

Compared to other types of authoritarianism that have been reviewed, pragmatic authoritarianism has its own distinct features, which help to distinguish it from these variants of authoritarianism. The above analyses have discussed the differences between the Party state in China on the one hand, and quasi-pluralistic authoritarianism, democratizing and pluralistic authoritarianism, bureaucratic authoritarianism, and fragmented authoritarianism on the other. The following section will focus on the differences between pragmatic authoritarianism on one hand, and soft authoritarianism and consultative authoritarianism on the other.

Pragmatic authoritarianism versus soft authoritarianism. Scholars have characterized the state in Malaysia and Singapore as soft authoritarianism. There are two crucial differences between soft authoritarianism in Malaysia, and especially Singapore, and authoritarianism in China. First, in Malaysia and Singapore there are formal and regular nationwide elections where the ruling party has to compete head to head against the legally existing opposition parties. In China, not only is there no nationwide election, but also no opposition party is allowed to register. There have been several attempts by Chinese activists to form opposition parties in the reform era. Each time they were quickly rounded up by the police and were later sentenced to jail terms. Second, as a legacy of the British colonial rule there is a fair degree of the rule of law in these two countries. In Singapore even the top leaders have to abide by the law especially in economic and social affairs. The law thus acts as a supervision of the power of leaders and helps reduce the abuse of power and especially corruption in Singapore.[14] In China law has not been an effective weapon on minimizing official corruption. The public in China often questions why the Party acts above the law. These two institutional constraints thus make authoritarianism in Malaysia and Singapore rather soft compared to the Party state in China. For these reasons a number of scholars prefer to call the state in Malaysia and Singapore illiberal democracy, instead of soft authoritarianism. In this sense pragmatic authoritarianism is much harder than soft authoritarianism. It is not as institutionalized, developed, and effective when compared with the state in Singapore. Nevertheless, very few states in the world are as effective as that in Singapore.

Pragmatic authoritarianism versus consultative authoritarianism. As stated, several China scholars, especially Baum, regarded the Party state in China as consultative authoritarianism. Indeed, pragmatic authoritarianism embodies elements of consultative authoritarianism. In the reform era the Party state in China, as suggested by Baum, had allowed the people's congress and the political consultative conference at all levels to play a greater role in offering advice, comments and even moderate adjustment in policies. It has also provided a few channels for the citizens to report official abuse of power, chiefly through the letters and visits (*xinfang*) offices. In addition and importantly, the Party state has permitted and even promoted village elections nationwide and has introduced a limited degree of intra-Party democracy.[15] These measures were regarded by Baum and Pei as soft authoritarian. In this light pragmatic authoritarianism in China is more liberal than consultative authoritarianism in the post-Khrushchev USSR.

As a concept, consultative authoritarianism was initially created to depict the Soviet Union after Khrushchev. Compared to the Soviet Union after Khrushchev (as well as bureaucratic authoritarianism), pragmatic authoritarianism in China has been more open and innovative in economic policies and governance. Unlike the post-Khrushchev Soviet Union, the Party state in China embraces the market economy and the linkage with the capitalist global economy. Moreover, it even uses its apparatus and controls of extensive resources to further the market-economy-based economic growth. For example, it institutes economic growth as one of the key criteria for official promotion. In addition, as to be explained, the state has formally accepted the concept of good governance and tried to improve administrative efficiency and accountability and embraces a degree of political transparency. It has also overhauled critical institutions such as crisis management and leadership succession. In sum, while consultative authoritarianism is mainly concerned with the relations between the state and social groups especially in the policy making process, pragmatic authoritarianism captures a much wider spectrum of the endeavor of the state. The latter includes not only social governance (state-societal relations), but also economic and political governance. The wider scope of the latter enables us to better understand the nature and capacity of the Chinese state.

Pragmatic authoritarianism in this book versus that in a few previous studies. There have been a few rare applications of the term pragmatic authoritarianism in the existing scholarly literature. A few scholars used this term to denote the authoritarian state in China in the reform era. In using this term they described the state's non-hostile interaction with the middle class in the 2000s, or the authoritarian and largely non-ideological rule by technocrats such as President Jiang Zemin since the end of 1990s.[16] I do share many of these observations about pragmatic authoritarianism in China. On the other hand, their use of the term is brief and non-systematic. I have thus taken a large stride further by analyzing the main features of pragmatic authoritarianism and dissecting and assessing the main areas of institutional innovations under it.

Outside the Chinese case, one main and related study was arguably "pragmatic unipartism" (or, the pragmatic one-party system) discussed by Giovanni Sartori. He used the term to describe authoritarian regimes that downplayed ideology, had room for pressure groups and some degree of expression and press freedom, and bargained and absorbed these social forces. Sartori placed Portugal until April 1974 and Spain after 1939 under this category. He specifically excluded Mao's China from this category and included it under the category of totalitarian unipartism. It was unclear how he would classify China in the reform era. It was likely that China after 1978 would lean toward authoritarian unipartism, which was characterized by weaker and nontotalitarian ideology, medium coercion, exclusionary policies toward outer groups, independence of non-political subgroups, and predictable limits on arbitrariness of the state.[17] Sartori's work captured two aspects of one-party systems, that is, the significance of ideology and the state-societal relations. However, as I shall detail in my book, these two aspects, which relate to only part of political governance and part of social governance, are insufficient for capturing the various, rich, and significant substance in institutional development and resilience of the authoritarian regime in China. As suggested below, we need to understand pragmatic authoritarianism in terms of economic, social and political governance.

In short, pragmatic authoritarianism in China in my account is a form of authoritarianism that is largely practical, flexible, and adaptive. As to be explained, pragmatic authoritarianism in China entails distinctive measures in economic governance, social governance, and political governance. The main objective of economic governance is to stimulate high economic growth and to provision public services in order to sustain public support for the regime.

Its social governance involves calculative and subtle management of the society with the aim of giving larger space for non-political social activities while containing organized and potentially independent social groups. Its political governance comprises overhaul of leadership succession and crisis management, schemes of grass-roots and intra-Party democracy, and initiatives to promote "good governance" and improve administrative efficiency and transparency. A pragmatic authoritarian state emphasizes actual economic results of its governance in order to bolster legitimacy, makes efforts to overhaul the most vulnerable component of its key institutions, introduces public gestures such as anti-corruption to tackle issues that arouse the strongest public resentment, and allows timid exercises of grass-roots democracy and intra-Party democracy to deflect criticisms of its authoritarianism. These efforts would make authoritarianism more responsive to the changing society and the increasingly complex economy.

The ultimate aim of the aforementioned programs and efforts of the state is to sustain the Party's monopoly of power and to prolong the life of authoritarianism. The Party has been constantly on guard against and readily suppressed nascent opposition parties, vocal dissidents, and well-organized yet disobedient social groups. As new technology, such as commercialized media, internet and mobile phones, opens up space for public and private expression, discussion and discourse, the state quickly responds with its own means and agencies to enforce censorship. By and large, the state has succeeded in preventing waves of technological revolution of popular expression from overrunning the dam of political control.

Therefore, despite the fact that since 1978 the CCP has shifted its focus away from Mao's zealous ideological campaign involving every walking Chinese, pragmatic authoritarianism in China is neither political-values-free, nor totally free of ideological elements. Indeed, the CCP has reformulated its ideology by downplaying class struggles and revolution, by playing up the representativeness of the Party for the whole population and the services the Party provides for the people. Now and then, the Party state in China warns cadres against western political infiltration and peaceful evolution, and launched political campaigns to indoctrinate Party members about the correct ideology and to guard against the influence of Western liberalism. At times the Party members and cadres have to undergo brief and internal political campaigns where they would declare their resistance to Western liberalism or erosive attraction of corruption.

Nevertheless, it is imperative for me to highlight the fact that in the reform era the Party state has given a lower priority to ideology and has transplanted traditional ideals as well as modern notions into the official ideology. These moves suggested that the authoritarian state has adopted a pragmatic stance and utilitarian approach toward ideology. In Mao's China ideological compliance was of utmost importance for cadres, urban workers and peasants, and ideology goaded officials and commoners into political campaigns for a utopian society. In contrast, in the reform era ideology has been largely a practical tool for the Party state to justify its rule and policy. Since the mid-1980s the Party has largely removed from its official ideology the core Marxist and Leninist components, namely, the condemnation of capitalism and of economic exploitation of workers and calls for the setup of a utopian communist society. In the 1980s the Party emphasized that China was and would remain at the primitive stage of socialism for a very long time where the primary tasks of the nation were to develop the economy and advance the technology. During 1992–1997 in order to promote the marketization program and subdue conservative criticisms, reformists led by Deng even halted major and open ideological debates and reduced ideology to a minor role. Since the late 1990s, in light of the surge of various rival ideologies such as Western liberalism, religions, and materialism and money worshipping, as well as rising corruption, the Party leaders have started to revert to ideology in order to cope with these problems and challenges. The main ideological formulations included the "three represents" under President Jiang, the harmonious society under President Hu, and the China dream under President Xi. A forthcoming section in this chapter will discuss in detail the Party's changes of its ideology from the 1980s to the early 2010s and will touch on all these aforementioned formulations. The main threads of these aforementioned formulations have been that the CCP is able to represent the interests of the majority of the Chinese and will strive to build a fair, just, prosperous and secure society as well as a strong and internationally respected country. As a result, the official ideology is used to serve very practical ends: to justify the relevance of the Party for the ever changing society and rapidly developing economy in China, to promote the ideal society (such as the harmonious society and the China dream) appealing to an overwhelming majority of the population, and to minimize the political space for rival ideologies (such as Western liberalism). In its ideological endeavor the Party state has thus become highly practical and pragmatic.

Components of pragmatic authoritarianism

After the above overview of pragmatic authoritarianism in China it is helpful to examine its main components. As stated, pragmatic authoritarianism comprises economic, social and political governance. Table 2.1 summarizes these three components as well as elements under each of these components. My analysis will start with economic governance of pragmatic authoritarianism, followed by social and political governance. The aim is not only to explain these components, but also to identify their advantages and drawbacks, thereby rendering a balanced view of pragmatic authoritarianism.

Economic governance: pro-growth policies and institutions

Undoubtedly, pragmatic authoritarianism has delivered the most impressive results in economic governance. This is manifested in a series of economic achievements documented in Chapter 1. They include the highest growth in

Table 2.1 Components of pragmatic authoritarianism in China

Component	Specific Components	Aims	Results
Economic Governance	Pro-growth policies and institutions: reform and opening; *growth as a criterion for official promotion; public investment in infrastructure; fiscal stimulus in economic crises*	Earn legitimacy through performance	Rapid economic growth; formation of a state-directed market economy; political legitimacy for the Party despite collective protests.
	Provision of basic welfare for disadvantaged groups	Ease social discontents	Provision of basic social welfare; ease of public discontents over this issue.
Social Governance	Differentiated treatment of social groups	Contain potentially antagonistic groups	The state keeps organized social groups on a short leash while giving space for non-political social activities.
Political Governance	*Eclectic borrowing of successful practices*	*Enhancing governance capacity*	It helps the state to improve its governance.
	Reformulation of ideology	*Showcase legitimacy; drive away rival political values*	The state fends off rival values but its ideology has met popular skepticism.
	Overhaul of crisis management	Earn legitimacy	Improved crisis management reduces the state's vulnerability.
	Institutionalization of leadership succession	Avoid devastating self-inflicted damage of the Party	Smoother succession reduces the state's vulnerability.
	The Party's control of key state branches (via appointments)	*Sustain the Party's monopoly of power*	The CCP controls key state branches.
	The Party's censorship of the media	*Sustain the Party's monopoly of power*	The Party keeps out unfavorable information.
Political Governance	Endeavor toward good governance: official accountability, administrative efficiency, and a fair degree of political transparency	Improve the Party's governance capacity; ensure economic growth	Some but not dramatic improvement in governance and efficiency.
	Grass-roots and intra-Party democratic initiatives	Defuse pressure for democracy	These initiatives improve governance but fail to defuse pressure for democracy.

Note: Italics represent elements of pragmatic authoritarianism that have been analyzed in detail in various existing studies and that will be surveyed in Chapter 2. Normal fonts represent elements that will be examined in this *and* subsequent chapters.

GDP and the living standard for the past 35 years and the biggest poverty reduction in world history.

The economic miracle in China has to be attributed to the economic governance of pragmatic authoritarianism that comprises of pro-growth policies and institutions specifically, the following four components.

The first element in pro-growth policies and institutions is the state's ability to push forward incremental reform and opening, and refrain from carrying out rushed reforms that could bring economic disasters. This is arguably the most important element of economic governance. Since the late 1970s and ahead of the Eastern European and Soviet bloc, China has pursued market-oriented economic reform. During 1979–82 a revolutionary change took place in the Chinese countryside whereby decades-old collective farming was replaced by family farming. This change, initiated by inland peasants in a few localities and encouraged by reformist leaders, was promoted nationwide. This change dramatically improved the productivity of agricultural production. Meanwhile, opening of the economy to the outside world was experimented with in four Special Economic Zones. In the following years the major coastal areas were gradually opened up. Meanwhile, reform spread to other sectors, including foreign trade, exchange rate, SOEs, distribution system, pricing, and finance. Non-state including foreign and private enterprises were gradually allowed to enter the market. In 1992 with Deng's strong intervention through his tour to southern China the CCP formally accepted the market economy as one primary objective of its economic governance. In 2001 China made a push in economic reform by entering the WTO.[18] By opening up its services, automobile, and telecommunication markets, China has gained secure access to international markets, and has taken its economy down the path of the market economy much further. In return, it has enjoyed noticeably higher growth throughout most of the 2000s than the years before the WTO accession.

The second element in China's pro-growth economic institutions in China is that promotion of economic reforms and economic growth records have become key criteria for official promotion. Deng himself promoted several reformist local leaders into the highest national positions. They included Zhao Ziyang (the Premier), Wan Li (Vice Premier), Li Ruihuan (a member of the Politburo Standing Committee), Jiang Zemin (the General Secretary of the CCP), and Zhu Rongji (Executive Vice Premier). As noted by Whiting, among dozens of the criteria for assessing the performance of local cadres in the outskirts of Shanghai in the 1990s, most of them related to economic growth.[19] A study by Zhiyue Bo on the mobility of provincial officials during 1978–98 concluded that local economic growth and revenue remittance to the national government were the most important factors that explained their promotion.[20]

The third component in pro-growth policies and institutions of pragmatic authoritarianism is, as widely noted by analysts, that the state in China has made massive investment in infrastructural development. As a result, China has arguably one of the best infrastructures in the developing world. Overall, according to the World Economic Forum in 2008, the quality of China's infrastructure was ranked number 58 out of 134 economies, just immediately behind Egypt but well ahead of all other nations in Table 2.2, including Brazil, India, Indonesia, and Vietnam. The reason for China's decent quality of infrastructure is its high quality of road (mostly paved road) and rail (speed trains covering critical lines between mega cities), ports and airports, frequent bus and truck services, as well as rapid expansion in energy generation.

Around the mid 2000s China's road transport system had a similar density to Indonesia's; China's road and rail was less dense than Vietnam, a much smaller neighbor. Nevertheless and very importantly, China's quality of road (reflected in percentage of paved road) was higher than both nations, and China's rail density more than doubled that of Indonesia (Table 2.2). More importantly, China's total length of high-quality road, such as highways and expressways, was eight to ten times as much as other populous economies such as Brazil and India (Table 2.3). China has the second longest highway system after the U.S. Good infrastructure allows goods and people to be transported rapidly and efficiently. China's pace of expansion of road networks in the developing world can be matched only by the fast growing economies, such as India and South Africa and surpassed by smaller economies such as Vietnam. Nevertheless, China's expansion in electricity generation far surpasses the former two (Table 2.3).

During the Beijing Olympic Games, China displayed its dazzling Olympic venues and new architectures in Beijing, including the new state-of-the-art terminal at the Capital Airport, the futurist CCTV office tower, the Olympic "bird-nest" stadium, and the "water cube" swimming stadium. In a similar vein, impressive and growing urban skylights and public transport (such as subways and within-city highways) in Shanghai and other major cities such as Shenzhen and Guangzhou provide necessary amenities for rapid urban development and for inflow of investment.

Even in terms of broadly-defined infrastructure China also excels in a global comparison. China provided better water supply access to its population than Vietnam and Nigeria; better sanitation access than Vietnam and India; far better electricity, phone, and internet access than Indonesia, India, Vietnam, and Nigeria. China's provision of these services except for electricity, however, lagged noticeably behind Brazil, a more developed economy. China was somewhat behind Egypt in terms of water supply and sanitation access (Table 2.2).

Empirical evidence from Asia suggests that the quality of infrastructure is associated with economic development. Good infrastructure reduces transportation and transaction costs, increases efficiency, and improves the population's access to work and jobs, and living standards and health through provision of clean water and sanitation.[21] The importance of infrastructure is captured in a Chinese saying: "The initial path to wealth is a road" (*yao zhifu, xian xiulu*). As a matter of fact, the province that developed the fastest and earliest in the reform era, i.e., Guangdong, experienced the earliest and the most explosive growth in the highway system, especially expressways, in China.

Why can China build up its infrastructure rapidly? The answer lies in the Chinese state's financing of infrastructural development. As a report by ADB

Table 2.2 Infrastructure in selected developing nations, 2004–05 (% of population for access data)

Country	Global rank of quality of infrastructure	Road network density (km per 100 sq km²)	Road quality (% paved road)	Rail network density (km per 100 km²)	Water supply access	Sanitation access	Electricity access	Telephone access	Internet access
China	**58**	**19**	**91**	**0.64**	**76**	**39**	**99**	**42**	**6.3**
Vietnam	97	29	25	0.97	49	25	81	9	4.3
Indonesia	96	20	58	0.25	78	55	55	13	3.8
India	90				86	33	57	13	5.5
Brazil	98				90	75	97	69	19.5
Nigeria	114				48	44	46	15	3.8
Egypt	57				98	70	98	32	8.4

Sources: Asian Development Bank, Japan Bank for International Cooperation and the World Bank, *Connecting East Asia: A New Framework for Infrastructure* (Manila, Washington, Tokyo, 2005), 9; The United Nations Development Programme, *Human Development Report 2007/08* (New York: UN, 2007); Klaus Schwab and Michael E. Porter, *The Global Competitiveness Report 2008–2009* (Geneva: World Economic Forum, 2008), 384. The global rank comes from the last source.

Table 2.3 Road network and electricity generating capacity (EGC)

Country	Road network in 2000 (km)	Growth in road network, 1990–2000 (%)	Highways, 2005–08 (km)	Expressways (km), 2005–08	EGC (GW), 2000	Growth in EGC, 1990–2000
China	1,679,848	63	1,930,543	41,005	299	136
Indonesia	355,951	23			25	98
Vietnam	215,628	104			6	180
India	3,319,644	66	198,489	5,000	108	51
Brazil	1,724,929	3	200,000		69	32
South Africa	362,099	95			40	28

Sources: *Connecting East Asia*, 5; *China Statistical Yearbook 2006*, 42; internet sources on highway and expressways in India and Brazil.

suggested, from 1990–2003 private sector investment in East Asia amounted to about $190 billion. It trailed that in Latin America, but was more than three times as high as in South Asia, Middle East and North Africa, Sub-Saharan Africa and was much higher than in Europe and Central Asia. Due to a host of reasons including path dependency, policy reform, and property rights issues, the private sector was not the main driver in infrastructural development in East Asia. Instead, the state plays a leading role.[22]

In China, about half of the expenditure on infrastructure came from the government, slightly less than half from state-owned enterprises (SOEs), and only about 3 percent from the private sector.[23] In East Asia, such as Japan, Korea, China and Thailand, the government provides the strategic vision and plan for development of national infrastructure and coordinates construction of the infrastructure. The state or SOEs finance the construction. The state-led developmental model seems to explain well the rapid infrastructural development in China, Thailand, and Vietnam. In these nations, the expenditure on infrastructure in 2003 amounted to 7.3, 15.4 and 9.9 percent of GDP, respectively, much higher than India's 5 percent (2005–06), the Philippines's 3.6 percent and Indonesia's 2.7 percent.[24] These economies were also growing faster than the latter two. China's annual GDP growth from 2000–2004 averaged 8.7 percent, Vietnam's 7.2 percent, and Thailand's 5.3 percent, compared to Indonesia's 4.6 percent and the Philippines' 4.2 percent.[25]

The fourth element in pro-growth policies and institutions of pragmatic authoritarianism is the state's fiscal stimulus during economic crises, which helps China to escape severe economic downturns and avoid an economic "hard landing." Since the 1990s the pragmatic authoritarian state in China has twice unfolded a massive stimulus package. The first fiscal stimulus package was introduced in the wake of the Asian financial crisis that occurred in 1997. GDP growth in China decelerated in 1998 and 1999, reaching 7.8 percent and 7.6 percent, respectively, over two percentage points lower than that during 1996 and 1997 (which was 10.0 percent and 9.3 percent, respectively).[26] In 1999 the Chinese leaders started a massive regional developmental program called "great western regional development" (*xibu dakaifa*). In 2000 mega projects were launched and the state injected a huge amount of funding into these projects. The western developmental program aimed directly to accelerate the economic growth of the most backward western region in China by improving its environment and infrastructure and by tapping into sectors that the region has advantages in, such as power generation, natural resources, and tourism.

For the western developmental program, the government invested a substantial amount in the western region. In 2000 national investment in basic construction in the region totaled 166 billion yuan (around US$20 billion). In the first half of 2001 alone, total investment in fixed assets in the twelve western provinces totaled 171 billion yuan (US$20.7 billion), 30 percent higher than in 2000, and more than 10 percent higher than the increase in the coastal and central regions.

In addition, the state increased the share of the western region in its budgetary allocation in order to boost economic growth and reduce income disparity between the prosperous coast and the backward west. Between 1999 and 2001, budgets for investment in capital construction were a corresponding 23.5 percent, 25.9 percent and 25.6 percent for the west and 34.4 percent, 29.2 percent and 29 percent for the coast. The gap between the west and the coast in the share of budgetary allocation for capital investment thus declined from 10.9 percent, to 3.3 percent and 3.4 percent during this period.[27]

Thanks to the state's fiscal stimulus program China's GDP growth in 2000 and 2001 sustained a high level, registering 8.4 percent and 8.3 percent, respectively. China avoided an economic hard landing and emerged as one of the few, if not the only country in Asia that was little affected by the Asian financial crisis.

In 2008, China introduced the second fiscal stimulus package. In 2007 the Western financial crisis was unfolding. In 2007 and 2008 China's exports suffered badly in the wake of the crisis. Exports fell by 21.7 percent January to June 2009 year-on-year. In 2008 GDP growth in China reached 9.6 percent, down by 4.6 percentage points from 2007. The crisis ended the double-digit growth that China had been enjoying since 2003. China's GDP growth in the 4th quarter of 2008 even slipped to as low as 6.8 percent. In response, in late 2008 China unveiled a 4-trillion-yuan ($585.6 billion) stimulus package. The package targeted development of transport and rural infrastructure, provision of low-cost housing, environmental protection, social security, technological upgrade and innovation, welfare of peasants and low-income urban residents, and rebuilding of the quake zones.

As a result of the massive injection of governmental funds into the economy, China's GDP growth sustained a high pace. It registered 8.7 percent in 2009, and accelerated to 10.4 percent in 2010 and remained a respectable 9.3 percent in 2011. China has become the best performing country among the largest as well as emerging economies.

Provision of social welfare and remedies of inequalities

In fact this component relates to both economic and social governance. It involves substantial economic and financial input and affects the state's management of the society. As Chapter 4 is devoted to this topic, a brief discussion will be sufficient here.

Rapid economic growth in the reform era has brought substantial improvement in the living standard of China. However, it has also been accompanied with two noticeable economic and social problems. The first is the erosion of the rudimentary state or collective-funded provision of welfare that was closely linked with the command economy. In the cities the old welfare provision included life-time tenure of employment, pension covering the excessively early retirement of the workers by as early as 50 in age for women and 55 for men, and medical and child care of the employees was provided by their work units. In the countryside, the people's communes provided rudimentary health care. With the closure of numerous small and medium-sized SOEs and the struggling of a number of large SOEs owned by the local government the welfare provision of SOEs shrank in the 1990s. In the countryside, with the abolition of the communes and the slow development of rural health care rural residents lived in a void of public welfare provision in much of the 1990s. Individuals or families had to bear the main responsibilities of financing their own medical care, retirement, and unemployment. For the unemployed and peasants working in less developed areas, the burden was dauntingly heavy.

The other severe downside of rapid growth is rising income inequalities. Mao's China was one of the egalitarian societies in the world, though the excessive stress on social equity helped result in one of the lowest levels of per capita GDP in the world. In the reform era, especially since the mid-1980s income inequalities have soared steadily. The Gini coefficient of income distribution in China registered a low 0.288 in 1981, but soared to 0.403 in 1998 and to 0.459 in 2001, on par with the United States' 0.466 in 2001.[28] The Gini coefficient at 0.40 and above suggests a serious level of income inequalities. The income inequalities have seemingly continued to be aggravated in the following years.

The decline in the public provision of social welfare, increasing competition in the labor market and mounting pressure on workers, and rising income equalities serve as a hotbed for social discontents. The urban workers and peasants lament the losses of economic security and rudimentary social welfare they once enjoyed in Mao's era. They resent the fact that in the reform era a segment of the society has amassed an astounding amount of wealth sometimes through illegal means such as corruption.

In order to ease public grievances, since the late 1990s the Party state has started to introduce a series of measures to rebuild the social safety net and to help out low-income groups including the peasants. These efforts were intensified under the Hu–Wen administration during 2002–2012.

In the cities a welfare scheme called minimum living allowances was introduced in 1998 to provide aid for the unemployed in the wake of the reform of state-owned enterprises (SOEs). Later the state expanded a subsistence aid program for the very poor and the unemployed in the cities. Pension benefits for retired people have been increasing. In addition, through a set of policies the state mandates the provision of medical care and pensions for the formal employees in the cities.

In order to reduce the rural-urban income gap and improve the material life of the peasants, the state encourages rural industrialization, promotes productivity in farming, reduces fiscal burdens on peasants, creates new cities, and helps rural residents find work and retrieve unpaid wages in the cities. Importantly, it has increased financial support for agriculture, and has built roads and infrastructure in the countryside. The state also finances free and compulsory basic schooling in the countryside. In recent years a rural cooperative health care scheme has been instituted and expanded nationwide.

Finally, in order to reduce regional developmental gaps the national government has unfolded and invested a tremendous amount of money into several regional developmental schemes. They include the aforementioned western developmental program targeting the western region, the northeast revival program to help out the rust-belt northeast, and the "rise of the central region" program to accelerate the growth of the central region.

These welfare and anti-inequalities programs serve several political objectives. The leadership demonstrates to the population that the state is indeed concerned with inequalities, the well-being of the low-income groups and development of inland areas. Moreover, these welfare programs, heavy fiscal inputs and regional developmental schemes serve to restrain the alarming growth in rural-urban and coastal-inland income gaps. To some extent, as will be discussed in Chapter 4, these measures have earned the national government support from significant segments of the population, especially peasants. Nevertheless, the Party state still faces the challenges of income inequalities and of adequate provision of social welfare programs.

Social governance: differentiated treatment of social groups

In this section we will focus on the state's policies toward and relations with non-governmental organizations (NGOs) in China. When we examine the state-societal relationship, we literally refer to two relations, that is, the state's relationship with social groups and with social activities. Chapter 5 will use religions as an example and examine the state's relations with religious groups and religious activities.

In order to facilitate economic growth in the reform era the state has relaxed its control of the society. As a result, social groups and activities have revived. In China social activities can be in a very organized form and can take place within social groups or with the sponsorship and leadership of a given social group. The fixed and clearly-organized form of social groups can be seen in non-governmental groups (NGOs). NGOs here refer to organizations that are neither an organic part of the Party state, such as an agency or department of the CCP or the administrative branch, nor are they for-profit business organizations. Nevertheless, we need to be aware that in China due to the state's extensive intervention in social activities the pure non-governmental groups, namely, those NGOs that are independent of the state, are few in numbers and weak in influence. In contrast, many NGOs have maintained ties of some kind with the state and its agencies. In a way this is similar in Europe as well. A key difference is that in Western countries the NGOs have greater autonomy in their registration and operation such as setting of their policy agenda. The government in the West is subject to periodic popular elections and the rule of law respecting the autonomy of NGOs. Consequently, the Western governments are less likely to intervene extensively in the NGOs. In China official statistics distinguish the following three main types of NGOs. In reviewing the analyses and the data below it is useful to keep in mind that some NGOs are actually government-operated organizations (GONGOs) or Party NGOs (PANGOs) (which are set up by the CCP to advance its political agenda). Thus the statistics on NGOs will include these NGOs:

1   Social associations (*shehui tuanti*). They are formed by citizens, enterprises or public services units (*shiye danwei*) and operate according to their own constitutions. The examples of social associations include sectoral associations, academic associations, professional associations, and comprehensive associations representing a specific social sector or large social groups, such as women's associations.
2   Civil non-enterprise institutions (*minban feiqiye danwei*). They refer to social services-providing enterprises, public services units, social associations, other social groups, and citizens who used non-state assets. The main service areas where civil non-enterprise institutions operate include education, health, science and technology, culture, labor, civil affairs, sports, intermediate services, and law.
3   Foundations (*jijin hui*). They refer to social associations that use donations for public charity works. They include public foundations and private foundations.[29]

As demonstrated in Table 2.4, the total number of formally registered NGOs in China grew from 175,000 in 1994 to 446,000 in 2010, registering a growth by 155 percent and a very robust average of 6.4 percent per annum for that period. Out of the NGOs, social associations increased from 175,000 in 1994 to 245,000 in 2010, a gain by 40 percent for the period or an average 2.3 percent growth each year for that period; civil non-enterprise institutions grew from 6,000 in 1999 to 198,000 in 2010, a phenomenal 32-fold increase during a period of 11 years, or 34 percent on average per year. During 2003–10, foundations grew from

Table 2.4 Officially registered NGOs and subcategories in China, 1994–2010

Year	Total NGOs	Social associations	Civil Non-Enterprise Institutions	Foundations
1994	175,000	175,000		
1995	181,000	181,000		
1996	185,000	185,000		
1997	181,000	181,000		
1998	166,000	166,000		
1999	143,000	137,000	6,000	
2000	154,000	131,000	23,000	
2001	211,000	129,000	82,000	
2002	244,000	133,000	111,000	
2003	266,954	142,000	124,000	954
2004	288,892	153,000	135,000	892
2005	319,975	171,000	148,000	975
2006	354,144	192,000	161,000	1,144
2007	387,340	212,000	174,000	1,340
2008	413,597	230,000	182,000	1,597
2009	430,843	239,000	190,000	1,843
2010	446,000	245,000	198,000	2,200

Note: Data on foundations prior to 2002 were included into social associations.
Sources: "Er 00 Yi Nian Minzheng Shiye Fazhan Tongji Gonggao" (Statistical Bulletin on the Development of Civil affairs in 2001), posted at: http://news.xinhuanet.com/zhengfu/2002-10/09/content_589751.htm; "2009 Nian Minzheng Shiye Fazhan Tongji Gonggao" (Statistical Bulletin on the Development of Civil affairs in 2009), posted at: http://cws.mca.gov.cn/article/tjbg/201006/20100600081422.shtml; both accessed on August 25, 2013. Huang Xiaoyong and Cai Liqiang, "Zhongguo Minjian Zhuzhi Fazhan Buru Quanmian Tupo Jieduan" (The Development of China's Civil Organizations Enters a Stage of Full Breakthrough), in Huang Xiaoyong *et al.*, eds, *Zhongguo Minjian Zhuzhi Baogao: 2011–2012* (*Annual Report on Chinese Civil Organizations*) (Beijing: Shehui Kexue Chubanshe, 2012), 2–7.

954 in number to 2,200, a growth by 131 percent, or 0.5 percent on average per annum for that period. In 2010, over half of the NGOs (54.9 percent to be exact) were social associations, and 44.4 percent were civil non-enterprise institutions, and only 0.5 percent were foundations (Table 2.4).

In 2010 the largest portion (19.5 percent) of social associations were devoted to agriculture and rural areas, followed by social services (13.4 percent), industrial and commercial services (9.6 percent), culture (8.5 percent), and science, technology and research (8.0 percent). Meanwhile, the pattern for civil non-enterprise institutions is quite different, as nearly half of them (49.5 percent to be exact) were in the functional area of education, compared to 5.1 percent of the corresponding share of social associations. The other largest functional areas for civil non-enterprise institutions included social services (14.9 percent, compared to 13.4 percent and the second highest share of social associations in this area), and health (12.7 percent, compared to 4.6 percent of social associations).[30]

The relationship between the state and NGOs is a significant issue that has attracted much attention from scholars and the media. There have been a number of studies on this topic and the scholarly views vary. The best approach to the topic is to examine the state's differentiated treatment of different types of social groups. This is done in Chapter 4 as religious groups and activities are used as a case study. Mainland Chinese scholar Kang Xiaoguang tried to provide the most comprehensive survey of this topic. He distinguished 15 types of NGOs and examined the state's interaction with each of them. Given the limited space I will only summarize the main types of state-NGO relations according to him, which is indicated in the third column ("Mode of State Control") in Table 2.5. I will describe them below by first summarizing Kang's view and then supplement it with my discussion and scholarly studies on the topics.

Briefly stated, out of a total 15 types of NGOs in China, only the last four types in Table 2.5 were free from the state's control. First, grass-roots hobby groups enjoyed no interference from the state. However, they were non-political and had little interest in and negligible effects on governmental policies. Second, non-profit organizations registered as enterprises were subject to ineffective control by the state. According to Kang, these NGOs have relatively well-defined internal governance structures and provide charitable public services for society. They relied on volunteers and were the key innovators in organizing activities and advocating ideas and values. Third, family churches, grass-roots advocacy groups, grass-roots rights organizations, and international organizations were subject to the state's ineffective control. The state did try to impose control on these organizations and periodically crack down on them. However, this result was mixed. While these groups failed to grow as large and strong as they could, the state also failed to wipe them out and prevent their existence and activities. Fourth, political and social oppositions were prohibited by the state. Out of all NGOs, the state has been most concerned with this type and has devoted considerable resources to banning it. It has been very successful in this regard, as activists who wanted to start a political opposition group were closely monitored, tracked, swiftly arrested and severely punished.

On the other hand, the first eleven types of NGOs in Table 2.5 were subject to control by the state ranging from a very large to a moderate degree. The first four types of NGOs were controlled tightly by the state. The first three types, namely, (1) the eight national people's organizations and 25 social associations exempt from official registration,[31] (2) officially-run religious associations, as well as (3) residential neighborhood committees throughout urban China and village committees throughout rural China, were treated by the Party state as quasi-governmental organizations. The state exercised heavy influence on them, especially on the appointment of their leaders and their

Table 2.5 The State's relations with various NGOs in China

Organizational Type	Types of NGOs	Mode of State Control	Model of NGO Development
1	8 National People's Organizations and 25 Social associations Exempt from Registration	The NGO is treated as a quasi governmental unit	Development of the NGO is supported by the state
2	Officially-Run Religious Associations	The NGO is treated as a quasi governmental unit	Development of the NGO is supported by the state
3	Residential Neighborhood Committees; Village Committees	The NGO is treated as a quasi governmental unit	Development of the NGO is supported by the state
4	Public Services Units	Appointment controlled by the Party or the state; activities managed by functional government agencies.	Development of the NGO is supported by the state
5	People-Run Non Enterprises Units	Dual management (by the Ministry/ Bureau of Civil affairs and by the corresponding functional departments of the government)	The NGO is co-opted by the state
6	State-Initiated Social associations and Foundations	Dual management	Development of the NGO is supported by the state
7	Associations, Chambers of Commerce and Societies	Dual management	Development of the NGO is supported by the state
8	Non-State Charities and Foundations	Dual management	The NGO is co-opted by the state
9	Organizations Affiliated to, as a Subsidiary of, or Managed by Legal NGOs	Management by Parent NGOs	The NGO is co-opted by the state
10	Socially-Initiated Social associations, Property Owner Committees, and Religious Organizations	Dual management	The NGO is co-opted by the state

Organizational Type	Types of NGOs	Mode of State Control	Model of NGO Development
11	Socially-Initiated Organizations Affiliated to, as a Subsidiary of, or Managed by Legal NGOs	Management by Parent NGOs	The NGO is co-opted by the state
12	Grass-roots Hobby Groups	No Interference	No support from the state
13	Non-Profit Organizations Registered as Enterprises	Ineffective Control	The NGO is not subject to state control
14	Family Churches, Grass-roots Advocacy Groups, Grass-roots Rights Organizations, and International Organizations	Ineffective Control	The NGO is not subject to state control
15	Political Oppositions or Social Groups in Confrontation with the State	Prohibition	The NGO defies or resists control by the state

Kang Xiaoguang, Lu Xianying, and Han Heng, "Gaige Shidai de Guojia yu Shehui Guanxi" (State-Society Relations in the Reform Era), in Wang Ming, ed., *Zhongguo Minjian Zuzhi 30 Nian: Zuo Xiang Gongmin Shehui* (*Thirty Years of China's Civil Organizations: Toward Civil Society*) (Beijing: Shehui Kexue Wenxian Chubanshe, 2008), 287–337. I have tried to incorporate his actual description (instead of his original labels) in producing the above table.

political stance, with a possible exception of village committees that were elected by villagers. The state also shouldered a large share of their finance. The fourth type, namely, (4) public services units, was also subject to tight state control in a similar degree, as the appointment of their leaders was controlled by the Party or the state and their activities were regulated and supervised by corresponding governmental departments in the same functional area.

There are differing views on the role of the four types of NGOs in defending the interests of the relevant segments of the society that they are supposed to represent. In a study of the All-China Federation of Labor Unions (ACFLU) (which is also known as the All-China Federation of Trade Unions) Tim Pringle argued that the ACFLU made top-down attempts to voice concerns about workers' rights, serve as a link between labor rights, labor union activities and social harmony, and gain credibility among workers. For example, migrant workers in the cities have been included in the working class since the 14th Labor Union Congress in 2003. The ACFLU took part in the law-drafting and experimental implementation of regulations on collective bargaining and collective wage consultation. It intervened in mediation, arbitration and the courts involving labor disputes. It promoted direct elections of labor union officials and committee members at the enterprise level. This activism of the ACFLU was attributable to the rising labor shortage and the rights consciousness among young workers, especially younger migrant workers.[32] Nevertheless, this optimistic assessment of the national labor union was contradicted by a study based on extensive surveys of labor union chairpersons in eight coastal, central, and western provinces during 2004–2006. Masaharu Hishida, Kazuko Kojima, Tomoki Ishii and Jian Qiao found that many of these chairpersons took up party and labor union positions at the same time. Although these chairpersons thought this arrangement gave them power bases and the network in the Party state to protect workers' interests and although they did embark on top-down initiatives for this purpose, collective negotiation for workers and democratic participation in union matters were a formality. Workers were not given a place by the state to protect their own interests.[33]

Another study of a national association for enterprises, namely, China Enterprise Confederation (CEC) (*Zhongguo Qiye Lianhehui*) revealed a growing trend of CEC in expanding its autonomy in finance, governance and operation, such as its own appointment of officials at the section (*chu*) level, expansion of regional and local branches, safeguarding of legal interests of entrepreneurs, the increasing portion of self-raised revenue, and promotion of innovations. In addition, along with the Ministry of Labor and Social Security and with the ACFLU, CEC was becoming one party of the triangle-arrangement in managing labor relations in China. Nevertheless, it is even clear from the study that CEC was still subject to extensive influence of the state. The leaders of CEC continued to be former governmental officials, appointment of senior officials of CEC had to be approved by the government, the association acted more as the implementer rather than an initiator of governmental policies, and a portion of revenue of CEC continued to come from the Ministry of Finance though it had been declining.[34]

The fifth to the eleventh types of NGOs in Table 2.5 were subject to a moderate degree of control by the state. They included (5) people-run non-enterprise units, (6) state-initiated social associations and foundations, (7) associations, chambers of commerce and societies, (8) non-state charities and foundations, (9) organizations affiliated to, as a subsidiary of, or managed by legal NGOs, (10) socially-initiated social associations, property owner committees, and religious organizations, and (11) socially-initiated organizations affiliated to, as a subsidiary of, or managed by legal NGOs. Most of these NGOs were under dual management, namely, management by the Ministry/Bureau of Civil Affairs and by the corresponding functional departments of the government. Yiyi Lu argued that these NGOs were in a state of dependent autonomy. In order to be officially registered, these NGOs had to maintain amicable relations with their formal sponsor associations or governmental agencies and depended on these patrons and the state for their development and survival. On the other hand, they also enjoyed a degree of operational autonomy as the central government could not monitor a large number of NGOs and as the Chinese state was fragmented. However, the lack of state supervision would also permit these NGOs to ignore rules and advance their own narrow self-interests at the expense of public interests that they were supposed to serve. This gave rise to an "uncivil society."[35]

In sum, the above analysis and a number of scholarly analyses of NGOs in China point to the dominance of the state in the NGOs, despite a possible trend of activism among certain NGOs, including the ACFLU. Qiusha Ma, in a study on the NGOs in China in 2006, proclaimed in an upbeat tone that legally and institutionally social institutions and civil non-enterprise institutions enjoyed a status outside the state system. Yet while she observed sensibly that these NGOs were "increasingly powerful instruments through which the Chinese people participate[d] in public affairs," especially in social and economic matters, she acknowledged the continued state supremacy in the state-civil society interaction, the "vulnerability of NGOs" and the absence of their voice in political and religious affairs.[36] Her last point was echoed by prominent China scholars such as Yongnian Zheng, Joseph Fewsmith, and Baogang He in a volume of articles on the NGOs in China.[37]

Overall, the pragmatic authoritarian state has succeeded in allowing NGOs to play a bigger role in social and economic affairs and to provide functional and formalistic (albeit non-independent and democratic) representation of functional segments of the society. By doing so, it has eased social tension to some extent, though it is far from minimized. It has also maintained its control over the majority of NGOs and has severely restricted the influence of defiant NGOs. Chapter 5 will explore and explain the subtle strategies of the state's management of social activities and social groups.

Political governance

Political governance is probably the most complex and substantial part of pragmatic authoritarianism, even though, compared to economic governance, it may not be the most successful. Table 2.1 lists several important components of political governance. When going over these elements, and conscious of the space, I will provide a brief overview in two circumstances. First, these elements have been analyzed in detail in the existing studies. These elements include eclectic borrowing, reformulation of ideology, and some of the elements in the endeavor toward good governance. Second, a number of other elements will be discussed in detail in the following chapters. The elements under this category include leadership succession, crisis management, and grass-roots and intra-Party democracy.

Eclectic borrowing of successful practices

Shambaugh observed that China's political and policy analysts studied very carefully the positive and negative lessons from "communist, ex-communist, and non-communist" ruling parties in the globe. For the purpose of improving the capacity of the Party state to govern, the Party state is willing to borrow "bits and pieces of the wide variety" of different political systems and institute them in its own institutions and practices.[38] It is clear in this strenuous endeavor the Party state is very pragmatic and is largely free from ideological shackles and political constraints. The Party state will adopt the effective institution and practice it has learned from abroad as long as they help to sustain its rule.

Ideological reformulation

Ideology is a primary tool for the Party to justify its policies and motivate and guide Party members in implementing them. Along with its organization, ideology enables the Party or the top Party leader to unite the Party members, mobilize the masses, extract resources and outmaneuver opponents of the Party or the opponents of the top Party leader.[39] In the reform era the Party state's stance toward ideology has been largely pragmatic. When ideology became an obstacle for furthering economic reform, it was downplayed and ignored. When the marketization agenda had been installed and the Party state confronted rival ideas including liberalism and excessive materialism, and when its legitimacy was questioned, it reformulated ideology in order to justify the relevance and "advanced nature" of the Party and to fend off rival ideas.

In Mao's times, ideological purity was regarded as the key barometer of social progress. The Party prided itself as a vanguard for the working classes, especially the proletariat in the cities and poor and lower-middle class peasants in the countryside. Mao launched numerous campaigns to condemn officials and citizens who favored elements of the market economy, such as household farming and material incentives for workers, and branded them negatively as "revisionist." Decades of Maoism had resulted in a stagnation of living standards. Ideological emphases were practiced at the expense of economic development and improvement in the people's material life.

Deng, in launching economic reform and opening up China, encountered stern resistance from a conservative coalition of top conservative veterans, ideologues, and segments of the population who came to accept Maoist praise for the superiority of public ownership, heavy industrial sectors, as well as inland provinces.[40] In particular, ideologues and the people who embraced Maoism persistently opposed Deng's economic experiments and reform initiatives, including special economic zones, the opening of China, promotion of private and collective enterprises, and reform of state-owned enterprises (SOEs). In order to overcome ideologues' opposition, Deng employed two strategies. First, he reinterpreted Maoism and the Party's ideology. In 1978, he proclaimed that the core of Maoism was to view practice, instead of blind application of Marxist-Leninist doctrines, as the main criterion for judging the success of policies. In the 1980s, he oversaw the development of the theory of the primitive stage of socialism. According to this theory, China was at the primitive stage of socialism and would remain there for a long time to come. At that stage, the primary task for the Party was to develop the productive forces (or the economy) so as to improve the political consciousness of the people and prepare them for communism. Second, in the early

1990s, especially in his final assault on conservatism in his southern tour in 1992, Deng called on the Party to stop the ideological debate over reform. He urged the Party to devote energy away from time-consuming debates toward economic development. He declared that development was the last word in Chinese politics.

Deng's downplay of ideology enabled him to overcome conservative opposition and secured the acceptance of the marketization agenda by the Party. Nevertheless, Deng's convenient emphasis on economic development and marketization and his brushing-aside of ideology had unintended consequences. A single-minded emphasis on marketization and commercialization resulted in the worship of money and excessive materialism. The neglect of the Party's ideology created a vacuum in the mind of cadres and officials and removed the ideological guide for them. Many Party members and officials turned to materialism, religions, folk religions, and Western liberalism. As a result of the ideological void and weak enforcement of law and rules, corruption was growing rampant within the Party. Some cadres resorted to religious cults such as Falun Gong as alternative beliefs. In 1999, Falun Gong even organized 10,000 followers to surround Zhongnanhai, the residential and office compound of the top state leaders. The populace also equated the Party with an agent of marketization and materialism.

Alerted by these developments, Jiang Zemin concluded that ideology needed to be rebuilt in order to provide cadres an ideological guide and discipline, to fend off alternative thoughts, and to earn political legitimacy for the Party among the population. Since 1995 he started a series of exploratory efforts to remake the Party's ideology. In 1995, Jiang emphasized that senior leading officials at the ministerial level and above should "stress politics" (*jiang zhengzhi*) and study the Party's political lines, instead of getting lost in a variety of unsanctioned thoughts. In March 1996, Qiao Shi, Jiang's arch rival in the Party and the Chairman of the Standing Committee of the NPC, formally proposed to "rule the country in accordance with law." In order to counter Qiao's dominant role in political discourse within the Party, Jiang urged in the same month senior leading officials to heed closely politics, virtue, and political studies (*san jiang*, or three stresses). He criticized the single-minded focus on economic construction. However, Jiang's "stress-politics" and "three-stresses" were received coldly by the Party, as they lacked originality and appeal. As a result, Jiang stepped up his search for an innovative and attractive ideological reformulation. In February 2000, he proclaimed in his visit to Gaozhou in Guangdong that the Party represented the most advanced mode of production, the most advanced culture and the interests of the majority of the people. This notion of new ideology was termed "three represents" (*sange daibiao*). Jiang also suggested that the rule by virtue should go hand in hand with the rule of law.[41] This new ideological formula contained an element of creativity as well as relevancy to the complex and changing China in the wake of marketization. It had thus evoked some resonation among segments of the cadres and intellectuals. At the Sixteenth Party Congress in November 2002, Jiang's "three-represents" theory was enshrined in the revised Party constitution as an ideological basis for the Party. At a session of the Tenth NPC in March 2003, this theory was also included in the amended constitution. The Party formally, though in a low-key fashion, recruits private entrepreneurs as fresh blood.

Upon coming into power, one of the first initiatives Hu undertook was to unfold ideological formulation bearing his marks. On the one hand, he sustained Jiang's efforts to remold the Party's ideology and paid formalistic tribute to the ideological legacy of his predecessor, i.e., Jiang's "three represents" theory. On the other hand, he gradually put forward an ideological platform that evaded the controversial elements of Jiang's notion, but revived populist elements in Mao's and even traditional Chinese political ideology.

Meanwhile, Hu immediately acted to pronounce his own ideological formulations. They served to distinguish his own conception of political ideals from that of Jiang's, overcome Jiang's innovative yet elitist ideology, and to establish his own political legitimacy. On his first trip outside Beijing, he made a pilgrimage to the Party's revolutionary site. Honoring Mao's call for a prudent and thrifty lifestyle, Hu proposed his trademark slogan: "Power should serve the people, compassion should be showered upon the people, and benefits should be sought after for the people." This was termed the "new three-people principle." Two months after his revolutionary pilgrimage, Hu also proclaimed a "two-for" principle, that is, "establishing the Party for the public, and governing the nation for the people." These two principles evoked Confucian emphasis on people in state affairs and on compassionate rulers. It also renewed Mao's call for cadres to serve the people. By proposing these two principles, Hu aimed to establish a pro-people and populist ideological platform, and distanced himself from Jiang's elitist ideology and controversial embrace of the rich (especially private entrepreneurs). It indicated the new leadership's concerns for common people and even "disadvantaged groups" during China's economic reform and their intention to help them out.

Hu tentatively proposed the "scientific concept of development" during the SARS epidemic in the middle of 2003 and did so formally in September 2004. This new formulation aimed to overcome a simplistic focus on economic development pioneered by Deng and installed by Jiang. He also called on officials to pay attention to the environment and people's actual living standard, physical and spiritual health. This notion served as a key instrument for the Hu–Wen leadership to reorient China's economic growth toward balanced and sustainable socio-economic development.

In February 2005, Hu called for the building of a harmonious society. According to Hu, a "socialist harmonious society" is one that is based on democracy, the rule of law, fairness, justice, trust, friendship and love, vitality, stability, order, as well as harmonious relations between man and nature. Ironically, his call was a direct response to sharply rising social disturbances and protests in China in recent decades. Supposedly, Hu's notion of a harmonious society served two purposes. First, it offered an ideological remedy for rising social protests by combining the Confucian ideals of a harmonious society, social order, and stability with universal ideals of democracy, the rule of law, and trust. Second, it signaled to the public that China's top leaders were keenly aware of its plight and acted promptly to address them, and that they could be trusted.

Not all Hu's ideological formulations are original and appealing to the public. Around August 2006 Hu also proposed "eight glories and eight shames." Hu espoused six good deeds such as law abiding, honesty, and helping others and criticized eight shameful acts, including dishonesty and law breaking. Hu used the behavior code to enhance Chinese "spiritual civilization" and morality. Within the Party, Hu has also launched two campaigns to improve the members' moral behavior. First, he goaded the Party to learn from model members who dedicated their lives to serving people under their jurisdiction and died in their duties. The primary example was former Huerhot Party Secretary Niu Yuru. Second, from January 2005 onward the Party launched an 18-month ideological campaign among its members to maintain their advanced nature. Members were required to evaluate themselves against the Party's proposed behavioral guide. They had to write a report to criticize themselves and subject themselves to comments by others. Nevertheless, these efforts easily resembled the Maoist styled political slogans and might be dismissed as political indoctrination. Analysts voiced their skepticism about their effectiveness.[42]

When Xi Jinping took over the helm of the Party state from Hu, he also started to search for his own ideological formulations while paying respect to Hu's. He proclaimed in November 2012 that the Chinese people, under the leadership of the CCP, would be able to live to see the fulfillment of the China dream (*zhongguo meng*) of the revival of the Chinese nation as a world-class prosperous and strong power. Simply put, the China dream refers to a fair, corruption-free, safe, secure, orderly and rich society at home and a strong, prosperous, and respected China abroad. Xi expected that the CCP could fulfill the China dream for the Chinese population by 2049.[43] He also called on the cadres and the people to establish "three confidences," that is, confidence in the theory, the path, and the institutions (*lilun zixing, daolu zixing, zhidu zixing*) that the CCP has chosen.

Xi went as far as to authorize the No. 9 document of the Party that was circulated within the Party in 2013. The document suggested the utmost danger for the Party is Western political liberalism, including Western constitutional democracy, the so-called universal values of human rights, free press, civil society, pro-market neoliberalism, and severe criticisms of the records of the CCP before 1978. He also ordered the Party members to return to the "masses line" publicized initially by Mao by relating their work to the common people's concerns.[44]

Overall, Jiang and Hu tried to remake the Party's ideology in order to earn political legitimacy for the Party, and improve the image of the Party and especially its top leaders to the public. They also made numerous efforts to inject Confucian ideals and populism into their ideological platform. They wanted to demonstrate to the nation that the Party's leaders were compassionate and enlightened and that the Party was adapting itself to the new circumstance while trying its best to serve the people. Through these efforts the Party has made itself appear adaptive and flexible. The Party's pro-people ideology has also earned its leaders, especially Hu, some sympathy from the public.

Nevertheless, the new ideological formulations also had their critical weaknesses. They are not necessarily backed by institutional adjustment that could effectively ensure that cadres at all levels live up to the ideology. The rule of law is not faithfully practiced. Cadres are subject to neither election nor pressure and supervision from the media, the parliament, and the people. Cadres thus lack the incentives to implement the Party's ideals. Over the years the Party's ideology may become more like talk than reality. Furthermore, some of the Party's ideological indoctrination and promotion seems like Maoist old-style campaigns. Their effectiveness has proved to be questionable.

On the other hand, by constantly reminding the cadres and the people of the Party's sanctioned ideological line, the Party state has warned its members not to embrace liberal ideologies and has signaled to the population the political values especially Western liberalism that it will not endorse. By doing so, it has maintained the Party's ideology as the official one in the nation and has rendered other ideologies illegitimate, thereby significantly reducing the political space for alternative ideologies. All in all, in the reform era ideology has been remade to be a tool to justify the Party's governance and its governance program, to install the code of conduct among officials, and to pre-empt the rise of rival ideologies. The Party has thus come to view and use ideology pragmatically.

Overhaul of crisis management

By crises I mean sudden events that occur outside the expectation of leadership in China and that have the potential for seriously disrupting the normal life of the people. Crises can be categorized in a variety of forms—national versus local; external versus internal crises; political, economic, environmental, and public health crises (such as epidemics); natural disasters versus human-error induced accidents. In China, a country of a continental size, local crises can take place on a daily basis, and national crises may take place occasionally. In particular, natural disasters, such as floods, droughts, and earthquakes, have been the most frequent and destructive form of crises.

Crisis management is one of the most important institutions for governance. As a national crisis can affect millions of people adversely, the ability of the state to manage crises can matter a great deal not only for the people whose life is disrupted and for their support for the state. It also matters for the other people who are judging how well the state is helping out people in need and whether the regime is worth their support. Improper management of crises can swiftly and severely undermine the credibility and legitimacy of the Party state. In the Severe Acute Respiratory Syndrome (SARS) epidemic in early 2003 the provincial authority in Guangdong failed either to contain it or to publicize it openly. As a result, the deadly and highly contagious disease spread to Hong Kong, Taiwan, Southeast Asia, and North America. It devastated the economy of these affected areas and caused public panic. Suddenly, global public opinion chided China's government for ineffectual and secretive management of the epidemic and for ignoring the well-being of its citizens and people outside China. Inside China there were also a growing number of people questioning the government's management of the epidemic in the early months. By decidedly reversing the secretive management of the disease and by quickly containing the epidemic, President Hu and Premier Wen won high marks for their leadership and seemed to consolidate their power within the first year of their assumption of power.

Prior to the SARS epidemic in 2003 institutions for crisis management in China were developed mainly in high-risk sectors and over natural disasters, especially floods. Comprehensive and systemic institutions for crisis management were largely underdeveloped. The preparatory plans were drafted and responsible agencies were set up in coping with accidents in the following three areas: (1) high risk sectors such as coal mining, the chemical industry, and nuclear power plants, (2) departments that tended to frequently experience crises, such as public security, fire fighting, and medical aid, and (3) in the 1990s earthquakes. The only locality that set up overall crisis management institutions was Shanghai in 2001.[45]

In practice when coping with natural disasters on an unprecedented scale the Party state did provide coordination and mobilization of various branches of the state and resources. This was necessary for minimizing the devastation of natural disasters. In the summer of 1998, for example, the Yangtze River experienced the largest flood since 1954 and the Sonhua and Nen Rivers in the northeast also experienced a high flood, which altogether endangered the lives and property of 18 million residents in 11 provinces. In May under the leadership of Vice Premier and its Director Wen Jiabao, the National General Headquarters for Preventing Floods and Droughts convened a meeting to make arrangements to minimize the damage of the flood. For three months in the summer the Party state mobilized 300,000 soldiers and armed police to help fight the floods. Along with Wen, President Jiang, Premier Zhu, and a number of members of the Politburo toured the dams along the Yangtze to supervise anti-flood efforts. They coordinated the flood-control efforts of the military, the police, governmental agencies and six provinces along the Yangtze.[46]

In addition, over sensitive and localized crises, such as epidemics and high casualty accidents, the Party state tended to take a secretive approach to management. It mobilized only the functional governmental agencies (such as the public health bureaus in the case of epidemics) to deal with the crises while hiding the news of the crises from the other agencies (other than the superiors of the responsible agency) and the population. This secret approach, which was adopted in the early weeks of the SARS outbreak in southern China, aimed to minimize social instability and threats to the Party state.

One of the bitter lessons the Party state learned from the SARS epidemic in early 2003 was that the lack of crisis management institutions helped produce ineffectual management of the epidemic. In the wake of the SARS epidemic the Chinese leaders endeavored to build comprehensive and nationwide institutions for crisis management and to improve transparency in this regard. In November 2003, under the leadership of Premier Wen Jiabao, a small working group for preparatory plans for sudden events was set up at the State Council, the administrative branch of the Party state. The General Office of the State Council distributed a Guide to the Framework for Relevant Departments and Units of the State Council to Formulate and Revise Preparatory Plans for Sudden Events in April 2004. The General Office also circulated a Guide to the Framework for Provincial People's Governments to Formulate and Revise Preparatory Plans for Sudden Events in May 2004. By the end of 2005 national and local preparatory plans for crisis management were largely completed. By the end of 2009 the number of these plans reached 2.4 million.

The preparatory plans for crisis management in China have six categories, namely national, special items, departmental, local, enterprise and public institutions, and large-scale events and activities. Crises were classified into four grades based on the level of the potential devastation—Grade I: grave (*tebie zhongdao*); Grade II: major (*zhongda*); Grade III: big (*jiaoda*); Grade IV: ordinary (*yiban*). The guidelines of preparatory plans for crisis management require that in the event of a crisis at Grade I or II the governmental administration at all levels should promptly, accurately, objectively, and comprehensively publicize the crisis and the corresponding measures to the society. Each crisis management preparatory plan has five components, namely, the command structure and responsibilities, prevention and early warning mechanisms, procedures and measures for handling crises, safeguard and support measures for crisis management, and measures for recovery and rebuilding after crises.[47]

By the end of 2009 all provincial, municipal, and county governments had formulated their overall preparatory plans for crisis management, and many functional agencies of the government also made their crisis management plans. The government, enterprises, and public institutions are obligated by the crisis management guidelines to publicize timely information on the crisis to the society. By doing so the Party state has significantly reduced its political vulnerability due to its improper and secretive management of crises. It has also greatly enhanced its ability to deal with major crises that may undermine itself.

Institutionalization of leadership succession

Leadership succession has been the most risk-fraught institution of the Chinese political system since the founding of the People's Republic of China (PRC). Succession prior to Hu Jintao has been fraught with purges. These purges exposed the rift within the top leadership. In the wake of these purges the Party suffered from political devastation. Three of the successors hand-picked by Chairman Mao Zedong, namely, Liu Shaoqi, Lin Biao and Hua Guofeng, all fell from grace. Although Hua was able to eventually succeed Mao, he was too weak a leader to ward off challenges from Deng Xiaoping, Mao's former friend-in-arms, in whom Mao lost confidence and denounced in 1975. Two of the favorite heirs apparent of Deng Xiaoping, namely, Hu Yaobang and Zhao Ziyang, were also purged due to their disagreements with Deng over political reform. Jiang, who was Deng's third and reluctant choice, was nearly replaced in early 1992. He managed to succeed Deng only after he vowed to follow Deng's marketization course.

Since then this crucial department of the Chinese political system has undergone much institutionalization. Hu's smooth ascendance as the top leader marks the first real smooth power transfer in the People's Republic of China.

The surprisingly rapid and smooth power transition from Jiang to Hu and later from Hu to Xi can be explained most importantly by ongoing institutionalization of China's leadership succession.[48] Institutionalization of China's leadership succession started in Deng's later years, especially after the 1989 Tiananmen movement. Before 1989, Deng, along with chief conservative Chen Yun, had been pushing for leadership renewal by retiring veteran leaders and promoting younger technocratic leaders. New selective criteria were set for young leaders—high education, young in age, professional training, and political reliability.[49] Meanwhile, Deng also favored young leaders embracing his market liberalism, with coastal working experience, and having served in both local and national posts.[50] However, leadership transition was incomplete, as a few top veteran leaders such as Deng and Chen continued to determine policies from behind the scene and even picked or sacked young front-line leaders such as Hu Yaobang and Zhao Ziyang.

These trends of institutionalization of retirement and promotion continued under Jiang. In the late 1990s the age and two-term limits were imposed on top posts, including the State President, the Premier, and the General Secretary of the CCP. In 1997 Qiao Shi, the powerful No. 2 of the CCP, retired as he reached 70, thereby setting an important precedent of retirement at 70. In 2002, Jiang also retired from the State Presidency and the Party General Secretary after he had served in both posts for two terms. Another secondary reason was that he well exceeded 70 in age.[51] In the last two Party Congresses in 2007 and 2012, respectively, 67 appeared to be the age threshold for new entrants into the Politburo and its Standing Committee.

A key component in the institutionalization of leadership succession that has been ignored by many China observers is the designation of the core leader and two-step assumption of the post. Deng brought about this arrangement after the 1989 Tiananmen Movement. He mandated that the core leader should control three posts at the same time and become the first among equals. However, he apparently made arrangements so that a new core leader could assume the post of the Chairmanship of the Central Military Commission (CMC) sometime after he took over the State Presidency and the Party General Secretary. Deng himself handed over the CMC Chairmanship to Jiang in November 1989, months after Jiang became the General Secretary of the CCP.[52]

Apparently, Jiang followed the arrangement of phased succession set by his powerful predecessor Deng. He handed over to Hu the posts of the State Presidency and the General Secretary of the CCP first at the Sixteenth Party Congress in November 2002. Less than two years later, he passed the CMC Chairmanship to Hu.

At the 18th Party Congress in late 2012 Hu made a surprising move by handing over all his three top posts to Xi Jinping, his successor. He also made a forceful call for ending old veteran leaders' uninvited interference in the policies of the new leaders. His move earned widespread applause by observers.

Through institutionalizing the process the CCP has thus so far avoided deadly conflict over succession especially between the incumbent President and the General Party Secretary and his predecessor. Since 1990 no successor-in-waiting has been purged. This can be regarded as one of biggest achievements of the Party in political governance.

The Party's control of key state branches

It has been well accepted that the CCP controls all the major branches of the state, including the administration, the military, the police, the judiciary branch, the legislature, the state banks, and even the largest national SOEs. It does so through controlling the appointments of key posts in these state branches and the major SOEs. In certain cases the formality of approval by other agencies will be followed after the Party nominates the only candidate for these posts. In these scenarios the Party, via its Department of Organization, tentatively chooses the final candidate for the post and a formalistic procedure will be gone through before the appointment is announced. For example, the appointment of the state and governmental (administration) posts such as the President, the State Chairman of the Central Military Commission, the Premier, and the head of the Supreme Court and of the Supreme Procuratorate, will need to be approved by the legislature at the same level (the National People's Congress) in this case. As the CCP controls the nomination and election of the legislators, the legislators will accept the Party's preferred candidates for these aforementioned posts. Otherwise, their legislative posts will be quickly reassigned by the Party. For this reason, even the legislative approval of the candidates decided by the Party is a mere formality.

Through dictating major appointments the CCP controls all the major branches and key components of the state, including the military, the police, the court, legislature, and over 100 of the largest SOEs. The CCP is thus able to translate its decisions and policies into policies and actions of each of these branches and units of the state.

In addition, the national leadership of the CCP, again through the Department of Organization, controls the appointment of local leaders at the provincial level, such as the provincial Party secretary (the No. 1 leader of a province), the provincial governors, and posts at the deputy-provincial rank. By doing so, the national government controls the localities. For example, in order to continue to serve in their posts provincial leaders will need to pledge loyalty to the national leadership and also keep their subordinates (such as leaders at the city and county levels in the province) in line with the national Party lines. This mechanism prevents any local tendency toward separation and keeps China united.[53]

Through the subtle control of key appointments the pragmatic authoritarian state exercises its power, permeates all areas and all levels of the state, and keeps the state machinery working to serve the interests of the Party.

The Party's censorship of the media and the internet

In addition to controlling the organization of the state, the CCP also tries to influence people's minds through censoring the media and the internet. The Department of Propaganda of the CCP regularly issues instructions to the chiefs and editors of major publications throughout the nation on what to report and how to report, especially over sensitive news events and topics. Editors of any publication that refuses to follow the instructions will be disciplined and removed and the contents of relevant issues of the publication will be forcefully changed. In addition, the state, through the Ministry of Public Security, also censors the internet by preventing the postings on the internet of commentaries that are highly critical of the top leaders, and blatantly call for change in the political regime, or until recent years even commentaries that continuously and relentlessly expose the wrongdoing and power abuse of a string of leading officials in a locality or a nation. In certain cases individuals who post these scathing comments on the Party state will be detained and punished. By keeping the media and the internet on a short leash the Party state has prevented the snowballing of messages that aim to instigate or coordinate large protests or upheavals, and undermine the image of the top leaders. It also reduces the accessibility and impact of values and ideologies rivaling the official ideology to the potential audience.

Endeavor toward "good governance"

The Party state in the reform era strives for good governance in order to sustain its legitimacy. The Party state sees good governance as both a viable way to deliver impressive economic growth and a politically safe alternative to political liberalization. The endeavor by the Party state toward good governance includes efforts to strengthen official accountability and improve administrative efficiency and transparency.

Official accountability

In the 2000s the Party state has introduced formal institutions to enforce accountability of officials. On April 21, 2001 the State Council promulgated the first document holding officials accountable for public and employee safety, i.e., "Regulation Regarding Pursuing Administrative Responsibilities for Particularly Large Safety Accidents," which was also coined No. 302 Document. The document stipulated that all leading cadres at all levels were responsible for public safety and should be disciplined for failing this duty. A number of provinces including Guangxi, Jiangsu, Fujian, Shanxi, Liaoning, Henan, Hunan, Guangxi, Sichuan, and Shaanxi, formulated their own rules for implementation.

According to official statistics, from April 2001 to August 2002, supervising authorities in China applied No. 302 document in 207 particularly large accidents, each involving more than 10 deaths. Out of these 207 applications 176 were closed. Altogether, 1,684 cadres were penalized, including six provincial and ministerial level officials, sixty-two prefectural and bureau-level cadres, 352 county-level ones, and 1,113 section or below level cadres. Furthermore, 340 people were turned over to legal agencies for legal investigation and prosecution.[54]

China's legislature also formulated a law to mandate safety in work. On June 29, 2002, the 28th meeting of the Ninth National People's Congress (NPC) Standing Committee approved the Law on Work Safety. The law was put into effect on November 1, 2002. Article 4 of the law requires production and business units to set up and improve the responsibility system for work safety and improve the conditions for it to guarantee work safety. Article 13 also stipulates that the State applies the responsibility investigation system in case of accidents related to work safety and pursues the legal responsibilities of individuals responsible for such accidents.[55]

The Party and the government also formulated rules regarding official accountabilities for their official duties. On July 9, 2002 the "Articles for Work in Selecting and Promoting Party and Government Leading Cadres" were promulgated by the Central Committee of the Party. This policy document stipulated that institutional sanctions could be imposed on officials so as to ensure the implementation of No. 302 Document. The articles specified four types of resignation, as well as demotion. The first two types of resignation were voluntary and normal—resignation due to official reassignment; voluntary resignation for personal and other reasons. The other two, self-censured resignation and commanded resignation, were meant to discipline incompetent officials. Cadres themselves could initiate self-censured resignation for failing to carry out their duties. In the case of commanded resignation, a cadre was ordered to resign by a higher authority that deemed the cadre incompetent or unfit for his/her duties. Commanded resignation might need to go through legally stipulated procedures if necessary. Cadres who lacked the ability to perform their duties should be demoted.[56]

The SARS epidemic was a critical event that had strengthened the Party state's drive to enforce official accountability. During the state-led anti-SARS campaign about 1,000 government officials were dismissed for failing to cope with the epidemic.[57]

In April 2004 the Party promulgated the first Party document that stipulated concrete and detailed procedures for official resignation and dismissals. It marked a significant step in enforcing official accountability. "Provisional Regulation on the Resignation of Party and Government Leading Cadres" clarified four types of resignation stipulated in the "Articles for Work in Selecting and Promoting Party and Government Leading Cadres" of July 2002, especially self-censured and commanded resignation. Chapter 4 of the regulation spelled out self-censured resignation. Article 14 of Chapter 4 required in principle that leading cadres who had committed serious errors and negligence, that caused severe losses or resulted in very serious social repercussions, or bore a major responsibility for serious accidents, should resign out of self-censure. Article 15 stipulated nine occasions where leading cadres should resign. They included leading cadres who bore leadership responsibilities for (1) grave collective incidents (referring to disturbances involving 50 participants or more),[58] (2) for severe errors in decision making which resulted in huge economic losses or serious social repercussions; (3) severe negligence in preventing and managing disasters and epidemics which resulted in huge economic losses or serious social repercussions; (4) severe negligence in safety work and for a series of or numerous grave accidents or for a serious accident; (5) severe negligence in supervision of markets, environmental protection, and social management and for causing a series of and numerous grave accidents or grave criminal cases which resulted in huge losses or serious social repercussions; (6) failure to carry out "Articles regarding Work in Selecting and Promoting Party and Governmental Leading Cadres"; (7) negligence in supervision and management of subordinates, allowing members of its leadership group or one's subordinates to commit a string of or numerous rule-infringing and unlawful acts that resulted in serious social repercussions; (8) failure to stop serious rule-infringement and unlawful acts by one's spouse, children, or staff, which resulted in serious social repercussions; (9) other cases where self-censured resignation was appropriate.

Article 19 of Chapter 6 also defined the use of commanded resignation in the case of cadres whose performance at work disqualified them from their current post.[59] The regulation stipulated that in the case of self-censured resignation and commanded resignation for the sake of official accountability, if cadres are appointed by the People's Congress or the People's Political Consultative Conference, their resignation should go through the legally stipulated procedures (namely, their removal should be approved by either of these two bodies). For cadres who undergo self-censured or commanded resignation, if they have violated Party disciplines, government regulations, or laws, they should also be held accountable for these infringements.[60]

Provisions on self-censured and commanded resignation were also included in the Law on Civil Servants that came into effect on January 1, 2006. The law contains the following stipulations in line with the aforementioned documents: leading officials should resign when they have committed serious blunders in their work, when their negligence of duties caused serious losses or resulted in serious social repercussions, and when they were responsible for serious accidents; leading officials should resign out of self-censure for serious accidents or errors; they should be ordered to resign if they failed to do so, or if they were no longer suitable for the current posts. Thus for the first time official accountability has been defined in national law.[61]

Under the Hu–Wen leadership a number of leaders resigned in order to take responsibility for serious accidents that took place under their jurisdiction. However, the career path of these disciplined leaders has aroused public discussion. In April 2003 Meng Xuenong, the then Beijing Mayor, along with the Minister of Public Health Zhang Wenkang, were dismissed for failing to contain the SARS epidemic in the national capital. Meng, who assumed the mayorship for only 93 days, was widely viewed as a scapegoat for the ineffectual management of the SARS outbreak that could be blamed on both the municipal leadership and Jiang's secretive management of the epidemic. In April 2004, Ma Fucai, the general manager of the CNPC, resigned out of self-censure in the wake of the gas well blowout in Kaixian County of suburban Chongqing in December 2003 that killed 243 people and injured 2,000 people. The gas-well was operated by the state-owned oil company China National Petroleum Corporation (CNPC).[62] Ma had earned applause for taking his formal responsibility. Afterwards Meng maintained their ministerial rank. Later, both were returned to new posts of the same rank. Meng was appointed in September 2003 as Deputy Director of the Office for the South-to-North Water Diversion Project Construction Committee. In August 2007 he was appointed as the Acting Governor of Shanxi. Unfortunately, his luck ran out again in 2008. After a deadly mining accident that claimed 254 lives in September 2008 Meng tendered a resignation. In June 2005 Ma Fucai was appointed at the Acting Deputy Director of the Office for the National Energy Leading Small Group. However, his rank was deputy minister, which was apparently lower than his former ministerial rank before his resignation.

Many scholars view their return to politics as a lack of transparency and ineffective enforcement of official accountability. However, officials who knew these senior officials and other officials who were disciplined and their abilities believed the root causes of the accidents were beyond the control of the disciplined officials. They thought the sanctions against these officials were unfair and were losses of talents by the state.[63]

Administrative efficiency

In the reform era the Party state has introduced seven administrative reforms in 1982, 1988, 1993, 1998, 2003, 2008, and 2013, respectively, in order to rationalize the structure of the government, downsize the bureaucracy, and increase efficiency. Each administrative reform involved at first the ministries, institutions, and offices under the State Council, and then spread to the administration at the provincial, city, and county levels. In each reform the number of commissions and ministries (ministries in short), institutions and offices under the State Council decreased. This was usually matched by corresponding changes in the subnational government. In addition, the posts at the national and local government also shrank.

For example, in the administrative reform in 1982 the number of commissions, ministries, institutions, and offices under the State Council was cut from 100 to 61, the number of departments of provincial governments declined from a range of 50–60 to 30–40, and that of county governments dropped from 40 plus to about 25. The number of bureaucratic posts at the national level decreased from 51,000 to 30,000, that at the provincial level dropped from 180,000 to

120,000, and the number of official posts at the county level declined by 20 percent.

After each reform the number of ministries and commissions under the State Council has declined. It totaled roughly 45 in 1982 after the administrative reform, decreased to 41 in 1988, but rebounded to 59 in 1993, and continued to drop to 29 in 1998, to 28 in 2003, to 27 in 2008, and finally to 25 in 2013 after the latest round of administrative reform (Table 2.6). Thanks to administrative reforms former ministries that served the state's heavy regulation of industries and sectors were abolished. They included the Ministries of Machinery Industry, Electronic Industry, Chemical Industry, Coal Industry, Metallurgical Industry, Textile Industry, and Forestry. The governmental structure

Table 2.6 Administrative restructuring in China in the reform era

	1982	*1988*	*1993*	*1998*	*2003*	*2008*	*2013*
Number of Ministries of the State Council Before the Reform		45	86	40			
Number of Ministries After the Reform	**45$^+$**	**41**	**59**	**29**	**28**	**27**	**25**
Reduction in the Number of Ministries		4	27	11	1	1	2
Number of Institutions Directly under the State Council Before the Reform		22					
Number of Institutions Directly under the State Council After the Reform		19	18*				
Reduction in Institutions Directly under the State Council		3					
Eliminated Posts at the National Level (or Decline by %)	21,000	9,700	20%				
Eliminated Posts at the Provincial Level	60,000						
Eliminated Posts at the City and County Level (or Decline by %)	20%						
Total Eliminated Posts			1.15 million				

Note: * Suggests that the number includes institutions directly under the State Council (*zhishu jigou*) and offices under the State Council (*banshi jigou*).
+ Suggests an inferred number from the existing reports.

in the later years reflected a move in the governmental work away from direct supervision of enterprises in each of these industries toward macroeconomic management, provisions of public services and welfare, selective intervention in strategic areas such as science and technology and education, and the regulation of the economy. Examples included the creation of the National Development and Reform Commission (NDRC), the Ministry of Commerce, the Ministry of Education, and the Ministry of Science and Technology.

In the 2013 administrative reform four new agencies were created. The National Health and Family Planning Commission was formed with the merger of the Ministry of Health and Family Planning Commission. The General Administration of Food and Drugs was created to step up supervision on the quality of food and drugs which has become a major public concern in recent years. The former Ministry of Railway was broken up into State Railway Administration and China Railway Corporation. The latter was a SOE rather than a governmental agency. The General Administration of Press and Publication, Radio, Film and Television was formed by merging the General Administration of Press and Publication with the General Administration of Radio, Film and Television. In addition, the State Council under new Premier Li Keqiang pledged to reduce restriction on the entry of firms into the market but would step up supervision of the firms and closely monitor the quality of their products and services.[64]

In addition, in many large cities the local government set up one-stop service centers to facilitate the submission of applications for administrative approval by the government. With the establishment of these centers, applicants can submit an application to multiple departments at the same location. In the past for each application they would have to travel to various governmental departments located in various places in the city.

Furthermore, over the years the government has gradually reduced the number of administrative approvals. With this change residents in China could conduct more of their daily business without having to seek governmental approval. For example, in the wake of China's entry to the WTO, during October to December 2002 the State Council reviewed 4,000 items of administrative approvals administered by 65 bureaucratic agencies, and annulled 789 items. This change was to comply with the WTO rules, reduce governmental interference in the economy, and avoid the abuses of administrative approvals.[65]

In sum, streamlining of the bureaucracy, reduction in the number of governmental agencies, the establishment of one-stop service centers, and streamlining of administrative approval all help to increase governmental efficiency and increase the convenience of people and businesspersons in conducting their daily routines.

Greater political transparency

Prior to the Hu–Wen leadership a series of topics were political taboos. They included serious accidents of public health, public safety, and social disturbances, details of corruption scandals, major socio-economic concerns of the population, and failures of public policies. They were deemed either too damaging to the image and legitimacy of the leadership, or as potentially explosive material for inciting public unrest. Most of them were left out in the media coverage, or the coverage or mention of them were carefully kept to the minimum.

This has changed since the Hu–Wen leadership came to power. Since late 2002, especially since the open campaign against SARS in April 2003, the Chinese media has frequently investigated and discussed issues of production accidents, epidemics, wasteful official image-making projects of development, the plight of peasants and migrant workers in the cities, corruption scandals and their sources, as well as failures of governmental policies in public health and higher education. Even the progress and limits in hallmark policies of the Hu–Wen New Deal, such as new policies on land management and housing prices, are discussed openly in the media.

Moreover, the leadership has also become more forthcoming in admitting existing socio-economic problems, defects in the institutions (other than the political regime), pending issues that require new public policies, as well as activities and attention of top leaders. For example, Hu publicized each group study of the Sixteenth Politburo, as well as the topics and background of each plenum of the Sixteenth Central Committee of the Party, giving the nation and the world a sense of major issues that interested the top leaders, and provided them a glimpse at the context of policies of the Central Committee.

This enhanced transparency reflected the vision and policy choices of the leadership. As the leadership stressed addressing the real concerns of the people, the media received a green light on shedding limelight on these issues. Rather than seeing public discussion of these policy issues as undermining the state, the Hu–Wen leadership viewed it as a publicity campaign to promote its pro-people image. It also regarded public discussion as a forum for soliciting public views, for probing the sources of the problems and for exploring effective solutions. In the first twenty months of its reign, the Hu–Wen leadership even tolerated the publication of some considerably critical reports on sensitive topics, such as *Investigations on Chinese Peasants* regarding the plight of peasants and hair-raising stories of abuse of power by rural cadres, or that of liberal calls for political reform, such as the historical drama of *Marching Toward the Republic*.

A significant change also took place under Hu. National and local media have abandoned the boring and formalistic long coverage of leaders' activities in its news reports. Instead, more coverage is devoted to policies and issues that concern the public.

In addition, as early as the early 2000s the State Council and provincial governments such as those in Beijing, Guangdong and Shanghai, extensively promoted e-government. Nowadays it is common for national governmental agencies and local governments to have their own websites where they publish their activities, main policy documents, and even procedures for applicants to seek administrative approvals on specific issues. E-government campaigns have greatly increased the volume of information on the government available to the public.[66]

Nevertheless, as stated above, the Party still retains its control over the media and the internet, although it has been scaled back. On highly sensitive topics, the media still has to follow the official scripts. Very high death tolls and very severe property damage from catastrophes are still deemed politically too sensitive to be publicized. Scandals implicating top leaders are forbidden from being publicized. Internal speeches by top leaders on external issues and even sensitive political issues are deemed state secrets. Appeals by rights activists against violations by local governments are largely brushed out from the media reports. Criticisms of the political regime targeting a broad audience are a criminal offense and subject to police arrests and legal prosecution.

The public also believed that the administration especially at the local level could do much more in improving transparency. In a national survey covering both urban and rural residents throughout China in 2011 only 37 percent of the respondents thought the government's informational transparency was satisfactory, whereas 44 percent regarded it as unsatisfactory. This item was the aspect of local governmental work that received the second lowest public approval.[67]

Democratic experiments

In the reform era the Party state has been under constant pressure for democratization. The first call for democracy came from intellectuals and political activists such as Wei Jingsheng in early 1979. The demand for democracy culminated in the Tiananmen movement in 1989. In the subsequent years, open-minded officials, intellectuals, and political activists continued to call for the opening of the political system. To fill the administrative void, check the abuse of power and quench the populace's thirst for democracy, the Party has permitted several forms of democratic experiments and initiatives. The earliest democratic scheme was the village election. In the recent decade outstanding forms of democratic experiments have been elections of township chiefs, publicized and competitive appointments of local officials, consultative local democracy (especially in Zhejiang), and intra-Party democracy at the local and national levels.

Since the early 1980s, the Party has gradually allowed the election of village chiefs and villagers' committees. The peasants in two localities in Guangxi Province initiated the elections of villagers' committees and village leaders in the wake of the dissolution of the communes. This practice won the approval of the state, as specified in Article 111 of the Constitution of the People's Republic of China in 1982. In 1987 the National People's Congress approved a trial version of the Organic Law on Villagers' Committees of the People's Republic of China and approved a finalized version of the law in 1998. Since 1987 villagers' elections were promoted and spread throughout the nation.

Over the years village elections have become freer as many candidates for the villagers' committees were primarily openly nominated, but not by the government. In many localities elected village officials felt compelled to satisfy the demand from peasants.

Village elections thus became the first form of genuine and open elections under the authoritarian regime in China. In the early 1980s the communes were abolished in the countryside. The end of communes left an organizational void in the villages, leaving no agency to take care of public services and affairs such as public goods, public security, and adjudication of disputes in the villages. The Party cell, being a Party unit instead of an administrative organ, was unable to effectively attend to these affairs. In this regard, elected villagers' committees became a pragmatic, convenient, low-cost, and effective replacement of the former communes in the governance of the countryside.

Since the mid-1990s the second type of democratic schemes have started to emerge in China. Electoral experiments were conducted in a number of provinces whereby residents directly elected the chief of townships or the head of township-level urban districts. Most of these elections occurred in Sichuan Province, and a small number of them took place in Jiangsu, Yunnan and Hubei.

The best known pioneering experiment with township-level elections took place in Suining City, Sichuan Province in 1998. The initiator of the experiment was Madame Zhang Jinming, who was then the Party Secretary of Shizhong District of Suining City. She explained her rationale for the elections of the (administrative/governmental) chief of Baoshi Town and the Party Secretary of Xinqiao Township as a way to restore villagers' confidence in the local authorities of these two localities after the exposure of cadres' embezzlement of funds raised by peasants in these two localities. It was revealed that after these scandals local peasants refused to pay taxes and fees to the town and the township. As a result, the governments of the town and the township came to a halt. Elections of the two posts seemed to be an ultimate though ingenious option out of this political impasse. This inside story of the best-known township elections in China suggested that officials under the pragmatic authoritarian state used local democratic experiments as one of the final options to defuse political tension and a governance crisis. In the wake of Baoshi Town elections, peasants resumed paying fees and taxes. With the resolution of the governance crisis more restrictions were imposed on the subsequent elections of the town. In the election of the chief of Buyun Township under Suining City in 1998, after 13 rounds of public debates Tan Xiaoqiu, the incumbent deputy chief of the township defeated two rivals, a high school teacher and a member of a villagers' committee, and won the election. Tan won the election again in 2001. Zhang, who creatively served the Party state, was later promoted to the Vice Mayor and Deputy Party Secretary of Suining City. In contrast, in another famous case in Dapeng Town, Shenzhen, Guangdong, the authority allowed the semi-competitve election to be held in 1998, but put an end to the experiement by 2001, due to absence of governance crises.[68]

Another major and widely noticed type of democratic experiment is local consultative schemes in several cities in Zhejiang, especially Wenzhou, Jiaojiang and Wenling. Three main forms of meetings/assemblies have emerged. The first was a consultative meeting (*minzhu kentanhui*), where 20–300 representatives and voluntary participants of local residents were invited to a meeting to discuss issues related to local social-economic development and planning. The second form was an evaluation meeting where 60–200 citizens were invited, heard a report on the performance of local leaders, asked questions, and then filled in a questionnaire to assess their performance. The third form was an urban or village representative assembly where 15–30 elected representatives of urban residents or villagers discussed local development or community-related issues. In Wenling local residents were also invited to discuss issues related to the local governmental budget.[69] These deliberative schemes did not involve election of officials. Rather, they concerned the deliberation of policies. They served to elicit citizens' feedback on governmental policies and obtain their input on policies being considered.

The third form of democratic schemes is open and competitive selections of local officials. In the past the Party secretary at each level has an indisputable and even dominant role in nominating candidates for governmental and Party posts under him and even appointing them. Since 2000 the Party has encouraged elements of democracy and competition. It also mandated several institutions on cadre appointment and evaluation, including public notices of candidates prior to final appointment, deliberation on the appointment at the local Party committee, and annual review of official performance. These measures aimed to reduce corrupt practice of applicants for these posts (such as their bribing the officials in charge of promotion) and ensure the appointment of qualified candidates. In several provinces competitive selections were introduced. During 1999–2002 the Party committees at the city and district levels in Meishan City of Sichuan Province cast ballots to decide on the appointments of 3088 officials in the city. In August 2002 the authority in Suihua City in Heilongjiang Province introduced an institution mandating that the number of candidates had to exceed that of the vacancies, that secret ballots were used to decide on the appointment, and that the results would be announced right after the ballot. In 2003 the authority in Yangzhou City of Jiangsu Province used open selection and written and oral exams to decide on the appointment of the Mayor of Jiangdu City under its jurisdiction.[70]

One of the last types of democratic initiatives to be reviewed here is intra-Party democracy at the national and local levels. Efforts have also been made to curtail the excessive concentration of power of the Party in the hands of a few party secretaries at each level. The earliest initiative under this category is an institution called permanent representation of delegates of the Party Congress, which was introduced in the mid-1980s. Instead of being elected in a large number, acting as ceremonial figures, and meeting only once every five years for a few days, in some localities delegates were competent and had a clear term limit. They exerted their power during their term by supervising and advising Party leaders after the Congress adjourned. They even obtained the power to approve major decisions of the local Party branch.

The leadership embarked on initiatives to introduce democracy in the CCP at the national level in the recent years. In 2003 Hu, on behalf of the Politburo, reported its work to the Central Committee, procedurally subjecting himself and the other Politburo members to the supervision of the latter. The latter's power has been formally included in the Party's constitution. In addition, the opinions of hundreds of the most senior members of the CCP were solicited before the successors to the President and the Premier were announced in the recent two Party Congresses. This point will be elaborated in Chapter 7.

From the perspective of the Party state, the aforementioned democratic experiments help to improve its rule. The CCP has realized that over-concentration of power has led to power abuse, corruption and problems in governance and that these democratic institutions can help to alleviate defects associated with the authoritarian regime.

On the other hand, these democratic experiments hardly constitute any major change of the structure of the authoritarian regime. According to the Chinese Constitution, villages do not constitute a level of the state; the lowest level of the state is township; and chiefs at all levels of the state from the township to the national level need to be selected by indirect election, that is, through ballots by legislators at the same level, not by residents in the township or cities. Furthermore, the Party has been very cautious in expanding direct elections. Township elections are largely restricted to selected localities in four provinces. No open election of posts above the township level has been reported. On balance the Party is also more comfortable with intra-Party democracy than inter-party democracy, as the latter could encourage the birth and expansion of opposition parties and make it possible for them to displace the Party.

In sum, the Party state has practiced pragmatic authoritarianism in a number of major aspects of its governance of the country. In economic governance it embraces highly practical and aggressive pro-growth policies. They help generate high growth and build an internationalized market economy. The Party state has also built a rudimentary social safety net, provides basic welfare coverage for the population and significantly eases popular grievances with their personal risks in the new market economy. These moves help the CCP to sustain its legitimacy among its population.

In social governance the Party state installs social organizations that provide formalistic representation for major functional sections of the society, such as labor, women, youth, entrepreneurs and religious people. These functional associations provide top-down initiatives to address some of the concerns of their constituents while operating within the strict parameters of the state. NGOs affiliated with these functional organizations and with the state bureaucracy enjoy a degree of autonomy, but are dependent on their institutional sponsors to survive. Only relatively smaller and fewer NGOs enjoy a high degree of autonomy, but have neither much influence on the state's policies, nor attract many followers Large and defiant groups face harsh supression from the state.

In political governance, the Party state is very adaptive in several aspects. It eclectically transplants successful policies and institutions from around the world, remakes its ideology, restricts rival political ideas, and importantly, has overhauled the institutions for crisis management and leadership succession. In addition, it has not loosened its control of the major state branches through tightly managed official appointments. It continues to censor the media and the internet. By doing so, it frees itself of the most immediate crises and forces that have the potential to critically undermine and even topple the regime. Furthermore, the Party state has adopted a number of measures to enhance official accountability, administrative efficiency, and political transparency. Even though in the public's eye much improvement is needed in all these areas, they have indeed compelled officials and cadres to heed issues that are of grave consequence to the Party state (such as serious accidents) and simplify procedures for administrative applications from citizens and businesspersons. Though far from perfect these measures are much needed for smooth economic activities and for sustaining economic growth. It is true that the Party state continues to be plagued by scandals, especially corruption cases, and frequent collective protests. It has come a long way in renewing itself and faces no immediate deadly challenge.

Notes

1 Sujian Guo, *Post-Mao China: From Totalitarianism to Authoritarianism?* (Westport, CT: Praeger Publishers, 2000).
2 Gordon Skilling and Franklyn Griffiths, eds, *Interest Groups in Soviet Politics* (Princeton, NJ: Princeton University Press, 1971).
3 H. H. Lai, "Religious Policies in Post-Totalitarian China: Maintaining Political Monopoly over a Reviving Society," *Journal of Chinese Political Science*, Vol. 11, No. 1, Spring 2006, 55–77.
4 See Juan J. Linz, *Totalitarianism and Authoritarian Regimes* (Boulder, CO and London: Lynne Rienner Publisher, 2000), especially 245–61; Gordon H. Skilling, "Leadership and Group Conflict in Czechoslovakia," in R. Barry Farrell, ed., *Political Leadership in Eastern Europe and the Soviet Union* (Chicago, IL: Aldine, 1970), 276–93. For earlier studies of totalitarianism, refer to Carl J. Friedrich and Zbigniew K. Brzezinski, *Totalitarian Dictatorship and Autocracy* (Cambridge, MA: Harvard University Press, 1956); Zbigniew Brzezinski, *Ideology and Power in Soviet Politics* (New York: Frederick Praeger, 1962).
5 Skilling, "Leadership and Group Conflict in Czechoslovakia," 224.
6 Skilling, "Leadership and Group Conflict in Czechoslovakia," 225.
7 Kenneth Lieberthal and David Lampton, eds, *Bureaucracy, Politics and Decision Making in Post-Mao China* (Berkeley and Los Angeles, CA: University of California Press, 1992), Chapter 1.
8 Guillermo O'Donnell, *Modernization and Bureaucratic-Authoritarianism: Studies in South American Politics* (Berkeley, CA: University of California Press, 1973).
9 For analyses of soft authoritarianism in Malaysia and Singapore, refer to Gordon P. Means, "Soft Authoritarianism in Malaysia and Singapore," in Larry Diamond and Marc F. Plattner, eds, *Democracy in East Asia* (Baltimore, MD: Johns Hopkins University Press, 1998), 96–112.

10 Minxin Pei, "China's Evolution Toward Soft Authoritarianism," in Edward Friedman and Barrett McCormick, eds. *What If China Doesn't Democratize?* (Armonk, NY and London: M.E. Sharpe, 2000), 74–98.
11 Pei, *China's Trapped Transition*, 2006, 5–16.
12 Baum, "The Limits of Consultative Leninism," 13–15.
13 Linz, *Totalitarian and Authoritarian Regimes*, 195.
14 This is based on the author's observation after working and living in Singapore for six years.
15 Baum, "The Limits of Consultative Leninism," 13–15.
16 For a discussion on the relations between the state and the middle class in China, refer to Li He, "Middle Class: Friends or Foes to Beijing's New Leadership," *Journal of Chinese Political Science*, Vol. 8, No. 1–2, Fall 2003, 87–100. For a discussion of pragmatic authoritarianism of the Chinese technocratic leaderships, see Gongqin Xiao, "The Rise of the Technocrats," *Journal of Democracy*, Vol. 14, No. 1, January 2003, 60–65.
17 For Sartori's work, refer to Giovanni Sartori, *Parties and Party Systems: A Framework for Analysis* (New York: Cambridge University Press, 1976), 198–202.
18 For an overview of China's economic reform, refer to Barry Naughton, *The Chinese Economy* (Cambridge, MA and London: MIT Press, 2007), 85–111; Hongyi Lai, *Reform and the Non-state Economy in China* (New York and London: Palgrave Macmillan, 2006), 2–29 (Chapter 1), 232–243 (Chapter 9) on debates on approaches to reform and 61–77, 83–85 (Chapter 3) for elite conflict in the reform era.
19 Whiting, *Power and Wealth in Rural China*, 72–120.
20 Zhiyue Bo, *Chinese Provincial Leaders: Economic Performance and Political Mobility Since 1949* (Armonk, NY: M.E. Sharpe, 2002).
21 Asian Development Bank (ADB), Japan Bank for International Cooperation (JBIC) and the World Bank (WB), *Connecting East Asia: A New Framework for Infrastructure* (Manila, Washington and Tokyo: ADB, JBIC and WB, 2005), 3.
22 ADB, JBIC, and WB, *Connecting East Asia*, 26, 37, 36–7.
23 Ibid., 215–16.
24 Ibid., Chapter 1 and Appendixes (especially p. 215). Data on India come from "India Must Hike Infra Spend to 9% of GDP," *The Financial Express* (Source: Reuters), December 4, 2007.
25 World Bank, *World Development Report 2006: Equity and Development* (Washington, DC: Oxford University Press, 2005), 296–7.
26 China Statistical Bureau, *China Statistical Yearbook 2012* (Beijing: China Statistical Press, 1992), Table 2–4 "Indices of Gross Domestic Product".
27 Data came from *China Statistical Yearbook 2002*; *China Investment Yearbook 2000, 2001*.
28 World Bank, *Sharing Rising Incomes* (Washington, DC: World Bank, 1997), 7. World Bank, *World Development Report 1997, 1999/2000; 2003; 2004* (Washington, DC: World Bank). The U.S. Gini coefficient in 2001 came from the website of the U.S. Census Bureau of the Department of Commerce.
29 "Shehui Tuanti" (Social associations), posted at: http://baike.baidu.com/view/1914.htm, accessed on August 25, 2013.
30 For data sources, refer to the last source of Table 2.5.
31 The former provided official representations of major functional groups (such as labor, youth, women, scientists, overseas Chinese, Taiwan compatriots, and business) with two associations representing the youth, including the Communist Youth League. The latter provided official representation for artists, writers, journalists, legal scholars, alumni of the Huangpu (Whampoa) Military Academy, Chinese students in Europe and America, legal scholars, the disabled people. In addition, the latter included associations the Madame Sun Yet-sin Foundation, the China Red

Cross, and associations for promotion of vocational education, political thought among workers, international trade, and people-to-people diplomacy.

32 Tim Pringle, *Trade Unions in China* (London and New York: Routledge, 2011).
33 Masaharu Hishida, Kazuko Kojima, Tomoki Ishii and Jian Qiao, *China's Trade Unions: How Autonomous Are They? A Survey of 1,811 Enterprise Union Chairpersons* (London and New York: Routledge, 2010).
34 Wang Yunfang, "Zhongguo Qiye Lianhehui Zizhuhua Jianshe de Diaoyan Baogao" (An Investigative Report on the Autonomous Construction of China Confederation of Enterprises), in Cai Tuo, ed., *Zhongguo Zhunzhengfu Zuzhi Fazhan Zhuangkuang Yanjiu* (*A Study of the Developmental Status of Quasi Governmental Organizations in China*) (Tianjin: Tianjin Renmin Chubanshe, 2011), 33–59.
35 Yiyi Lu, *Non-Governmental Organizations in China: The Rise of Dependent Autonomy* (London and New York: Routledge, 2009).
36 Qiusha Mao, *Non-Governmental Organizations in Contemporary China: Paving the Way to Civil Society?* (London and New York: Routledge, 2006), 2–3.
37 Yongnian Zheng and Joseph Fewsmith, eds, *China's Opening Society: The Non-State Sector and Governance* (London and New York: Routledge, 2008).
38 Shambaugh, *China's Communist Party*, 101–2.
39 See Franz Shurmann, *Ideology and Organization in Communist China* (Berkeley and Los Angeles, CA and London: University of California Press, 1968); Philip Selznick, *The Organizational Weapon: A Study of Bolshevik Strategy and Tactics* (New York: McGraw-Hill Book Company, Inc., 1952), 8–12.
40 For an in-depth discussion of the conservative coalition, refer to Susan Shirk, "The Politics of Industrial Reform," in Elizabeth Perry and Christine Wong, eds, *The Political Economy of Reform in Post-Mao China* (Cambridge, MA: Harvard University Press, 1985), 195–222; Lai, *Reform and the Non-State Economy in China*, 61–76.
41 For a detailed discussion about ideological decay under Deng and ideological reformulations under Jiang, see Yongnian Zheng and Hongyi Lai, "Rule by Virtue: Jiang Zemin's Revival of the Party's Ideology," in Wang Gungwu and Yongnian Zheng, eds, *Damage Control: The Chinese Communist Party in the Jiang Zemin Era* (Singapore: Eastern Universities Press, 2003), 350–64.
42 "Central Committee of the Chinese Communist Party's Opinion regarding Starting Educational Activities to Maintain the Advanced Nature of Party Members," posted at: http://politics.people.com.cn/GB/1026/3106750.html on November 7, 2004, accessed on January 9, 2005; Jim Yardley, "Chinese Party Tries to Get its Mao Back," *The New York Times*, March 10, 2006.
43 See "Zhongguo Meng" (China Dream), posted at http://baike.baidu.com/link?url=a7a9I-xCcXYqLy8B4uGwUhc8dVc3PgSJpa27xm6S8B7r_QIXbabR9TN6VCTUlvS2i2ZzdQ6PPBRduN9OZ13CEqq-gYJYWa8Vkybp3LGA9vu, accessed July 31, 2015.
44 "Xi Jinping: Yishixingtai Gongzuo Jiduan Zhongyao" (Xi Jingping: Ideological Work Is of Utmost Importance), posted at: http://china.dwnes.com/news/2013-08-20/59317030.html, on August 19, 2013, accessed on August 21, 2013; Chris Buckley, "China Takes Aim at Western Ideas," *New York Times*, posted at http://www.nytimes.com/2013/08/20/world/asia/chinas-new-leadership-takes-hard-line-in-secret-memo.html?pagewanted=all&_r=0 on August 19, 2013, accessed on August 26, 2013.
45 Yingdui Tufa Shijian Keti Yanjiuzu (Research Group on Managing Sudden Events), ed., *Geji Lingdaozhe Yingdui he Chuzhi Tufa Shijian Bibei Shouce* (*A Must Handbook for Leaders at All Levels to Manage Sudden Events*) (Beijing: Zhongguo Shangye Chubanshe, 2012), 138.

46 "Dazai zhong Ningju Minzu zhi Hun: 1998 Nian Zhongguo Kanghong" (A Catastrophe Unites the Soul of the Nation: China's Fight against the Flood in 1998), in Gui Weimin, ed., *Yingji Guanli 100 Li* (*100 Cases of Management of Sudden Events*) (Beijing: Zhonggong Zhongyang Dangxiao Chubanshe, 2009), 1–7.

47 Yingdui Tufa Shijian Keti Yanjiuzu, *Geji Lingdaozhe Yingdui he Chuzhi Tufa Shijian Bibei Shouce*, 138–42, 146–51.

48 For an earlier discussion on the institutionalization of leadership succession, refer to John Wong and Zheng Yongnian, eds, *China's Post-Jiang Leadership Succession* (Singapore: World Scientific), 2002. For a brief and recent discussion, refer to Hongyi Lai, "Institutionalization of China's Power Transfer Behind Dramatic Reports," *Hsin Pao* (*Hong Kong Economic Journal*), October 11 2004, 23.

49 For a study of the promotion of young cadres in the 1980s, refer to Melanie Manion, *Retirement of Revolutionaries in China* (Princeton, NJ: Princeton University Press, 1993); Hong Yong Lee, *From Revolutionary Cadres to Party Technocrats in Socialist China* (Berkeley and Los Angeles, CA and Oxford: University of California Press, 1990).

50 For a study on Deng's promotion of young leaders, refer to Lai, *Reform and the Non-State Economy in China* ("Installing Technocratic Young Leaders"), Chapter 5.

51 For discussion on quasi-institutional "rules" for succession, refer to Frederick Teiwes, "The Politics of Succession," in Wong and Zheng, *China's Post-Jiang Leadership Succession*, 21–58.

52 For detailed discussion on China's leadership succession and Hu's power consolidation, refer to Lai Hongyi, *Hu–Wen quan toushi: Hu–Wen shizheng neimu quan jiedu ji Zhongguo weilai zhanwang* (*Hu–Wen under Full Scrutiny: A Comprehensive Inside Story of Governance Under Hu and Wen and Prospects for Future China*) (Hong Kong: Wenhua yishu chubanshe, 2005), 16–41, 64–6, 319–64.

53 For an analysis of this national appointment of provincial leaders, see Huang, *Inflation and Investment Control in China* ("The Local Officials in the Bureaucratic Hierarchy"), Chapter 4, 89–124.

54 "Zhongguo dui anquan zhong teda shigu shixing xingzheng zeren zuijiu jilue" (A Short Account of Pursuit of Administrative Accounabilities of Severe and Particularly Large Accidents in Safety and Production in China), posted at: http://news.xinhuanet.com/newscenter/2004-05/09/content_1459145.htm on May 9, 2004, accessed on August 23, 2006.

55 See "Law of the People's Republic of China on Work Safety," posted at: http://english.gov.cn/laws/2005-10/08/content_75054.htm, accessed on March 19, 2007.

56 "Dangzheng lingdao ganbu xuanba renyong gongzuo tiaoli" (Article for Work in Selecting and Promoting of Party and Government Leading Cadres), posted at: http://news.xinhuanet.com/ziliao/2003-01/18/content_695422.htm on June 26, 2006.

57 "2003 nian yilai woguo xingzheng wenze shijian" (Cases of Administrative Accountability in Our Country Since 2003), posted at: www.03964.com/read/c10dd1bc22cc8f99e80ce004.html, accessed May 12, 2015.

58 The Party state has been concerned with official acts that produce negative social repercussions as they could generate grievances and protests and undermine its own political legitimacy.

59 "Guanyu zhuanfa 'Dangzheng lingdao ganbu cizhi zanxing guiding'" (A Notice regarding Distributing 'Provisional Regulations on the Resignation of Party and Governmental Leading Cadres'), posted at: www.cas.ac.cn/html/Dir/2005/06/23/0431.htm on June 23, 2005; accessed on October 16, 2006.

60 "Dangzheng lingdao ganbu gongkai xuanba, cizhi zanxing guiding deng wenjian banbu" (Provisional Regulations on Open Selection and Resignation of Party and Government Leading Cadres Are Promulgated), posted at: http://news.sohu.com/20040908/n221943272.shtml on September 8, 2004; accessed on the same day. For an analysis on the regulation, refer to Szu-chien Hsu, "Reforming the Party and

State under Hu Jintao," in John Wong and Hongyi Lai, eds, *China into the Hu–Wen Era* (Singapore: World Scientific, 2006), 178–9.

61 "Gongwuyuan fa mingnian shishi, lingdao chengyuan gongzuo shiwu ying yinjiu cizhi" (Law on Civil Servants Goes into Effect Next Year and Members of the Leadership Should Resign out of Self Censure for Blunders in Work), posted at: www.sina.com.cn on April 28, 2005; accessed on the same day.

62 "Guowuyuan yansu chuli sanqi teda anquan shigu Ma Fucai cizhi" (The State Council Sternly Handles Three Particularly Large Safety Accidents and Ma Fucai Resigns), posted at: http://news.xinhuanet.com on April 15, 2004.

63 See, for example, "Ma Fucai Didiao Renzhi Nengyuanban, Cengshi Zhongshiyou de Tianwen Lingxiu" (Once an Iron-Fist Leader of CNPC, Ma Fucai Assumes Post at the Energy Office in a Low-Key Way), posted at: http://finance.sina.com.cn/leadership/CXOconduct/20050916/08031973062.shtml, accessed on August 26, 2013; "Meng Xuenong Zaici Quzhi Yinfa Wen Wenzai Guanyuan Fuchu Zhidu Taolun" (The Second Resignation of Meng Xuenong Invites Discussion on the Institution of Re-Appointment of Officials Subject to Discipline Due to Official Accountability), posted at: http://news.sohu.com/20080917/n259610277.shtml, accessed on August 26, 2013.

64 "Guowuyuan Jigou Gaige" (Reforms of Agencies of the State Council), posted at: http://baike.baidu.com/view/9850446.htm, accessed on August 26, 2013.

65 Hongyi Harry Lai, "Local Governments and China's WTO Entry," *American Asian Review*, Vol. XXI, No. 3, Fall 2003, 153–186.

66 For a discussion on e-government, refer to Yang, *Remaking the Chinese Leviathan*, 165–75.

67 The item with the lowest public approval was official honesty and punishment of corruption. See Li Wei *et al.*, "2011 Nian Zhongguo Minsheng yu Chengshihua Diaocha Baogao" (An Investigative Report on the People's Well-being and Urbanization in China), in Rui Xin *et al.*, eds, *2012 Nian: Zhongguo Shehui Xingshi Fenxi yu Yuce* (*2012: An Analysis and Forecast on the Conditions of China's Society*) (Beijing: Shehui Kexue Wenxian Chubanshe, 2012), 122.

68 Lai Hairong, *Zhongguo Nongcun Zhengzhi Tizhi Gaige: Xiangzhen Banjingzhengxing Xuanju Yanjiu* (*Reform of Political System in China's Countryside: A Study of Semi-Competitive Township Elections*) (Beijing: Zhongyang Bianyi Chubanshe, 2009), 71–2, 21–2, 85–9, 95.

69 Baogang He, "Participatory and Deliberative Institutions in China," in Ethan Leib and Baogang He, eds, *The Search for Deliberative Democracy in China* (Basingstoke and New York: Palgrave Macmillan, 2006), 183–7.

70 Xu Xianglin, "Dangguan Ganbu Tizhi xia de Jiceng Minzhu Shigaige" (Experimental Reforms with Local Democracy under Party-Managed Nomenclature), in Tang Jin *et al.*, eds, *Daguoce: Tongxiang Daguo zhi Lu de Zhongguo Minzhu* (*Great Power Stratagem: China's Democracy on Its Path Toward Great Power*) (Beijing: Renmin Ribao Chubanshe, 2009), 19–30.

Part 2

Economic and social governance

3 Pro-growth governance and protests
Results and resentments of governance[*]

Introduction: uneven opening of the society, economy, and politics

Indisputably, the greatest strength and achievements of China's model of governance lie in its economic governance. Since 1978 the state has engineered the transformation and opening of the economy. It has ushered in an average annual nearly double-digit growth of the economy since 1978. The Chinese model of economic governance attracted global limelight in 2008 when Beijing hosted the Olympic Games. The glowing success of the Beijing Olympic Games allowed China to showcase its economic success. Highlights of the Beijing Olympic Games included the smooth completion of the games, fantastic sports ventures, and the mega media show of the opening ceremony, which has been widely accepted around the world as the greatest opening ceremony in the Games history and for decades to come and which has been the most watched and acclaimed global media event ever.

Nevertheless, even in this strongest department the Chinese model of economic governance has its Achilles' heels. While generating sustained, robust high economic growth that is admired around the world, the Chinese state has also aroused much public discontent. As will be shown in this chapter this strange mixed blessing of high growth plus high popular resentment has to do with the uneven opening of the economy, society and politics in China, which constitutes the weakest link in the Chinese model of economic governance and the Chinese model of governance as a whole.

The transformation in China has been uneven across spheres. China's society has also been opened up significantly. The Chinese are no longer ignorant about the outside world. They are attentive to the popular culture, especially movies, TV programs, music, entertainment, dresses, and lifestyle of the West. More importantly, the Chinese have become accustomed to individual initiatives, such as economic entrepreneurship and volunteering for the Olympic Games. Importantly, they are aware of their legal rights and keen to defend them. This marks a sharp departure from their docile or passive submission to the state in the pre-reform period. In the economic realm, China's opening has been most impressive. After over three decades of reform China has been transformed from one of the most isolated economies in the world into one of the most open in the developing world. However, in the political realm, despite overhaul of the governmental structure, agencies, and work style, the state has not been changed fundamentally. The Chinese Communist Party still dominates politics, and the policy-making process remains largely inaccessible to the public. As a result, the state and officials often ignore people's rights, legitimate interests, due processes and relevant laws. Therefore, ironically, in the last two decades frequent collective protests have gone hand-in-hand with high economic growth.[1]

The purpose of this chapter is to analyze the features and limits of the mode of development, especially the model of governance in China. China's model of development is marked by the uneven economic, social and political opening of China. China's model of governance can be characterized by pro-growth authoritarianism. I suggest that the Chinese model of governance is character-ized by a gap between fast economic and social opening and slow political opening. As far as governance is concerned, the Chinese state is indeed very effective in opening up and modernizing the economy. However, it is very ineffective when it comes to protecting and respecting citizens' legitimate social and economic rights, controlling rampant corruption, and enforcing the rule of law. As Gilley dramatically puts it, "China's performance in rights and freedom [author's note: predominantly political freedom] is much worse than most developing countries, excepting those where political disorder cancels out any formal freedoms."[2] High growth is thus not necessarily followed by a decrease in social protests. On the contrary, flagrant violation of citizens' rights in official aggressive pursuit of high growth results in public outrages and protests.

This chapter will first discuss the opening of society in China. It will then examine the rapid opening of the Chinese economy and the positive aspects of governance in China. This is followed by a discussion of slow political opening and the severe limits of governance in China, as well as of the con-sequences of uneven opening, i.e. frequent protests in the wake of high eco-nomic growth in China. The chapter concludes by summing up the findings of the chapter and emphasizing the need for greater political opening in China.

Social opening and rights consciousness

In the reform era the former and onerous restrictions on society have been lifted or eroded. People have fewer restrictions in migrating across counties and provinces and even outside China; they no longer need the state's approval in finding a job and getting married; they are free to engage and even indulge in a variety of entertainment and hobbies and choose their favorite fashions.

Associated with economic opening is social opening. In the 1980s the state dismantled collective farming and reformed state-owned enterprises. As a result, collectivism declined. Individual economic initiatives were promoted and rewarded, reflected in the state's encouragement of private enterprises and the rise of private entrepreneurs. Both private enterprises and entrepreneurs were prohibited during the late Mao era. The Chinese are more interested in personal and family material well-being than they were in Mao's era.

The Chinese have become more conscious of their legal rights, especially economic and social rights. A small sample survey of Chinese from various professions from 2005–6 suggested that over 60 percent of urban Chinese and 38 percent of rural Chinese were aware that the Constitution protected citizens' legal private property and that 90 percent of urban Chinese and over 60 percent of peasants believed correctly that the Constitution served to regulate state power and protect citizens' rights.[3]

Their awareness can be traced to a number of factors—people's greater concerns with their material interests as their living standard improves and their wealth accumulates, greater media coverage of people's legal rights, and the state's recent efforts to protect citizens' social and economic rights through constitutional amendment, such as that which protects their private property. In addition, it is likely that citizens are increasingly aware of the "best practice" regarding state protection of citizens' rights and citizens' initiatives in defending their rights in more developed economies, including Hong Kong, which is adjacent to Guangdong Province, as well as Taiwan, South Korea, Japan, and the West. This change suggests rising Chinese consciousness as citizens, a slow maturation of the Chinese society and its growing embrace of international norms for citizens' rights.

The Chinese are more willing to turn to legal action, complaints and protests in order to safeguard their rights. This change in public consciousness of the law and legal rights can be found in results of surveys over the years. One survey of 1,460 residents in four cities in 1999 suggested that in addressing disputes with state authorities, 67 percent of urban residents chose appeals to high level state authorities, 44 percent contacted the media, and 30 percent resorted to the law. A nationwide survey in 2005 suggested that the percentage of urban residents willing to use the law to resolve their disputes with the state went up to 51 percent, that those who would approach leaders of an agency in a dispute and leaders at the upper-level declined to 15 percent and 18 percent, respectively, and that the number of those who intended to approach the media dropped to 6 percent.[4] The growing awareness of the Chinese people of their rights and legal assertiveness is also reflected in the growing number of cases for re-trial in China in recent years. A senior judge at the Chinese Supreme Court attributed it to the growing Chinese consciousness of their legal rights, their unhappiness with improper legal procedure in the first trial and their resort to retrial for justice.[5]

Meanwhile, the Chinese are less willing to trust the state authorities or the media in their recourse. They are also more willing to act in a group in order to enhance their bargaining power vis-à-vis the state and protect each individual in the process. As a result, the percentage of Chinese petitioners in person grew from 60 percent in 1998 to 76 percent in 2001. The aforementioned national survey in 2005 indicated that 13 percent of Chinese did use collective petition to solve their disputes with the state.[6]

The growing rights and legal consciousness apparently suggests that Chinese society is maturing, although slowly. Chinese citizens are becoming conscious of their legitimate rights as citizens, increasingly reluctant to place their hope for defense of their rights on state authorities and officials, and increasingly willing to use the court, which is seen as less partial than other state branches, to resolve their disputes with the state and assert their independence from the state. This trend indicates Chinese citizens' (especially urban Chinese citizens') growing awareness of the utility of the legal system. It also demonstrated an alarming decline in citizens' trust in the state authorities, local leaders, and the media. This dwindling trust has a grave implication for social stability in China.

Fast economic opening and the positive side of governance

As stated earlier, China's model of development is characterized by fast social and economic opening but slow political opening. One of the defining features (or components) of China's model of development is its model of governance. There are two sides of the same "coin" of Chinese governance. On one hand, the Chinese state is very effective in opening up the economy, building a market economy, and generating economic growth. On the other hand, and as will be elaborated in the coming section, the Chinese state has been slow and ineffectual in protecting citizens' social and economic rights, in easing popular grievances, and in enforcing the rule of law. These two conflicting sides of the coin make up what I call pro-growth authoritarianism.

The positive side of Chinese governance helps to explain why the Chinese state has been very effective in opening up the economy, mobilizing resources, reforming the inefficient economic system, and paving the way for high economic growth. Specifically, the Chinese state outperforms many other developing countries in the following two important areas.

First, dramatic economic opening and promotion of trade (especially exports). Economic opening is regarded as a key to success in East Asia, including China.[7] China has been one of the few developing nations that have made rapid and decisive strides toward opening up its economy. Within less than three decades, China has transformed itself from one of the most isolated economies to an economy closely integrated with the world economy. China's promotion of exports that confirm China's comparative advantage has helped transform the economy into a powerhouse of exports and a major manufacturing base.

From the 1960s to the late 1970s China pursued self-reliance and isolated itself from the market-oriented world economy. Between 1955 and 1978, China was almost completely free of foreign direct investment (FDI). During this period, tensions created a rift in China's relations with the United States and after 1960 with the USSR, thereby preventing the mass introduction of investment from Eastern and Western countries and the USSR. Foreign loans, a politically less sensitive form of foreign capital, played a minor role in development, especially between 1960 and 1976.

Since the late 1970s, with firm support initially from Deng Xiaoping and later his successors, China has decisively opened up its closed economy and steadily integrated with the world market. There have been several landmark developments. First, in 1979 four special economic zones (SEZs) were approved. Second, in 1984, 14 coastal port cities which accounted for 23 percent of the nation's industrial output, including Tianjin, Shanghai, Dalian, Qingdao, Ningbo, Wenzhou and Guangzhou, were opened up. Then from 1985 to 1988 major coastal economic areas were also opened up. From 1992 onwards, in the wake of Deng's reform-promoting tour, inland border cities and provincial capitals were opened up. In 2001, China took a historical step in its opening. It joined the World Trade Organization, subjecting itself to the rules governing international trade, and linking itself closely with the world economy.[8] China agreed to reduce average tariff levels for agricultural products to 15% and for industrial products to 8.9 percent by 2004. China also agreed to open significant service markets such as tele-communications, banking, insurance, securities, audiovisual, professional services, and importantly, wholesale and retail trade, post-sale service, repair, maintenance, and transportation.[9] Finally, in the reform era China has also actively promoted its exports and attracted FDI. One primary measure, as described above, is incremental and steady opening of localities and economic sectors and fiscal incentives for foreign investors.

China's promotion of exports has helped transform the economy into a powerhouse of exports and a major manufacturing base. China's exports grew from US$18.2 billion in 1980 to US$968.9 billion in 2006, and China's FDI grew from US$1.96 billion in 1985 to US$69.5 billion in 2006, a 34.5-fold increase.[10] In 2003, China's FDI inflows reached US$53,505 million, the largest in the developing world. It was five times as much as that of Brazil (US$10,144 million) and 12 times that of India (US$4,269 million).[11] China quickly surpassed other developing nations to become a major exporter of manufactured goods. By 2004 the share of manufactured goods in China's exports reached 91 percent, similar to that of South Korea (93 percent). It far surpassed that of India (77 percent), Vietnam (50 percent), Indonesia and Brazil (52 percent), and Egypt (31 percent).[12]

According to the *Global Competitiveness Report*, in 2007 China's external market size, measured by values of exports of goods and services, was ranked No. 1 worldwide, ahead of the U.S., Germany, and Japan. In 2004, China's exports amounted to US$593,369 million. It was six times that of Brazil (US $96,474 million), and eight times that of India (US$72,530 million) and Indonesia (US$69,710 million).[13]

Second, capacity to undertake reform and development. The Chinese state is capable of undertaking major tasks during reform and development. For example, it overcame political opposition and successfully spread the household farming and economic opening nationwide. It has made noticeable progress in reforming its restriction of non-state business and inefficient SOEs. Since the early 1980s the Chinese government has also identified areas (such as counties) of poverty and introduced economic and social programs to lift the population there out of poverty.

One of the most important factors underlying the effectiveness of the Chinese state is that it has a relatively able leadership and bureaucracy. The Chinese leaders in the reform era, Deng in particular, possessed adroit political skills in overcoming and negotiating through obstacles and opposition and pushing through reform policies. For example, he pushed hard for reform and opening when the opportunities were ripe (from 1978 to 1980 and from 1984 to 1987) or critical (such as in 1992). He retreated temporarily when reform was faced with setbacks, such as in 1989–1991. In addition, he strategically selected localities that had the greatest local popular and official support and best geo-economic conditions to experiment with reform and opening. He also appointed able leaders to lead those localities. These localities included Guangdong in the 1980s and 1990s and Shanghai after the mid-1980s. He also allowed these localities to retain a higher share of fiscal income during their experimental reform. Success of these provinces stimulated reform efforts and demands for liberalization from other provinces.[14] Under the reformist leadership, the bureaucracy and the Party apparatus have been transformed from ones that were suited to political control and ideological indoctrination to ones that maintain stability, encourage rapid economic growth and deliver decent macroeconomic management. For example, a key measure that the Chinese leaders such as Deng Xiaoping adopted was to promote younger officials with knowledge in economic management and who had successfully generated rapid economic growth in the units or localities under their jurisdiction. This practice helped transform Chinese officials from ideological indoctrinators into official entrepreneurs.[15] In global comparison, the Chinese bureaucracy is relatively efficient at processing business cases and welcoming foreign investment. According to *The Global Competitiveness Report 2008–2009*, it took 35 days in China to start a business in 2007, much better than Vietnam (50), Indonesia (105), and Brazil (152). It lagged slightly behind India (33 days) and Nigeria (33 days). In terms of rules favoring foreign direct investment, China was ranked No. 55 out of 134 economies, behind Vietnam (No. 38), and slightly behind the U.S. (No. 53). China was ahead of India (No. 61), France (No. 65), and Thailand (No. 68), and well ahead of Brazil (No. 82).[16] Some scholars, like Bruce Gilley, questioned that the Chinese authoritarian state helped to drive China's high economic growth.[17] Nevertheless, as the aforementioned analysis and literature indicate, authoritarianism did play a positive role in the Chinese miracle. Ogden's view, which Gilley criticized, thus made sense. She faulted the Indian government for failing to solve social problems and credited the Chinese state for carrying out policies in the long-term interest of the population.[18] As far as quickly lifting the population out of poverty is concerned, the Chinese state has been more effective than the Indian state. From 1981 to 2001 the percentage of the population in poverty declined by about 40 percentage points in China, doubling that in India in the same period.[19]

Overall, thanks to the aforementioned strengths of the Chinese governance, China has been enjoying the highest economic growth for the past three decades in the world. China's GDP per capita at exchange rate increased from US$227 in 1978 to US$2,485 in 2007. China's economic performance even dwarfs that of India, which has attracted international attention for its starlet growth performance. From 1995 to 2004 China's annual GDP growth reached 9.1 percent, 3.1 percent higher than that of India.[20]

Slow opening of politics and limits of governance

Despite the aforementioned advantages, the limits of China's model of governance are also apparent. They are reflected in a host of serious problems, including weak rule of law and official corruption, violations of citizens' rights by the powerful and the rich, unequal distribution of the fruits of high growth, as well as environmental degradation. As a result, the rich and powerful benefit more from development than do the lower classes.

In many ways, the positive and negative sides of China's pro-growth governance are intricately interrelated. A single-minded pursuit of high growth and refusal to open up the political system are interlocked core features of pro-growth authoritarianism. In 1979, in response to the Democracy Wall Movement in Beijing, Deng spelled out the "four cardinal principles." The most important principle was to uphold the CCP's leadership of the nation. The "four cardinal principles" were cemented as the political pillars of the Party in the following decade, with the purges of two liberally-minded Party General Secretaries, i.e. Hu Yaobang in 1987 and Zhao Ziyang in 1989, and with the consolidation of power of orthodox reformists led by Deng, who embraced rapid economic opening and reform but slow political opening.[21]

Growth-oriented authoritarianism is based on all-out efforts to promote high growth for the Party's continued dominance. Deng, as well as his successors whom I term orthodox reformists, believed that the Party could sustain its political power through promoting economic growth and improving people's material well-being.[22] Simply put, until recent years, the prevalent view among China's leaders and officials has been that high economic growth and a good living standard will be sufficient to earn the Party political legitimacy.[23]

In actual policy making and implementation officials perceive that respect for citizens' social and economic rights, economic justice, and environmental protection would increase considerably the difficulties in producing high growth within a short time span and would even slow down economic growth. As the Party dominates politics and can implement policies without political opposition and with little social resistance, officials are able and in fact tend to push forth their pro-growth agenda without taking into account people's legitimate concerns. Meanwhile, free from public supervision and monopolizing political power, officials were tempted to trade their control of market entry and economic resources for wealth from the rich or gangsters. This has given rise to corruption and criminal gangs. Nevertheless, violations of citizens' rights, unequal distribution of wealth, and limited channels for public grievances lead to mass popular protests. In the following paragraphs, the major problems that have arisen in governance will be discussed briefly.

Lack of rule of law and rampant corruption

China's top leaders started to actively and publicly promote the rule of law back in the late 1990s. At the closing ceremony of the annual session of the National People's Congress (NPC) in March 1996, Qiao Shi, the chief of the Chinese legislature, that is, NPC, formally called on the Party to "rule the country in accordance with law, and build a legally institutionalized socialist country." One month after his assumption of the post of Party General Secretary, Hu Jintao declared at a meeting of the twentieth anniversary of the implementation of the Constitution of the People's Republic of China that the Party should abide by the Constitution.[24] Nevertheless, in reality, the courts at all levels are dominated by a political and legal committee of the Party at the same level and the courts are hardly independent in reaching verdicts.[25] The courts and judges cannot independently make legal decisions and are subject to political interference.

In the international perspective China's performance in the rule of law is mediocre and falls well short of its economic competitiveness. Judicial independence is a key indicator of the rule of law. In this aspect, China ranks No. 69 out of 134 economies worldwide. It is far behind Egypt (No. 42) and India (No. 43) and very similar to Brazil (No. 68). This contrasts sharply with China's status as the thirtieth most competitive economy in the world.

Concentration of power into the hands of a few leading Party officials at each level, their important role in economic decisions, as well as the rapidly expanding economy, create ample opportunities for the officials to enrich themselves. On the other hand, institutional and public restraints on official behavior are ineffectual due to the lack of genuine rule of law, closedness of the political process, lack of public supervision, and the absence of an independent press. Very often, several top local leaders, especially the Party Secretary, control key personnel appointments,[26] including the members of the political and legal affairs committee and the head of the Department of Propaganda, and even the top managers of leading local newspapers and TV stations (which are usually state owned). They thus indirectly dictate local legal decisions. No local courts or local media dare to challenge the decisions and policies formulated by local leaders; nor will they take up cases or stories suggesting corruption of these leaders. This usually gives a green light for abuse of power and corruption by local leaders.

In addition, as *guanxi* plays a key role in official promotion, candidates for office may resort to bribery and nepotism in order to gain office. Furthermore, officials whose career advancement is less promising may also concentrate on rent-seeking activities, instead of polishing their performance records in order to advance their careers. These traits of official behavior only induce corruption.[27]

Transparency International, a reputed international agency, ranked China No. 78 out of 159 countries and areas in the corruption perception index in the world in 2005. Mainland China earned a meager 3.2 out of a scale of 10, where 10 stood for no corruption. Its low score was in sharp contrast with other high-scoring Asian economies—Singapore's 9.4, Hong Kong's 8.3, Japan's 7.3, Taiwan's 5.9, and South Korea's 5.0. It also lagged behind several other developing Asian economies—Malaysia (5.1), Thailand (3.8), and even very backward Laos (3.3). It was also behind several major emerging economies such as Brazil (3.7) and Poland (3.4). The only comforting fact was that China was slightly ahead of other slightly poorer Asian economies, i.e. India (2.9), Vietnam (2.6), the Philippines (2.5), and Indonesia (2.2). In 2014 Transparency International ranked China No. 100 out of 175 countries and areas in the corruption perception index in the world in 2014. Mainland China earned a meager 36 out of a scale of 100 (compared to 3.2 out of the best and full score 10). So only small improvement has been made in China compared to 2005.[28]

The severity of corruption in China was also confirmed by a survey from late 2006 to early 2007 among private entrepreneurs in coastal China who had more intimate knowledge about official rent-seeking behavior. Some 19.0 percent of the respondents agreed with the statement that most officials in their county or city were corrupt and 63.1 percent agreed that some officials in their county or city were corrupt.[29] Official rent-seeking and corruption is thought to be more severe in inland areas. Therefore, overall corruption in China remains serious.

Unequal distribution of wealth

In the reform era, under Deng's call, some areas, especially the coastal region, were encouraged to grow earlier and faster than the rest of the nation, and certain social groups, especially entrepreneurs and managers, were encouraged to get rich first. This uneven growth policy was to break Mao's egalitarianism that discouraged individual entrepreneurship, productive activities, and innovations. As a result, income inequalities in China have grown. The Gini coefficient of income distribution in China registered a low 0.288 in 1981, yet soared to an alarming 0.403 in 1998; it continued to rise to 0.459 in 2001, on a par with the U.S.'s 0.466.[30] China's Gini coefficient further rose to 0.496 in 2005. In 2006, in a nationwide public opinion survey, income inequalities were regarded as the third most serious social problem.[31] Income inequalities developed along three dimensions—the rural–urban gap, inter-regional gap (most noticeably coastal–inland gap), and inter-strata gap.[32] Nevertheless, weak state institutions for income redistribution do not help to stem the income gaps. As a result, inequalities along these three dimensions continue to grow. Of the three dimensions the most alarming is the rural–urban income gap. The disposable income of an average peasant was equivalent to 53.8 percent of that of an average urban resident in 1985. It declined sharply to 34.9 percent in 1994 and registered a deplorable 30.5 percent in 2006.[33] The issue of inequalities will be discussed further in Chapter 4.

Until recent years the state, especially at the local level, has tried much harder in catering to the needs of entrepreneurs than offering economic assistance and providing welfare to the lower classes. Social spending out of the governmental budget is viewed as economically wasteful and unhelpful for generating high economic growth. Many officials would rather concentrate on wooing investment in order to generate GDP than on collecting and channeling revenue into the financing of local welfare programs and for equal income distribution.

Violation of citizens' rights in development

Many officials view high growth as the ultimate barometer of governance of their localities. They often regard local residents' legitimate demand for protection of their interests as obstacles to the rapid economic development. For example, they favor swift confiscation of rural land for industrial parks and estate development and make low compensation to peasants in order to reduce business costs and woo investors. In addition, they treat local people's complaints about infringement of their social–economic interests (such as resettlement, pollution and noise from plants) by local developmental projects as trouble making and detrimental to their pursuit of high growth. They rely on public security or even the mafia to suppress protestors.

One of the most serious and widespread cases of infringement of rights arises from the use of agricultural land. It was estimated that from 1987 to 2001, 34–51 million peasants lost their land to non-agricultural use of land. According to a survey of 10 provinces, 69 percent of the land of industrial parks was taken over by local authorities illegally. In many of these cases, inadequate compensation was quite common. In particular, in inland provinces such as Henan, Yunnan, and Shanxi, peasants' income declined by 25 percent, 26 percent, and 9.4 percent, respectively. Even in coastal provinces such as Tianjin and Liaoning, despite higher income after compensation, peasants who lost land suffered from a real decline in income due to their moving into urban areas where living expenses were higher. There were cases where village cadres enriched themselves whereas villagers received only a portion of compensation that was deemed reasonable. These cases of official corruption in land use served to instigate social tensions and conflict.[34]

Limited channels for remedies of public grievances

From the beginning of reform, China's leaders rejected any conspicuous attempt to open up the political system and introduce democracy. The only exception is the direct and relatively open elections of village chiefs and villager committees.[35] As a result of this political strategy, China has indeed avoided the political upheavals and instability that the former Soviet Union (such as Russia and its former Republics in Central Asia), as well as democratized Asian nations such as Indonesia, the Philippines and Thailand, experienced.

However, the development-first strategy has entailed grave political, social and even economic consequences. The ruling Chinese Communist Party has maintained the closed political system. There have been few channels for the public and concerned parties to influence and shape public policy. As Bernstein and Lü observed in their study on protests in rural China, peasants protested, sometimes even violently, because local officials arbitrarily imposed economic burdens on them through illicit taxation, fees and projects and target meeting without consulting peasants.[36] As a result of the closed political system and largely closed policy-making process, policies that are implemented can be short-sighted and do little to improve people's well-being. In addition, new officials may pursue a whole set of policies different from their predecessors in order to claim political credits. Officials have weak incentives to help out disadvantaged groups. These groups include rural migrants and the poor, as well as a portion of the Tibetan and Uighur population. These groups benefit modestly from economic development. These groups inevitably feel that they lag far behind other groups in the course of rapid economic development and are neglected by the government.

The pro-growth authoritarianism that has been discussed inevitably leads to social grievances. As their legitimate rights are violated urban residents and rural residents try to seek justice.[37] One form of action is individual or collective appeals to officials. Nevertheless, citizens' channels for complaints and grievance airing are restricted due to the institutional barriers the state has set up. As Cai put it, "workers and peasants have experienced significant failures using appeals in their struggles against abusive cadres."[38]

Most importantly, the institutional setup largely discourages officials from responding promptly and effectively to citizens' complaints. Officials are appointed by their superiors; getting along with colleagues and other officials is thus important for leaving a good impression upon superiors. Addressing infringement of legitimate economic and social rights by officials and the rich would require decisive action that may risk alienating colleagues, subordinates and local powerful groups and may invite retribution. Without effective institutions of public supervision and censorship such as free elections of officials and a free press, local officials and courts are under no public pressure to address public grievances. Some local officials even call upon the police and gangsters to prevent disgruntled people from airing their grievances to their superiors. In response, discontented citizens resort to disrupting public order and destroying public property and governmental offices in order to vent their grievances and anger. Their rationale may be that by escalating the tension protesters would attract the attention of some higher authority to their grievances and that the higher authority will then force the local official to change their behavior.

High growth coupled with frequent protests in China

China has maintained rapid economic growth during the past three decades. From 1978 to 2008 China's GDP grew at a brisk 9.8 percent per annum, and increased 15-fold. From 1993 to 2006, China's GDP annual growth rate ranged from 7.6 percent to 14 percent. The average growth at nearly 10 percent (9.96 percent to be exact) was higher than the average growth rate of 9.6 percent from 1978 to 1992.[39] One may be tempted to conclude that thanks to higher economic growth China should witness fewer popular protests in the later period than the earlier period.

However, what actually happened was the opposite. From 1993 to 2005, China witnessed a steady and rapid growth in collective grievances and protests. The number of petitions to the national government, a key Chinese form of expressing grievances especially at the local level, was only 297,900 in 1984; but it started to grow in 1994, totalled 586,400 in 2000 and had reached 603,000 by 2005.[40]

China's GDP grew on average at 9.8 percent a year from 1994 to 1999 and 9.5 percent from 2000 to 2006. As the economic performance in these two periods was very impressive and comparable, popular protests in these two periods should have been stable in number and small in total. In China a more direct and explosive form of expression of public grievances is collective protests, which refer to protests by over five participants. The number of collective protests registered at 10,000 in 1994; it increased to 32,000 in 1999. Instead of declining during the period 2000–2006, it increased further to 40,000 in 2000 and grew steadily to an estimated 90,000 in 2006.[41] The period from 2000 to 2006 witnessed more frequent collective protests than that from 1993 to 1999. In 2006 the number of collective protests was 10.3 times that in 1993, averaging nearly 20 percent growth per annum, more than twice as fast as the GDP growth rate.

Thus it is apparent that high economic growth does not necessarily lead to solid political legitimacy of the ruling elites, nor does it preempt popular dissatisfaction with the political regime. Even though high economic growth may increase the level of popular support for the regime, it does not preclude outbreaks of popular protests. Indeed, this is the hardest lesson the CCP learned in the summer of 1989 and from 1993 to 2006. The following is an analysis of one of the most-noticed riots in China in 2008, which can help shed light on the negative implications of uneven opening in China in the economy, society and politics for social stability and the society, as well as pro-growth authoritarianism. It also suggests Chinese leaders' awareness of societal opening and their more pragmatic approach to social protests.

Weng'an: protests against erroneous pro-growth governance

Among recent protests during the 2000s, few match the scale of the riots in Weng'an in June 2008. The riots in Weng'an illustrate well the side effects of the blatant pursuit of high economic growth at the expense of people's social and economic rights, as well as the dark side of pro-growth governance in China. They also shed light on the dynamics of interaction between discontented people, predatory officials, and the usually far-away central government. As the riots in Weng'an became a national and international news headline, top leaders in China were so alarmed at the appalling errors in governance in Weng'an that they immediately acted to address the popular grievances there.

The trigger and the riots

Weng'an is a county in Guizhou, one of the least developed provinces in China. On June 21, 2008, Li Shufen, an almost 16-year-old junior high school female student, committed suicide by jumping into a river at night. Liu, a friend of Li's boyfriend Chen, tried to rescue her but failed. Earlier all three went to the riverside after a drinking session. Miss Wang, Li's classmate, who was also at the scene, stated that Li had long resented her parents' prejudiced treatment of her as a girl and that this could be a cause for her death.[42] Later rumors spread in the county that Li was raped by Chen and Liu, murdered and thrown into the river, that Chen and Liu were relatives of local ranking officials and that the local police covered up the case and protected them. For days Li's parents refused to accept the official verdict that Li had committed suicide and placed the body of their daughter at the scene of the incident. Rumors were also circulated in the county that Li's uncle, aunts, grandparents and mother had been beaten by the local security.

On the afternoon of June 28, 300 people gathered near Li's body and marched to the office of the county's public security. By 4 pm, nearly 10,000 people had assembled outside the office. The confrontation between police and protesters, however, went out of control. At 4:30 pm protesters and spectators started to break into the office building, smashed and burned the offices, and broke into the offices of the nearby People's Government (the administration), the bureau of finance, and the Party committee of the county. By 6 pm the crowd had reached 20,000. Police vehicles were set on fire. A crowd of about 10,000 remained outside the governmental office buildings until 3 am on June 29. Early the next morning a crowd of about 6,000 gathered again and tried to break into the governmental offices. They were dispersed by armed police. The rioters destroyed much of the office buildings belonging to the county's Party committee, the people's government (the administration) and the public security, as well as 42 cars; 150 people were injured.[43]

Sources of protests

In fact, in the preceding years the economy of the county had been growing rapidly thanks to a number of economic initiatives. However, the controversial death of Li directly triggered the mass riots in the county. According to emerging official in-depth investigations, the real sources of tensions lay in the erratic governance of the county. Shi Zongyuan, Guizhou's Party Secretary, pointed out three main causes for the riots. The first two are particularly relevant for my argument here. The first cause was that the interests of the Weng'an residents were violated in the extraction of minerals and resettlement and that the local leaders often used public security forces to suppress people's grievances. The second cause was that the county's leaders and public security failed to crack down on local crime and criminal gangs, that many local crimes remained unsolved and that local people lost their trust in the public security.[44]

Several cases show vividly how the local government's reckless pursuit of high growth and blatant transgression of people's rights sowed the seeds of unrest. One case was the extraction of phosphorus ore, one of the rich minerals in the county, in Yan'gen Village. Back in 1998 Weng'an County Phosphorization Company started to extract minerals from beneath the village. By 2003, the operation had caused a drop in the water level in the Tianba Group of the village. As a result, a paddy field of 285 mu could not be irrigated, the spring villagers used as their drinking water source was polluted, and the livelihood of 280 villagers was threatened. The villagers appealed to the township government in vain. In January 2007 the county granted the rights to Aisikai Company to extract ores in the village, and a provincial commercial newspaper estimated the output of the extraction would be worth 200 million yuan. Villagers made collective appeals to local government and demanded that the issues regarding drinking water, paddy field irrigation and sinking of the ground be addressed before the extraction started. Villager representatives even travelled to Guiyang, the provincial capital, but again there was no solution to their satisfaction. In March villagers blocked representatives from the township and county governments from entering the village. In April the county government summoned villager representatives to the county office to discuss a resolution of the dispute. However, seven representatives were arrested upon arrival on criminal charges. Upon learning the news, over 100 villagers went to the county office and entered into a row with the police. In December 2007 the seven villager representatives were sentenced by the county court to prison terms of between two and seven years for disrupting public order, for causing losses of 2 million yuan in the operations of the Aisikai Company. Their appeal was rejected by the prefectural court.

The second case had to do with run-away crime, especially against teenagers. Crimes in the county ran out of control. Since 2006 several crimes victimizing teenagers had occurred in the county. In 2006 a nine-year-old boy was kidnapped by human smugglers. When his uncle reported the case to the public security, he got into a quarrel with the police and was beaten up. In December 2007 a girl student was raped and murdered 200 meters outside her home, and the culprit remained at large. In addition, there were over 10 known criminal gangs that rampaged in the county. They included the Jade Mountain Gang, the Ax Gang, and the Kitchen Knife Gang. Local residents refrained from going out after 7 pm out of fear of robbery. As many crimes remained unsolved, local residents were greatly dissatisfied with the local security. Their distrust played a role in the spread of rumors about a police cover-up of the rape and murder of Li and the outbreak of the riots.[45]

Aftermath

The mass riots in Weng'an shook the nation. Hu Jintao, the Chinese President and the General Secretary of the CCP, urged quick and proper management of the protests. He also subtly blamed the local authority for not resolving popular grievances in the past and for too readily using the police to suppress angry citizens. In the wake of the protests, the Party secretary, the magistrate, and the chief of public security of Weng'an County were dismissed. The official media subtly portrayed these incompetent officials as a primary cause of the mass riots. Immediately after the riots, the Guizhou Provincial Party Secretary spent several days in the county investigating the causes of the riots. One of the conclusions he drew was that the riots invalidated one of the theories once popular among Chinese officials that once the economy grew rapidly the society would be stable.[46] The moderate and restrained response from the Chinese national and provincial leadership suggested that even the leadership was aware of the growing openness of the society and the need for changing the management of state–societal relations. However, and unfortunately, this change does not apply to the political system as a whole.

In retrospect, the people in Weng'an claimed a moral victory by taking dramatic action. They exposed the long-existing problems of misgovernance in the locality and gained much-needed attention from the top leaders to the embedded problems. In addition, they gained a far fairer treatment in the aftermath of the riots than most previous riots. In the past the state authority would have blacked out news reports and would have sent in the military to crush the protests, which would result in the loss of numerous lives. The state would have arrested the protest leaders, sentenced them to heavy prison terms if not death sentences, and would have condemned the riots as "anti-revolutionary" or "subversion of the state."

Development after 2008: a short note

There have been rare reports or revelations of China's official statistics on collective protests after 2006. One likely reason is that these statistics have been viewed as secrets by the Chinese state and have been closely guarded. Nevertheless, one estimate placed the number of collective protests at 180,000 in 2010,[47] doubling the 90,000 protests registered in 2006. This data represented 19 percent growth per year during 2006–10 and was slightly below the 20 percent annual growth in collective protests during 1993–2006. In addition, in the 2000s and the 2010s the Chinese state is apparently spending a large amount on maintaining social stability. In 2010, for example, the state spent 548.6 billion yuan ($83.5 billion) on internal security, a 15.6 percent growth over 2009, compared to 533.5 billion yuan on national defense.[48] Even though internal security expenses might include items for public safety such as fire fighting the bulk was likely on items such as detection and management of social grievances and protests. Therefore, it seems that the collective protests in China continue to increase at a phenomenally fast pace and that the Chinese state even views domestic protests as a greater threat than external military threats in its spending priority.

Xi's anti-corruption campaigns, which will be discussed in Chapter 10, may have restrained official corrupt practice and may have hence eased public grievances to an extent. However, it is unclear or even doubtful that it has reversed the strong momentum in the growth of collective protests in China. Reportedly, hundreds of petitioners appeal to national offices of the Chinese government, after their appeals to local offices failed even after Xi assumed power in 2013. One of the new offices for petitions is the Central Disciplinary and Inspection Commission of the CCCCP, as its main mission is to investigate corruption of officials and impose punishment.[49]

Conclusion

In the reform period China's economy and to a lesser extent society has undergone considerable opening. In contrast, much of the political process and political system has remained closed, despite much progress compared to Mao's era. This chapter investigates the uneven opening of China's economy, society, and politics as well as the positive and negative sides of China's pro-growth governance. It suggests that Chinese society has benefited from the opening and that the Chinese themselves have become conscious of their legitimate social and economic rights and are willing to defend them. It also points out that the Chinese state has been very capable of rapidly opening up the economy, overcoming obstacles to economic development, and achieving growth.

The negative aspects of China's pro-growth governance, however, cannot be ignored. Negative by-products of pro-growth authoritarianism include the weak rule of law, official corruption, violation of people's rights, and few channels for public inputs in policy and public grievances. These defects of the Chinese governance help to account for outbursts of frequent protests during the period of high economic growth.

As China's economy rapidly expands and the Chinese living standard rises, the Chinese society is changing, becoming increasingly mature and open. As discussed above, the Chinese citizens are increasingly aware of their legal rights and have learned to forge social bonds within small groups for their own protection. They must also be aware of the good practice of rights protection and citizens' action in defending their rights in developed economies.

For these reasons, in the reform era high economic growth goes hand-in-hand with a rise in popular protests in China. In the 1980s democracy protests were the norm; into the 1990s and 2000s social protests have become a daily occurrence. The case of Weng'an illustrates that high economic growth at the great expense of people's legitimate demands for economic survival and public security will incite social protests, instead of generating popular support. Therefore, the argument which has long been accepted by Chinese officials and even leaders that high economic growth would automatically translate into popular support and social stability is flawed.

On the other hand, the moderate state responses to riots in recent months, such as those in Weng'an, indicate a growing strength of Chinese society. Importantly, it points to national leaders' growing understanding of the increased opening of the society and social tensions, and their improvement in the handling of social conflicts.

The seemingly viable way for China to escape the quandary of rising instability amidst high economic growth is to reform its pro-growth authoritarianism. A number of modifications of the tight authoritarian governance are vital for the reduction of public discontent. An effective remedy of the sources of public grievances requires the opening of the political process for public participation, political transparency, media supervision, direct and public election of representatives, and greater independence of the legal system. Specifically, greater public inputs in economic policy making are needed, fair compensation for material losses in the execution of developmental projects is necessary, public yearning for low-crime and economic security has to be satisfied, and public supervision and election of official policies needs to be implemented. Furthermore, the media's open and truthful reports on political events and supervision of officials should be tolerated, and the court should be allowed to play a bigger role in resolving disputes, including those involving the state and citizens. Only by addressing the negative side of China's governance can China experience genuine social stability in the course of high growth. Otherwise, a state effective in pushing forth economic opening and generating growth but ineffective in protecting rights will continue to be harassed by social protests.

Notes

* An earlier of the chapter was published as "Uneven Opening of China's Society, Economy, and Politics: Pro-Growth Authoritarian Governance and Protests in China," in *Journal of Contemporary China*, Vol. 19, No. 67, November 2010, 819–835 (DOI: 10.1080/10670564.2010.508581). Reprint by permission © 2010, Taylor & Francis. The first section and the last two sections of the chapter are newly written or revised segments.

1 For a discussion of protests and instability in China, refer to Steven F. Jackson, "Introduction: A Typology for Stability and Instability in China," in David Shambaugh, ed., *Is China Unstable?* (Armonk, NY: M.E. Sharpe, 2000), 3–15. For a recent discussion, see Susan Shirk, *China: Fragile Superpower* (Oxford and New York: Oxford University Press, 2007).

2 Bruce Gilley, "Two Passages to Modernity," in Edward Friedman and Bruce Gilley, eds, *Asia's Giants: Comparing China and India* (New York and Basingstoke: Palgrave Macmillan, 2005), 20.

3 See Wang Guiyu, *Zhuanxing shiqi Zhongguo gongmin xianzheng yishi de shizheng yanjiu* (*An Empirical Study on the Chinese Citizens' Constitutional Awareness*), posted at: http://article.chinalawinfo.com, accessed March 20, 2009.

4 See Yongshun Cai, "Social conflicts and modes of action in China," *The China Journal*, No. 59, January 2008, 106, 102.

5 *Gong Ming: Zaishen anjian shuliang zengzhang fangying le gongmin quanli yishi zengqiang (Increase in Retrial Cases Reflects Growing Citizens' Consciousness with Rights)*, posted at: www.chinacourt.org, accessed March 14, 2008).

6 Yongshun Cai, "Social conflicts and modes of action in China," 102–3.

7 Shujie Yao, *Economic Growth, Income Distribution and Poverty Reduction in China under Economic Reforms* (Abingdon and New York: RoutledgeCurzon, 2005), 84–99; Jeffrey Sachs, *The End of Poverty: How We Can Make it Happen in Our Lifetime* (London and New York: Penguin Books, 2005), 264.

8 For a discussion on the topic, refer to Hongyi Lai, *Reform and the Non-state Economy in China*, 45–59.

9 Nicholas Lardy, *Integrating China into the Global Economy* (Washington, DC: Brookings Institution Press, 2002), 65–6.

10 National Statistical Bureau of China (NSB), *China Statistical Yearbook 2006* (Beijing: China Statistical Press, 2006), Table 18–5 – Exports value by category of commodities and Table 18–14 – Utilization of foreign capital.

11 World Bank, *World Development Report 2006* (Washington, DC: World Bank, 2005), 298–9.

12 Betina Dimaranan, Elena Ianchovichina and Will Martin, "Competing with giants," in L. Alan Winters and Shahid Yusuf, eds, *Dancing with Giants: China, India, and the Global Economy* (Singapore: The World Bank and Institute of Policy Studies, 2007), 73–4.

13 Klaus Schwab and Michael E. Porter, *The Global Competitiveness Report 2008–2009* (Geneva: World Economic Forum, 2008), 471.

14 For an in-depth analysis of China's reform strategies, refer to Lai, *Reform and the Non-state Economy in China*, Chapters 3, 5, 6 and 7 (61–90; 109–90).

15 For studies on the topic, refer to ibid., Chapters 4 and 9 (91–108; 236–241); Lance Gore, *Market Communism: The Institutional Foundation of China's Post-Mao Hyper-Growth* (Hong Kong: Oxford University Press, 1998); and Susan Whiting, *Power and Wealth in Rural China: The Political Economy of Institutional Change* (New York: Cambridge University Press, 2001).

16 Schwab and Porter, *The Global Competitiveness Report 2008–2009*, 428, 433.

17 Gilley, "Two Passages to Modernity," 19–54.

18 See Suzanne Ogden, *Inklings of Democracy in China* (Cambridge, MA: Harvard University Asia Center, 2002), 369, 371.

19 Sachs, *The End of Poverty*, 154, 182.

20 Winters and Yusuf, eds, *Dancing with Giants*, Table 1.1.

21 For an analysis of leadership conflict over political opening and of the rise of orthodox reformists, refer to Lai, *Reform and the Non-state Economy in China*, Chapter 3, 61–90.

22 For an analysis of orthodox reformists headed by Deng, refer to ibid.

23 For a discussion and critique of the Party's approach to legitimacy, refer to Lynn White, "Introduction: Dimensions of Legitimacy," in Lynn White, ed., *Legitimacy* (Singapore: World Scientific, 2005), 3–4; Yongnian Zheng and Liangfook Lye, "Political Legitimacy in Reform China," in White, ed., *Legitimacy*, 186–96; and Zhengxu Wang, "Political Trust in China: Forms and Causes," in White, ed., *Legitimacy*, 128–38, 118, 121.

24 Hongyi Lai, *Hu Wen quan toushi: Hu Wen shizheng neimu quan jiedu ji Zhongguo weilai zhanwang (Hu–Wen under Full Scrutiny: A Comprehensive Inside Story of Governance under Hu and Wen and Prospects for Future China)* (Hong Kong: Wenhua yishu chubanshe, 2005), 75–9.

25 Minxin Pei, *China's Trapped Transition: The Limits of Developmental Autocracy* (Cambridge, MA and London: Harvard University Press, 2006), 69–72.

26 Yang Zhong, *Local Government and Politics in China: Challenges from Below* (Armonk, NY: M.E. Sharpe, 2003), 105–9.

27 Ibid., 109–26.

28 Transparency International Secretariat, *Transparency International Corruption Perceptions Index 2005* (Berlin: 2005), posted at: www.transparency.org. For data on China in 2014, refer to www.transparency.org/country/#CHN, accessed May 14, 2015.

29 Jie Chen and Bruce J. Dickson, "Allies of the State: Democratic Support and Regime Support Among China's Private Entrepreneurs," *China Quarterly*, Vol. 196, December 2008, 17.

30 Hongyi Lai, "Growth with Rising Income Inequality: China's Response to the Problem," *EAI Background Brief No. 227* (Singapore: East Asian Institute, 16 February 2005).

31 Li Peilin, Chen Guangjin and Li Wei, "A Report on a Survey on the Conditions of Social Harmony and Stability in China in 2006," in Ru Xin, Lu Xueyi and Li Peilin, eds, *2007 nian: Zhongguo shehui xingshi fenxi yu yuce* (*Analyses and Forecasts on China's Social Development*) (Beijing: Shehui Kexue Wenxian Chubanshe, 2007), 24–5.

32 See World Bank, *Sharing Rising Incomes* (Washington, DC: World Bank, 1997), 7. For studies on income inequality in China, refer to Carl Riskin, Zhao Renwei and Li Shi, eds, *China's Retreat from Equality, Income Distribution and Economic Transition* (Armonk, NY: M.E. Sharpe, 2001).

33 My own computation using data from the National Bureau of Statistics, *China Statistical Yearbook 2007* (Beijing: China Statistical Press, 2007), Table 10–2.

34 Xiaoyun Li, Lixia Tang and Keyuan Zhang, "Conditions of Land-losing Peasants from 2003–2004", in Xiaoyun Li, Ting Zuo and Jingzhong Ye, eds, *2003–2004 Zhongguo nongcun qingkuang baogao* (*A Report on the Conditions of China's Countryside*) (Beijing: Shehui Kexue Wenxian Chubanshe, 2004), 287–304.

35 For a discussion on rural elections, refer to Yang Zhong and Jie Chen, "To Vote or Not to Vote: An Analysis of Peasant Participation in Chinese Village Elections," *Comparative Political Analysis*, Vol. 35, No. 6, 2002, 686–712; Tianjian Shi, "Voting and Nonvoting in China: Voting Behavior in Plebiscitary and Limited Choice Elections," *The Journal of Politics*, Vol. 61, No. 4, November 1999, 1115–1139; Kent M. Jennings, "Political Participation in the Chinese Countryside," *American Political Science Review*, Vol. 91, 1997, 361–72.

36 Thomas Bernstein and Xiaobo Lü, *Taxation without Representation in Contemporary Rural China* (Cambridge and New York: Cambridge University Press, 2003), 12–5, 250–1.

37 For a study on rural protests, see Kevin O'Brien and Lianjiang Li, *Rightful Resistance in Rural China* (Cambridge and New York: Cambridge University Press, 2006).

38 Yongshun Cai, "Managed Participation in China," *Political Science Quarterly*, Vol. 119, 2004, 444.

39 *China Statistical Yearbook*, 2006, 2007.

40 Yongshun Cai, "Social Conflicts and Modes of Action in China," 97.

41 For data on protests from 1993 to 2006, refer to Jae Ho Chung, Hongyi Lai and Ming Xia, "Mounting Challenges to Governance in China: Surveying Collective Protestors, Religious Sects, and Criminal Organizations," *China Journal*, No. 56, July 2006, 6; Xunlei Xu, "*Dui qunti shijian diyibu yao zuodao 'tuomin'*" (*The First Step Toward Collective Incidents Should be to "Desensitize" Them*), posted at: http://blog.zjol.com.cn/, accessed December 20, 2008.

42 "Three Eye Witnesses in the Death of Li Shufen Reconstructed the Original Scene," posted at: http://bbs.phoer.net, accessed January 30, 2009.

43 "The Beginning and the End of the Weng'an Incident and the Provincial Party Secretary Apologized to the Common People Three Times," *Xinhua*, July 5, 2008.

44 Ibid.

45 "Weng'an Before the June 28 Incident," *Liaowang Dongfang Weekly*, No. 29, July 2008.

46 "The Beginning and the End of the Weng'an Incident."
47 "China's Spending on Internal Policing Outstrips Defense Budget," posted at www.bloomberg.com/news/articles/2011-03-06/china-s-spending-on-internal-police-forc e-in-2010-outstrips-defense-budget on March 6, 2011, accessed May 14, 2015.
48 Ibid.
49 See the following report for an example of recent protests and petitions: "Chuang Zhongjiwei sa chuandan, si fangmin beizhua" (Four Petitioners Were Arrested for Breaking into Central Disciplinary and Inspection Commission and Distributing Leaflets), posted at: http://kt99.kanxing04.cf/?dua=D3D3Lm50ZHR2LmNvbs94D HIvZ2IvMjaXNC8wOs8wNi9hMTEzNjIyMi5oDG1S on September 6, 2014, accessed November 11, 2014.

4   Defusing discontent through welfare and aid

One of the biggest achievements by the CCP in the reform era is that it has engineered a massive poverty reduction throughout the nation and a rapid lift in the population's living standard. Nevertheless, since the mid-1980s China's rapid growth has been overshadowed by rising income inequalities and a struggle for subsistence by social underclasses such as peasants and the urban laid-off workers.

Income inequalities and subsistence struggles by these underclasses have resulted in widespread discontent. In particular, in the 1990s peasants in central China resisted ruthless extraction of labor, taxes and fees by tyrannical cadres. The urban unemployed aired their grievances in front of the governmental offices in the cities, and even provincial and national capitals. Elites in interior regions complained about the lack of favorable treatment that the national government bestowed on the coastal provinces. Arguably, in the 1990s the Party state confronted the most daunting social crises and the most devastating waves of social discontent since 1989.

In response, the national government has introduced a set of economic policies to facilitate agricultural development and to subsidize grain production. It has also installed a range of welfare programs for the rural and urban residents. I argue that through these measures the Party state has made noticeable progress in tackling rural-urban and interior-coastal gaps and has engineered a set of remedies of the side effects of growing income inequalities. Most importantly, the Party state has eased the hardship and grievances from these rural and urban underclasses. The Party state has thus demonstrated its surprisingly strong abilities to weather this wave of mass discontent.

In the remainder of the chapter I will first draw attention to the escalating income inequalities and the resulting explosion of grievances and protests by the rural and urban poor. This will be followed by a detailed documentation of the responses from the state. The effects of the remedies introduced by the state will then be analyzed.

Rising inequalities amidst income growth from an international perspective

China under Mao Zedong was probably one of the most egalitarian countries due to a number of peculiar factors. Under the command economy, personal assets were very limited. Importantly, Mao's egalitarian policies in regional development and his control of wage differentials led to an even distribution of income. Furthermore, the country was so poor that few people could amass wealth. Equality was thus achieved at the expense of efficiency and prosperity.

Since the reform started in 1978 the Chinese population has witnessed an unprecedented pace of improvement in their material life. During 1978–2012 per capita gross domestic product in China improved from 381 yuan to 38,499 yuan, or expanded from US$227 to US$6,099 in current prices. Meanwhile, on average per capita consumption in China grew 12 fold.[1] In 1981, the number of Chinese living below the international poverty line of daily income of US$1.25 in purchasing power parity terms stood at a massive 837.5 million. Thanks to the rapid growth in living standards and especially the highly successful rural reform in the 1980s, the population in poverty fell to 84 million by 2011. The share of the Chinese population under the international poverty line of US$1.25 daily income declined dramatically from 84.3 percent to 6.3 percent (see Figure 4.1).[2] Within the three decades of 1981–2011 753.5 million people had graduated out of poverty. This magnitude of poverty reduction was unprecedented in the world. For this reason, the vice-president of the World Bank for the Asia-Pacific Region commented: "Since 1980, China has achieved poverty reduction on a scale that has no parallel in human history."[3]

In the international context, China could be viewed as a stellar example of economic growth and poverty reduction. During the period of 1978–2002 China was among the fastest growing economies. By 2002 China's per capita

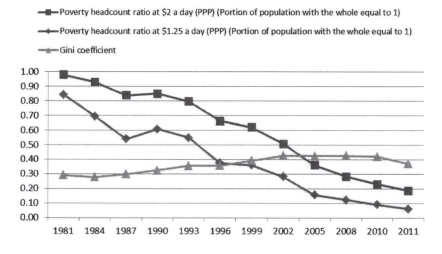

Figure 4.1 Poverty reduction and income inequality in China, 1981–2011
Note: Data came from http://databank.worldbank.org/data/views/reports/tableview.asp x, accessed on February 16, 2015. As this chapter aims to analyze social grievances in the late 1990s and China's governmental provision of social welfare in the period after 2002, the improvement of China's economic conditions *before and after 2002* is thus worth closer attention.

GDP reached US$940, higher than that of India (US$480), Sri Lanka (US$840), and Indonesia (US$710).[4] China also outperforms India, Indonesia, the Philippines, Thailand, Brazil, Russia, and Nigeria in life expectancy; it is far ahead of India and Nigeria in reducing adult illiteracy (Table 4.1).

Worldwide, however, China appears to be an intermediate case of poverty when compared to other developing countries around 2002. The share of the population in China living below US$1 a day was smaller than that of India, the Philippines, and Nigeria, but far higher than that of Poland, Thailand, Malaysia, Sri Lanka, Russia, and Brazil (Table 4.1).

China also constituted an intermediate case of inequality when compared to other developing countries, especially the populous ones. China's income inequality in the late 1990s, measured by the Gini coefficient, was worse than India, Sri Lanka, Indonesia, and Poland. It was, however, better than Thailand, the Philippines, Malaysia, Russia, and much better than Nigeria and Brazil (Table 4.1).

Turning our attention back to the economic successes and limits of China during 1978–2002, the living standard in China had also been significantly raised. During the 1978–2002 period, the Engel coefficient of rural households (or the share of food expenses in these households' expenditure) declined from 68 percent of total consumption to 46 percent; the Engel coefficient of urban households declined from 58 percent to 38 percent (Table 4.2). A 2002 national health survey even suggested that 22.8 percent of Chinese adults were over-weight and 7.1 percent obese.[5] Clearly the Chinese had moved beyond a state of living merely on or below subsistence.

"Relative poverty," however, emerged as a new problem. According to an income survey in China in 2002, 3.5 percent of the population (or 45 million) had annual per capita disposable income of 20,000 yuan (US$2,416) and lived a luxurious life. Some 450 million, or 35 percent of the population, came under the middle-income group, garnering annual per capita disposable income of 6,000–7,000 yuan (around US$785), and living a relatively well-off life. Half of the population resided in the countryside, had annual per capita disposable income of 2,000 yuan (US$242) and lived a simple life just above subsistence.[6] The absolute number of people in poverty in China was large, partly due to its large population. The World Bank estimated in 2004 that 200 million Chinese (or 15 percent of the population) lived below the international poverty line of US$1 daily income.[7]

In addition and importantly, income inequality in China has risen sharply since the late 1980s and rising income is distributed rather unevenly, especially since the late 1990s.[8] The Gini coefficient of income distribution, a major indicator to measure the distribution of income from the highest to the lower income-earning groups in the population, suggested that income inequalities in China were rising at a rapid pace from the mid-1980s to the 2010s.[9] In 1981, an early year of economic reform, the lingering effect of Mao's egalitarian policy still affected income distribution in China. The Gini coefficient of 0.291 then suggested a fairly equal income distribution. In 1984, with the huge success of

Table 4.1 Development and income distribution of selected countries

Country	Population (million), 2002	GDP per capita, US$, 2002	GDP Per Capita, purchasing power parity, US $, 2002	GDP annual growth, 1990–2001, %	a. Population below national poverty line, %	b. Population below $1 a day, %	c. Population below $2 a day, %	d. Gini co-efficient	e. Share of income or consumption of the highest 10%	Survey years for columns a; b-c; d-e.	Life expectancy, 2000	Adult illiteracy rate, % of people 15 and above, 2000
China	1281	940	4,390	10.0	4.6	18.8	52.6	.403	30.4	1998; 1999; 1998	70	16
India	1048	480	2,570	5.9	35.0	44.2	86.2	.378	33.5	1994; 1997; 1997	63	43
Sri Lanka	19	840	3,390	5.1	25.0	6.6	45.4	.344	28.0	1995	73	8
Indonesia	212	710	2,990	3.8	27.1	12.9	65.5	.317	26.7	1999	66	13
Philippines	80	1,020	4,280	3.3	36.8	26.9	62.8	.462	36.6	1997; 1994; 1997	69	5
Thailand	62	1,980	6,680	3.8	13.1	<2	28.2	.414	32.4	1992; 1998; 1998	69	5
Malaysia	24	3,540	8,280	6.5	15.5	4.3	22.4	.492	38.4	1989; 1995; 1997	73	13
Poland	39	4,570	10,130	4.5	23.8	<2	<2	.316	24.7	1993; 1998; 1998	73	<0.5

Country	Population (million), 2002	GDP per capita, US$, 2002	GDP Per Capita, purchasing power parity, US $, 2002	GDP annual growth, 1990–2001, %	a. Population below national poverty line, %	b. Population below $1 a day, %	c. Population below $2 a day, %	d. Gini coefficient	e. Share of income or consumption of the highest 10%	Survey years for columns a; b-c; d-e.	Life expectancy, 2000	Adult illiteracy rate, % of people 15 and above, 2000
Russia	144	2,140	7,820	-3.7	30.9	7.1	25.1	.487	38.7	1994; 1998; 1998	65	<0.5
Brazil	174	2,850	7,250	2.8	17.4	11.6	26.5	.607	48.0	1990; 1998; 1998	68	15
Nigeria	133	290	780	2.5	34.1	70.2	90.8	.506	40.8	1992–3; 1997; 1996–7	47	36
South Korea	48	9,930	16,480			<2	<2	.316	24.3	1993	73	2
Australia	20	19,740	26,960	4.0				.352	25.4	1994	79	
Singapore	4	20,690	23,090	7.8				.47		1999	78	8
U.S.A.	288	35,060	35,060	3.5				.408	30.5	1997	77	

Sources: World Bank, *World Development Report 1997, 1999/2000; 2003; 2004* (New York: Oxford University Press). Information on Taiwan comes from CIA, *The World Factbook*, posted at: www.cia.gov/cia/publications/factbook. The Gini coefficient for Singapore came from *Straits Times*, June 10, 2000, cf. Lim Chong Yah 2004, *Southeast Asia: The Long Road Ahead* (Singapore: World Scientific Publishing Co.), 15.

Table 4.2 Per Capita Annual Income of Urban and Rural Households in China, 1978–2012

Year	Per Capita Rural Income		Per Capita Urban Income		Engel Coefficient of Rural Households	Engel Coefficient of Urban Households
	Yuan	*Index (1978=100)*	*Yuan*	*Index (1978=100)*	*% of food in total consumption*	*% of food in total consumption*
1978	134	100	343	100	68	58
1980	191	139	478	127	62	57
1985	398	269	739	160	58	53
1990	686	311	1510	198	59	54
1995	1578	384	4283	290	59	50
1998	2162	456	5425	330	53	45
2000	2253	484	6280	384	49	39
2002	2476	528	7703	472	46	38
2008	4761	793	15781	816	44	38
2012	7917	1177	24565	1147	39	36
Growth						
1978–85		169%		60%	-10%	-5%
1985–2000		80%		140%	-8%	-15%
2000–2012		143%		199%	-5%	-2%

Note: The data in the last three rows are from the author's own calculation.
Sources: *China Statistical Yearbook 2003*, p. 244; *China Statistical Yearbook 2013*, Table 11–2.

household farming that had reduced much of the food scarcity and had improved dramatically the livelihood of hundreds of millions of peasants who constituted the overwhelming majority of the population, the Gini coefficient dropped further to 0.277, the most egalitarian period in the reform era. It was equivalent to that in Norway in 1995 (0.276). However, in the following years urban living standards improved drastically with deepening of urban reform, whereas the rural ones rose modestly due to the lack of governmental efforts. The Gini coefficient reached 0.324 in 1990, jumped to 0.392 in 1999, rose to 0.426 in 2002 and stayed in the range of 0.42 during 2002–2010 (Figure 4.2). The critical threshold of 0.4 suggests severe inequalities. China had thus been transformed from an egalitarian into a highly unequal country. It is worth mentioning that around 2002 the Chinese leaders were probably aware of the following portrait of income inequalities published by the World Bank: The Gini coefficient of per capita residents' income started at a very low 0.288 in 1981, reached an alarming 0.403 in 1998, and rose further to 0.459 in 2001, on par with that in the U.S. (0.466) (Figure 4.2).[10]

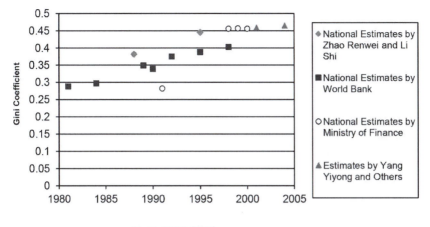

Year, 1978–2005

Figure 4.2 Gini coefficient of income distribution in China, 1978–2005
Note: See endnote 10.

As China is a geographically large country regional and urban-rural developmental gaps contribute a great deal to income disparities. According to a World Bank study, three dimensions accentuated rising disparities in the reform era. The urban-rural gap of development has increased. By the Chinese categorization of countryside 60 percent of the population were rural residents around 2002.[11] In 1978, an average rural resident's consumption was equivalent to 34.1 percent that of an average urban resident. It improved to 43.3 percent in 1985. This ratio decreased drastically to 33.9 percent in 1990 and to an alarming 27.8 percent in 2001 (Figure 4.3). In contrast, in many other countries the rural income level was equivalent to two-thirds of the urban level; few countries witness a ratio below 50 percent. Moreover, regions have developed at highly different paces. Per capita resident income in the interior region in 1985 was 67 percent that of the coastal region. This ratio declined to 55.8 percent in 1995 and reached a much lower 46.5 percent in 2001 (Figure 4.3).[12] Finally, the income gap of different strata has enlarged, as levels of skills of labor vary and wage differentials widen. Disparities within the cities and in the countryside have thus grown. The urban Gini coefficient rose from 0.16 in 1978, to 0.30 in 1994 and to 0.33 in 2001; the Gini coefficient in the countryside grew from 0.21 in 1978, to 0.33 in 1994 and to 0.42 in 2000 (Figure 4.4).[13]

Grievances from the rural and urban poor

Inequality breeds instability in rural and urban China. In the provinces in central China with a significant agricultural sector (central agrarian provinces in short) a significant number of peasants were struggling economically. Yet their economic hardship was linked to two elements, namely, (1) lack of subsidies

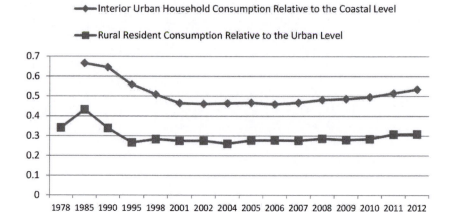

Figure 4.3 Interior-coastal and rural-urban inequalities, 1978–2012

from the national government which it gave to poor western provinces and (2) predatory cadres who tried to squeeze funds out of agriculture to finance local development and basic public services such as education, roads, and health care.[14] What is worse, as will be detailed, people with insight on these agrarian provinces suggested that a significant number of cadres were care-free in spending hard-earned tax money from the peasants, but were ruthless in forcing peasants to pay taxes and fees. This gave rise to massive discontent from rural residents in these provinces. Meanwhile, in the cities in the late 1990s and early 2000s a large number of workers of state-owned enterprises were laid off

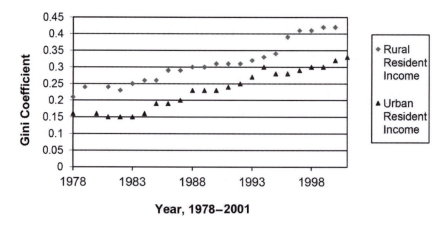

Figure 4.4 Gini coefficient of urban and rural income distribution in China, 1978–2001
Note: See endnote 10.

and lost their secure income and welfare services. Many were forced to find various ways of supporting themselves, including prostitution. Economically desperate, they blamed the government for their hardship. Laid-off workers and displaced peasants frequently protested or petitioned in front of the local governmental offices. Some even travelled to Beijing to protest and appealed to the central government. Economic hardship was thus linked with rising crimes, discontent and instability. Rural migrants commit many violent crimes in the cities, including burglaries, robberies, ransoms, and murders. The plights of interior rural residents and the urban poor will be discussed in detail below.

Plight of and resistance by rural residents in the inland provinces

Rural residents, who constituted 60 percent of the population, lived a basic life until the early 2000s. As stated, peasants in the central agrarian provinces had inadequate social services and welfare yet had to shoulder a relatively heavy fiscal burden and endure frequent transgression of their economic and social rights in the hands of local cadres. In China scholars and officials referred to rural issues as three rural issues (*sannong wenti*), namely, the issues of the countryside, peasants and agriculture. The aforementioned problems are also confirmed by data collected on the national level.

Chinese peasants bore a heavy burden of social services including health care and education. A nationwide survey on public health in 1998 suggested that only 12.7 percent of the peasants received medical insurance, including 6.6 percent covered by cooperative health schemes, and that 87.3 percent of rural residents relied solely on out-of-pocket payment to cover their medical expenses. During 1991–2000 rural residents, who made up 60–70 percent of the population, consumed only 32–37 percent of total medical expenses of the nation.[15] During 2000–1 health care and medical services rose from 3.25 percent of per capita consumption expenditure of rural households to 5.24 percent.[16] Despite their rising income and an escalating share of medical expenses in overall expenditure, 36.7% of rural residents did not seek medical treatment and 64 percent were not hospitalized due to financial constraints. As to be detailed below, rural residents also had to pay for extremely high schooling expenses for their children out of their own pocket, which could take up 15–50 percent of the average income of a peasant.

In addition to the imperative of footing the bill for medical and schooling expenses, peasants in China also bore a hefty burden of fees and expenses. A nationwide random survey of 5,000 rural households in 1997 revealed that on average a peasant paid 195 yuan in fees and taxes, equivalent to 12.4 percent of their net income and that the fees were 3.2 times as much as taxes.

Understandably, economic predicaments amounted to a hotbed for discontent in rural China. In addition, in central China predatory officials who forced peasants to shoulder a heavy load of fiscal charges often fueled the discontent of peasants.

In a number of areas peasants refused to pay fees and taxes in protest. In Nan County of Hunan Province, for example, the fees and taxes compliance rate declined from 95 percent in 1995, to 53 percent in 1998 and less than 50 percent in 1999. Similar phenomena were found in Anhui, Henan, Hubei and Shandong Provinces.[17]

In 2000 Li Changping, the Party Secretary of Qipan Township, Jianli County, Hubei Province, wrote a report to Premier Zhu Rongji. Based on his own personal observations he exposed the following severe problems in his township in a book he published in 2002, which he believed was typical of an area that was agrarian. I also provide additional evidence for these problems from other sources.

1   Heavy fiscal burdens. In 1998 in Qipan Township on average a peasant earned 1910 yuan, but had to pay 232 yuan in fees and taxes in 1999 (they could only use their income from the previous year to pay the current charges). Thus the fiscal burden amounted to 12% of their income from the previous year.[18] In addition to these fees and taxes, peasants also shouldered a hefty amount of tuition for their children. Despite the local government stipulation that tuition should range from 50 yuan to 160 yuan a year, a primary school student was charged 300–500 yuan (equivalent to 15.6–26.0 percent of the average income of a peasant in 1998). An average student in junior high school was billed over 1,000 yuan, roughly 52.0 percent of the average income of a peasant in 1998. One school even imposed a tuition fee of 1,300 yuan. As revealed by a Hong Kong news report in 2002 nearly 20 percent of rural children dropped out of school or terminated their schooling due to inability to afford the expenses. As a result, one in ten of the new laborers from the countryside were semi-illiterate or illiterate.[19]

2   Loss-making or scant revenue income. Due to heavy fiscal burdens, high production costs, and low grain prices, peasants made little money and even incurred losses from grain production. About 25 percent of the peasants had no income to continue grain production. As a result, a good number of them refused to grow grain.[20] This severely hampered self-sufficiency and security of grain and food in China.

3   Heavy indebtedness and inability to cover health expenses. As a result of low income or losses in their production many peasant households were heavily indebted. A high percentage of the rural households, ranging from 30–80 percent, were in heavy debts. They often borrowed at a very high interest rate. As many as 75 percent of the peasants could not afford to seek medical treatment.[21]

4   Embezzlement of cadres. Cadres indulged themselves in gambling and entertaining guests. In order to cover their expenses (sometimes as much tens of thousands of yuan in a gambling loss) they embezzled public funds.[22]

5   Abuses of power by cadres. In order to cover the fiscal burdens cadres resorted to force to extract payment from unwilling peasants, including illegal detainment and beating. During three months from late 2000 to

early 2001, four peasants lost their lives in Jianli County. Among them one committed suicide after being beaten and after his complaint was ignored, two died in an illegal and cold jail, and a woman died after a blow on her head when she tried to reclaim money that she lent to a township government in order to pay off her outstanding debts.[23]

As a result of the heavy fiscal burdens and violent treatment of peasants by cadres, peasants in Jianlin County were very cynical about the local government and politics. A popular saying circulated in the county revealed their strong discontent about the government: "Growing up in new China, lost the life at the office of township government. With no place to have the grievances addressed, who would act on behalf of the people?"[24]

The gravity of these problems was also echoed in several well-read accounts published around that time. They included Cao Jinqing's account of his field work in central China in 1996, as well as a report on the miserable economic conditions of rural residents in Anhui Province in the 1990s and early 2000s authored by two daring Chinese journalists. According to that journalistic report entitled *An Investigation on Peasants in China*, peasants ate plain rice and vegetables on a daily basis and could afford meat only occasionally. That report contained gruesome stories where tyrannical cadres forcefully extracted money from peasants in order to meet their dining and personal expenditures and where they detained, tortured and even murdered resisting peasant activists.[25]

A story circulated among grass-roots cadres in central China revealed the depth of rural discontent. In the mid-1990s President Jiang Zemin visited the countryside. Afraid that peasants would not tell him the truth he assured them that he would try his best to meet any of their demands. A peasant told Jiang that they needed Chen Sheng and Wu Guang. Both were two rebel leaders best known in China for starting the nationwide rebellions that eventually overthrew the once mighty Qin Dynasty that unified the warring states into the first Chinese empire. Afterwards, Jiang confessed at internal Party meetings that he could not sleep soundly whenever he thought of the rural issues. Premier Zhu Rongji also stated frankly that his biggest concern upon China's admission into the World Trade Organization was the issues with peasants.[26]

Hardships of and protests from the urban unemployed

Urban residents, especially the poor (a significant number of whom were the unemployed) and sick, suffered from thin and inadequate social services. The Chinese leaders, especially Premier Zhu Rongji, decided in 1998 to complete the reduction of redundant workforce and to enable a drastic restructuring of loss-making SOEs within three years. From the mid-1990s to the early 2000s tens of millions of urban residents who worked at SOEs suddenly found themselves jobless. The lack or inadequacy of social security of the laid-off workers accentuated their sense of helplessness and their discontent.

According to an estimate where the definition of employment recommended by the International Labor Organization was applied, the actual urban unemployment rate in mainland China rose steadily from 6.3 percent in 1995 to 9.2 percent in 1999 and 10.9 percent in 2001.[27] This high level of unemployment exceeded the overall unemployment rate in Indonesia, Taiwan, the U.S., and U.K. the According to a national census in 2000, the unemployment rate in China's urban areas reached 8.3 percent (including that in the cities 9.4 percent and that in the townships 6.2 percent), and that in the countryside 1.15 percent. Ten provinces (about one-third of mainland China's provinces) experienced a high urban unemployment rate above 10 percent. They are Liaoning (17.7 percent), Heilongjiang (15.4 percent), Tianjin (14.0 percent), Jilin (13.9 percent), Hainan (13.4 percent), Qinghai (12.3 percent), Shanghai (12.0 percent), Inner Mongolia (11.4 percent), Jiangxi (10.3 percent), and Chongqing (10.8 percent). During 1995–2001 a total of 43.3 million workers were laid off in China, 78.6 percent of whom (or 34.0 million) were from SOEs. An estimate based on data on personal income suggested that in 1998 14.7 million (or 4.7 percent) of urban Chinese were in poverty while an estimate based on the data on personal expenditure placed the figure at 37.1 million (or 11.9 percent) of the urban Chinese population. Another alarming fact was that the proportion of laid-off workers from SOEs being able to find jobs declined from 50 percent in 1998 to merely 30 percent in 2001.[28] Similarly, a representative survey of urban households in 2000 suggested that as many as 19 percent of the households and 11 percent of the workers had experienced layoff, indicating the widespread impact of restructuring.[29]

This tidal wave of urban unemployment in the late 1990s triggered massive discontent among urban workers, resulting in petitions and protests by laid-off workers at the governmental office and even in Beijing, the national capital. Not surprisingly, during the period of 1993–2003, the number of collective protests had experienced the most rapid growth in 1998, a year when the drastic SOEs restructuring was launched. The number of collective public security incidents (CPSI) where a group of people illegally gather, disrupt public order and destroy public properties grew from 15,000 in 1997 to 25,000 in 1998, registering a massive rise by 67 percent, dwarfing the annual growth rate of 9 percent to 25 percent during 1994–1997. In Fujian Province during 2000–2 laid-off workers were the largest group (49 percent) of 37,513 workers who participated in CPSI.[30]

During the late 1990s and the early 2000s local protests and petitions became a daily event in many cities in the provinces hard hit by waves of lay-offs (such as the three northeastern provinces). In Benxi of Liaoning Province, for example, petitioners visited the government daily and lodged their complaints over unpaid medical benefits and insurance. Some of the protests were very large in scale. In March 2002, 5,000 workers from six bankrupt factories in the aging industrial city of Liaoyang of Liaoning Province demonstrated, demanding more than one year's unpaid wages and pensions and accusing officials of embezzling public funds. Later the number of protesters escalated to 30,000. In the same month, 50,000 workers in the Daqing Oilfield were unhappy over their severance agreement and staged protests.[31]

The unemployed also travelled to Beijing and petitioned the central government. According to provincial officials, in those years petitioners went to Beijing every day; Beijing asked local officials to bring back their petitioners on a daily basis; petitioners from Liaoning going to Beijing topped all provinces. According to a Chinese policy analyst, over half of the petitioners in Beijing came from the northeast;[32] one-third of the women working in the red-light business in the nation also came from the region.[33] In 2003, for example, petition to Beijing only stopped during the period of the SARS rampage.[34] It is not surprising that Jilin, a northeastern province with high unemployment, was where Falun Gong founder Li Hongzhi successfully attracted the first echelon of followers, and where his followers protested against the state three years after the state outlawed the sect.[35] Severe unemployment thus threatened social stability, raising grave concerns from the central government.

Public and officials' concerns with stability

Concerns with income inequalities, urban unemployment, fiscal burdens on peasants, and official corruption were also shared by the public and cadres. In 2002 the Chinese Academy of Social Sciences conducted a nationwide random sample survey of Chinese urban and rural residents. The respondents said that the following issues had experienced the biggest deterioration after the reform: corruption (1.70 on the scale 1 to 5), income gaps (1.85), and public security and crimes (2.67). The score 1 represented sharp deterioration, 2 moderate deterioration, 3 neutral, 4 moderate improvement, and 5 sharp improvement.[36] In a survey of leading cadres who were studying at the Central Party School in Beijing in the same year, 66.8 percent respondents regarded corruption as the top concern, followed by unemployment (64.5 percent), income gaps (57.1 percent), burdens on peasants (43.7 percent), state-owned enterprises (39.2 percent), public security and crimes (33.8 percent), people's behavior and conduct (30.8 percent), and regional gaps in development (25.6 percent).[37]

Viewed from Beijing the grievances and protests from peasants in central China and from laid-off workers of SOEs in five provinces near to Beijing, including three northeastern provinces, Tianjin, and Inner Mongolia, as well as Shanghai and Jiangxi were major political challenges to the national government. The ruling CCP built and expanded its political influence in China through gaining initial support from the workers in cities in coastal and central China (such as Shanghai, Wuhan, and Jiangxi) in the late 1920s and especially from poor peasants in central China in the 1930s. From its own political journey it thus knew all too well the importance of maintaining peace and easing social discontents from these groups and these areas.

Outside China many China scholars were acutely aware of the severe political implications of these and other challenges for the regime. This was reflected in the publication in 2000 of an edited volume of analyses of instability in China by a group of leading scholars in the field entitled *Is China Unstable?*[38] In a sensational and doomsday prediction of the Party state published in the following year Gordon Chang wrote: "Then there are the armies of the unemployed roaming China, the single most immediate threat to the continued existence of the Party and the government it dominates."[39] Obviously, Beijing confronted political challenges that if mishandled could well turn into a nationwide upheaval that could bring down the Party state. At that time, China observers such as Gordon Chang saw an immediate demise of the regime, though others were less pessimistic.[40]

Responses from the state

In the 1990s under the leadership of the President and Party's General Secretary Jiang Zemin and Vice Premier and then Premier Zhu Rongji, China started to address the grievances from laid-off workers, inland peasants, and people suffering from the lack of social protection. Three measures were most noticeable. First, during 1993–2002 minimum living allowances were gradually institutionalized in urban China in order to aid the laid-off workers. This policy will be documented in detail in a section below. Second, during 2000–2 experiments with reduction of rural fees and taxes were implemented and then expanded gradually in the nation. The first experiment was conducted in Anhui Province in 2000. The maximum rate of agricultural tax was set at 7 percent and all the other additional surcharges were set at 20 percent of agricultural tax. Within one year the state rescinded over 50 fees and surcharges on peasants amounting to 1.69 billion yuan. On average fiscal charges per capita on rural residents declined by 31 percent from 109.4 yuan to 75.5 yuan.[41] In 2001 Jiangsu became the second province to undergo the experiment with the reform of rural taxation and fees. In 2002 the experiment was spread to eighteen provinces.[42] In Jiangxi, for example, cities and counties dispatched nearly 15,000 cadres to ensure that two to three cadres would assist each village with the reform. The province introduced a supervision card for each of the 8 million rural households of 32 million rural residents. At the end the provincial and national governments regarded the reform as a clear success as fiscal burdens had been reduced while no single petitions or protests were reported.[43]

Third, in 2000 the national government launched the most ambitious regional developmental program since the mid-1980s that aimed to accelerate the growth of the most backward region, namely, the western region.

President Hu Jintao and Premier Wen Jiabao came to power in March 2003. They regarded the plight of poor rural and urban residents in the inland areas, laid-off workers and rising inequalities as top challenges in governance. Like President Jiang they worried that hardship by the farmers and the urban unemployed, lingering poverty and east-west regional disparity, coupled with official corruption, would cause mass protests and instability.[44]

Acutely aware of the plight of inland peasants and laid-off workers both leaders had adopted a new stance by distancing themselves in public from the rich, entrepreneurs, and most advanced areas in China. President Hu and Premier Wen carefully projected an image of caring for the common people and helping out low-income groups. At the 82th anniversary of the founding of the Party in 2003, Hu, the General Secretary of the Party, called on cadres to use power for the people, show concern for the people and seek benefit for the people (权为民所用、情为民所系、利为民所谋 *quan wei min wei yong, qing wei min suo xi, li wei min suo mou*). He reminded officials that the country was governed and the Party set up for the people (执政为民 立党为公 *zhizheng wei min, lidang wei gong*). Specifically, Hu asked cadres to heed and mitigate difficulties encountered by the common people. He urged cadres to sincerely implement the state's measures for reducing poverty and eco-nomic hardship. Hu and Wen spent their Chinese New Year with commoners (miners and peasants, etc.), checking out their material conditions and assuring them a better future. Their populist approach, which was covered exten-sively by the Chinese news media, earned them respect from a good number of the common Chinese and some legitimacy for the central government. This view also conformed with the conventional Chinese belief that the top rulers of the nation are benevolent and that the political trouble is made by lower-rank officials. Hu and Wen's populist approach also helped defuse discontentment from low-income earners for the time being.

President Hu and Premier Wen unfolded a rural reform package to address the rural grievances, especially during 2004–9. This rural reform package was regarded by Chinese analysts as the most sweeping in China since the pro-motion of household farming during 1979–81. Concomitant with the rural reform were efforts to protect the material interests of migrant workers in the cities. President Hu and Premier Wen toured backward areas, showed their compassion for the poor in the countryside and in the cities, and adopted policies to improve public services to the poor. In addition, fiscal input into and institutional building for social security was accelerated. Measures were also taken to reduce the regional developmental gap through developing the western region and the rust-belt northeast. By the end of the Hu–Wen admin-istration the leaders boasted of installing a comprehensive though basic rural public health and education scheme, comprehensive health and pension coverage for urban residents, and basic programs for easing rural and urban discontent.

In the following sections I will start with the rural reform package that covers rural production, fiscal burden reduction, as well as education, health, and retirement pension provision. I will then examine the state's efforts to provide aid for laid-off workers and other disadvantaged groups and build up health and retirement pension coverage for urban residents. Finally, I will briefly review the regional developmental programs.

Rural reform to reduce the plight of inland peasants

At his first interview upon becoming Premier Wen Jiabao expressed his concern that uneven development in China, especially between the cities and the countryside could lead to a "tumble" in development. He also revealed that he visited 1,800 counties including the poorest ones in China. This amounted to 63 percent of this vast nation with a continental size.[45] During the two terms of President Hu and Premier Wen rural issues were made the top priority in the formal policy documents issued by the Party. This policy stance was complemented by a range of policies promoting economic development and providing for social services in the countryside.

The most important policy document targeted rural issues during 2004–13

In China the most important policy documents each year is arguably the No. 1 Document issued by the Central Committee of the Chinese Communist Party (CCCCP), usually at the very end of the previous year or the very beginning of that year. For ten years in a row from 2004 to 2013, the No. 1 Document had been about rural issues. These ten years coincided with the two-term tenure of President Hu and Premier Wen during 2003–13. The last time the Party state laid such a heavy emphasis on rural issues was during 1982–6 when it issued five No. 1 Documents on these issues.[46] Thus in terms of the number of the No. 1 Document predominantly about rural issues the Hu–Wen leadership surpassed their predecessor in the reform era by a wide margin. This new focus in the Party's No. 1 Documents signaled to the cadres at all levels that it was imperative to ease the plight of the peasants. The No. 1 Document also outlined the key measures to address pressing rural issues such as the growing rural-urban income gaps, heavy fiscal burdens on peasants, lack of health insurance and irrigation works, and high tuition fees (Table 4.3).

Reducing fiscal burdens on peasants

One of the first priorities for Premier Wen was to reduce the fiscal burdens on peasants. In 2003 experiments with reforms of rural fees and taxes were spread throughout the nation. In order to support the reduction of rural fees and taxes the national government made payment in fiscal transfers of 35 billion yuan. In 2004 when the first No. 1 Document on rural issues in the Hu–Wen administration was issued, the leadership decided to abolish agricultural taxes within five years and experimented with abolition of the taxes first in Jilin and Heilongjiang. In this year authorities in five provinces including Beijing, Tianjin, Shanghai, Zhejiang, and Fujian abolished agricultural taxes; the agricultural tax rate was reduced by 3 percentage points in eleven provinces that were regarded as the primary grain production areas in China; in the remaining provinces in mainland China the agricultural tax rate was cut by one percentage point. In 2005 in the aforementioned eleven provinces the agricultural tax rate was cut by two percentage points

Table 4.3 The theme of the No. 1 Policy Document of the Central Committee of the
　　　　　 CCP, 2004–10

Year	Theme	Key words
2004	Reverse the increasing urban-rural income gap through "taking less, giving more, and loosening control"	Reduce the urban-rural income gap
2005	Agricultural infrastructure, scientific and technological progress in agriculture, and comprehensive agricultural production capacity are major and pressing strategic tasks	Agricultural infrastructure, technology and production capacity
2006	"Balance urban and rural economic and social development and steadfastly advance construction of new socialist countryside"	New socialist countryside
2007	"Effectively increase the agriculture investment, actively promote the construction of modern agriculture, strengthen rural public services, and deepen comprehensive rural reform"	Invest in and modernize agriculture and provide rural public services
2008	Increase the income of peasants	Increase rural income; permission of long-term land lease and payment for transfer of land use rights
2009	Heed the decline in grain production, pay attention to income of peasants, and ensure social stability in the countryside.	Stabilize grain production and growth in peasants' income
2010	"Strengthen the efforts of coordinative urban-rural development and further consolidate the basis of agricultural and rural development"	Ensure rural development catch up with urban development
2011	"Accelerate irrigation works reform and development"	Irrigation works
2012	"Accelerate agricultural technological innovation and continued to improve the capabilities to supply and support agricultural products"	Agricultural technological innovation
2013	"Accelerate the development of modern agriculture and further enhancing the vitality in rural development"	Modernize agriculture

Notes: Information on the No. 1 Policy Document of the Central Committee of the CCP came
from the Chinese Central Television Project Group for a Memorandum of the National Conditions, *Guoqing beiwanglu* (*A Memorandum of the National Conditions*) (Shenyang: Wangjuan
chuban she, 2010), 90–1. Information on the document during 2010–13 comes from various
online news reports in Chinese. Phrases in speech marks are original official formulations translated
into English.

and in the latter provinces it was cut by four percentage points. By 2005 28
provinces had already terminated agricultural taxes. During 2000–6 the national
government allocated 260 billion yuan to support the reforms (Table 4.4). In 2006
the national government formally abolished the agricultural taxes that had been
collected in China for 2,600 years. This marked the fulfillment of one of the main
objectives of rural reform, that is, the reduction of fiscal burdens on peasants.
Compared with 1999, fiscal collections from peasants around 2006 were reduced
by 125 billion yuan, or 140 yuan per rural resident.[47]

Reducing financial losses in crops production

The next task the government undertook was to help peasants to avoid financial losses in their production of main crops such as grain, cotton, and edible oil. The state adopted multiple measures. First, the government has introduced substantial subsidies for production of primary agricultural products since 2004. Three subsidies were created to cover (1) grain production, (2) grain-producing peasants' purchase of machinery and certified seeds. In 2004 the governmental spending on these two subsidies amounted to 11.6 billion yuan and 14 billion yuan, respectively. Second, in subsequent years the government also provided peasants comprehensive subsidies for prices in agricultural capital goods.[48] During 2004–8 the governmental subsidies on grain production, subsidies for purchases of machinery and certified seeds, and comprehensive subsidies for adjustment in prices of agricultural capital goods (termed the four subsidies in China) amounted to 102.8 billion yuan.[49] In 2009 the four subsidies totaled 127.45 billion yuan, registering a 23.7 percent growth from the previous year. In addition, the state increased the minimum purchase prices for wheat and rice. All the measures helped the peasants to reduce losses and make profits in their production of these basic products and incentivized them to produce these products.[50]

Third, the government stepped up its investment and fiscal input into rural infrastructure, production facilities, and informational support in order to facilitate agricultural production and minimize losses of peasants. In 2004 the state's budgetary expenditure on agricultural support amounted to 200 billion yuan. The funding supported the development of new seeds and fine breeds, technological innovation and application, protection of animals and plants, product quality and safety, ecological protection, as well as development of information systems, product markets, and agricultural resources.[51]

Protecting migrant workers

In recent decades an increasing number of rural residents have sought employment outside their villages and towns and their earning has been a major source of their family income. In 2003 113.9 million peasants worked outside their home town, and their wages constituted 35 percent of the net income of an average rural resident in the country. By 2008 the population of migrant workers grew to 230 million. It was estimated by some analysts that each employed migrant worker on average generated a net value of 19,000 yuan a year after deducting their own labor costs. A report by the Chinese Academy of Social Sciences suggested that in the first three decades of economic reform migrant workers contributed to 21 percent of China's GDP and that in the late 2000s migrant workers constituted 52.6 percent of the labor force of commerce and restaurants and food catering, 68.2 percent of that in manufacturing, and 79.8 percent of that in construction.[52]

Table 4.4 Governmental funding for rural production and public services (billion yuan, current price)

Year	Reduction of Rural Fees and Taxes	Subsidies for Production of Main Crops	Funding for Agricultural Infrastructure and Technology	Rural Education	Rural Health Care	Government Budgetary Funds for the Countryside (% of governmental expenditure)
2002						190.5 (13.5%)
2003	30.5					214.4 (13.7%)
2004		11.6 (plus 14 for purchase of machinery and certified seeds)	200	59.3		262.7 (14.3%)
2005		17.2			3.52	297.5 (14.7%)
2006	103 (260 for 2000–6)	12	31.4 (plus 7.1 for farmland transformation and 6.9 for tax reduction for rural credit cooperatives)	184.0	9.52?	351.7 (15.0%)
2007		42.7 (plus 15.2 for pig rearing)	39 (plus 380 in power grid building during 1998–2007 and 10 for construction of methane pits during 2006–10)	223.5	20?	431.8 (14.6%)
2008		103.03				595.6 (16.4%)
2009		127.45 (plus 13 for purchase of machinery)	269 (including 204.4 for road building)			725.3 (16.5%)
2010		115.3	49.5			818.3 (10.7%)
2011		140.6 (plus 20.5 for rewarding, subsidizing and insuring grain and husbandry production)	252.8 (including 181.1 for irrigation, 27.16 for farmland transformation, 40.3 for road, and 4 for environment)			1040.9 (9.1%)
2012		164.3		533.9 (including health expenditure)		1238.8

Sources: RDRI and RSEST, Zhongguo nongcun jingji xingshi fenxi yu yuce (Analyses and Predictions on Rural Economic Conditions in China), (Beijing: Shehui kexue chubanshe, 2002–2012); "Zhongguo nongcun feishui gaige he nongcun zonghe gaige de huigu yu sikao" (A Review and Deliberation over Reforms of Rural Fees and Taxes and Rural Comprehensive Reform in China), posted at: http://znzg.xynu.edu.cn/Html/?14751.html, accessed on February 27, 2015; collected news reports on government's fiscal spending in the countryside posted at: http://blog.sina.com.cn/s/blog_6b9c2615010iim97.html, accessed on March 1, 2015; Li Xiaoxi and Hu Biliang, Zhongguo jingji xin zhuanxin (New Transformation of China's Economy) (Beijing: Zhongguo dabake quanshu chubanshe, 2011), 49–50.

Nevertheless, in 2002 unpaid wages of migrant workers amounted to 40 billion yuan as employers abused the rights of migrant workers in order to save costs, maintain or improve their capital flow, or to cope with financial difficulties. In 2003 Premier Wen, in talking to a rural woman on his unplanned stop at a village in Chongqing, learned that the wage of 2,240 yuan of her husband in his construction job at the nearby county had not been paid for over a year and that the amount was equivalent to 40 percent of annual income from a construction job of a migrant worker in the area. Premier Wen helped the peasant to retrieve his wage on the same night. During 2003–5 he led a nationwide campaign to help migrant workers to retrieve their overdue wages.[53]

In recent years, the state has allowed rural residents to work in the cities through relaxing the residential household registration (户口 *hukou*) system. The center also asks localities to make provisions for the health care and work safety of migrant workers, for schooling the children of migrant workers, and for employment training of migrant workers. The state also introduced measures to protect peasant workers in the cities. In 2003, the central government (the center) reformed shelter and repatriation stations (收容遣送制度 *shourong qiansong zhidu*) where station clerks used to detain, physically abuse and financially exploit migrants from the countryside who were looking for jobs and finding residence in the cities.

Waiving tuition fees in the countryside

Moreover, in light of the fact that peasants had to pay out of their pockets to cover a hefty bill for the schooling of their children, the Hu–Wen leadership had endeavored to extend basic and free provision of compulsory education for peasants. In 2003 the national government made a formal declaration to develop rural education. From 2004 onwards the national government had started to increase funding for rural compulsory education by allocating 59.3 billion yuan to this end in its budget. In December 2005 the General Office of the State Council promulgated "A Circular Concerning the Deepening of the Reform of the Mechanisms that Safeguard the Funding of Rural Compulsory Education." The proposed reform focused on the central and western provinces and covered a number of counties in poverty in the coastal provinces. According to the arrangements the national government would provide 80 percent of funding for waiving of tuition and other fees for schooling in the western provinces and 60 percent of the funding in central provinces. The provincial and local governments of western and central provinces would provide 20 percent and 40 percent, of the funding respectively. In September 2006 the national government convened a meeting to make arrangements for nationwide implementation of the rural comprehensive reforms that aimed to downsize the government, reform fiscal institutions, and provide for basic education free of charge in the countryside.[54]

By the end of 2007 52 percent of the townships in the country had made substantial progress in the rural comprehensive reform. Rural compulsory education was largely free of charge, benefiting 150 million students. As a result, on average a student in an elementary school was waived tuition of 140–180 yuan and a student in a junior high school 180 yuan to 230 yuan. In addition, 38 million students whose family were in economic difficulties received free textbooks and 7.8 million students whose families were in poverty received a living allowance.[55] In that year 223.5 billion yuan in the governmental budget was allocated for rural education. In 2011 the government conducted an experiment among 26 million students in rural schools in 680 counties and cities where a daily meal allowance of 3 yuan was introduced.[56]

Building rural health insurance and pensions schemes

New rural cooperative medical scheme

Prior to 2002 the national government promulgated several policy documents aiming to build a new rural cooperative medical scheme (NCMS).[57] However, due to the lack of complementary policy measures and especially the funding, little actual progress was made. In 2002 the national government issued "A Decision on Further Strengthening Rural Health." It mandated that the government at all levels should ensure that growth in funding for public health should be no less than that of the budgetary expenditure. It was also decided in 2002 that the NCMS aimed to provide a coordinated coverage of serious illnesses (*da bing tongchou*) and that for each rural resident the insured peasant would pay 10 yuan and the local government 10 yuan. In the following years experiments were conducted in selected localities. In 2004 80 million rural residents joined the NCMS. In 2005 the government injected 540 million yuan to fund the expansion of the experiments. By September 2005 the experiment with the rural cooperative health scheme had been conducted in 671 counties, covering 233 million rural residents, or 26.3 percent of the rural population in China. The scheme was jointly financed by contributions from peasants, local government and national government. By September 2005 funds of 6.4 billion yuan, including 3.52 billion yuan of subsidies from the budget of the government at all levels, was raised for the NCMS. The scheme covered a higher percentage of medical bills at the township clinics than at the hospitals at the counties or cities.[58] In 2006 the government increased its fiscal support for the scheme. In most places where the scheme was trialed a rural resident would pay 10 yuan, and local and national governments each paid him/her 20 yuan a year.[59]

By 2007 the rural cooperative health scheme covered 80 percent of rural residents. In 2008 815 million, or 91.5 percent of rural residents were covered by the scheme. By 2012 805 million residents were covered by the NCMS. The government increased the annual subsidies per rural resident in the scheme from 50 yuan in 2006 to 200 yuan in 2011, to 240 yuan in 2012, and further to 380 yuan in 2015. On average a rural resident needed to contribute 90 yuan a year to the scheme in 2015. The proportion of reimbursed hospitalization costs rose from 48 percent in 2008 to 75 percent in 2013. Around 2012 the maximum payment of medical bills under the scheme was 6 times the average annual income of a rural resident.[60]

Rural retirement pension schemes

In December 1986 the Ministry of Civil Affairs (MCA), as well as several other ministries of the State Council convened a meeting in Shazhou of Jiangsu Province. It was decided that townships, towns and villages in developed areas in the nation should develop community pension schemes. In 1990 the State Council designated the Ministry of Civil Affairs as the ministry responsible for rural pension schemes. In January 1992 the Ministry of Civil Affairs promulgated "A Basic Program for County-Level Rural Pensions." It was stipulated in this document that funding for rural pensions should be based primarily on contribution from individuals, complemented by subsidies from villages and that personal pension accounts should be established. In the 1990s coastal provinces, including Beijing, Jiangsu, and Zhejiang, had started to explore schemes of retirement pensions for migrant workers in the cities, as well as rural residents who worked in the rural enterprises, and those residents whose cultivated land had been used for non-agricultural purposes.[61] In 1993 30.4 million rural residents joined rural pension schemes and this number surged to 80.3 million in 1998. The State Council decided to overhaul the schemed after detecting various loopholes and problems. The number of participants in the schemes declined to 54.6 million in 2002.[62]

In the following years the national government was focusing on reduction of fiscal burdens on peasants, subsidizing rural production, and establishing new rural cooperative health schemes. It did not formulate any major policies on rural pensions. Progress in establishing local rural pensions schemes occurred mainly in provinces such as Guangdong and Shandong.

In 2008 the State Council decided to allow 10 percent of the counties to undergo an experiment with the new rural social pensions (NRSP) scheme in 2009. In 2009 it decided to expand the scheme nationwide by 2020. Under this scheme pensions are comprised of two parts: (1) a basic pension starting from a national base line of 55 yuan a month plus any additional amount set by provinces and (2) personal pension accounts. The funding of pensions comes from personal contributions ranging from 100 to 500 yuan a month for a minimum of 15 years and from village and governmental subsidies.[63] In 2011 the national government decided to conduct the experiment with the NRSP in 60 percent of the localities and implement the scheme throughout the nation in 2012.[64] In 2011 326 million peasants joined the NRSP.[65]

Aiding the poorest in the countryside

In the reform era the state has stepped up its support for those who fail to catch up with the increasingly competitive rural and urban economy. Starting from 1986 the State Council has made aiding the poor in the countryside a routine task. In that year it established an Aiding-the-Poor and Development Leading Small Group (APDLSG) (国务院扶贫开发领导小组 *Guowuyuan fupin kaifa lingdao xiaozu*) and an office for the group. In the 1990s the state implemented a vigorous developmental program to lift the rural poor from poverty. It built infrastructure, developed human capital, extracted local resources, protected the local ecology and environment, employed rural residents in developmental projects, enforced family planning, and forged cooperation with international organizations.

In 2007 the national government introduced the rural minimum living allowances (RMLA) scheme in the country, covering 20 million rural residents in poverty. The threshold income level for being qualified for the RMLA scheme ranged from 1,000 yuan to 2,000 yuan across localities.[66] In 2011 the state published "A Program for Poverty Alleviation and Development in the Countryside for 2011–20," making geographically connected areas in exceptional poverty the focus for poverty alleviation in the nation. It also set a target that by 2020 residents in these poor areas would be fed and clothed and would enjoy free compulsory education, basic medical care and housing. In 2011 the government also increased the line of rural poverty from 1,196 yuan in 2009 by 93 percent to 2,300 yuan in 2010 prices and qualified a much larger number of residents for governmental assistance.[67] As a result of this change, the percentage of the rural population below the official poverty line rose from 2.8 percent in 2010 to 12.7 percent in 2011, and the number of rural people in poverty soared from 26.9 million to 122.4 million (Table 4.5). A much larger number of rural residents, whose living standard was far below the average of the nation, qualified for support from the government.

The state's remedies of urban discontents

Instituting minimum living allowances and unemployment insurance

As stated earlier, in the course of drastic downsizing of SOEs unemployment soared in the cities. A significant percentage of the unemployed (50 percent in 1998 and 70 percent in 2001) could not be re-employed quickly. Many of them were plunged into poverty. The sudden spread of poverty among the laid-off workers of SOEs necessitated a social welfare program that could provide aid for these jobless workers, as well as those who lacked the abilities to cope with demand from an increasingly competitive job market, and old people who had neither pensions nor family support. It was under the tenure of Premier Zhu Rongji and President Jiang Zemin of 1998–2002 that the

Table 4.5 Population in poverty in China

Year	Rural Population in Poverty, Official Statistics (million)[a]	% of Rural Population, Official Statistics [a]	% of Rural Population, Scholarly Estimates	% of Urban Population, Official Estimates	% of Urban Population, Scholarly Estimates
1978	250	33.1			
1980			40.8 [b]		20.1 (1981) [b]
1985	125	14.8	14.0 [b]	0.4 [c]	12.7 [b]
1988	97	11	16.1 [b]	0.2 [c]	
1992	80.7	8.8	13.6 [b]		4.7 (1991) [b]
1993	75	8.2	14.1 [b]		
1994	70	7.6	13.6 [b]		5.9 [b]
1995	65	7.1		5.4 [c]	
1996	58	6.3			
1997	50	5.4			
1998	42	4.6		3.9 [c]	
1999	34.1	3.7		3.5 [c]	
2003	29[d]	3[d]		5.9 [c] (2002)	
2010	26.9[e]	2.8[e]		4 [f] (2009)	8 [f] (2009)
2011	122.4[e]	12.7[g]			

Notes: (1) The official line of rural poverty during the 1985–1987 period was per capita annual income of 200 yuan in 1984 price. This poverty line was adjusted upward to 206 yuan in 1986, 236 yuan in 1988, 500 yuan in 1990, 540 yuan in 1995, and 637 yuan in 2003. (2) The scholarly definition of rural poor population was provided by A. R. Khan, an expert for the ILO. Khan defined the rural poor as people who spent over 60 percent of income on food to obtain daily subsistence requirement of per capita 2,150 calories. In 1995 the scholarly poverty line in the countryside in monetary terms was 1,157 yuan, and that in the cities 2,291 yuan. (3) The national official urban poverty line was set at 215 yuan of monthly income in 1985, 289 yuan in 1988, 2,107 yuan in 1995, 2,310 yuan in 1998, 2,382 yuan in 1999, and 624–2,310 yuan (depending on the cities) around 2003. The urban poverty rate has gone up due to the relaxed definition. Information source is cited below. (4) In 2011 the government raised the rural poverty line to per capita income of 2,300 yuan in 2010 constant price, resulting in a massive surge in rural population in poverty.

Sources: [a] State Investigative Team on Rural Society and Economy, State Statistical Bureau, 2000. *Zhongguo Nongcun Pinkun Jiance Baogao* (*A Report on Surveillance on Rural Poverty in China: 2000*) (Beijing: State Statistical Press), 7. [b] Information on the official line of rural poverty comes from See Li Qiang, *Zhongguo Fupin zhi Lu* (*China's Road toward Aiding the Poor*) (Yunnan: Yunnan Remin Chubanshe, 1997), 120–1; Anti-poverty Project Group of China Reform and Development Research Institute in Hainan, *Zhongguo Fanpinkun Zhili Jiegou* (*The Structure in China's Anti-Poverty Governance*) (Beijing: Zhongguo Jingji Chubanshe, 1998), 39; Liu Chunbin, "Install Aid-the-Poor Tax on Upscale Entertainment Places to Solve the Problem of Too-low Poverty Standard," *Xiang Gang Chuanzhen* (*Hong Kong Fax*), No. 2004–21, 2004. Data on scholarly rural and urban poverty come from A.R. Khan, "Analyses of China's Poverty in Reform and Development," in Zhao Renwei, Li Shi and Carl Riskin, eds, 1999. *Zhongguo Jumin Shouru Fenpei Zaiyanjiu*, 350. [c] See Hong Dayong, 2003. "Urban Poverty Population in China since the Reform," *China Net*, January 20, 2003, cf. in Yan Hao, "Urban Poverty in China," paper presented at the Workshop on Urban Poverty in East Asia, Beijing, April 2004, p. 25. [d] Liu Chunbin, "Levy Aid-the-Poor Tax on Upscale Entertainment Sites to Rectify the Excessively Low Standard for Defining Population in Poverty," *Xianggang Chuanzhen* (*Hong Kong Fax*), No. 2004–21, June 11, 2004, 2. [e] *Guojia tongji jiu zhuhu diaocha bangongshi* (*Office for Household Survey, National Statistical Bureau*), ed. *Zhongguo zhuhu diaocha nianjian* (*Yearbook of the China Household Survey*) (Beijing: Tongguo tongji chubanshe, 2012), 85. [f] "Woguo chengshi pinkun renkou 5000 wan" (Urban Population in Poverty 50 Million), posted at: www.fawan.com/Article/gn/jd/2011/08/03/122946124972.html on August 3, 2011, accessed May 20, 2015. [g] World Bank data, posted at http://data.worldbank.org/, accessed February 16, 2015.

urban unemployment soared. Not surprisingly it was under their leadership that the social welfare program for the urban poor was installed.

In June 1993 Shanghai paved the way in the nation for institutionalizing a program of minimum urban living allowances (MULA) (*chengshi jumin zuidi shenghuo baozhang*). In the next year the MCL affirmed Shanghai's MULA program and made arrangements to conduct experiments with the program in coastal areas. By June 1995 the program was installed in Shanghai, Xiamen, Qingdao, Dalian, Fuzhou, and Guangzhou and by the end of the year it was set up in 12 cities. By March 1997 165 cities had established the MULA program, including three out of the four nationally-administered municipalities (NAMs), 49 percent of the prefecture-level cities and 13 percent of the county-level cities. In August 1997 the State Council promulgated "A Circular Regarding Establishing a Minimum Living Allowance Scheme for Urban Residents in All Areas." The next month the State Council required all localities to set up the MULA program. By the end of 1998 the MULA program was introduced in 581 cities, including all the NAMs, 90 percent of the prefecture-level cities, 85 percent of the county-level cities, and 90 percent of the counties in the country. By 1999 the program was instituted in 668 cities, providing aid to 2.82 million people.[68]

Around October 1999 the monthly MULA had been raised by 30 percent in the cities, and 80 percent of the funding for this increase came from the national government, with the exception of the seven most developed coastal provinces. From October 1999 onwards, the following urban residents could claim full or partial support from the MULA: 1) those with formal residency (or *hukou*) and the average per capita income of their family fell below the urban minimum living allowances threshold; 2) those who lacked earning, working abilities, a legal guardian, and supporters (i.e., people with "four withouts").[69]

In 1999 21 percent of the MULA recipients were people without working abilities or old people without family support for their retirement, and 79 percent of them the new urban poor.[70] As of October 2002, 13 percent of 19.6 million MULA recipients were laid-off workers, 15 percent the registered unemployed people, 10 percent current employees, 5 percent retirees, 29 percent dependents of these poor individuals, and 5 percent individuals with "four withouts." The majority of the recipients were in the northeastern, central, and western provinces such as Liaoning, Jilin, Heilongjiang, Jiangxi, Henan, Hubei, Hunan, and Sichuan.[71]

Prior to June 2001 the MULA had been hamstrung by limited governmental funds. Despite governmental funding for MULA growing from 300 million yuan in 1996 to 1.2 billion yuan in 1998 and to 3 billion yuan in 2000, its share in the governmental budgetary expenditure was 0.38 percent, 1.11 percent, and 1.89 percent, respectively. Thus despite rapid increase during these years the funding for the MULA program only accounted for a small portion of the governmental budget. In the second half of 2001 the State Council decided to rapidly increase the funding for the MULA. The national government increased its funding by 1.5 billion yuan, and the provincial governments by 300 million yuan. Together with funding from cities and counties eventually the funding for the MULA program grew to 5.3 billion yuan in 2001, up by 76.7 percent from 2000 and accounting for 2.8 percent of the budgetary expenditure, compared to 1.89 percent in 2000. In 2002 the MULA funding rose further to 10.4 billion yuan. Out of this total 44.2 percent came from the national government and 55.8 percent from local governments. This amount nearly doubled the funding for the MULA in the previous year (5.3 billion yuan) and pushed the share of MULA funding in the budgetary expenditure to an all-time high of 4.72 percent. In 2003 when the Hu-Wen leadership assumed power the total MULA funding grew by 50 percent to 15.6 billion yuan and its share in budgetary expenditure rose further to 6.43 percent.

As a result of improved funding the number of urban residents covered by the MULA grew from 0.85 million in 1996, to 1.84 million in 1998, to 3.82 million in 2000. The largest increase in the recipients of the MULA occurred in 2001, as it reached 11.32 million, nearly three times as much as the previous year. The number grew by 70 percent to 19.32 million in 2002 and rose by 16.3 percent to 22.5 million in 2003.[72] By 2008 the starting year of the second term of the Hu–Wen administration the MULA recipients grew to 23.35 million. Obviously after 2002 the growth in the recipients of the MULA had moderated significantly, likely due to the fact that the MULA had managed to cover a much large number of the urban poor. In 2008 the funding for the MULA grew to 39.3 billion yuan, 60 percent higher than that in 2002, the year right before the Hu–Wen leadership came to power.[73]

In order to provide economic assistance to unemployed workers in the cities, in addition to building the MULA the government also promoted the unemployment insurances. In the 1990s laid-off workers of SOEs in China still maintained their affiliation and linkage with the enterprises, as they were hoping to resume their jobs in the future and importantly, maintained their entitlement to health care and pensions. They were reluctant to formally register as the unemployed (thereby being counted as the "officially registered unemployed") and lose these entitlements. In 1999 the State Council issued "Articles on Unemployment Insurance," replacing laid-off insurance with unemployment insurance, and expanding the insurance coverage from employees of SOEs to employees of all enterprises and public institutions. According to the Articles employees and employers jointly contributed to the insurance and the benefits of the insurance were linked with the minimum wage and the minimum living expenses.[74]

In 2000 the number of recipients of benefits for the layoff peaked at 6.57 million. From 2000 onwards, laid-off workers were gradually subject to the new regulations regarding the unemployed, instead of those regarding the laid-off workers. The former would thus be registered as the unemployed. By the end of 2003 the remaining laid-off workers shrunk to 2.7 million.[75] In 2013 the registered urban unemployed people totaled 9.26 million and the official urban employment rate was 4 percent.[76]

Despite a slight decline during 2001–2, the participants in the unemployment insurance had been growing steadily since 1999. They grew from 98.5 million in 1999, to 104.1 million in 2000, and dropped slightly to 101.8 million in 2002. The number then grew to 103.7 million in 2003, reached 124 million in 2008 and registered 164 million in 2013. The recipients of unemployment insurance totaled 3.12 million in 2001, climbed to 4.4 million the next year and declined to 4.15 million in 2003, and rebounded to 4.19 million in 2004. In the following years the number declined noticeably to 2.61 million in 2008, and further to 1.97 million in 2013. Meanwhile, the surplus of the unemployment insurance accounts grew from 16 billion yuan in 1999 to 25.4 billion yuan in 2002, to 30.4 billion yuan in 2003 and to 131 billion yuan in 2008 and 368.6 billion yuan in 2013.[77]

Expanding urban medical and pensions insurance schemes

As the analysis of the state's responses to urban grievances in this chapter focuses on the urban unemployed and, to a lesser extent, the urban poor, the discussion on urban medical and pension schemes will thus be very brief.

Urban medical insurance schemes

During 1988–97 the national government oversaw experiments with urban medical care that was coined the urban employee medical insurance scheme (UEMI). The aim of the UEMI was to contain the runaway medical expenses as medical care was provided free of charge to urban employees. In 1988 eight ministries of the State Council led by the Ministry of Health and the National Economic Structure Reform Commission (NESRC) drafted a plan for reforming urban employee medical coverage. The next year experiments were conducted in Dandong, Siping, Huangshi, and Zhuzhou. In 1994 four ministries led by the NESRC proposed to combine socially pooled funds with personal accounts and selected Jiujiang and Zhenjiang to undergo an experiment from late 1994. From the end of 1996 the State Council expanded the experiment to 57 prefecture-level cities.[78]

In December 1998 the State Council issued "A Decision regarding the Establishment of the Urban Employees Basic Medical Insurance Scheme (UEBMIS)." In this document the State Council outlined a course of action to move from experiments in selected cities to national implementation of the UEBMIS scheme that would provide wide and rudimentary medical care coverage of urban employees. In that document the State Council also required contribution from both employees and employers, at 2 percent and 6 percent of wages, respectively, and suggested that socially pooled funds would be combined with personal accounts. The maximum of the reimbursed medical bills was capped at four times the annual wages. By 2000 the scheme was set up in the nation, covering employees of SOEs, governmental agencies and public institutions. Employees of non-state enterprises were required to join the UEBMIS. During 1999–2002 the schemes were being expanded throughout the nation and the number of employees covered by the UEBMIS grew from 14.3 million in 1999, and 94 million in 2002. In 2002 the surplus of funds of the UEBMIS totaled 45.1 billion yuan. Surveys in 20–30 cities by the Ministry of Labor and Social Security (MLSS) found that in 2002 the UEBMIS with the maximum reimbursement cap instituted was set up in 76.7 percent of the cities and that the UEBMIS covering civil servants was installed in 43.3 percent of the cities, and that only 22 percent of the enterprises in financial difficulties joined the UEBMIS. In 2003 the State Council extended the coverage of the scheme to self-employed individuals, employees of enterprises of mixed ownership, and migrant workers in the cities. In 2006 the MLSS called for the comprehensive inclusion of migrant workers in the UEBMIS. In the decade of 2003–12 under the Hu–Wen leadership the urban employees covered by the UEBMIS grew to 274.4 million in 2013, nearly three times as much as that in 2002. In 2013 50.2 million migrant workers also joined the scheme and the UEBMIS fund ran a surplus of 580.4 billion yuan.[79]

During 2005–2007 the government extended medical care coverage to urban residents who were jobless and had no financial and family support. In 2005 experiments with urban medical aid were implemented in selected cities whereby medical assistance was offered to urban residents with financial difficulties. In 2007 the State Council called on the establishment of the urban residents basic medical insurance scheme (URBMIS) in order to cover the urban jobless people. The funding was based primarily on contributions from the insured family and secondarily governmental subsidies. In the same year the people covered by the URBMIS totaled 42.9 million and the surplus of the fund was 3.3 billion yuan. In the following years the scheme was expanded to cover an increasingly larger number of urban residents. The urban residents covered by the scheme grew to 116.5 million in 2008 and to 296.3 million in 2013. The URBMIS fund had a surplus of 98.7 billion yuan in 2013.[80]

Urban pensions insurance schemes

Provinces and localities made various efforts to build pensions schemes for urban employees after the government's decision to press ahead with reforms of SOEs nationwide in December 1984. In June 1991 the State Council decided to build socially pooled funds for pension insurance mostly at the city and county level. In May 1995 it adopted a modified scheme of combining socially pooled funds with personal accounts. In July 1997 the State Council implemented a further revised scheme nationwide. In its document entitled "A Decision to Establish a Unified Enterprise Employees Basic Pensions Scheme" it specified the funding sources and payment for pensions. Funding sources included a deposit of an amount of 11 percent of the wage of an employee into a personal pension account, which consisted of personal contributions from the employees starting from 4 percent of their wages and eventually increasing to 8 percent and a contribution from the employers. The total contribution of employers was capped at 20 percent of wages of employees. The payment of pensions included (1) a basic pension of 20 percent of the averaged annual wage of the localities and (2) monthly payment equivalent to 1/120 of savings from the personal account.[81] This scheme was initially applied in SOEs and collective enterprises. A similar scheme was then adopted in governmental agencies and public institutions. Between 1999 and 2005 the government required this scheme to be adopted in foreign and private enterprises, individual household businesses and self-employed individuals.[82] In 2013 322.2 million urban employees or retired employees as well as 49 million migrant workers were covered by the basic pensions scheme, and the basic pensions scheme ran a surplus of 2.83 trillion yuan. The average monthly payment for a retired employee in the cities had grown noticeably over the years, from 544 yuan in 2000 to 623 yuan in 2002, 1,144 yuan in 2003, and 1,914 yuan in 2013.[83]

Addressing regional developmental gaps via aiding backward regions

The regional gap described above can only be reduced through proper macroeconomic policy and long-term plans. In light of this, since the late 1990s China has shifted its regional developmental focus away from the coast toward the inland regions. These inland regions include the vast western region, the northeast that is viewed as the rust-belt, and the central region that is regarded as the national granary. During 1999–2003 the national government had unveiled three regional developmental programs to accelerate the economic growth in each of these three inland regions, respectively.

Western developmental program

The western region was redefined in 2000. The re-configured western region comprised of 12 provinces such as Tibet, Xinjiang, Inner Mongolia, Sichuan and Shaanxi. Covering 71 percent of China's land areas and 29 percent of the population in 1995 and 2003, the western region was the most backward in China. Nevertheless, accounting for 86 percent of the population of ethnic minorities in China, the region is the home to China's ethnic minorities. As the movement for ethnic autonomy and even separatism turned vocal and even violent in the 1990s in Xinjiang and to a lesser extent Tibet, the importance of this region for China's unity and territorial integrity was heightened.[84] The state implemented western development in 2000. The government identified mega infrastructure, energy, environmental, and resources extraction projects in the 12 western provinces in order to generate sustainable development in the region. By the end of 2009 the government had invested over 1 trillion yuan in 70 mega projects. The government poured into the region 550 billion yuan of fiscal funds for construction, 750 billion yuan through fiscal transfers and 310 billion yuan in long-term construction treasury bonds.[85] In 1999 the averaged GDP growth rate in the western provinces was 1.8 percentage points behind that of the coastal provinces. By 2002, the former was 0.8 percentage points behind; by 2008 the former was 1.1 percentage points ahead of the latter, and by 2012 the former was 2.9 percentage points ahead.[86]

It thus appears that in the wake of the western developmental program the national government has succeeded in reversing the slower growth of the western region compared to the coast.

Revival of the Northeast (振兴东北)

The northeast in China refers to Liaoning, Jilin and Heilongjiang Provinces. This region hosted the first batch of the largest SOEs that were built with the help of Soviet aid in the 1950s. It was once one of the primary heavy industrial bases of the People's Republic of China. In the reform era, however, the economy that was dominated by SOEs in this region faltered, and the region's share in the nation's gross value of industrial output declined from 16.5 percent in 1978 to 9.3 percent in 2003. As stated earlier, this region had the highest urban unemployment rate due to the poor performance of numerous SOEs.

In late 2003 and early 2004 the national government unfolded a program to rejuvenate the rust belt. This program focuses on restructuring SOEs and helping cities that rely heavily on SOEs to undergo economic transformation. The national government offered exemption of consumption-related value added taxes to selected enterprises in the region that would save them up to 10 billion yuan per year. In November 2003, the central government approved 100 large projects totaling 61 billion yuan, most of which were in equipment manufacturing as well as processing raw materials and agricultural commodities that were among the most competitive industries in the region.[87] By February 2015 the government had invested 382 billion yuan in 139 major projects covering infrastructure, public services, and strategic industries in the region.[88] In 2003, right at the moment when the program was launched, the averaged GDP growth rate in the northeastern provinces was 1.9 percentage points behind that of the coastal provinces. Thanks to the program, by 2008 the former was 2.3 percentage points ahead of the latter. This edge declined slightly to 1.5 percentage points in 2009 and further to 1 percentage point in 2012.[89]

"Rise of the central region" (中部崛起 *zhongbu jueqi*)

After the introduction of the coastal developmental strategy in the 1980s, the western developmental program in 2000, and the northeast revival program in 2003, the central region was the only region in China that had not benefited from the national government's developmental programs. The central region includes Shanxi, Henan, Anhui, Jiangxi, Hubei, and Hunan. Central China is a major national base for production of grain and energy materials. In 2003–4, central China produced 30, 31, and 32 per cent of the nation's fertilizer, coal, and grain, respectively.[90]

To make up for the neglect of central China, Premier Wen Jiabao declared in March 2004 that Beijing would accelerate the development of this region in order to attain more balanced development in the nation.[91]

Since then, the rise of central China (*zhongbu jueqi*) has become a popular term in China's media. In contrast to its extensive investment and fiscal transfers in the western region and the northeast, the national government has not injected a huge amount of funds or investment into the central region. Rather, its support for the region mainly assumes the forms of policies and calls for the attention from the public and business to central China. The national policies that have been introduced to speed up growth in central China include tax reduction and exemption similar to that in the western region and the northeast, rural reform as described earlier, development of infrastructure and clusters of cities, as well as facilitation of reforms of SOEs and the grain production and trading.[92]

In 2003, right at the moment when the program was launched, the average GDP growth rate in the northeastern provinces was 1.7 percentage points behind that of the coastal provinces. Partly as a result of the program, the former was 0.9 percentage point ahead of the latter by 2008 and was even 1.5 percentage points in 2012.[93]

Ease of grievances over rural fiscal burdens and urban lay-off

As stated, between the late 1990s and the early 2000s inland peasants overburdened by high taxes and fees and low revenue income from production of main crops, as well as tens of millions of workers laid off by SOEs constituted the gravest nationwide challenge to the Party state since the 1989 Tiananmen protests. Grievances were widespread among peasants in central China, and discontents were acute among tens of millions of unemployed workers in cities throughout the nation and especially in the northeast and central China. Between 1994 and 2000 the number of CPSI grew three fold to 40,000 in China, registering an average 26% a year.[94] In addition, in 2000 rural residents accounted for half of the petitions and CPSI in the nation for the first time, suggesting the severity of rural restlessness.[95]

As far as rural residents in the inland areas (including those in the inland provinces and in inland areas of coastal provinces) are concerned, economic survival has been a daily struggle. Fiscal burdens imposed by the local government accounted for 12.7 percent of peasants' income in 1997, which was very taxing given their already low average income. In addition, all peasants would need to bear the full tuition costs of their children and faced low profits or even losses in grain production as late as 2003. Moreover, they enjoyed very scant social services. Less than 13 percent of peasants were covered by health insurance and only 9.2 percent of peasants covered by pensions in 1998 (Table 4.6). As late as 1994, nearly 14 percent of rural residents were still in poverty (Table 4.5). Despite the fact that peasants were spending increasingly less of their income on food in the reform era, peasants in central and western China were still struggling economically. During the decade of 1985–95 the share of food in consumption expenditure of rural residents even grew slightly by 1 percent (Table 4.2).

In the cities the unemployed had also suffered dearly since the mid-1990s. During 1998–2001 an estimated 27 million workers lost their jobs in the restructuring of firms, especially SOEs. In 2000 alone the number of jobless workers amounted to 21 million, pushing the actual unemployment rate in the cities in 2001 to double digits. While experts estimated that among the urban Chinese population at least 14 million and as many as 37 million were in poverty in 1998, only 2.8 million of them could receive the minimum living allowances provided by the government in 1999 (Table 4.6), and many of the remaining urban poor were struggling for subsistence. Not surprisingly there had been frequent petitions and protests by the laid-off workers in the cities since the mid-1990s.

Both the inland peasants and the urban laid-off workers confronted a crisis of economic survival, their discontent was high, turning inland provinces and the northeast into a political volcano that would readily explode. It seemed that the Party state was trapped in a boiling pot of societal anger and would not escape for a long period to come.

However, it is rather surprising that within a number of years the Party state had managed to implement a range of rural reforms and build a basic set of social security systems in the countryside and the cities, thereby easing many of the grievances from the inland peasants and urban employed. In the countryside, the government invested 103 billion yuan during 2000–6 and abolished the agricultural taxes by 2006, years ahead of its own schedule.

From 2004 onwards it devoted a large sum of money to subsidizing production of main crops and increased the amount over the years. The

Table 4.6 Plights of rural residents and urban unemployed and poor

Rural Residents				
Share of fees and taxes in disposable income, 1997 (%)	% covered by health insurance, 1998	% in poverty, 1994	% covered by pensions, 1998	% of peasants paying for children tuition in central and western region, 2003
12.4	12.7	13.6	9.2	100 (estimate)
Urban Unemployed and Poor				
Urban unemployment rate, 2001	Total unemployed, 2000	Laid-off SOE workers, 1998–2001	Urban residents in poverty, 1998	Recipients of minimum living allowance, 1999
10.9%	21 million	27 million	14–37.1 million	2.8 million

Sources: For data sources on taxes and feeds and on health insurance coverage of rural residents, refer to the relevant sources in text. The rural poverty rate came from Table 4.5. The remaining data come from Chen Jiagui *et al.*, *Zhongguo shehui baozhang fazhan baogao (1997–2001) (A Report on the Development of China's Social Security)* (Beijing: Shehui kexue chubanshe, 2001), 127, 222; *Zhongguo shehui baozhang fazhan baogao (2001–2004)*, 48, 157–8.

subsidies amounted to 12 billion yuan in 2004 and 164 billion yuan in 2012 (Table 4.4).

In addition, after 2004 the state invested a significant amount of funds to build infrastructure and develop technology including informational technology for agriculture. In 2004 the funding for this purpose was a massive 200 billion yuan. In 2009, when the government unfolded a massive stimulus package to reverse the decelerating economic growth, it earmarked 269 billion yuan for agriculture, including 204 billion yuan for road building. In 2011 the government allocated 253 billion yuan into these areas, including 181 billion yuan for irrigation works (Table 4.4). The aforementioned subsidies and massive investment and spending on agricultural infrastructure and technology would enable peasants to reduce production costs, improve productivity and increase income.

Moreover, the government has injected a huge amount of funding in providing for compulsory education in the countryside since 2004. The amount was 59 billion yuan in 2004, grew to 184 billion yuan in 2006 and further to 223.5 in 2007 (Table 4.4). By 2007, rural compulsory education was free of charge, benefiting 150 million students.

The government had also managed to build a rudimentary health and pension insurance scheme in rural China. The health insurance scheme covered 94 percent of rural residents in 2009 (Table 4.7), compared to a meager 13 percent in 1998. This progress has significantly eased peasants' concerns with poverty or bankruptcy should they fall severely ill for months. In addition, the government has made steady progress in building and expanding coverage of pensions among rural residents from 9.2 percent in 1998 to 50 percent in 2011 (Table 4.7).

In the cities, the efforts to help out the unemployed and the poor started in the mid-1990s, much earlier than the rural reform. First of all, the government had quickly introduced minimum living allowances throughout the nation. The recipients of the MULA were merely 2.8 million in 1999, yet skyrocketed to 20.7 million in 2002, and grew modestly to 22.8 million in 2011. Given the estimated urban population in poverty in the range of 14 to 37 million in 1998, 21 million recipients in 2002 suggested that the majority of the poorest in the cities could receive governmental aid. Moreover, the government has been sustaining 43 percent unemployment insurance coverage of urban employees despite the number of urban employees doubling from 82 million in 1995 to 164 million in 2012 (Table 4.7).

Furthermore, the government has vastly expanded the coverage of health insurance and pensions among urban residents. In 2013, 78 percent (or 571 million) of urban residents were covered by basic urban medical scheme, compared to merely 4 percent and 17 million in 1998. In the same year 52 percent of urban employees (or 200 million workers) were covered by work injury insurance, compared to 17 percent and 38 million being covered back in 1998. In 2013, 84 percent of (or 322 million) urban employees were covered by urban employees pension scheme, nearly doubling the 44 percent coverage rate and 110 million insured employees in 2002 (Table 4.7).

As a result of these major remedies, the boiling anger from inland peasants and the urban laid-off workers due to their personal crises over economic survival has been much eased. Between the late 1990s and the early 2000s petitions and protests by laid-off workers in Beijing and in major cities in the provinces, especially in the northeast, were frequent. Nowadays they are far less noticeable. The unemployed could resort to insurance or local government offices for the MULA, instead of taking to the street or protesting at Tiananmen Square.

Similar observations can be made about rural grievances. Inland peasants have seen their income improved noticeably. During 2000–2012 per capita income of rural residents grew by 143 percent. Even though it was moderately less than the 199 percent growth in per capita income of urban residents in the same period, it was far higher than 80 percent improvement in rural income during 1985–2000 (Table 4.2).

In terms of income inequalities, the government has apparently managed to reverse the aggravating trends of the urban-rural gap and coastal-inland gap since the mid-2000s (Figure 4.3). Per capita rural resident consumption relative to the urban level declined from a peak of 43.3 percent in 1985 consistently to 33.9 percent in 1990 and to the all time low 26.6 percent in 1995. With the help of rural reforms and the introduction of rural public services it improved to the range of 27.5–28.6 percent during the decade of 2001–10, except for 2006 when it dropped to 26.0 percent. During 2011–12 the ratio even improved to 30.7–30.8 percent. Per capita interior urban household consumption relative to the coastal level declined steadily from 66.6 percent in 1985 to 50.8 percent in 1998 and to 46.5 percent in 2001. It further declined to 45.9 percent in 2006. In the following years, however, the ratio has consistently improved, going up to 51.4 percent in 2011 and 53.4 percent in 2012. According to the World Bank China's Gini coefficient registered the first drop in 2011 since 1984, as it declined from 0.421 to 0.370 (Figure 4.1).

According to Nobel Laureate Simon Kuznets, inequality would be mild at a low level of development, would reach its peak at an intermediate level of development, and would decrease at an advanced level of development. This is what is called the inverted U-shaped curve. The data from China's government and the World Bank thus imply that along the three dimensions of income inequalities (namely, urban-rural, coastal-interior, and intra-strata), inequalities in China seem to be passing the peak and have started to decline.

There are apparent limits in the provision of social services and the containment of inequalities in China. Nevertheless, China continues to face daunting challenges. First of all, China needs to follow through industrialization and move most of its peasants into non-farming jobs. Given that 47 percent of the population resides in the countryside, China has a long way to go in raising the income of its peasants and cutting the rural-urban income gap that stands at about 69 percent (per capita rural resident income was 31 percent of the urban

Table 4.7 Results of the state's remedies of hardship of rural and urban residents

Rural Residents	Fees and taxes as % of peasants' disposable income	% of peasants covered by health insurance	% of rural residents in poverty by national standard	% of peasants covered by pensions	% of peasants to pay for tuition for their children in central and western region,
Status after remedies (year in parenthesis)	0.1–0.3 (2005–11)	91.5 (2008) 94 (2009)	1.6 (2007)	50 (2011)	0 (2007)
Status prior to remedies (year in parenthesis)	12.4 (1997)	12.7 (1998)	13.6 (1994) 4.6 (1998)	9.2 (1998)	likely 100 (2002)
Urban Social Security	% of urban employees covered by unemployment insurance, (million and/or year in parentheses)	% of urban residents covered by basic urban medical scheme (million and/or year in parentheses)	Recipients of minimum living allowance (million and/or year in parentheses)	% of employees covered by urban employees pension scheme (million and/or year in parentheses)	Urban employees covered by work injury insurance (million and/or year in parentheses)
Status after remedies	43% (164.2 in 2012)	78% (570.7 in 2013)	22.8 (in 2011)	84% (322.2 in 2013)	52% (199.7 in 2013)
Status prior to remedies	43% (82.3 in 1995)	4% (17 in 1998)	2.8 (1999); 20.7 (2002)	44% (110 in 2002)	17% (37.8 in 1998)

Sources: For data sources on taxes and fees and on health insurance coverage of rural residents, refer to the relevant sources in text. The rural poverty rate came from Table 4.5. The remaining data come from Chen Jiagui et al., *Zhongguo shehui baozhang fazhan baogao (1997–2001)*, 127, 222; *Zhongguo shehui baozhang fazhan baogao (2001–2004)*, 48, 157–8; "2013 niandu renli ziyuan he shehui baozhang shiye fazhan tongji gongbao" (A Statistical Bulletin on Labor and Social Security in 2013), posted at: www.chinanews.com/gn/2014/05-28/6223421.shtml, accessed on March 3, 2015; "2011 nian guojia xinxing nongcun shehui yanglao baoxian shidian diqu canbao renshu 3.3 yi" (In 2011 330 Million Joined the National New Rural Social Pensions Scheme), posted at: www.askci.com/news/20120816/105129_46.shtml, accessed on March 2, 2015.

level in 2012). Second, China's current social security is very thin. For example, experts estimated that in 2009 about 50 million urban Chinese lived in poverty, accounting for 8 percent of the urban population. This population was twice as large as that which received the MULA in China in that year (Table 4.5).

Nevertheless, for the CCP, the most important objective for its rural reform and provision of social security for rural and urban residents since the late 1990s was to avert the apparent explosion of nationwide protests. Apparently it has met this objective by defusing this massive societal time bomb. The results of a survey that was conducted by Singapore-based Chinese newspaper *Lianhe Zaobao (United Morning Post)* in China in 2012 were revealing. In this survey nearly 90 percent of the rural respondents were far happier in the recent decade and said that they enjoyed many favorable policies. Rural respondents in the survey had a very high regard for President Hu and Premier Wen.[96] Undeniably the CCP had achieved a surprising political feat of avoiding a nationwide upheaval by rural and urban residents who were facing subsistence crises. This feat illustrates that the Party state has the authoritarian flexibility and resilience to tackle pressing social-economic challenges despite widely-discussed flaws in its structure.

In this chapter we have seen the ample ability of the state in managing a sizable segment of the society that was disgruntled and rebellious due to their subsistence crisis. In the next chapter we will turn our attention to how the state responds to the segment of the society and populous social groups that are not directly linked with economic issues. In the wake of economic liberalization and of the lifting of pervasive, excessive, and draconian surveillance and control of the society practiced in the late Mao era, these social groups and activities revive, resurge and even pose stern challenges to the political control of the Party state.

Notes

1 National Statistical Bureau of China, *Zhongguo tongji zaiyao* (*China Statistical Abstracts*) (Beijing: Zhongguo Tongji Chubanshe, 2013). RMB to the US dollar exchange rates are obtained from "Renminbi (Chinese Yuan) Exchange Rates 1969–2011," posted at: www.chinability.com/Rmb.htm, accessed on February 16, 2015.
2 The data or the data that were used in computation in arriving at the report data came from http://databank.worldbank.org/data/views/reports/tableview.aspx, accessed on February 16, 2015.
3 "Wiping Out Poverty Galvanizes China," *China Daily*, October 18, 2004.
4 *China Statistical Yearbook* 2003, 72; China's Government Report at the 10th NPC, Table 4.1.
5 "Assessing Status of Nation's Health," *China Daily*, October 12, 2004.
6 "Who Belongs to the High-income Group in China? A Large Nationwide Survey of Wages and Remuneration in 2002," posted at: www.manager.cn, accessed on August 21, 2004.
7 "China Reports First Rise in Poverty Since Start of Reforms," *Straits Times*, July 19, 2004. The World Bank devises two lines of international poverty, i.e., US$1 a day and US$2 a day. While the World Bank might use US.$1 a day as the criterion

here, it would take into account the low consumer prices in China. Later it raised this threshold to US$1.25 a day.

8 Several estimates of income inequality in China are available. They may have three problems. First, one or two Gini coefficients may not be a meaningful measure of income distribution of so vast a country as China. Second, as stated, income in the early years of reform included mainly wages. In the 1990s, however, income also encompassed income from property as well as in-kind income such as housing and medical subsidies. Third, the measure of income varied among scholars, sometimes even in the same years. Some scholars and governmental agencies include only wages, bonuses, and in the case of farmers, income from sales of products; more prudent scholars also include in-kind income as well as income from property. Estimates thus may vary and may not be comparable.

9 The Gini coefficient data cited here is the Gini index from the World Bank divided by 100. "Gini index measures the extent to which the distribution of income or consumption expenditure among individuals or households within an economy deviates from a perfectly equal distribution." "Thus a Gini index of 0 represents perfect equality, while an index of 100 implies perfect inequality." See the notes on the definition of the Gini index at the World Bank website http://data.worldbank. org/indicator/SI.POV.GINI?page=1, accessed February 16, 2015.

10 Data sources for Figure 4.2 are as follows: World Bank data during the 1981–95 period came from World Bank, *Sharing Rising Incomes* (Washington, DC: World Bank, 1997), 2, 10. Data for 1998 come from World Bank, *World Development Report: Attacking Poverty* (New York: Oxford University Press, 2001), 282. Estimates by Zhao Renwei and Li Shi came from Zhao Renwei, Li Shi and Carl Riskin, eds, *Zhongguo Jumin Shouru Fenpei Zaiyanjiu* (*Income Distribution of China's Residents Revisited*) (Beijing: Zhongguo Caizheng Jingji Chubanshe, 1999), 11. Estimates by the Ministry of Finance (MOF) were cited in "Conditions of Income Distribution of Residents in Our Country and Fiscal Adjustment," *Jingji Ribao* (*Economic Daily*), June 16, 2003, 6. Series by Chen Zongsheng, Liu Xiaodong and Lu Qing, Xiang Shujian, and Research and Development Council come from Zhao Manhua, Wang Shangyi, Hao Yunhong, and Wang Minghua, *Shouru Chaju yu Liangji Fenhua Wenti Yanjiu* (*A Study of Income Gaps and Polarization*) (Beijing: Zhongguo Jihua Chubanshe, 2002), 152; Yang Yiyong and Huang Yanfen, "New Situation in Income Distribution of China's Residents," in Ru Xin, Lu Xueyi, and Shan Tianlun, eds, *2003 Nian: Zhongguo Shehui Xingshi Fenxi yu Yuce* (*2003: Analyses and Predictions of China's Social Situation*) (Beijing: Shehui Kexue Wenxian Chubanshe, 2003), 226–34. Study by Gu Yan and Yang Yiyong, cited in "Resident Income: A Beautiful Upward Curve," *Zhongguo Xinxibao* (*China Information Newspaper*), January 24, 2005.

11 Unlike the functional categorization used widely in the West, the Chinese urban-rural categorization is administrative in nature.

12 For further discussion on regional inequality, refer to TIAN Xiaowen, "China's Regional Economic Disparities under Economic Reform," *EAI Background Brief No. 33* (Singapore: NUS), May 14, 1999.

13 For a comprehensive overview of income inequalities in China in the reform era, refer to John Knight, "Inequality in China: An Overview," *Policy Research Working Paper* 6482 (Washington, DC: The World Bank), June 2013.

14 For an analysis, refer to Thomas P. Bernstein and Xiaobo Lü, *Taxation without Representation in Contemporary Rural China* (Cambridge and New York: Cambridge University Press, 2003). Their analysis, however, was based on secondary Chinese and western-language literature.

15 Chen Jiagui, Wang Yanzhong, *et al. Zhongguo shehui baozhang fazhan baogao (2001–2004)* (*A Report on the Development of Social Security in China during 2001–4*) (Beijing: Shehui kexue wenxian chanbanshe, 2004), 9–10.

16 National Statistical Bureau of China, *National Statistical Yearbook 2006* (Beijing: China Statistical Press, 2006), 373.

17 Rural Development Research Institute of the Chinese Academy of Social Science (RDRI) and Rural Social and Economic Survey Team of National Statistical Bureau (RSEST), *2002–2003 nian: Zhongguo nongcun jingji xingshi fenxi yu yuce (Analyses and Predictions on Rural Economic Conditions in China during 2002–3)* (Beijing: Shehui kexue chubanshe, 2003), 20–1, 22.

18 Li Changping, *Wo Xiang Zongli Shuo Shihua (I Tell Premier the Truth)* (Beijing: Guangming ribao chubanshe, 2002), 69.

19 See Hongyi Lai, *Hu Wen quan toushi: Hu Wen shizheng neimu quan jiedu ji Zhongguo weilai zhanwang (Hu–Wen under Full Scrutiny: A Comprehensive Inside Story of Governance under Hu and Wen and Prospects for Future China)* (Hong Kong: Wenhua yishu chubanshe, 2005), 239.

20 Li Changping, *Wo Xiang Zongli Shuo Shihua (I Tell Premier the Truth)*, 67–70, 75.

21 Li, *Wo Xiang Zongli Shuo Shihua*, 71–2, 75.

22 Li, *Wo Xiang Zongli Shuo Shihua*, 71–2, 75.

23 Li, *Wo Xiang Zongli Shuo Shihua*, 318–26.

24 Li, *Wo Xiang Zongli Shuo Shihua*, 331.

25 See Cao Jinqing, *Huahe bian de Zhongguo (China along the Yellow River)*. Shanghai: Shanghai wenyi chubanshe, 2000; Chen Chundi and Chun Tao, *Zhongguo Nongmin Diaocha (An Investigation on Peasants in China)* (Beijing: Renmin wenxue chubanshe, 2004).

26 See Hongyi Lai, *Hu Wen quan toushi* (Hong Kong: Wenhua yishu chubanshe, 2005), 239. The story was circulated among cadres in Hubei Province.

27 Another study portrayed a similarly rising trend with somewhat lower figures of annual urban unemployment: 1995, 4.3 percent; 1996, 4.8 percent; 1997, 5.5 percent; 1998, 4.5 percent; 1999, 5.6 percent; 2000, 7.9 percent. See John Knight and Lina Song, *Towards a Labour Market in China* (Oxford and New York: Oxford University Press, 2005), 35.

28 Chen Jiagui, Wang Yanzhong, *et al.*, *Zhongguo shehui baozhang fazhan baogao (2001–2004)*, 165, 163, 157–8.

29 See Knight and Song, *Towards a Labour Market in China*, 130.

30 Jae Ho Chung, Hongyi Lai, and Ming Xia, "Mounting Challenges to Governance in China: Surveying Collective Protestors, Religious Sects, and Criminal Organizations," *China Journal*, Vol. 56, 2006, 6–7.

31 "Leaner Factories, Fewer Workers Bring More Labor Unrest to China," *New York Times*, March 19, 2002.

32 Interview with an official at the State Council in November 2004.

33 Interview with an analyst at the Research and Development Center of the State Council, September 2003.

34 "Millions of Laid-Off Workers Were the Biggest Headache for the Provincial Government,"*Ming Pao*, August 13, 2003.

35 For news report on protests of Falun Gong, refer to "Falun Gong chabo an, Changchun duoren beibu" (In the Case of TV Program Interruption by Falun Gong, a Number of Arrests are Made in Changchun), *Ming Pao*, April 3, 2002.

36 Xu Xinxin, "2002 nian Zhongguo chengxiang jumin shehui taidu, zhiye pingjia yu zeye quxiang diaocha" (A Survey of Chinese Urban and Rural Residents on Social Attitudes, Assessment of Occupations, and Tendency toward Job Selection), in Ru Xin *et al.*, eds, *2003 Nian: Zhongguo Shehui Xingshi Fenxi yu Yuce (Analyses and Predictions on Social Conditions in China in 2003)* (Beijing: Shehui kexue wenxian chubanshe, 2003), 122.

37 Qing Lianbin, "Zhongguo dangzheng lingdao ganbu dui 2002–2003 nian shehui xingshi de jiben kanfa" (Basic Assessment of Social Conditions by Leading Party and Administrative Cadres in China during 2002–2003), in Ru Xin *et al.*, eds, *2003*

Nian: Zhongguo Shehui Xingshi Fenxi yu Yuce (*Analyses and Predictions on Social Conditions in China in 2003*) (Beijing: Shehui kexue wenxian chubanshe, 2003), 128.

38 See David Shambaugh, ed., *Is China Unstable?* (Armonk, NY and London: M.E. Sharpe, 2000).

39 Gordon Chang, *The Coming Collapse of China* (New York: Random House, 2001), xvii.

40 For example, Steven Jackson regarded China as in the state of "disruption" along the stability spectrum that ranged from stagnation, stasis, dynamic equilibrium, disruption, rebellion, revolution, and collapse. However, he refused to rule out the possibility of collapse. See Jackson, "Introduction," in Shambaugh, ed., *Is China Unstable?*, 13.

41 Xie Peixiu, *Zhongguo nongcun gaige guiji yu qushi: Anhui nongye fazhan yu nongmin zengshou shizheng yanjiu* (*The Track and Trend of China's Rural Reform: An Empirical Analysis of Agricultural Development and Growth in Peasants' Income in Anhui*) (Beijing: Zhishi chanquan chubanshe, 2004), 239.

42 "Zhongguo nongcun feishui gaige he nongcun zonghe gaige de huigu yu sikao" (A Review and Deliberation over Reforms of Rural Fees and Taxes and Rural Comprehensive Reform in China), posted at: http://znzg.xynu.edu.cn/Html/?14751.html, accessed on February 27, 2015.

43 See Hongyi Lai, *Hu Wen quan toushi* (Hong Kong: Wenhua yishu chubanshe, 2005), 239.

44 Ren Huiwen, "Wen Jiabao Ponders over Relieving Populace Hardship and Stabilizing the Country," *Xinbao* (*Hong Kong Economic Journal*), September 10, 2004, 6. For an early discussion of an explosive mix of social problems, refer to Lai Hongyi, "Retiring from the Sixteenth Party Congress and Leaving a Name in History," *Lianhe Zaobao* (*United Morning Post*), September 4, 2002, 26. For a report of Premier Wen's concerns with the predicament of peasants and urban laid-off workers, refer to "Wen Preoccupied with Rural Areas, Unemployment, Poverty," posted at: www.xinhua.org on March 18, 2003; "Wen Jiabao on Major Problems Facing New Government," post at: http://english.peopledaily.com.cn on March 18, 2003, accessed on August 27, 2004.

45 The Chinese Central Television Project Group for a Memorandum of the National Conditions, *Guoqing beiwanglu* (*A Memorandum of the National Conditions*) (Shenyang: Wangjuan chuban she, 2010), 93.

46 Ibid., 90.

47 "Zhongguo nongcun feishui gaige he nongcun zonghe gaige de huigu yu sikao" (A Review and Deliberation over Reforms of Rural Fees and Taxes and Rural Comprehensive Reform in China), posted at: http://znzg.xynu.edu.cn/Html/?14751.html, accessed on February 27, 2015.

48 Rural Development Research Institute of the Chinese Academy of Social Science (RDRI) and Rural Social and Economic Survey Team of National Statistical Bureau (RSEST), *2004–2005 nian: Zhongguo nongcun jingji xingshi fenxi yu yuce* (*Analyses and Predictions on Rural Economic Conditions in China during 2004–5*) (Beijing: Shehui kexue chubanshe, 2005), 22.

49 Chen Xiwen, Zhao Yang and Luo Dan, *Zhongguo nongcun gaige 30 nian huigu yu zhanwang* (*A Review of Rural Reforms in China in the Past Three Decades and Their Prospects*) (Beijing: Renmin chubanshe, 2008), 4.

50 RDRI and RSEST, *Zhongguo nongcun jingji xingshi fenxi yu yuce (2009–2010)* (*Analyses and Predictions on Rural Economic Conditions in China during 2009–10*) (Beijing: Shehui kexue chubanshe, 2010), 27.

51 RDRI and RSEST, *2004–2005 nian: Zhongguo nongcun jingji xingshi fenxi yu yuce*, 22.

52 The Chinese Central Television Project Group for a Memorandum of the National Conditions, *Guoqing beiwanglu*, 83–4.

53 Ibid., 85–6.
54 RDRI and RSEST, *2005–2006 nian: Zhongguo nongcun jingji xingshi fenxi yu yuce* (*Analyses and Predictions on Rural Economic Conditions in China during 2005–6*) (Beijing: Shehui kexue chubanshe, 2010), 29–30.
55 "Zhongguo nongcun feishui gaige he nongcun zonghe gaige de huigu yu sikao" (A Review and Deliberation over Reforms of Rural Fees and Taxes and Rural Comprehensive Reform in China), posted at: http://znzg.xynu.edu.cn/Html/?14751. html, accessed on February 27, 2015.
56 RDRI and RSEST, *Zhongguo nongcun jingji xingshi fenxi yu yuce (2011–2012)* (*Analyses and Predictions on Rural Economic Conditions in China during 2011–12*), 36.
57 The new rural cooperative medical care scheme is named to differentiate itself from the old scheme in place during Mao's China. The old scheme consisted a three-tier medical care arrangement for peasants. The first tier provided the easiest access for basic medical treatment and prevention through barefoot doctors. The second tier was small, outpatient clinics at township that were staffed by medical professionals and were subsidized by the government. The third tier was government-funded county hospitals that treated the most seriously ill patients. See Yuanli Liu, William C. Hsiao, and Karen Eggleston, "Equity in Health and Health Care: The Chinese Experience," *Social Science & Medicine*, Vol. 10, 1999, 1349–56.
58 RDRI and RSEST, *2005–2006 nian: Zhongguo nongcun jingji xingshi fenxi yu yuce*, 32–4; Chen Jiagui *et al.*, *Zhongguo shehui baozhang fazhan baogao (2010)*, 42.
59 RDRI and RSEST, *2006–2007 nian: Zhongguo nongcun jingji xingshi fenxi yu yuce*, 36–7.
60 RDRI and RSEST, *Zhongguo nongcun jingji xingshi fenxi yu yuce (2011–2012)*, 36; Chen Jiagui *et al.*, *Zhongguo shehui baozhang fazhan baogao (2010)*, 42; Central News Interview Center of Xinhua News Agency, *Zhongzheng Zhongguo* (*Governing China*) (Beijing: Renmin chubanshe, 2012), 67, 101; "Xinxing nongcun hezuo yiliao" (New Rural Cooperative Medical Scheme), posted at: http://baike.ba idu.com/link?url=MltrbYAdInkIdY2sPfJa3Bkfj0fvhdenUyelngLg_l0rbkcb4SSsxTY 60aJhbWOhTB8rbqLkRN35SoPhPVeqdK, accessed on March 1, 2015.
61 Chen Jiagui *et al.*, *Zhongguo shehui baozhang fazhan baogao (1997–2001)*, 251–2.
62 Chen Jiagui *et al.*, *Zhongguo shehui baozhang fazhan baogao (2001–2004)*, 48.
63 "Xinxing nongcun shehui yanglao baoxian" (New Rural Social Pensions), posted at: http://baike.baidu.com/link?url=a-1J_joJ3bGQaUL6RPWt1XG9WaBKHCXMp_ 6ewiIwPPqn2zP4QHIWwXTXv3Ueut3PbZhXBwWiE3qJZbAm0TiCdK, accessed on March 2, 2015.
64 RDRI and RSEST, *Zhongguo nongcun jingji xingshi fenxi yu yuce (2011–2012)*, 37.
65 "Chengzhen jumin yanglao baoxian canbao renshu shouci 'suoshui' yi chuxian guaidian" (For the First Time People Covered by Urban and Rural Basic Pensions Shrank in Number, Suggesting a Turning Point), posted at: http://news.xinhuanet. com/politics/2014-06/19/c_126641079.htm, accessed on March 4, 2015.
66 RDRI and RSEST, *2007–2008 nian: Zhongguo nongcun jingji xingshi fenxi yu yuce*, 28.
67 RDRI and RSEST, *Zhongguo nongcun jingji xingshi fenxi yu yuce (2011–2012)*, 35.
68 Chen Jiagui *et al.*, *Zhongguo shehui baozhang fazhan baogao (2001–2004)*, 28–30.
69 Chen Jiagui *et al.*, *Zhongguo shehui baozhang fazhan baogao (2001–2004)*, 28–30.
70 Chen Jiagui *et al.*, *Zhongguo shehui baozhang fazhan baogao (2001–2004)*, 30.
71 Tang Jun, "Leap-like Development in the Institution of Minimum Living Allowances for Urban Residents in China," in Ru Xin, Lu Xueyi, and Shan Tianlun, eds, *2003 Nian: Zhongguo Shehui Xingshi Fenxi yu Yuce*, 243–46; 231; 40–41.
72 Chen Jiagui *et al.*, *Zhongguo shehui baozhang fazhan baogao (2001–2004)*, 30–3.
73 Chen Jiagui *et al.*, *Zhongguo shehui baozhang fazhan baogao (2010)*, 46.

74 Chen Jiagui *et al.*, *Zhongguo shehui baozhang fazhan baogao (2010)*, 43.

75 Chen Jiagui *et al.*, *Zhongguo shehui baozhang fazhan baogao (2001–2004)*, 135–6.

76 "2013 niandu renli ziyuan he shehui baozhang shiye fazhan tongji gongbao" (A Statistical Bulletin on the Development of Human Resources and Social Security in 2013), posted at: www.chinanews.com/gn/2014/05-28/6223421.shtml, accessed on March 3, 2015.

77 Chen Jiagui *et al.*, *Zhongguo shehui baozhang fazhan baogao (2010)*, 43; "Woguo shehui baozhang fazhan xianzhuang yu qianjing zhanwang" (The Status of Development and Future Prospects of Social Security in Our Country), posted at: www.cet.com.cn/ycpd/sdyd/1325408.shtml, accessed on March 3, 2015; "2013 niandu renli ziyuan he shehui baozhang shiye fazhan tongji gongbao."

78 Chen Jiagui *et al.*, *Zhongguo shehui baozhang fazhan baogao (1997–2001)*, 127, 222.

79 Chen Jiagui *et al.*, *Zhongguo shehui baozhang fazhan baogao (2001–2004)*, 106–8; Deng Dasong and Liu Changping, *2006–2007 nian Zhongguo shehui baozhang gaige yu fazhan baogao* (*A Report on the Reform and Development of Social Security in China*) (Beijing: Renmin chubanshe, 2008), 123; "2013 niandu renli ziyuan he shehui baozhang shiye fazhan tongji gongbao."

80 Chen Jiagui *et al.*, *Zhongguo shehui baozhang fazhan baogao (2010)*, 43; "2013 niandu renli ziyuan he shehui baozhang shiye fazhan tongji gongbao."

81 Chen Jiagui *et al.*, *Zhongguo shehui baozhang fazhan baogao (2001–2004)*, 178–81.

82 Chen Jiagui *et al.*, *Zhongguo shehui baozhang fazhan baogao (2010)*, 36–7.

83 "2013 niandu renli ziyuan he shehui baozhang shiye fazhan tongji gongbao"; Li Xiaoxi and Hu Biliang, *Zhongguo jingji xin zhuanxin* (*New Transformation of China's Economy*) (Beijing: Zhongguo dabake quanshu chubanshe, 2011), 271.

84 Hongyi Lai, "National Security and Unity, and China's Western Development Program," *Provincial China*, Vol. 8, No. 2, October 2003, 118–143.

85 "Xibu dakaifa zhanlue" (Western Development Strategy), posted at: http://ba ike.baidu.com/link?url=9y2x1ZyfXvFVSCjcWhXZkqVqFYkPYEW8I8JkAOREZ HGIDVBWs-SJ0gLlLA6G49pg, accessed on March 4, 2015. For further analyses, see Hongyi H. Lai, "China's Western Development Program: Its Rationale, Implementation, and Prospects," *Modern China*, Vol. 28, 2002, 432–66. For an evaluation of China's western development in the early years, refer to Lai Hongyi, "China's Western Development (I): Progress in the First Two Years"; "China's Western Development (II): Problems Ahead," *EAI Background Briefs Nos. 156–157* (Singapore: East Asian Institute, NUS, May 26, 2003).

86 The author's own computation based on data from *China's Statistical Yearbook* in multiple years.

87 "Northeast Revival Enters a Stage of Practical Execution," *Beijing Qingnian Bao* (*Beijing Youth Daily*), November 27, 2003.

88 "Gujia fagaiwei: Dongbei zhenxing yi touzi 3820 yi" (NDRC: 382 billion yuan invested in northeast revival), posted at: http://news.sohu.com/20150227/n409193664. shtml, accessed on March 4, 2015.

89 The author's own computation based on data from *China's Statistical Yearbook* in multiple years. For an in-depth analysis and tentative assessment of the program, refer to Jae Ho Chung, Hongyi Lai, and Jang-Hwan Joo, "Assessing the 'Revive the Northeast' (zhenxing dongbei) Programme: Origins, Policies and Implementation," *The China Quarterly*, Vol. 197, 108–25.

90 The author's computation using data from Zhongguo Tongjibu (National Statistical Bureau of China), *Zhongguo tongji zaiyao* (*China Statistical Abstract*) (Beijing: Zhongguo tongji chubanshe, 2004), 129–30, 122.

91 "Relief for Depressed Central Region", *Beijing Review*, April 21, 2005, 22–4.

92 For an analysis of the program, refer to Hongyi Lai, "Developing Central China: A New Regional Programme," *China: An International Journal*, Vol. 5, No 1, 2007, 109–35.

93 The author's own computation based on data from *China's Statistical Yearbook* in multiple years. For an in-depth analysis and tentative assessment of the program, refer to Hongyi Lai, "Developing Central China: A New Regional Programme".

94 Chung, Lai, and Xia, "Mounting Challenges to Governance in China," 6.

95 Lu Xueyi, "Nongcun yao jinxing di erci gaige" (A Second Reform Is Needed in the Countryside), in Ru Xin, Lu Xueyi, and Shan Tianlun, eds, *2003 Nian: Zhongguo Shehui Xingshi Fenxi yu Yuce*, 190.

96 "Diaocha xianshi: Hu Wen zai nongmin xinzhong xiangyou hengao weixin" (A Survey Reveals that Hu and Wen Are Held in High Regard by Peasants), posted at: http://18.dwnews.com/news/2012-10-11/58899650.html, accessed on October 14, 2012.

5 Differentiated treatment of religious groups

Maintaining monopoly over a reviving society[*]

In the post-Mao decades China has experienced widespread revival of religious faith and practice. This is evident in a growing number of new religious sites and an increasing attendance at religious services, as well as the rise of numerous unofficial and unorthodox religions, including Falun Gong. According to official reports, followers of the five religions, namely, Buddhism, Daoism, Islam, Catholicism, and Protestantism, totaled 136 million in 1999, or 11 percent of the population.[1]

Empirical data on religious revival in China, including the state's policies to it, is growing and informative.[2] Scholars note that the state has introduced a series of laws and regulations regarding religion,[3] that the state cracks down on sects such as Falun Gong,[4] and that the state tries to maintain political control while showcasing its tolerance.[5] Nevertheless, systematic and logical answers to the following questions are still required: How does the Chinese state deal with a variety of religions? Which theoretical framework, totalitarianism or post-totalitarianism, better describes such policies? What rationales do they offer for state policies toward specific religions? Can large religious groups function independently of the Chinese state? Taking the post-totalitarianism framework as a point of departure, I argue in this chapter that in China, the state acts as a calculating monopolist, distinguishing religions on the basis of their ideological assertiveness and organizational independence. This calculated and differentiated treatment of social groups is a trademark of pragmatic authoritarianism. The argument is deployed to explain key policies toward major religions.

State and society under totalitarianism and post-totalitarianism

Three major views may be identified in the existing literature on the relations between state and society under communism. One view holds that the communist state is a totalitarian regime. The Party state controls two sets of political tools, soft (ideology) and hard (bureaucracy, police, and army), and polices all aspects of social life. It is essentially hostile to organized religions and co-opts and subjugates them.[6] The Chinese state is probably no exception even in the era of reform.[7] Nevertheless, this image of strict totalitarianism, while closely modeled on the Soviet Union under Stalin, fell short of realization in fact. With subsequent development, the Soviet regime itself was rationalized and decentralized, and social spaces opened up.[8]

Hence, a second school, adopting the framework of post-totalitarianism, suggests that the subsequent communist regime allows considerable participation by social groups, arbitrates social interests, and regulates and limits their expression.[9] Studies on China echo this argument while pointing to specific Chinese characteristics. In the years following the Tiananmen crackdown in 1989 the regime has undergone similar changes—the Party courts intellectuals,[10] the state's capacity to control society declines,[11] while the society remains "fragmented and fragmenting."[12]

Since the 1990s, a growing number of scholars of Eastern Europe have attributed the demise of communism there to the rise of civil society.[13] Several also insist that China's civil society, as a state-societal intermediate, is rising, as is reflected in the registration of social groups, and revival of local rituals.[14] The civil society approach rightly points to increased space for social groups and activities. However, it has underestimated severe limits in the case of China. Conventionally, civil society denotes a sphere that exists independent of the state's control that can promote democracy and orderly political transition.[15]

Unfortunately, there is no civil society in China that satisfies the two features. First, advocates of the civil society approach in China usually have to reformulate the concept itself. The late Gordon White, a leading proponent of this approach, had to settle for a much watered-down version, in his words, a "partial and patchy 'civil society'."[16] Others, however, like Kenneth Dean and Yanqi Tong, deny the existence of a Chinese civil society outright.[17] Second, known candidates for inclusion in civil society fail to promote transition to a modern and democratic state based on the rule of law. "Single-clan villages," for instance, are closed and exclusionist: they engage in feuds and traditional, obstructionist religious practices. Similarly intolerant and closed are communities like the Catholics.[18] At the extreme end of this spectrum are *hei shehui* (underworld) brotherhoods and gangs on the model of the traditional triads, which fail basic requirements of legitimacy.

The Chinese state as a rational monopolist

Among the above three approaches, post-totalitarianism is the most able to describe the state-religion relations. It points to the rising influence of social forces including religions on the one hand, and the regime's abilities to co-opt and control them on the other. Other than co-optation, post-totalitarianism, however, has yet to adequately explain the state's other tactics in controlling social groups and their possible differentiation.

To fill this gap, this chapter seeks to develop a pragmatic authoritarian explanation accounting for the interaction between the communist state and the reviving society. It acknowledges the state's ability to suppress any social force that openly challenges it, as well as its clear limits. Post-Mao China, we argue, is a circumspect and shrewd monopolist as far as organization and ideology are concerned. Religions are regarded as potential rivals for organizational, ideological and, indeed, economic resources. Given its limited resources, however, the state is poorly placed to suppress religion *in toto*, as was attempted futilely in the Mao era. Differentiated management, co-optation and selective suppression thus become necessary. The state discriminates among religions according to their organizational (and even fiscal) strength, their political compliance, and their theology. It co-opts large, established and organized religions, cracks down on dissenting sects, especially those that are well-organized and non-compliant, and leaves cooperative groups or unorganized group activities largely untouched.

An authoritarian state like the PRC can be seen in economic terms as a power monopoly.[19] The Chinese Communist Party (CCP) has no legal challenge to its leadership. Satellite parties may offer loyal advice, but have no share of ruling power. The Party monopolizes the military, judiciary, police, administration, legislature, and media, and tightly monitors mass organizations and religious activities. Thus the Chinese state can be viewed as a mono-organization: a monopoly of political and social control mechanisms, i.e., organization and ideology.[20] Ideology justifies the Party's policies and motivates and guides party members in implementing it; organization enables the Party to unite its members, mobilize the masses, extract resources and outmaneuver its opponents.[21]

The CCP jealously guards its monopoly of power and views religions as potential rivals on ideological, organizational, and even fiscal grounds. First, religion needs a theology (or a set of religious beliefs) in order to supply the populace with a view of the world, such as an afterlife, and gain believers. Accepting Marx's materialism, the CCP claims that religion provides anxious people a supernatural yet unfounded account for natural and social events. It views religion as a spiritual opium that helps the non-communist ruling class to anaesthetize and govern the people. It officially defends atheism and asserts that religion will disappear with the progress of history.[22]

Second, religions need personnel, facilities, funding, and institutions in order to attract converts, serve adherents and train their clergy. Thus, religions constitute potential rivals for the CCP organizationally (and even fiscally). Religions sap the talent pool available to the state and set up institutions and facilities that deprive the states of relevance and popularity. Furthermore, the state may be considered a monopolist of rents that specializes in extracting revenue from the population.[23] Religious groups may, if uncurbed, attract huge donation incomes from the population, and may (as is the case in many countries) reduce the state's revenue base by claiming fiscal exemption. For this reason the CCP, on coming into power, prohibited all religious groups from occupying large stretches of arable land that could be cultivated only by hired tenants. It also prohibited the renewal of religious prerogatives or "exploitation" (read economic prerogatives and major commercial interests) enjoyed in the past.[24]

Third and perhaps most importantly, the organizational capacity and mass following of religions pose a serious threat to the CCP rule. The active role of the Catholic Church in bringing down communism in Poland provided a powerful precedent. That is among the reasons why the CCP views the Catholic Church, especially its underground branch, with suspicion. By the same token, Falun Gong was seen as a hostile rival after 10,000 of its followers surrounded the Chinese leadership's Beijing enclave in protest.

As a sophisticated political monopoly and a pragmatic authoritarian ruling party, the CCP carefully invests its resources in neutralizing potential rivals and avoids over-stretching itself. The state's policies toward religion are based on the three following considerations. First, religions as a whole have survived state repression. Wiping out religions *in toto* would consume more resources than the regime can afford. Second, citizens demand a non-political sphere of social goods and services,[25] such as worship of ancestors, attending prayers at open churches, and group efforts to protect the environment, maintain community order, or pursue hobbies. An indiscriminate crackdown on all religious activities and groups on the part of the state would alienate the population.

Third, it is not worthwhile for the CCP to seek to dominate religions having poor organizational capacity and posing little ideological and political threat, or that are costly to suppress. The threat from a religion comes less from its ideology than from its organizational strength and independence. Therefore, the CCP prefers to tighten its grip on organized religions rather than on non-organized ones.

As stated above, China also lacks a mature, civilized, and capable civil society. Some of the candidates for inclusion in a potential civil society, such as "brotherhoods," underground societies and clan villages have an unsavory tendency to promote illegal activities and narrow, sectarian loyalty while discriminating against and harming outsiders. This readily provides a rationale for frequent state intervention in society.

Religious policy in the post-Mao era

Before proceeding to analyses, a definition of religion is needed. Religion refers to a set of beliefs, symbols, and practices, which is based on the idea of the sacred and an afterlife.[26] Four categories of religions in China fall under this encompassing definition.[27] First, established religions, i.e., Buddhism, Islam, Protestantism, Catholicism, and Daoism. As a label, "established" implies that these religions have relatively clear theologies, well-defined procedures to train professionals, and well-specified sites for worship. The five are represented by state-sanctioned religious associations. Second, underground churches, especially the underground Catholic church and the Protestant house church. Third, unofficial and unorthodox sects, including Tibetan Buddhist and Xinjiang Muslims who favor independence for their regions, as well as Falun Gong. Fourth, folk religions, termed "feudal superstitions" by the CCP, and found in a plethora of diffuse forms, including ancestor worship, local god worship, geomancy, witchcraft, physiognomy, and taboos.[28]

While there are other ways of identifying religions, I identify these four clusters for the following reasons. First, as convincingly demonstrated in the case of the Catholic Church, the growth of religion in China has been deeply shaped by its relationship with the state.[29] The fate of Falun Gong again provides us with a vivid and recent case. Second, it is reasonable to correlate my first, second and third, and fourth categories with the three-fold division of religions in China into *official*, *heterodoxy*, and *popular* categories made familiar by Myron Cohen.[30] Third, my four categories are largely distinguishable by the state in terms of their organizational strength and theological and organizational independence, which, as we have asserted, are key to the state's differential response to them. State policies toward religions in Mao's China traversed three periods: 1949–1957: cooptation; 1958–1965: vacillation; 1966–1979: prohibition.

After 1979, the state permitted religious activities. The following differentiated strategies or stances toward different religious groups were adopted, in order of "softness": cooptation, discouragement, restriction, and suppression. Note that it was possible to adopt more than one of these stances toward a specific group. It was generally the case, however, that the state employed a single main strategy, supplemented on occasion with others. The more coherent and larger a religious organization, the less propensity it would have to comply with the state supervision or authority, and the more deviant from official ideology or policy its religious doctrines, the harsher the state's adopted stance.

Specifically, the following displays the state's basic repertoire of tactics in the handling of religions. First, it seeks to *coopt* the five established religions through official religious associations and political representation. Second, it *cracks down* on sects that are politically defiant toward and deviant from religious models sanctioned by the government, Falun Gong, and pro-independence Buddhists in Tibet and Muslims in Xinjiang are prime cases in point. Third, the state *restricts and suppresses* the underground Catholic and Protestant churches. Fourth, it *discourages* various types of localized and disorganized superstitions while tolerating folk religions that tends to be localized and disorganized.

A series of institutions and capacities are available to the state in implementing these strategies. First, it has the power to frame laws and regulations governing religions. Second, to enforce these rules and oversee religious affairs, it has key agencies including the United Front Department (UFD), the Propaganda Department of the CCP, as well as the Religious Affairs Bureau (RAB), the Ministry of Public Security, and, within the core administrative body, the State Council, the Ministry of Civil Affairs. Official religious associations are likewise powerful arms of the state in implementing its policies and (loyally) voicing the concerns of religious believers.

Coopting the established religions into official associations

The five religions have survived decades, if not centuries, of political and social adversity, not least the Cultural Revolution. In the 20th century the five were able prior to communist rule to co-exist with state authority without much trouble.[31] On the other hand, the five established religions provided formal, rational, and easy-to-monitor revenues for religious activities. Therefore, the post-Mao Chinese state recognizes Buddhism, Daoism, Islam, Protestantism, and Catholicism on the one hand, while striving through official associations persistently to control them on the other.

In the post-Mao period, the state has revived the official associations of the five religions that were set up in the 1950s, but abolished during the Cultural Revolution. The "No. 19 Document" issued by the Party Central Committee and the State Council in 1982 was the first major pronouncement on religion in the reform era. It stipulated official associations for the five established religions: the Chinese Buddhist Association (CBA); the Chinese Daoist Association (CDA); the Chinese Islamic Association (CIA); the Chinese Catholic Patriotic Association (CCPA), the China Catholic Administrative Committee (CCAC), the Bishop's Conference of the Catholic Church in China (BCCCC); the National Committee of Three-self Patriotic Movement of the Protestant Churches in China (NCTPMPCC, Three-self Church or TSC in short), and the Chinese Christian Council (CCC).

In 1994 the State Council issued a "Document No. 145," i.e., the *Regulations for Administration of Sites for Religious Activities.* Before a site could be used for religious purposes it was required to be legally registered in accordance with regulations formulated by the State Council Religious Affairs Bureau.[32] Local religious sites were subject to administration by religious affairs agencies at the county level or above. In 2004 the State Council issued a "Document No. 426," entitled *Regulations on Religious Affairs,* which was to take effect in March 2005. These 2004 regulations replace those of 1994. Religious sites are again required to be legally registered, this time in accordance with the *Articles on Administering Registration of Social Groups.*[33] As the above-listed official religious associations for the five religions are sanctioned by the state, they have no difficulty in obtaining the requisite registration.

Local governments (including at provincial and major municipal level(s)) have also formulated their own regulations on religious affairs in line with those issued by the State Council (such as Document No. 145 of 1994). In late 1997, for example, Guangzhou's Municipal government issued its *Regulations for Administering Religious Affairs* in the city, containing clauses very similar to those in Document No. 145. It identified local official religious associations as the main legal ones, including the Municipal Buddhist Association, the Guangzhou Municipal Daoist Association, the Municipal Islamic Association, the Municipal Catholic Patriotic Association, Guangzhou Catholic Diocese, the Municipal Christian Three-Self Patriotic Movement, and the Municipal

Christian Association. It required that sites for religious activities be approved and registered with county- or city-district governments and that religious activities take place in registered religious sites or sites approved by religious affairs agencies of the government.[34]

In order to ensure its ideological and organizational dominance the state has taken two steps, as stipulated in the above Document No. 19. First, the associations are required to pledge their support for the CCP, love the motherland and educate their followers and clergy into doing so. Thus, they foster ideological conformity of their followers with the regime. Second, through asking these associations to manage religious affairs under the leadership of the Party and the government and assist with implementing religious policies, the state exercises considerable control over the established religions.[35] In reality, official associations play a dual role that eventually helps to strengthen state supervision of the religious community. On the one hand, they help the state to manage religious affairs and local religious organizations, for example, by setting the number of Buddhist temples to be opened and by preventing religious groups and believers from stepping outside the official lines.[36] On the other hand, they voice the concerns (regarding, for example, religious freedom) of their adherents and believers to governmental agencies and the top leadership. In the post-Mao period, with help from the government, official religious associations have also helped train young religious professionals, reclaim and renovate religious sites and estates, popularize their doctrines, and engage in public and charity works, including aiding the poor and people in disasters, providing medical care, building infrastructure, and planting trees.[37] The dual role of official religious associations helps to ensure that believers and the state maintain smooth relations and that religious activities do not turn into anti-governmental protests. In the following paragraphs, I review the official associations of two of the five religions.

Buddhism among the Hans. Buddhism appears to be the most popular religion in China, claiming over 90 million followers around the late 1990s.[38] Yet the identity of Han Buddhists is rather diffused. A noticeable activity among Buddhists is pilgrimage to temples, which is mostly spontaneous, peaceful, and non-political. For example, in 1988 about 10,000 people visited the Wenshuyuan Temple in Chengdu on the first and the fifteenth days of each lunar month (days for Buddhist ceremony), and in two days in the same year, 30,000 celebrated the Guanyin's birthday at the Nanputuo Temple in Xiamen. While some of these visitors may well have been tourists, Buddhist devotees were certainly not lacking.[39] It is comparatively much easier to identify and document monks, nuns, and *jushi* (lay devotees). While Buddhists far outnumber all other religions combined, due to their weak identity and loose organization, as described above, they present no clear and present political threat to the CCP.

Partly out of the desirability of resuming contact with Buddhist organizations in Japan, the state allowed the CBA to resume activities in 1972, the first of such approvals.[40] It also established its branches at the provincial, prefectural, and even county level. Buddhist associations at provincial level and below supervise work in temples and monasteries and, on behalf of the RAB, monitor compliance with religious laws and regulations. Meanwhile they try to ensure that temples and monasteries enjoy autonomy regarding the administration of religious events and subsistence of temples.[41] Serious political troubles have yet to surface.

Catholicism. Due to antagonism between Beijing and the Vatican dating back to the 1940s, Catholicism has suffered most among the five religions. In the 1950s, the CCP encouraged the "Three-self Patriotic Movement" (TSPM) in order to minimize the Catholic church's ties with the Vatican that was hostile toward the communist regime. Pro-Vatican bishops, priests and nuns were arrested and many pro-Vatican Catholics driven underground. The Vatican has responded by rejecting archbishops and bishops appointed by the official church, and recognizing Taiwan instead of the People's Republic. Even official priests were persecuted during the Cultural Revolution, and for believers the underground church became the only avenue of the faith.

In 1980, the Chinese Catholic Patriotic Association (CCPA) was restored. Like the TSPM, the CCPA suffered from its track record as a mouthpiece for state policies and denunciation of pro-Vatican Catholics. As in the case of the Protestants, two new associations, the CCAC and the BCCCC, were set up in 1980 in a bid to regain the support of Catholics who were skeptical of the CCPA. The BCCCC was headed by more respectable religious leaders. Along with the CCAC, it was devoted to practical and relatively non-political pastoral work. As a result, it earned more trust from adherents. Between the 1950s and 1999, these official associations appointed 135 bishops in 115 dioceses. Given their allegiance to the Pope and experience of the state's past rough handling, however, many Catholics continued to distrust the official church. In the early 1990s, it has been estimated, only a fifth or less of Catholics visited official churches; in some provinces the underground church attracted twice as many followers as the official one. However, the state may have succeeded in reversing this situation in later years.[42]

Suppressing radical, separatist, or openly non-compliant religions

Before turning to state policies toward unofficial religion as a whole it is helpful to outline its regulations and tools for suppressing separatist and openly defiant religions, restricting unofficial churches and sects, and restraining folk religions. Document No. 19 of 1982 provided that religions failing to comply with the state's authority or its administration of religious affairs would incur legal sanctions. Specifically, religious activities that endangered "unity between ethnic groups" would not be condoned; illegal, criminal or anti-Party (or "counter-revolutionary," which was re-defined in the constitutional amendment as "subversion of state power" in later years) activities in the "guise of religion" should be struck down; unsanctioned sects should be banned; religious interference with the judiciary, administration, and schools and public education should be strictly prohibited.[43] Document No. 145 of 1994 and No. 426 of 2004 inherited similar provisions. A green light was thus given for the public security apparatus to apply laws and regulations to prosecute religious activities taking place outside the demarcated boundary.

Another tool used by the state to curb unofficial sects and churches is the denial of registration of religious sites. As stated above, according to the State Council Document No. 145 of 1994 and its replacement State Council Document No. 426 of 2004, all such sites have to be registered before they can legally host religious activities and no organized religious activities are allowed beyond the premises of religious sites. Undesirable sects and churches are thus conveniently denied an official existence. Should they operate, they would be deemed illegal and become subject to penalties and prosecution by the state, even though limits in resources and information render state crackdown on all illegal religious activities impossible. In 1996 the RAB promulgated the *Methods for Annual Inspection of Sites for Religious Activities*, mandating annual checks of religious sites for obeying laws, regulations, and policies, conducting religious activities, contact with foreign parties, management of finance, etc. In the same year provincial bureau chiefs were explicitly instructed by the RAB that organized churches refusing to be registered could be treated as evil cults (*xiejiao*); they could be abolished, and relevant religious leaders could be fined or sentenced to reform through labor.[44]

Maintenance of stability is among the criteria by which the state assesses the performance of its officials. Protests and activities by underground churches and unofficial sects are regarded as disrupting stability. Hence officials at all levels try hard to limit and suppress, activities by the underground church and unofficial sects.

Pro-independence or radicalized Islamic followers. Due to limited space, I will restrict discussion of pro-independence Islamic sects or extremist Islam to those coming from Xinjiang, as followers of radicalized Islam are most active in this region, where nine of ten Muslim ethnic minorities reside. In Xinjiang Muslims total over 10 million, equivalent to 60 percent of the population and 95 percent of the religious followers in the province. Sunni Muslims worship at most of the 24,000 mosques in Xinjiang. Pan Islam made inroads in Xinjiang in the 1930s, and seems to have revived with the rise of post-Soviet Central Asian countries dominated by Islam and support from several Middle Eastern Muslim countries. Militant separatists were able to receive training in some Middle Eastern countries, especially Afghanistan and Pakistan, and enter China for sabotage. The influx of Han immigrants and competition from the politically powerful Han also stimulates resentment and even pro-independence sentiment among Uighurs.[45]

Southern Xinjiang and Yining are hotbeds of the pro-independence movement. The population of Southern Xinjiang is overwhelmingly non-Han and Muslim; unemployment and economic underdevelopment are severe. With 500 years of Islamic tradition, Kashi hosts the largest mosque (Atigar Mosque) in Xinjiang. In the 1990s the Kashi area witnessed numerous violent incidents against Beijing. Yining was the capital of the former Eastern Turkestan, and a significant number of its Uighur residents still remember the history and privately express pro-autonomy and even independence sentiments. Urumqi, the capital of Xinjiang, also becomes a new base and a target of violent activities staged by local and more often outside radical Islamic followers.

The 1990s saw frequent protests and violence.[46] Chinese official sources suggest that explosions, assassinations, and other acts of violence in the 1990s totaled several thousand, and that in 1998 alone, over 70 serious incidents occurred, resulting in more than 380 deaths.[47] Many of the pro-independent activists deliberately chose to operate under the banner of Islam. Working as professional religionists, they condemned the CCP and the government, and claimed Koranic support for an Islamic state and even for a militant jihad.

In response to growing ethnic animosities, pro-independence sentiments or protests, and militant Islam, the government took a series of measures. First, it ruthlessly and systemically suppressed illegal religious and pro-independent activities. In particular, it severely punished leaders and activists by means of imprisonment and even execution. Following a violent riot in February 1997 in Yining when Uighur youths blocked the arrests of "separatists," called for the independence of East Turkestan and the expulsion of the Hans, and killed people on the street, the state tried 30 "separatists" in April. Three received death sentences. The government also purged local officials and cracked down on "underground" Muslim religious activities. Security organs arrested 44 "core participants in illegal religious activities" in the Yili region, broke up more than 100 "illegal classes" teaching the Koran, sacked five school principals, and warned numerous teachers of dismissal for allegedly stirring up sentiments for separation. In 1999, the authorities reportedly detained over 100 Muslims in Urumqi for demanding enactment of Islamic law, and closed a facility in Urumqi for printing "illegal religious propaganda."[48] Second, all new mosques and expansion of religious sites were required to apply for official authorization; building of new mosques was curbed. In the wake of the Yining riots of 1997 the construction or renovation of 133 mosques was banned. Third, supervision and education of religious professionals was stepped up. Religious leaders were reminded of the importance of love of the motherland and the subordination of religion to law and the state. Fourth, Muslims were urged to adopt modern lifestyles and values and abandon backward religious ideas.[49]

Into the late 2000s, after nearly a decade of lower-level violent activities, large-scaled violence with possible links with radical Islam in Xinjiang exploded into media limelight. One of the major starting points was the bloody mass riots in Urumqi in July 2009, resulting in 197 deaths and 1,721 injuries, most of whom were Han Chinese. In March 2014 about a dozen radicalized Uighurs were reportedly responsible for knifing 29 people to death and for injuring 131 people at the railway station of Kunming, the capital of Yunnan Province. Since then there have been numerous and constant reports about violent confrontations between the authorities and radical or armed Uighurs in Xinjiang. The government has been on high alert over activists of radicalized Islam and for Xinjiang independence and has resorted to stern measures to suppress the unrests.

Falun Gong.[50] Falun Gong is based on an unorthodox and exclusive theology and tight and extensive organization. Founded by Li Hongzhi, Falun Gong is an eclectic blend of Daoist meditation and Buddhist doctrines. Li implicitly preaches about an impending doomsday,[51] encourages mystic and exclusive cultivation, and attracts followers by claims to supernatural capabilities on the part of himself and his followers. He preaches truthfulness, kindness, tolerance, and morality, and denounces the corruptive influences of the marketplace.[52] The cult has provided millions of despairing and insecure followers temporary spiritual peace and medical relief amidst drastic changes. It has had notable success in attracting considerable funds and volunteer work and an international following and building a world-wide organization.

Nonetheless, prior to its official suppression, Falun Gong appears to have propagated itself through questionable means, sometimes in contradiction of its axioms. Li Hongzhi claimed that he and close devotees could single-handedly postpone the coming explosion of the earth. He claimed to have supernatural abilities, even though his mother, colleagues, and even he himself have privately denied the assertions.[53] His writings display many errors regarding science and history. Li accumulated a large amount of wealth, yet evaded income taxes. The cult's audacious and exclusive claims to the ultimate truth and salvation, blunt denunciations and ridicule anger many mainstream Buddhists. In a more open society like Taiwan and Hong Kong, Falun Gong had very limited popular appeal. In Taiwan mainstream Buddhism co-exists with the state, yet maintains its autonomy. It has made significant advances in its organization, innovative interpretation, and social work. It thus remains the most popular religion, attracting over 4 million believers, followed by mainstream Daoism. Falun Gong attracted no more than 100,000 followers.[54]

Falun Gong persistently challenged the state and public institutions through numerous open protests. Three developments prompted the state to outlaw it. First, Falun Gong had a large and extensive organization throughout China, and had rivaled and even penetrated the CCP and the state. Its core organization, the Falun Dafa Research Society, was established in Beijing in 1992. Subordinate to it were 39 provincial-level assistant general stations, 1,900 assistance stations, and 28,000 exercise sites. As the indisputable leader, Li, even when abroad, could readily issue instructions by fax, phone, or e-mail to each layer of the vast organization. His followers included many national, provincial, and local cadres, who even supplied inside information regarding the government's policies toward the cult. Next, between April 1998 and July 1999, Falun Gong had staged at least twenty public protests in front of the buildings of six national, provincial or municipal newspapers, three national or provincial TV stations, and three provincial governments.[55] Finally and crucially, the largest demonstration on April 25, 1999 dramatically demonstrated Falun Gong's strength and its determination to maintain its independence from the state. The CCP leaders and public security agencies were shocked to the core when tens of thousands of followers surrounded Zhongnanhai, China's "White House." After the early 1990s, with numbers of urban unemployed increasing and peasants' income growth slowing, protests by unemployed workers and disgruntled peasants began to occur almost daily across the country. The CCP leaders, especially Jiang, not unreasonably concluded that Falun Gong was organizationally capable of providing leadership for millions of such disadvantaged groups and challenging the regime.

In July 1999, Falun Gong was declared an "evil cult" (*xiejiao*) and outlawed by the state. The CCP forbade its members from any expression of belief in or adherence to it. In October, the Supreme People's Court, the Supreme People's Procuratorate, and the NPC passed a law against evil cults. The government issued an arrest warrant for Li and arrested key organizers. Official media launched a nationwide campaign exposing the "dirty secrets" of the sect, as well as staggering statistics and gruesome stories of 1,400 followers who died due to "acts of blind adherence." Followers protesting in Tiananmen Square and in other high-profile public places were subsequently subject to immediate arrest. By August 2000, at least 151 Falun Gong followers had been convicted of leaking state secrets, creating chaos, or other crimes.[56] In early 2001, several Falun Gong followers, in response to Li's call for action, set themselves on fire in protests at Tiananmen. The official media used the footage as vivid evidence of the cult as a suicidal evil in the eyes of the public.

Compared to the pro-independence movement in Xinjiang Falun Gong's style in confronting the state was less violent. Despite a nationwide campaign launched against the sect in 1999, suppression of the movement has been considerably less severe than in the latter case; few Falun Gong followers have received capital punishment, for example, though there have been unconfirmed reports of imprisonment and even maltreatment of Falun Gong activists.

The state also uses its apparatus to enforce crackdowns on unofficial sects. One of the three critical policy issues that the state uses to evaluate performance of officials (including local ones) is their abilities to maintain social and political stability. During 1999–2004 the state made suppression of Falun Gong a top-priority issue related to stability for central, prefectural, and local governments. It held Party and governmental officials responsible for open activities by the sect in the locale and especially for Falun Gong protesters in Beijing who come from their locality. Many localities thus acted swiftly to prevent open activities by the sect.[57] In the following years (after Jiang's formal retirement in 2004) the crackdown on the sect might have gained less political urgency, but the ban on the sect has continued.

Having defied and set itself on a collision course with the state, Falun Gong in fact lost much ground in China. Nevertheless, its followers continue to skirmish with the state through various acts, such as broadcasting messages of the sect through loud-speakers in public and interrupting cable TV programs.

Other sects. Falun Gong is one of the many unorthodox and unofficial sects in post-Mao China. Such movements became targets of state suppression as early as the mid-1990s. Unorthodox and unofficial sects include unofficial Christian groups such as the Lord God Sect (Zhushen Jiao), as well as unofficial Buddhist-like, Daoist-like, and folk-religious sects, such as Guanyi Famen, Yiguan Dao, and Zhong Gong (led by Zhang Hongbao, claiming 38 million adherents, and possessing extensive business networks). Some of these sects deviate from the officially-recognized religions, and a number of them rival officially-sanctioned churches, temples, or mosques. According to sources both official and unofficial, a significant number of them tend to have some of the following characteristics: (1) secretive activities and elaborate organizations; (2) personal cult of sect leader; (3) warnings about doomsday; (4) tight control of members; (5) hostility toward the CCP, by viewing it as the enemy of the sect or religion; (6) condemnation of official religious associations and the official church, such as the TSPM; (7) spreading of mysticism and supernatural abilities of the sect; (8) links with the West, Taiwan, South Korea.

Since these sects are highly secretive and autonomous and have international links, and since some of them hold an antagonistic view of the state and the official church, the state fears that they may disrupt official religious communities and undermine political stability. Predictably, the state's policy toward unorthodox sects parallels that toward Falun Gong. They are termed "evil cults," swiftly banned, and their leaders arrested and harshly sentenced.[58] In Hunan Province, for example, nearly 10,000 "cults" were eradicated in five campaigns over the span of a few years in the 1990s. One of the recent legal tools for the authorities to carry out this policy was provided by a law against "evil cults" passed in October 1999.

Suppressing and restricting the unofficial church

Underground Catholic Church. Due to limited space, the section focuses on the state's handling of the underground Catholic Church in discussing the unofficial church. The state is slightly more flexible and lenient toward the underground Catholic Church than its outright suppression of Falun Gong and other unorthodox sects. The reasons for the state's less stringent approach are as follows: much of the theology of the underground Catholic church related closely to the established Catholicism, rather than unorthodox sects; the underground church does not challenge the state's power as openly and assertively as religious advocates of independence of Xinjiang and Tibet and Falun Gong; as the Cultural Revolution suggested, total elimination of the underground church seems impossible.

With the Vatican's authorization, the underground church consecrated new bishops and ordained priests, and organized a national episcopal conference. Some elements of the underground church, however, might have over-used the Vatican's authorization over consecration and might have been more confrontational toward the state than Rome expected them to.[59] The underground Catholic Church has probably the oldest and best organized nationwide network among the unofficial religions. It had 46 archbishops and 1000 priests nationwide in 2004. The Vatican estimated that around that time underground

Catholics total 10 million, dwarfing the 5 million membership of the official Catholic Church.[60] The underground church exists mainly in the rural area of Hebei, Shaanxi, Guangxi, Gansu, and Xinjiang.

What has worried the state is the organizational independence and unchecked growth of the underground church. The underground Catholic Church has maintained secret contact with and has remained loyal to the Pope. The Vatican has not officially recognized the PRC; the underground church criticizes and tries to replace the official one. It also refuses the state's administration of religious affairs, has organized followers to protest, and might mobilize peasants who have been politically disorganized.

The CCP's concern is aggravated by its knowledge that the Vatican joined hands with the U.S. in toppling the communist regime in Eastern Europe and by its fear that they may apply the strategy in China. In 1977 the U.S. Central Intelligence Agency worked with the Vatican in producing a plot to overthrow communism in Poland. In June 1982 U.S. President Reagan met secretly with the Pope at the Vatican Library. Both agreed to stage a secretive movement to break up the communist bloc by starting with Poland.[61] The CCP thus feels compelled to restrict the underground church and even suppress it occasionally.

Document 19 in 1982 contained clauses that legalize sanction against the underground Catholic Church. It required religion to be self-reliant and independent of foreign influence and prohibited any foreign religious group from conducting missionary work in China. Document 145 in 1994 and its replacement Document 426 in 2004 stipulated that no religious sites should be subject to control by groups or individuals outside the PRC. In 1994, the State Council specifically promulgated Document 144, i.e., the *Provisions on the Administration of Religious Activities of Aliens within the Territory of the PRC*. It prohibited foreigners (or individuals from outside the PRC) from establishing religious groups, agencies, sites, or schools, gaining followers, and appointing clergy. Foreigners can host religious ceremonies or activities only with the approval of religious affairs agencies at the county-level or above.[62] These regulations open the gate for the state's restriction and suppression of foreign missionary work in China, the underground Catholic Church that owes its allegiance and clergy appointments to the Vatican, as well as any house church and unofficial sect that maintains close links with foreign religious groups.

Since 1981, the state has started to tighten its control primarily through suppression and restriction and secondarily, cooptation. Public security authorities arrested a number of pro-Vatican bishops, priests, and laymen reportedly in 1981, 1982, 1989, 1992 and 1994. They periodically arrest believers and priests for their unauthorized religious activities. In October 2000, the authorities held at least seven Catholic bishops in custody, and many of them had been held for years.[63]

Provincial and local governments also undertake measures to crack down on the assertive and sometimes antagonistic underground Catholic Church. For example, in early 1997 Zhejiang Provincial Party and Government instructed the localities to make stopping illegal Catholic and Christian activities a special task. In response, the Bureau of Public Security and the Party United Front Department of Tongxiang City ordered all townships and city agencies to launch a campaign, aiming at abolishing independent Catholic and Christian churches that evaded official registration and accused official churches for not being able to provide salvation.[64]

The state also supplies generous funding to the official church and helps it to compete against the underground church. The former is allowed to build new church buildings and seminaries, and the pro-Beijing bishops and priests to establish contact with each other and even overseas Catholics. Official seminaries also train young priests who are independent of the Vatican and install them in the official church. The official church seems to have attracted more members since the 2000s.[65] In contrast, the underground church relies on limited contributions from its members. Its resources for expansion are very limited, and its contact with overseas churches poor; the capable clergy are aging and the younger ones poorly trained and intolerant. Many Catholics attend both the official and underground church.[66]

Discouraging non-organized folk religions

Anecdotal evidence suggests that folk religions quickly regained their popularity in the countryside in the early and mid-1980s. In 1986 393 ancestor halls were erected in a market town in Guangdong Province where local residents regularly sought good luck for the living descendants through worship of the ancestors' spirits. In the 1990s some villagers in Shaanxi, Hebei and Zhejiang worshipped local gods (such as a Dragon King believed to control droughts) and rebuilt temples for local gods. A survey in the 1990s provides circumstantial evidence for the popularity of such beliefs and practices. Of all the respondents, more than 38 percent believed wholly or partly in, or had practiced, some form of superstition; 19 percent had both believed and practiced.[67] Folk religions continue to be popular in China. In particular, fortune telling and geomancy (*fengshui*) are very popular among both commoners and officials.

The state has several concerns with regard to such religious practices. First, if unchecked, they may promote clanship, dividing communities and challenging local governments. Second, there is a possibility that witches and sorcerers may utilize them to spread hostility toward the state and gain a sizable following, as occurred under the dynasties of old. Third, folk religions also tend to encourage wasteful and backward practices that obstruct the state's rational developmental policy. For example, *fengshui* results in the building of elaborate graves for the deceased in order to bring good luck for the living descendants, wasting hard-earned funds and precious arable land. Fourth, less rational and more primitive beliefs in gods and supernatural forces than established religions, such as extravagant worship of ancestors and local gods, with less commitment to charitable and social services on the part of believers, are promoted. For these reasons, folk religions are always referred to dismissively as feudal superstitions by the CCP and refused legal status. Document No. 19 of 1982 banned witchcraft and sorcery; these specific prohibitions appear, however, to have been dropped in Document No. 145 of 1994.

Compared to the established religions, folk religions are more localized, less organized, and more diverse. In many places, they are non-organized, or practiced exclusively by local residents on a spontaneous basis without a popular leader. Therefore, they pose for the most part a far less coherent ideological and organizational threat to the regime. Article 165 of the Criminal Code stipulates prison terms of up to seven years for persons convicted of swindling people though superstitious practices, and calls for re-education for their patrons. Given the popularity of folk religions in many areas, tremendous resources will need to be invested to eradicate them. Aware of this problem, the CCP has shown preference for discouragement through the mass media, and has focused on curbing the influence of folk religions among party cadres. The media recurrently carries articles criticizing and exposing superstitions. Fearing superstitions may weaken its ideological grip, the Party insists publicly that Marxism is the best way to cure and combat them, and singles out cadres who practice them and attract public attention.[68] The RAB also discourages local officials from using folk religions as platforms for hosting trade shows or business conventions aimed at attracting investment and boosting trade. In the "worst-case" scenarios when folk-religion professionals attract a large following, the state, sensitive to their potential use of their popularity for political aims, may restrict their activities and even arrest them.[69]

Despite reports of nationwide revival of folk religions from the 1990s into the 2010s and despite a 1993 estimate of 1.8 million witch doctors in China, however, few professionals practicing folk religions are said to have been prosecuted, and no systemic campaign against them has been reported.[70] Fortune telling is common, for example, in the temples along popular tourist routes in Sichuan, or in temples in popular tourist sites in Guangdong.[71] Rare reports of prosecution of folk-religion practitioners are in stark contrast to the often reported cases of mass detainment and prosecution of pro-independence and unofficial sect activists. Some cadres may view folk religions as "superstition" and allow police to ban local activities. Others, meanwhile, see them as a heritage, local custom, tourist attractions, tradition, or cultural capital. Therefore, as Feuchtwang put it vividly, folk religious activities are "subject to being forbidden by policy, but more often … are tolerated in a kind of legal and ideological limbo of uncertainty as far as official policy and its terms are concerned."[72] In some localities in Guangdong, ancestor halls are even beautifully renovated and made tourist attractions with local cadre support.[73]

Updates on state-religious interaction in the 2010s

In this section I will provide an update on the several new tendencies in the state's interaction with religions in China in the 2010s. Based on my field trips in China in the 2010s, especially 2012, and on published annual reports on religion in China this update aims to highlight a few noticeable developments. It is by no means comprehensive.

Several quick observations can be made here. First, the religious revival has continued and religious believers have reached an unprecedented number. Second, the state has much relaxed its policy toward the charitable activities engaged in by the religious associations and churches/temples. In addition, its restrictions on the activities of the legally registered religious sites seem to be much relaxed, encouraging to a fair degree these sites to engage in normal and non-political religious activities. Third, both the state and religions confront the issue of the commercialization of religious activities, especially those organized by Buddhist organizations or clergy. The problematic ethics of segments of Buddhist monks has tarnished the image of Buddhism, as well as that of official and non-official Buddhist organizations. This invites the population to cast doubt on the overall state of social morality in China. Fourth and importantly, despite a rapid surge in the number of believers the state continues to impose political restrictions on religions, notably by requiring religions to support the political regime and maintaining tight restrictions on religious sites and religious preaching.

Continued and widespread revival of religions in China

Compared to the population of religious followers in 1999 cited at the start of this chapter religions have gained far greater popularity in China in the 2010s. Two surveys conducted in 2007 suggested that 31.4 percent to 85 percent of the Chinese at the age of 16 or above believed or engaged in some form of religion. The lower estimate was based on the findings of the survey conducted by the East China Normal University in Shanghai. The higher estimate is based on the survey conducted by the Center on Religion and Chinese Society (CRCS) of Purdue University and by the Horizon survey firm and on the analysis of scholars at the CRCS. If we extrapolate the number of religious followers based on the Chinese population figure by assuming these two percentages applied to the whole population of 1.321 billion, there were 414.8 million to 1.123 billion of religious believers in China. According to the latter survey 18 percent of the adult Chinese (aged 16 and above), or 185 million, identified themselves as Buddhists, 30 million as Protestants, 3 million Catholics, 12 million Daoists, and 23 million Muslims (CIA estimates). Thus the self-identified followers of major religions totaled 253 million, about 19.2 percent of the population. Thus by the conservative estimate the population of the followers of the five aforementioned beliefs nearly doubled that in 1999 (which was 136 million).[74]

My own fieldwork in 2012 confirmed this trend. At one of the Christian churches I visited in a major city in northern China, I learned that the number of people attending worship at the church has grown rapidly, especially since 2008. Prior to 2008 the church conducted 1–2 sermons a week and had about 1,000–2,000 people attending the services in total. In 2012 the church offered five services (including four in Chinese and one in Korean for the Korean minorities from Jilin working in the city). In total about 5,000 people attended the services at the church, representing a 1.5 to four fold increase in attendance from 2008, which was a truly extraordinary development.

Among the attendants several hundred attend the regular activities of the church actively. Now, in addition to the main hall, there was a secondary hall and a basement. I noticed the basement could hold 400 people; the main hall 500 people and the secondary hall 100. About half of the people attending the church were older people, ranging from those in their late forties to eighties, and among them natives of the city were the majority. The other half was young people mostly in their 20s and 30s. Many of them were very well educated and have university and master's degrees. Most of the young people are from outside the city. They were very mobile. After several years, they may relocate to somewhere else. Many people knew about the church through its website. People could find services and other information on churches on websites.[75]

Greater tolerance of charitable activities by the state

One of the most liberal changes in the state's regulation of religion and social organizations is that since 2008 the government has adopted a much more relaxed and tolerant stance toward the charitable work of religious organizations. As a result, there has been a major upsurge in volunteering and donation activities by religious believers and religious organizations.

In the wake of the devastating Wenchuan earthquake in Sichuan in May 2008 that claimed nearly 70,000 lives, the Chinese government and Premier Wen welcomed donations and volunteering efforts from society to help aid the victims of the quake. This event and the state's relaxed stance toward donations triggered an unprecedented tsunami of donations and volunteers from all over China.

In the following years donations from various individuals and organizations for charitable causes have become common in China. In 2008 the China Buddhist Association (CBA) donated 1 million yuan for the victims of the Sichuan earthquake, and numerous local Buddhist associations also made donations. In May alone Muslims in 22 provinces in China raised 23.8 million yuan. In 2010 in the wake of the earthquake in Yushu, Qinghai claiming nearly 2,700 lives the CBA raised 2.33 million yuan, Hongfa Temple in Shenzhen raised 2.6 million yuan, and the Buddhist Association in Putuoshan raised 2 million yuan.

In 2010 the two main official Christian associations invested 5.5 million yuan in 25 of their sponsored charitable projects in 15 provinces. These projects covered health, disaster management, residential district development, elderly care, scholarship and educational aid, welfare and volunteering by followers.[76]

In recent years charitable foundations are also permitted to register and operate in China. For example, in 2006 the Ren'ai Charitable Foundation that was first established in Taiwan was registered with the Bureau of Civil Affairs in Beijing with a start-up capital of 2 million yuan. Inspired by Buddhist belief to aid people in need the foundation attracted 10,000 volunteers by 2011. It raised 11.1 million yuan through donations in 2009. It introduced a high degree of transparency in its use of funds, as donors could choose to donate to any of the operating projects of the foundation, and could check on the destination and use of donated money. Its projects include schooling aid, poverty and disaster relief, and elderly care.[77]

While the state's relaxed policy toward charitable work by religious groups seems quite enlightened, the state is also pragmatic in adopting this liberal stance. In the course of marketization and economic development since 1978, China has confronted a wide range of social issues, including rising inequalities between the countryside and the cities, between localities and between different social groups within the same localities. The coverage and infrastructure for social welfare and services in rural or underdeveloped areas and for migrant workers are rudimentary. Therefore, there is a dire need for social groups to offer assistance to these segments of the society. President Hu and Premier Wen promoted the idea of a "socialist harmonious society" from 2005 to 2012 in light of rising inequalities and grievances from disgruntled citizens about various social problems including lack of social services. The involvement of religious organizations and followers to engage in charitable activities represents a daring but calculated move of the Chinese state to allow religion to help the state to fill the holes in the provision of social welfare and social services, ease public discontent and maintain political stability.

It is worth noting that religious organizations are prohibited from engaging in activities to promote religious doctrines and converting new followers in their charitable activities. For example, the aforementioned Buddhism-inspired Ren'ai Foundation followed the state's regulations and refrained from using religious language and acts, distributing Buddhist scriptures and multimedia items, and preaching Buddhism in their charitable activities.[78] This also reveals the calculation of the pragmatic authoritarian state in utilizing religions to help ease social grievances while restraining their influence.

Commercialization undermining the integrity of religion

A rising level of material prosperity throughout China has brought a mixed blessing to religions. On the one hand, both the church/temple and its followers have more resources at hand to build up the hardware and facilities for the religious site and could fund more activities. On the other hand, unchecked commercial involvement by religious organizations and followers tarnish the image of religion and undermine its moral appeal, inviting public skepticism about the purity and integrity of religion.

In the recent years there has been a growing public perception that some of the best known religious sites (such as Buddhist temples where tourists flocked to visit) have degraded into sites where monks enrich themselves through offering simple prayers and, in outrageous cases, by coaxing followers to pay a handsome fee in order to escape the so-called foretold misfortunes. In the last decade the author has encountered at least two cases of such incidents, one being mild, and the other being outrageous. The first case involved a well-known temple known as a holy site of Zen Buddhism in Guangzhou about 10 years ago. There a senior visiting monk would offer peace and blessing to visitors by touching the head of a follower and by passing them an ordinary lucky charm. In return each follower would pay about 50 yuan. They lined up to see him. Thus within a day on weekends the senior monk could easily earn 50,000 to 100,000 yuan. There was no explanation about how the money would be used. The later case involved a Buddhist temple along the tourist coach routes from Chengdu to Jiuzaigou around 2004. All tourists on the coach were invited to visit the temple. Each visitor would be led into a room behind closed doors where the resident monks would give a free fortune telling service. However, through learning from visitors from the same coach the author realized that all visitors were warned of an imminent mishap and that they were advised to pay 50 yuan for a set of large incenses or pay 360 yuan for a couple of large candle sticks to be burned in order to escape them.[79] The latter case represented a blatant deceit and subtle coercion.

On the other hand, there have been efforts by religious organizations to reduce the possible undermining effects of commercialization and rely on donations and volunteering work of their followers to meet their material needs. For example, the aforementioned church where I did the fieldwork in 2012 rejected the commercialization of the site. Many people and some agencies offered to pay the church a decent amount in order to use it and hire its clergy to conduct marriage ceremonies. The church refuses. It only conducts free marriage ceremonies for its members. If someone is not a follower and a worshipper of the church, the church would not provide such a service. Nor would its clergy conduct ceremonies outside the church to earn income. The church was largely self-financed. It relied on its members for the revenue. When a project in the church needed finance, it would call on its members to donate and to contribute their skills.[80]

Allegiance and progressiveness in return for permission and limited sites

The state continues to impose restrictions on a variety of aspects of religious activities. As stated, religious organizations are prevented from preaching religions in conducting philanthropic work. There are several major restrictions the state has imposed on religions.

First of all, since the 1990s the state has introduced a new policy toward religion. This policy was coined "guiding religions to adapt to socialism" in 2001. At the national work conference on united front (which was a CCP platform to coopt various social groups including religions, ethnic minorities, and businesses) in 2001, State President and the General Secretary of the CCP Jiang Zemin elaborated on this policy. He made two requirements on religious leaders and followers and offered them two types of support. They were required not only to "love the motherland, support the socialist system, and the CCP leadership, and abide by laws, regulations and policies of the state," but also "to subordinate their religious activities to the supreme interests of the state and the overall interests of the nation." In return, the state would support religious leaders and followers to "interpret religious scriptures in line with social progress" and to "oppose illegal activities that use religions to endanger the interests of socialist motherland and the people" and to "contribute to the union of ethnicities, social development, and union of the motherland."[81]

Second, the state has maintained an archaic restriction on the number of religious sites which officially recognized religious groups can legally and openly use for their normal religious activities such as preaching and sermons. The law, regulations and policy on religions in China made three stipulations. First, religious activities should be held on legally approved religious sites and no conversion activities should occur outside them. Second, citizens have the right not to believe in religion, however, they should not preach their atheist beliefs or Marxism at the religious sites in order to prevent conflict. Third, religions in China should be run independently and be free from foreign intervention.[82]

Despite the rapid surge in the religious believers in China the state still maintains a regulatory regime that discourages the building of new religious sites, especially Buddhist and Daoist temples. The initial rationale of conflict prevention concerning preaching on religious sites seems increasingly unpractical and obstructive in light of the mass popularity of religions in China.

According to Wang Zhiyun, an expert on Chinese religions at the Chinese Academy of Social Sciences, the RAB promulgated "A Notice Concerning Halting Rampant Construction of Buddhist and Daoist Temples" in 1994. Similar policies were issued each year since 1996. Wang observed that in 1958 there were 2,666 temples in Beijing. By 2010 200 temples were left and only 20 of them were open for worshippers (and the rest were for tourism). Wang reasoned that given an estimated 2.2 million Buddhists in Beijing each of the 20 temples would have to accommodate 110,000 believers, which was physically impossible. Thus, official restrictions on religious sites have only resulted in unbearable congestion in legal sites and the emergence of illegal sites to meet the demand of believers. On the Chinese New Year in 2010, the busiest day of pilgrimage in the year at the most popular Buddhist temple Yonghegong in Beijing, 66,000 worshippers visited the temple and police had to impose traffic control. Wang also reported that there were only 5,000 legal religious sites for a vast number of Buddhists in the nation which was estimated to be at least 185 million in one of the aforementioned 2007 surveys. The illegal sites totaled 4,000, which could well be an under-stated figure. In

Jingzhou City in Hubei Province of central China the illegal Buddhist and Daoist temples were more than twice as many as the officially registered temples (63 versus 29).[83]

While the state's restriction on temples seems unreasonable and out-of-date, it does fit into its rationale to restrain the growth of ideology that rivals that of the CCP. In fact, the expansion of organized religions has already far out-numbered the membership of the CCP. In 2013 the CCP had nearly 86.7 million members, accounting for 6.3 percent of the population, far below the 19.2 percent self-identified believers of the five major religions in China in the aforementioned 2007 survey. The state's restrictions on religious sites also target Christian churches. In 2014 several churches in Wenzhou of Zhejiang Province that attracted thousands of followers were asked by the government to remove conspicuous crosses for the reason of their exceeding the legal heights. In another incident four stories of the six-story annex of the San-jiang Church in Wenzhou was dismantled by the local authority. The authority insisted that part of the complex was built illegally on farmland that it did not own, despite strong protests by hundreds of the church believers. In addi-tion, under the surface may exist the official concerns with foreign influ-ence and infiltration.[84] The author's reading of a field report and his own field work revealed that Christian, and Catholic churches have attracted con-siderable followings in Jiangsu, Zhejiang and Fujian and that many expatri-ates who work or study in China engage in preaching of religions including Christianity, Catholicism, and Buddhism. Subtly the Chinese government seems to be concerned with the unchecked growth of religions driven by acti-vists who had extensive foreign linkages and has cracked down on religious activities periodically.

Conclusions

As the Chinese state moves away from the pervasive totalitarian control of the Maoist era, religions are reviving. The revival demonstrates inherent psychological and social needs of segments of population for communal expression and spiritual fulfillment, especially amidst rapid social transition and emerging social problems.

A satisfactory account of state-societal relationship in post-Mao China is still lacking in the literature. None of the images in vogue—either of the omnipotent totalitarian state or of an autonomous civil society—accurately captures the changes. The religious revival indicates—as "post-totalitarian" models rightly underscore—the decline of the totalitarian state, its loss of all-pervasive power, the rising influence of social groups and an expanding sphere for citizens' activities. The populace can no longer be prevented, as in the Mao era, from expressing religious adherence. Nor can the emergence of religions and sects refusing compliance with its authority be totally elimi-nated. However, it is too tempting and too early to declare a victory for civil society. The post-Mao Chinese state continues to constrain religious movements within tight limits. Co-optation apart, the post totalitarian model has yet to adequately explain the state's other tactics for controlling social groups and activities; it has yet to unravel the logic behind the gradation of state tactics toward booming societal forces. In this chapter I propose pragmatic authoritarianism in explaining the Chinese state's management of religious groups and activities.

The Chinese state has indeed developed relatively effective strategies and tools for the differentiated management control of mushrooming social groups. Shrewd calculation in their deployment is in clear evidence. Religious groups and their agents are coopted, deterred, restricted, or suppressed, depending on their potential political threat as measured by their ideological assertiveness and, especially, their organizational strength, independence, and readiness to challenge the state. This discriminating suppression allows it to uphold its monopoly of power without dangerously exhausting itself.

Largely due to these shrewd tactics of a calculating monopolist, China today is full of seeming antitheses. While the society becomes increasingly pluralistic, the regime's monopoly of power continues; the populace enjoys a certain degree of religious freedom, yet a full-blown religious civil society (an independent and organized religious community) fails to emerge; ordinary citizens are free to criticize the regime on private occasions and even in conversation with acquaintances in public places, yet full citizen rights legitimizing organized political opposition are denied.[85] Ironically, the presence of "uncivil" and disruptive social elements, such as gangs, clans, and heretical cults, provides the state with a reason as well as an excuse to intervene heavily into social affairs.

These puzzles have to do with the pragmatic authoritarian state's redefinition and differentiated management of two types of zones. On the one hand, the parameters have been widened to allow a zone of social activities (such as folk religious practice and peaceful religious activities in sanctioned religious sites), low-profile political activities (such as talks among friends in public), and low-political activities (such as peaceful and brief local protests against pollution and even brief and unorganized protests by laid-off workers). It allows people to act relatively freely within the non- or low-political zone. Over the years the zone open for public activities has been enlarged.[86] As stated earlier, the most enlightened inclusion of items into this low-political zone is philanthropic work by religious organizations and individuals. Its inclusion, the state hopes, would help it to address the inadequacy of social services provision and to achieve social harmony.

On the other hand, the state has defined the political "no-go" zone more narrowly than under the totalitarian regime. This "forbidden" (or highly political) zone now includes mainly sensitive, high-profile and potentially influential political activities, such as (1) large, sustained, or sensitive protests in public, with Tiananmen Square most taboo of all; (2) moves to form political parties or open opposition groups, and (3) speeches critical of the regime targeting large audiences. The state continues to guard these zones vigilantly, swiftly eliminating intruders. In addition, the state is subtly guarding against possible backlashes from rapidly expanding religions by imposing tight and unreasonable restrictions on the number of religious sites, on conversion activities and on religious activities and organizations that have extensive international ties.

Such selective interventions in the reviving society, especially in behavior intruding into the above forbidden zone, enable the state to claim control of high-politics. The image projected by this chapter—of the state as a discreet and exclusive owner of the instruments of political control, namely, organization (including means of fiscal extraction) and ideology—captures its complex, uneasy relations with the society in a non-democratic, yet non-monolithic era. This explains the intriguing and uneasy co-existence of a reviving and expanding societal sphere and a predominant state.

Notes

* An earlier version of this chapter was first presented as a paper entitled "Religious Movements in Post-Mao China" at a Conference on "Civil Society, Social Movement, and Democratization on Both Sides of the Taiwan Strait" at Boston University on April 24–25, 2001. It was later published as "Religious Policies in Post-Totalitarian China: Maintaining Political Monopoly over a Reviving Society," *Journal of Chinese Political Science*, Vol. 11, No. 1, Spring 2006, 55–77. Reprint with permission from Springer. The introduction, various other sections and especially the last part of the chapter has been updated using latest information from publications and from a field trip to China in 2012.

1 The statistics come from Donald Argue, "Zongjiao ziyou: Meiguo zongjiao lingxiu daibiaotuan fanghua baogao" (Religious Freedom: A Report by the U.S. Delegation of Religious Leader to China), *Zongjiao* (*Religion*), No. 6, 2000, 57–62; Jing Hui, Min Zhiting, Wan Yaobin, Liu Yuanren, and Han Wenzao, "Zongjiao de mingyun shizhong yu guojia mingyuan jinmi xianglian" (The Fate of Religions Has Always Been Closely Linked with That of the Nation), *Liaowang* (*Outlook*), No. 21, 1999, 23–7.

2 For research on religious revival in China, refer to individual articles in *China Quarterly*, No. 174, June 2003. For studies on earlier years and religious policies, refer to Alan Hunter and Kim-Kwong Chan, *Protestantism in Contemporary China* (Cambridge: Cambridge University Press, 1993); William Liu and Beatrice Leung, "Organization Revivalism: Explaining Metamorphosis of China's Catholic Church," *Journal for Scientific Study of Religion*, Vol. 41, No. 1, 2002, 121–38.

3 For an earlier study, see Donald E. MacInnis, *Religion in China Today: Policy & Practice* (Maryknoll, NY: Orbis Books, 1989); for a later study, refer to Jason Kindopp and Carol Lee Hamrin, eds, *God and Caesar in China: Policy Implications of Church-State Tensions* (Washington, DC: Brookings Institution Press, 2004).

4 See Ronald C. Keith and Zhiqiu Lin, "The 'Falun Gong Problem': Politics and the Struggle for the Rule of Law in China," *The China Quarterly*, No. 175, 2003, 623–42; Benjamin Penny, "The Life and Times of Li Hongzhi: Falun Gong and Religious Biography," *The China Quarterly*, No. 175, 2003, 643–61; James Tong, "An Organizational Analysis of the Falun Gong: Structure, Communications, Financing," *China Quarterly*, No. 171, 2002, 636–60.

5 Refer to Pitman Potter, "Belief in Control: Regulation of Religion in China," *China Quarterly*, No. 174, June 2003, 318.

6 Earlier analyses of this school include Carl J. Friedrich and Zbigniew K. Brzezinski, *Totalitarian Dictatorship and Autocracy* (Cambridge, MA: Harvard University Press, 1956); Zbigniew Brzezinski, *Ideology and Power in Soviet Politics* (New York: Frederick Praeger, 1962). An excellent recent analysis is Juan Linz, *Totalitarian and Authoritarian Regimes* (Boulder, CO: Lynne Rienner, 2000).

7 Sujian Guo, *Post-Mao China: From Totalitarianism to Authoritarianism?* (Westport, CT: Praeger Publishers, 2000).

8 Gordon Skilling and Franklyn Griffiths, eds, *Interest Groups in Soviet Politics* (Princeton, NJ: Princeton University Press, 1971).

9 For analyses of this approach, refer to Gordon Skilling and Franklyn Griffiths, *Interest Groups in Soviet Politics*; Chalmers Johnson, ed., *Change in Communist Systems* (Stanford, CA: Stanford University Press, 1970), and Linz, *Totalitarian and Authoritarian Regimes*, 2000, 245–59.

10 Edwin A. Winckler, ed., *Transition from Communism in China: Institutional and Comparative Analyses* (Boulder, CO: Lynne Rienner Publishers, 1999).

11 Andrew G. Walder, ed., *The Waning of the Communist State: Economic Origins of Political Decline in China and Hungary* (Berkeley, CA: University of California Press, 1995).

12 See Merle Goldman and Roderick MacFarquhar, eds, *The Paradox of China's Post-Mao Reforms* (Cambridge, MA: Harvard University Press, 1999), especially the introduction and conclusion.

13 A classic treatise on civil society is Jürgen Habermas, *The Structural Transformation of the Public Sphere* (Cambridge, MA: MIT Press, 1989). For discussion of civil society in Eastern Europe and the USSR, refer to Robert Miller, ed., *The Development of Civil Society in Communist Systems* (Sydney: Allen and Unwin, 1992) and Frederick Starr, "Soviet Union: A Civil Society," *Foreign Affairs*, Spring 1988, 26–41.

14 See Gordon White, "The Dynamics of Civil Society in Post-Mao China," in Brian Hook, ed., *The Individual and the State in China* (Oxford: Clarendon Press, 1996), 196, 198; Timothy Brook and B. Michael Frolic, eds, *Civil Society in China* (Armonk, NY: M.E. Sharpe, 1997), 3. Robert Weller advanced a softer view of civil society in China by arguing that local religion (or folk religions) could give birth to an independent society once an authoritarian regime democratized. See Robert Weller, "Worship, Teachings, and State Power in China and Taiwan," in William Kirby, ed., *Realms of Freedom in Modern China* (Stanford, CA: Stanford University Press, 2004), 285–382.

15 The two characteristics come from Gordon White, Jude Howell, and Shang Xiaoyuan, *In Search of Civil Society: Market Reform and Social Change in Contemporary China* (Oxford: Clarendon Press, 1996), footnote 6; Phillippe Schmitter, "Civil Society East and West," in Larry Diamond *et al.*, eds, *Consolidating the Third Wave Democracies: Themes and Perspectives* (Baltimore, MD: Johns Hopkins University Press, 1997), 239–62.

16 Treatments of questionable social groups as elements of civil society are in White, Howell, and Shang, *In Search of Civil Society*, 1996, 1; Hook, *The Individual and the State in China*, 1996; White, "The Dynamics of Civil Society in Post-Mao China," 1996, 207.

17 Kenneth Dean, "Ritual and Space: Civil Society or Popular Religion?" in Brook and Frolic, *Civil Society in China*, 1997, 172–97; Yanqi Tong, "Political Development in Reforming China," in Joseph Cheng, ed., *China in the Post-Deng Era* (Hong Kong: The Chinese University Press, 1998), 101.

18 These elements are mentioned in White, "The Dynamics of Civil Society in Post-Mao China," 1996, 216. The Chinese Catholic community appears to be intolerant and not open to outsiders. See Richard Madsen, *China's Catholics: Tragedy and*

Hope in an Emerging Civil Society (Berkeley and Los Angeles, CA: University of California Press, 1998).

19 For examples of the conception of the market applied to politics, see Anthony Downs, *An Economic Theory of Democracy* (New York: Harper, 1957); Mark Ramseyer and Frances M. Rosenbluth, *Japan's Political Marketplace* (Cambridge, MA: Harvard University Press, 1993); Robert Keohane, "The Demand for International Regimes," in Stephen Krasner, ed., *International Regime* (Ithaca, NY and London: Cornell University Press, 1983), 141–72; David A. Lake, *Entangling Relations: American Foreign Policy in its Century* (Princeton, NJ: Princeton University Press, 1999). In a study published around the same time as the earlier version of this book chapter, Fenggang Yang applied the economic approach to religions in China. He differentiated three types of religions in China: a red market denoting officially permitted religions, a black market referring to officially banned religions, and a gray market consisting of religions with an ambiguous legal/illegal status and noninstitutionalized religiosity. His triple religion/market concept echoes my argument in this chapter about the Chinese state's cooptation of organized religious groups into official religious association, its suppression of unofficial and defiant organized religions and its tolerance of non-organized religions. See Fenggang Yang, "The Red, Black, and Gray Markets of Religion in China," *The Sociological Quarterly*, Vol. 47, No. 1, February 2006, 93–122. Please note that the main and original idea in my chapter was first presented at a conference at Boston University in April 2001, attended by China scholars such as Yongnian Zheng and Joseph Fewsmith.

20 For a discussion on mono-organization, refer to Thomas Henry Rigby, *The Changing Soviet System: Mono-organisational Socialism from its Origins to Gorbachev's Restructuring* (Brookfield, VT: E. Elgar Publisher, 1990).

21 See Franz Shurmann, *Ideology and Organization in Communist China* (Berkeley and Los Angeles, CA and London: University of California Press, 1968); Philip Selznick, *The Organizational Weapon: A Study of Bolshevik Strategy and Tactics* (New York: McGraw-Hill Book Company, Inc., 1952), 8–12.

22 For the Marxist view on ideology and religion, refer to Karl Marx and Friedrich Engels, *The German Ideology*, edited by C.J. Arthur (New York: International Publishers, 1986). For an analysis of the tension between communism and religion in general and in China, refer to Friedrich and Brzezinski, *Totalitarian Dictatorship and Autocracy*, 1956, 247–63; Chen Jinlong, "Zhongguo Gongchandang chuli zongjiao wenti de jiben jingyan" (The Chinese Communist Party's Basic Experience over Handling Religious Issues), *Shehui Kexue Zhanxian* (*The Battlefront of Social Sciences*), No. 4, 1999, 167–73. Shue argues that both the CCP and Falun Gong claim to possess ultimate ethical truths and thus become ideological rivals. See Viviene Shue, "State Legitimization in China," Paper presented at the Annual Meeting of the American Political Science Association, San Francisco, 2001.

23 See Margaret Levi, *Of Rule and Revenue* (Berkeley, CA: University of California Press, 1989).

24 See stipulations in Document 19 in 1982. Refer to Zhonggong Zhongyang Wenxian Yanjiushi Zonghe Yanjiuzu and Guowuyuan Zongjiao Shiwujiu Zhengce Faguansi (WXYJS and ZJSWJ), eds, *Xin shiqi zongjiao gongzuo wenxian xuanbian* (*Selection of Documents on Religious Work in the New Era*) (Beijing: Zongjiao Wenhua Chubanshe, 1995), 60.

25 The concept of this non-political social sphere is borrowed from Yanqi Tong. She distinguished a non-political civil society that provides social goods and services from a political society that seeks to influence the state's power and decisions. See Tong, "State, Society, and Political Change in China and Hungary," *Comparative Politics*, Vol. 26, No. 3, April 1994, 334.

26 This definition is a revised version of that in Gordon Marshall, ed., *A Dictionary of Sociology* (Oxford and New York: Oxford University Press, 1998), 562.

27 For a variety of religions in China, see, for example, Julia Ching, *Chinese Religions* (Hong Kong: MacMillan Press Ltd, 1993); Arthur Wolf, ed., *Religion and Ritual in Chinese Society* (Stanford, CA: Stanford University Press, 1974).

28 See MacInnis, *Religion in China Today*, 1989, 367–74, 385–410. For historical studies of China's folk religions, refer to Stephan Feuchtwang, *Popular Religion in China: The Imperial Metaphor* (Richmond: Curzon Press, 2001) and David Faure and Helen Siu, eds, *Down to Earth: The Territorial Bond in South China* (Stanford, CA: Stanford University Press, 1995).

29 Liu and Leung, "Organization Revivalism," 2002.

30 See Myron L. Cohen, "Religion in a State Society: China," in Myron L. Cohen, ed., *Asia: Case Studies in the Social Sciences* (Armonk, NY: M.E. Sharpe, 1992), 17–31.

31 An important exception is the period when Protestantism and Catholicism backed by foreign powers set foot in China under the Qing Dynasty. As a result, both churches' conflict with the populace occurred prior to the 20th century and escalated into the Boxer Rebellion in 1900.

32 For Documents 19 and 145, refer to WXYJS and ZJSWJ, *Xin shiqi zongjiao gongzuo wenxian xuanbian* (*Selection of Documents on Religious Work*), 1995, 65–6.

33 "Guowuyuanling: Zongjiao shiwu tiaoli" (Ordinance of the State Council: Regulations on Religious Affairs), posted at: www.xinhuanet.com on December 20, 2004.

34 See the Guangzhou Municipality's Regulations for Administering Religious Affairs. Refer to the Xingzhengyuan Dalu Weiyuanhui, *Dalu zongjiao gaikuang (1996–2001)* (*A Concise Introduction to Religion in Mainland: 1996–2001*) (Taipei: Xingzhengyuan Dalu Weiyuanhui, 2002), 173–84.

35 For official stipulations on these issues in Document 19 in 1982, refer to WXYJS and ZJSWJ, *Xin shiqi zongjiao gongzuo wenxian xuanbian*, 1995, 65–6.

36 MacInnis, *Religion in China Today*, 1989, 147.

37 Jing Hui, Min Zhiting, Wan Yaobin, Liu Yuanren, and Han Wenzao, "The Fate of Religions," 1999; MacInnis, *Religion in China Today*, 1989, 134–5.

38 He Kemin, "Zhongguo de zongjiao he zongjiao zhengce" (Religions and Religious Policies in China), *Zhongwai Jiaoliu* (*Sino-foreign exchanges*), No. 3, 1999, 40–1.

39 MacInnis, *Religion in China Today*, 1989, 125.

40 The state openly reaffirmed its policy of religious freedom only in 1979. See Zhao Kuangwei, *Woguo de zongjiao xinyang ziyou* (*Freedom of Religious Belief in Our Country*) (Beijing: Huawen Chubanshe, 1999), 100, 114.

41 Xingzhengyuan Dalu Weiyuanhui, *Dalu zongjiao xianzhuang jianjie* (*A Concise Introduction to the Current Situation of Religion in Mainland*) (Taipei: Xingzhengyuan Dalu Weiyuanhui, 1996).

42 Hunter and Chan, *Protestantism in Contemporary China*, 1993, 236–41.

43 Refer to WXYJS and ZJSWJ, *Xin shiqi zongjiao gongzuo wenxian xuanbian*, 1995, 68–9, 60.

44 For the regulations and the RAB instruction, refer to appended documents in Xingzhengyuan Dalu Weiyuanhui, *Dalu zongjiao xianzhuang jianjie*, 2002, 305–8, 62.

45 See reports from the following sources: *Ming Pao*, posted at: www.mingpao.com on September 2, 1999; *Kaifang* (*Open*), July 1998, 58; *Far Eastern Economic Review*, April 13, 2000, 25; *South China Morning Post*, August 28, 2000. Also see Colin Mackerras, *China's Minorities: Integration and Modernization in the Twentieth Century* (Hong Kong: Oxford University Press, 1994), 194–6; Nicolas Becquelin, "Xinjiang in the Nineties," *The China Journal*, No. 44, July 2000, 65–90.

46 Gardner Bovingdon, "The Not-So-Silent Majority," *Modern China*, Vol. 28, No. 1, January 2002, 39–78.

47 Becquelin, "Xinjiang in the Nineties," 2000, 87.
48 Human Rights Watch, "World Report 1998: China and Tibet" and "World Report 2001: China and Tibet," posted at: www.hrw.org/hrw in 1998 and 2001, respectively.
49 Zhang Xukai, "Yindao zongjiao tong shehuizhuyi shehui xiang shiying de lilun he shijian shikao" (Theoretical and Practical Reflection on Guiding Religions to Adapt to Socialist Society), *Xinjiang Sheke Luntan* (*Social Forum in Xinjiang*), No. 4, 1999, 9–12; *Zhonggong nianbao* (*An Annual Report on Chinese Communism*), 1998, 1-130–1-131.
50 Li Hongzhi, *Zhuan falun* (*Turn the Dharma*) (Beijing: Zhongguo Guangbo Dianying Dianshi Chubanshe, 1994); Hua Chu and Zhong Han, *Falun Gong fengbao* (*The Storm of Falun Gong*) (Hong Kong: The Pacific Century Press Limited, 1999), 84–5; 86–111; 151–68; 138–9; a video tape by the Chinese government criticizing Falun Gong.
51 Li did claim himself as a propagator of the true Dharma before the last millennium in his much-publicized *Zhuan falun*. See Li Hongzhi, *Turn the Dharma*, 1994, 33, 11.
52 Shue, "State Legitimization in China," 2001, 19.
53 Hua Chu and Zhong Han, *The Storm of Falun Gong*, 1999, 132, 99–101, 148–56.
54 Interviews with Buddhist nuns in Foguangshan Temple in Taiwan in 1991, and interviews with Taiwan scholars and officials in December 2002. For information on Taiwan Buddhism, see the Government Information Office, Taiwan, *Religions in the Republic of China on Taiwan* (Taipei: The Government Information Office of Taiwan, 1998).
55 Despite reports about these protests, Jiang Zemin paid little attention to and took no action against the sect before June 1999. Jiang probably was not aware of the organizational strength of Falun Gong until it surrounded Zhongnanhai in protest in April 1999. This puzzling fact is supplied by an insider's account of politics in China in 1999. See Zong Hairen, *Zhu Rongji zai 1999* (*Zhu Rongji in 1999*) (Hong Kong: Mirror Books, 2001), 48.
56 Human Rights Watch, "World Report 2001: China and Tibet," posted at: www. hrw.org/hrw in 2001.
57 See Yang Zhong, *Local Government and Politics in China: Challenges from Below* (Armonk, NY: M.E. Sharpe, 2003), 132–3.
58 Cao Guanghui, "Xiejiao Zhushen Jiao fumie ji" (A Story of the Demise of the Evil Cult the Lord God Sect), *Liaowang*, No. 17, 1999, 29–30; Tan Songqiu and Kong Xiangtao, "Dangdai Zhongguo xiejiao toushi" (A Fluoroscopy of Cults in Contemporary China), *Zhongguo Zongjiao* (*China's Religions*), No. 1, 2000, 28–30.
59 Hunter and Chan, *Protestantism in Contemporary China*, 1993, 241.
60 Information posted at: www.hsstudyc.org.hk/T134-E10.htm, accessed on December 4, 2004.
61 This account can be found in a book written by a senior official of the State Council Religious Affairs Bureau. See Wang Zuo'an, *Zhongguo de zongjiao wenti he zongjiao zhengce* (*China's Religious Issues and Religious Policies*) (Beijing: Zongjiao Wenhua Chubanshe, 2002), 222–3.
62 See WXYJS and ZJSWJ, eds, *Xin shiqi zongjiao gongzuo wenxian xuanbian*, 1995, 70, 275, 273; "Guowuyuanling: Zongjiao shiwu tiaoli," 2004.
63 Human Rights Watch, "World Report 2001: China and Tibet," 2001.
64 See Xingzhengyuan Dalu Weiyuanhui, *Dalu zongjiao gaikuang*, 2002, 119–25.
65 Liu and Leung, "Organizational Revivalism," 2002; interviews with a Chinese religious-affairs official, 2003.
66 Hunter and Chan, *Protestantism in Contemporary China*, 1993, 236–51.
67 Le Guo'an and Jiang Guoping, "Fengjian mixin yu shehui wending" (Feudal Superstitions and Social Stability), *Gangnan Shifan Xueyuan Xuebao* (*Academic Journal of Gangnan Normal Colleage*), No. 1, 1998, 73–5. The surveyors defined

superstitions as physiognomy, fortune telling, worshipping deities for help, divining, and believing in lucky numbers, that is, various forms of folk religions.

68 MacInnis, *Religion in China Today*, 1989, 385–410. This seems to be the case even into the 2010s.

69 This reaction is similar to that toward unofficial sects, described above.

70 Liu Jinghuai and Yun Shan, "Zhongguo de zongjiao zhuangkuang he zongjiao zhengce" (China's Religious Situation and Policies), *Liaowang*, No. 21, 1999, 18–21.

71 The author's observation and interviews in 2004 with a tourist guide on routes to Jiuzhaigou and Hailuogou in Sichuan, two of the best-known nature scenic sites in China; the author's interview in 2002 and 2003 with tourists to a temple in Feilai Gorge, a well-known tourist site in Northern Guangdong.

72 Feuchtwang, *Popular Religion in China*, 2001, 217.

73 Interview with a scholar who traveled to Guangdong, November 24, 2002.

74 See Katharina Wenzel-Teuber (Translated by David Streit), "People's Republic of China: Religions and Churches Statistical Overview 2011," *Religions & Christianity in Today's China*, Vol. II, No. 3, 2012, 29–54, ISSN: 2192–9289, posted at: www.china-zentrum.de, accessed on November 18, 2014.

75 Information collected by the author during his fieldwork in a Christian church in a major city in northern China in the summer of 2012.

76 See Wang Zhiyuan, "Jiji Wenjian de 2010 Nian Zhongguo Fojiao" (Positively and Stably Developing Buddhism in China in 2010); Ma Jing and Min Junqing, "2010 Nian Zhongguo Musilinjiao Gaikuang ji Dangdai Musilin de Zongjiao Cishan Shiye Fenxi" (An Overview of Islam in China in 2010 and an Analysis of Contemporary Course of Religious Charity by Muslims), in Jin Ze and Qiu Yonghui, eds, *Zhongguo Zongjiao Baogao 2011* (*Annual Report on Religions in China 2011*) (Beijing: Shehui Kexue Wenxian Chubanshe, 2011), 36; 85–6.

77 See Feng Bo and Le Ruizi, "Lun Cishan Jigou Zuowei Shehui Guanli Zhuti and Hefaxing: Yi Ren'ai Jijinhui weili" (On the Legality of a Charitable Organization as a Subject in Social Management: The Case of Ren'ai Foundation), paper presented at the 5th International Forum for Contemporary Chinese Studies, Beijing University of Technology, August 7–9, 2012.

78 See Feng and Le, "On the Legality of a Charitable Organization as a Subject in Social Management: The Case of Ren'ai Foundation."

79 Author's fieldwork in a Christian church in a big city in northern China in 2012.

80 Author's fieldwork in a Christian church in a big city in northern China in 2012.

81 For a detailed discussion on this policy, refer to Lai Hongyi, "Religions and Chinese Socialism: China's Religious Policies since the 1990s," in Yang Lijun and Shan Wei, eds, *Governing the Chinese Society: How the State Responds to the Rising Civil Society* (Hackensack, NJ, London and Singapore: World Scientific, 2016).

82 For a detailed discussion on these policies, refer to Lai, "Religions and Chinese Socialism," in Yang and Shan, eds, *Governing the Chinese Society*.

83 See Wang Zhiyuan, "Jiji Wenjian de 2010 Nian Zhongguo Fojiao" (Positively and Stably Developing Buddhism in China in 2010), in Jin Ze and Qiu Yonghui, *Zhongguo Zongjiao Baogao 2011*, 19–53.

84 See "Chinese Authorities Demolish Sanctuary of Wenzhou Church," posted at: www.ucanews.com/news/chinese-authorities-demolish-sanctuary-of-wenzhou-churc h/70807 on April 28, 2014, accessed on November 19, 2014.

85 Jean Oi discussed the complex coexistence of firm authoritarian control and expanded realm of freedom in the post-Mao era. See Jean Oi, "Realms of Freedom in Post-Mao China," in *Realms of Freedom in Modern China*, 2004, 264–84.

86 For related discussion, refer to the concept of zone of indifference discussed in Tang Tsou, *The Cultural Revolution and Post-Mao Reforms: A Historical Perspective* (Chicago, IL: University of Chicago Press, 1986), 18; Pitman Potter, "Belief in Control," 2003, 318.

Part 3

Political governance

6 Overhauling crisis management

Epidemics and beyond[*]

The ability of the Party state to promptly and effectively manage crises is an important indicator of its ability to govern the nation. Crises would throw up unexpected emergencies for the regime. Often these are critical but rare events, but the magnitude and scale of their impact far surpasses usual and daily matters. In the case of crises, the regime has very limited time to decide on its response. Should it misjudge the extent of the crises and fail to respond appropriately, it would incur extremely negative results. Excessive responses will cause unnecessary disruption and costs to the population and may result in mobilization of excessive institutional staff and people, leading to widespread alarm, panic, and extraordinary waste of resources. Inadequate and belated responses, in contrast, would not be sufficient to contain the crisis and may allow it to spread. Should the state fail to contain the crisis the populace will blame the state for its ineffectualness in handling crises in general and will question the regime's ability to protect the population and govern the nation.

For this reason an examination of crisis management of the current regime and the evolution of institutions of crisis management in China in the reform era provide a critical perspective of the regime's governance ability. Bruce Dickson acutely commented on an edited volume to which I contributed as follows: "The ultimate tests of a state's ability to survive comes from crises, whether a natural disaster or a man-made political crisis. For all those interested in the survival of the incumbent regime, this unique and informative book will be required reading."[1]

In this chapter I will review the transformation of the crisis management institutions in China in the reform era. In particular, this chapter will analyze the major transformation institutions for managing crises in this period. Institutions refer to the legal and administrative framework, entrusted jurisdiction and duties of agencies and units, and prescribed and practiced norms at the stages of preventing, monitoring, and containment of crises. Understandably, institutions are the key in effective and successful management of crises. Thus a look at institutional development in crisis management will provide a good picture of the state of crisis management in China.

I will cover major changes in the institutions of crisis management in China in the post-1978 period especially since 2003. Given the wide scope of the topic of crisis management, I will use pandemics and epidemics as a primary example in analyzing the changes in crisis management in China. In April 2003 the continued rampage of severe acute respiratory syndrome (SARS) triggered the most systemic reform of the management of epidemics and other crises in China. In April 2003 the Chinese leadership launched an open campaign to fight against SARS.[2] In the subsequent years China's institutions for managing major crises (including but beyond epidemics) have been over-hauled. As the change in epidemic management encapsulates the transforma-tion of crisis management in China, an analysis of the management of pandemic and epidemic crises thus provides a critical glimpse of the major overhaul in its crisis management in the past decade. In addition to document-ing and assessing the evolution of epidemic management in China before and after 2003, I will also discuss the establishment of a comprehensive nationwide crisis management system in 2006, a landmark event in crisis management in China. I will also provide a brief overview of several main changes in the management of crises essential to the survival of the regime.

In this chapter I will first give a brief overview of the main changes in Chinese crisis management prior to and after 2003. I will then conduct an in-depth analysis of the transformation of epidemic management in China before and after 2003. Finally, I will discuss the implications of the transformation of crisis management for the survival of the Party state.

Main changes in crisis management prior to and after 2003

The Chinese government categorized major crises in China into four types, namely, (1) natural disasters such as flood, earthquake, drought, and severe storms, (2) accidents such as plane crashes, train collisions, nuclear radiation leakage, mining accidents, and explosions in factories or mines; (3) public health crises especially pandemics and epidemics; and (4) public security incidents such as riots and demonstrations.[3]

Indeed, as exemplified by epidemic management to be discussed below, prior to 2003 crisis management mechanisms existed for major crises due to existing laws and corresponding regulations and the presence of relevant governmental agencies and posts. For example, the Ministry of Health was entrusted with fighting against the epidemics.

Yet, prior to 2003 crisis management institutions in China tended to be fragmented and not well institutionalized. Comprehensive and robust crisis management could be found mainly in a few high-risk functional areas. It was mainly agencies handling a high likelihood of crises, such as public security, fire fighting, and medical emergencies that had made very detailed emergency response plans. For example, between the late 1980s and 1991 the National Bureau of Seismology formulated quake response plans for areas highly prone to quakes. In 1996 the State Council published a State Preparatory Plan for Responding to Emergencies of Destructive Earthquake. About the same time, the National Defense Science and Industrial Commission coordinated the for-mation of a State Plan for Responding to Nuclear Emergencies. In the same vein emergency response plans were drafted mainly in industries with high risks, such as coal mining and chemical production. No or few plans for crisis management were drafted outside these industries and agencies. Moreover, comprehensive crisis preparation was conducted within one out of about 30 provinces. By 2001 only Shanghai had drafted a Comprehensive Preparatory Plan for Handling Disasters and Accidents.[4]

As a result, crisis management in this period failed to take into account the inter-agency demand for crisis management as well as the usually comprehensive impact of major crises. Very importantly, for many other sectors and other agencies as well as all but one province there was a lack of a comprehensive emergency response plan. These sectors, agencies and provinces confronted grave institutional defects such as unclear lines of command and ambiguous responsibilities at each layer of the bureaucracy for preparing for and handling crises, poorly specified routines and requirements for internal reports and public dissemination regarding crises, and even lack of procedures for handling crises and lack of daily precautionary methods against re-occurrence of crises. Understandably such a lack of a well-defined institution for crisis management often resulted in ineffectual and belated management of crises.

Moreover, the primary method for managing crises tended to be traditional. For example, information distribution failed to take the modern form of press release and often assumed the propaganda format of official announcements or public broadcasts, or internal documents circulated tightly among a small group of officials in charge of crisis management. One of the preferred methods for handling major crises such as flood and earthquakes was mass mobilization. That was the method the CCP tended to employ in the decades of its political struggle and military campaigns against the nationalists. This method, however, tends to be very costly as it involves mobilization of a tremendous amount of manpower and material input.

In the wake of the SARS epidemic in early 2003 the Chinese leadership became painfully aware of the hard fact that lack of crisis management institutions had undermined the local government's initial responses to crises and eventually hindered the central government's management of crises. Since then it had made considerable efforts to mend this institutional loophole. It had stepped up the building of crisis management institutions. In late 2003 the State Council set up a Small Working Group for Preparatory Plans for Emergency Responses (*yingji yu'an gongzuo xiaozu*). In January 2004 the State Council convened a work conference for drafting and perfecting preparatory plans for emergency responses at all agencies and work units. Since then the efforts for drafting emergency plans at all levels of the state and in all provinces had officially started. In May and June 2005 the state promulgated 25 preparatory plans for responding to the aforementioned four types of crises (natural disasters, accidents, public health events, and public security crises) and 80 preparatory crisis management plans drafted by agencies of the national government. By the end of 2005 localities had by and large completed their crisis management plans.[5] Eventually, in January

2006 the State Council promulgated the Comprehensive Preparatory Plan for Responding to National Public Emergent Events (*Guojia tufa gonggong shijian zongti yingji yu'an*). By November 2009 2.4 million crisis management plans had been made, covering provincial, municipal and county level governments.[6]

In short, crisis management in China prior to 2006 was scattering and sketchy and concentrated on a few high-risk sectors or a few regions, particularly Shanghai. In 2003 the Chinese leadership had launched unprecedented efforts to build a comprehensive, nationwide and multi-level crisis management system. By early 2005 this system was set up.

As stated, the aim of this chapter is to use epidemic management as a major case to illustrate the evolution of crisis management in China. The contrast in epidemic management, especially its institutions before and after April 2003 echoes the aforementioned point on crisis management. Prior to 2003, despite existing laws, regulations, agencies, and defined procedures, the institutions for managing epidemics were not well-defined and not comprehensive and lacked intra-agency and inter-regional coordination. This inadequacy in epidemic management systems was accentuated further by the secretive and half-hearted official attention to epidemics. Prior to April 2003 the Party leadership emphasized economic growth and social stability. As a result, the administration and the health department (the Ministry or Bureau of Health) managed the epidemics secretively and were reluctant to report epidemics publicly and respond swiftly and firmly to them. Adding to this defect were poor interagency coordination and the loopholes in the 1989 epidemic law and official accountability. Since April 2003 these institutional deficiencies have been incrementally addressed and national and local epidemic crisis management institutions have been strengthened. As a result, epidemic management has become more open, swift, and effective.

The following section of this chapter examines China's epidemic management before and after April 2003. For both periods, the following elements integral to epidemic management will be examined: laws and regulations that make up the legal framework; classification of epidemics; and the types of agencies that were entrusted with the duties. Furthermore, for both periods the three stages of epidemic management will be reviewed, i.e., preventive, monitoring, and containment stages.

Pandemic/epidemic management prior to April 2003

My analysis will start with the relevant laws and regulations, classification of epidemics, and agencies for managing epidemics. In a sense these three components help define the norms for epidemic management. The analysis will then move on to cover the preventive, monitoring, and containment stages. In the analyses both the prescribed norms and actual practice will be examined so as to provide a complete picture of epidemic management in China.

Legal framework of epidemic management

The epidemic management institutions prior to April 2003 were formally stipulated by the Epidemic Law of 1989 and the Implementing Measures of 1991. The Law on Prevention and Control of Epidemics (the Epidemic Law in short) came into effect in February 1989. The Ministry of Health promulgated the Implementing Measures for the Law on Prevention and Control of Epidemics (the Implementing Measures in short) in December 1991. The Epidemic Law of 1989 was the main law of the People's Republic of China regarding epidemic management, while the Implementing Measures were the main policy document regarding epidemic management.[7] Both documents, especially the Epidemic Law, stipulated epidemic management institutions. The Epidemic Law spelled out the duties and measures for each level of the government regarding epidemic management, including early warning and monitoring, reports, and management.[8]

Classification of epidemics

In particular, the Law stipulated three categories of epidemics. Class A included plague and cholera. Class B included 22 epidemics, such as AIDS, anthrax, dengue fever, typhoid and paratyphoid, gonorrhea, syphilis, measles, diphtheria, scarlet fever, epidemic hemorrhagic fever, rabies, and malaria. Class C included 11 epidemics, including pulmonary tuberculosis, schistosomiasis, filariasis, echinococcosis, leprosy, and influenza (Article 3). The Law authorized the State Council to add or remove Class A epidemics and the Ministry of Health to add or remove Class B and Class C epidemics (Article 3).

Agencies for managing epidemics

The prescribed agencies for epidemic management in the Epidemic Law of 1989 and the Implementing Measures of 1991 can be summarized as follows. Under the leadership of the Party Committee, especially the Party Secretary, the administrative branch at all levels was responsible for managing epidemics and announcing major anti-epidemic measures under their jurisdiction, and the health department was in charge of coordination of epidemic management by health bureaus and medical units. Below these governmental bodies, disease-control agencies played a key professional role in monitoring and detecting epidemics, and local medical units or disease control units took charge of quarantining patients with class-A or other epidemics, treating patients and suspected patients, and properly handling epidemic waste and items.

Overarching epidemic management agencies

The administrative branch at all levels, i.e., the State Council at the national level and the People's Government at the local level, was responsible for the overall epidemic management in the areas under its jurisdiction. Its role included interdepartmental coordination, drafting of epidemic plans, and organization of the implementation of the plans. Local administration could also adopt emergency measures for epidemic management after reporting them to the next higher level, whereas the State Council could adopt emergency measures directly (see Articles 4, 5, 9, 25, and 26, the Epidemic Law of 1989). In practice, the epidemic management was subject to the influences and instruction of the Party (especially the Party Committee and the Party Secretary) at the same level of the state. This was in line with the principle of the Party leadership. The Party or the Party Secretary could issue orders or guidelines on how to manage an epidemic.

In addition, in practice small groups might be established to coordinate epidemic management, provide technical guidance, and offer advice on etiological tests. The SARS management in Guangdong served as an example. In early February 2003 the Guangdong authority established the Guangdong Provincial Coordinating Group for Preventing and Controlling Unexplained Pneumonia, a Provincial Small Group of Experts for Guidance concerning Medical Aid, a Small Group for Guidance in Investigation in Epidemiology, and a Small Group for Technical Guidance at Etiological Tests. Moreover, the authority urged all localities to form corresponding groups and report their memberships and contact information by February 20.

Top medical agencies in charge of epidemic management

The health department took care of medical aspects of epidemic management. They included supervision and inspection of prevention, control, monitoring, and containment of epidemics; issuing of an order to any units or individuals to improve their anti-epidemic efforts; and imposition of compulsory measures on units or individuals who failed to adopt necessary anti-epidemic sanitary measures. The health department was responsible for reporting the epidemic conditions to the health department at the next higher level and the administration at the same level (Articles 5, 23, 27, 32, and 35, the Epidemic Law of 1989).

Meanwhile, the animal husbandry and veterinary departments of governments at each level were entrusted with responsibility for preventing, treating, and controlling infectious diseases of domestic animals and fowl that could be transmitted to human beings and animals (Article 18, the Epidemic Law of 1989).

Medical agencies providing technical expertise and guidance for epidemic management

The disease-control agencies, which later became the Centers for Disease Control and Prevention (CDCs), monitored, tested, and tracked the epidemic conditions, reported epidemic conditions to the health departments, and guided and supervised the anti-epidemic work. They might also participate in the quarantine of infectious patients (Articles 5, 15, 17, 24, and 27, Epidemic Law of 1989).

Medical units directly involved in epidemic management

Hospitals and clinics were directly involved in the prevention and control of epidemics and treatment and quarantine of patients. They should report epidemic cases to the local CDC. Medical suppliers were supposed to furnish sufficient equipment and medicine (Articles 5, 11, 17, 24, 27, and 35, Epidemic Law of 1989).

Prevention of epidemics

In China efforts for preventing epidemics have usually involved the government, the medical and health institutions, other social units and individuals. These efforts have included but are not limited to immunization programs, educational campaigns, sanitary measures, and proper procedures at medical units for minimizing virus transmission. These efforts will be detailed concisely below.

For decades the Chinese government has implemented immunization among children. Building on its immunization efforts from the 1950s to 1978, the Chinese government furthered its child immunization program in the reform era. By 1988, as much as 85 percent of children in all provinces were immunized against tuberculosis, poliomyelitis, measles, whooping cough, diphtheria, and tetanus. In 1990 and 1995, the majority of children in each county and township were immunized against the aforementioned diseases. In addition, efforts were made to contain the spread of hepatitis B, and by 1997, 50 percent of the children in China under one year old had been injected with the hepatitis B vaccine. Mass immunization of the population against these diseases (most of which were on the aforementioned list of Class B and Class C epidemics) helped to reduce the incidence of these infectious diseases.[9]

In addition, in the reform era the state continued the sanitary campaigns that it introduced in the 1950s. During the campaign, work units, neighborhood committees, and governmental organizations in all localities, especially cities, would be mobilized to clean up streets and buildings and kill four kinds of pest, namely, rodents, flies, mosquitoes, and cockroaches, as they were believed to transmit infectious diseases. In addition, localities were asked to establish or maintain public health facilities, provide better management of sewage, waste, and feces, and improve the hygienic condition of drinking water so that it met the national standard. In addition, in 1980 China joined the United Nations project for clean water by introducing tap water to the countryside. By 1995 tap water was said to reach 43.5 percent of the rural population. These efforts have helped to improve the sanitary conditions of the population and contain epidemics.[10] All municipalities, municipal districts, and counties were required to designate hospitals, clinics, and wards for treating infectious diseases (Article 11, Epidemic Law of

1989). However, during the SARS campaign it was revealed that the above requirement was not met, as many cities and counties lacked a designated hospital or ward to handle epidemic cases.

In addition, health departments at each level were required to have health organizations or personnel to take charge of prevention and control of infectious diseases for their respective units or their respective communities (Article 11, Epidemic Law). Three health stipulations were also imposed by the national government through the Epidemic Law to minimize the spread of epidemics. First, infectious disease patients, pathogen carriers, and suspected infectious disease patients were barred from jobs which the health administration department suspected could cause the spread of epidemics (Article 14). In addition, all health related institutions or units with samples of pathogenic microorganisms were required to rigorously abide by the requirements and operation procedures stipulated by the health department under the State Council (Article 15) in order to prevent release of the pathogen. Third, units should take effective measures to protect medical professionals engaged in anti-epidemic work from being infected (Article 20). However, again, as seen in SARS when an epidemic was largely new these cautious preventive measures might not be well implemented. Sometimes medical professionals might let their guard down because they are unfamiliar with the disease.

Monitoring of epidemics

According to the 1989 Epidemic Law the health department (the Ministry of Health at the national level and the Health Bureau at the local levels), as well as disease-control agencies, took charge of monitoring and inspecting epidemics, and supervising the medical and health work related to epidemics. Article 21 of the 1989 Epidemic Law also required immediate reporting of epidemic conditions by informed individuals to nearby medical care institutions, and health department disease-control agencies. The article also required medical, health, or anti-epidemic personnel on duty to report the following epidemic situations to the local health and anti-epidemic agency within the time limit prescribed by the health administration department under the State Council: patients, pathogen carriers, or suspected patients of Class A or Class B infectious diseases, or patients, pathogen carriers, or suspected patients of Class C infectious diseases. When a health and anti-epidemic agency found the spread of infectious diseases or received a report on the epidemic occurrence of Class A epidemic or of AIDS or pulmonary anthrax (Class B infectious disease), it should immediately report to the local health department, which should immediately report to the local government and the health department under the State Council. Article 22 of the Epidemic Law also prohibited governmental officials or health personnel from covering up or making a false report on the epidemic situation. Article 23 required the national health department to promptly release and publicize the epidemic situation and authorized local health departments to publicize local epidemic conditions.

In December 1991 the Ministry of Health issued the Implementing Measures for the Law on Prevention and Control of Epidemics. It imposed time limits for epidemic reporting and categorized AIDS and smallpox under Class A according to the nature of germs and viruses.[11]

During the SARS epidemic from January to early April, however, localities and the military were slow to report the SARS conditions to the national government. Some of them even noticeably underreported the SARS statistics. Guangdong during the early months of the outbreak of SARS provides an example regarding the monitoring of epidemics. Since mid-December 2002 a mysterious respiratory disease (which later was confirmed to be SARS) appeared in Heyuan City. The city authority reported it to the Guangdong Bureau of Health (GDBH) only in early January 2003. After mid-January 2003 the GDBH received a report on a mysterious infectious disease from Zhongshan City. In both cases the GDBH and Center for Disease Control and Prevention of Guangdong Province (GDCDC) dispatched a team of experts to investigate. The experts coined the disease atypical pneumonia (ATP) (or unexplained pneumonia).[12] Days before and during the Chinese New Year in late January the SARS cases grew rapidly in Guangdong. On February 7 the Acting Vice Governor Li Hongzhong submitted the SARS report from the GDBH to the Party Committee and the People's Government of Guangdong Province.

Containment of epidemics

The 1989 Epidemic Law authorized local government to take the following dramatic measures to contain epidemics after reporting to a higher-level of government: suspension of markets, assemblies, and cinema shows; closure of schools and factories and halting of business operations; temporary requisition of houses and transport vehicles; closure of contaminated drinking sources (Article 25). It also authorized the local government at the county level or above to impose health inspections on people or goods entering or leaving epidemic areas after reporting to the government at a higher level. Furthermore, it authorized provincial government to impose quarantines on areas of Class A epidemics within the province and authorized the State Council to impose quarantines on epidemic areas across provinces or quarantine the national border (Article 26). But in reality the local government was reluctant to take dramatic measures, such as suspension of markets and business and closure of schools and factories, as it would scare away tourists and investors and dampen local economic activities. This was seen in the SARS management in China prior to April 2003.

Article 24 of the Epidemic Law also required medical, health, and disease control personnel to quarantine patients and pathogen carriers of Class A infectious diseases and patients of AIDS and of pulmonary anthrax (Class B infectious disease) for treatment; take necessary treatment and control measures for patients of Class B and Class C epidemics (other than AIDS and pulmonary anthrax); and keep suspected patients of any Class A infectious disease under medical observation in designated places until the results of a diagnosis were available. These personnel should take necessary sanitary disposal and preventive measures regarding places and objects contaminated by patients, pathogen carriers, and suspected patients of infectious diseases and persons in close contact with them. Concerned patients of infectious diseases, and their relatives, friends, and work units, as well as the local organizations, were required to cooperate.

Again, the SARS management in Guangdong offers an illustrative example regarding the responses to epidemics by local governments and local health departments. On January 23, 2003 the GDBH issued a document to all health agencies at the prefecture level and above. It notified them that SARS (coined ATP) had occurred in the province, and advised these agencies to take preventive measures and quarantine patients. The document, however, was delayed for days and could only be viewed by senior officials at each recipient agency.[13] On February 3 the GDBH issued a document, calling on all hospitals to report SARS cases to CDCs and all CDCs to report SARS cases to the CDC of the next higher level.[14]

Before and during the Chinese New Year the SARS cases grew rapidly in Guangdong. On February 10, amidst widespread rumors, panic purchasing took place.[15] On February 11, Zhang Dejiang, Guangdong Party Secretary, inspected Guangdong Bureau of Health. Zhang set the following three guidelines: no efforts should be spared to save patients; the cause of the epidemic should be quickly ascertained and the epidemic should be effectively contained; normal work, life, and social order should not be disturbed.[16] Upon Zhang's suggestion, Guangzhou and Guangdong Bureaus of Health (GZBH and GDBH) hosted a live-televised press conference on the same day, and maintained that the epidemic was well under control.[17]

However, on February 12, panic purchasing occurred again in a dozen major cities in Guangdong. In response to the criticisms by national leaders, the administration and the Party committee in Guangzhou and Guangdong published SARS statistics and allowed temporary open discussion in the media. Governmental departments in charge of prices, industry, and commerce mobilized a large quantity of goods to stabilize supplies and prices. Governmental agencies organized daily disinfection and cleaning of public places such as shopping malls, railway stations, taxi stations, and bus stations. However, no quarantine and health checks at the border or mass transport hubs were imposed. Many travellers to and out of Guangdong were not aware of potential risks of infection, which resulted in the transmission of SARS outside Guangdong to Shanxi, Beijing, Hong Kong, Southeast Asia, and North America.[18] Moreover, open discussion lasted about two weeks. During February 11–16, the Department of Propaganda (DOP) the Party Committee of Guangdong mandated the news outlets throughout the province to follow its scripts in reporting SARS. In addition, from then on statistics on SARS were kept secret.[19]

Thus while the authority in China acted to cope with epidemics, it was unwilling to push for higher-profile measures and publicize the epidemic conditions and anti-epidemic methods. This severely limited the effectiveness of anti-epidemic efforts.

Drawbacks of epidemic management prior to April 2003

It is clear from the aforementioned discussion and management of SARS in the early months that several noticeable deficiencies existed in the epidemic management institutions prior to April 2003.[20] They related to the reluctance of the authority in charge in undertaking dramatic and decisive measures to contain epidemics and in publishing truthful epidemic statistics. They also concerned coordination of agencies and units for epidemic management across regions and soundness of laws and regulations.

Political concerns

Management of epidemics could be undermined by political concerns, especially the need to showcase stability. Prior to April 2003 social stability and economic growth were paramount concerns for local Party and even administrative leaders. These concerns led to downplaying of epidemic conditions and underestimation of destruction from epidemics. This defect was shown clearly in the initial management of the SARS epidemic.[21]

Restriction of Information

The usual approach of governmental and even medical agencies was to restrict information on the epidemic conditions to senior medical officials at all levels and downplay the epidemic conditions to the public, despite the fact that it violated the Epidemic Law (Articles 22 and 23). These agencies did so out of fear of affecting economic growth or derailing major political events. As late as early April the Ministry of Health and the Bureau of Tourism maintained that the SARS epidemic in China was well under control and that the situation was safe for foreign tourists and visitors.[22] The cover-up of epidemic conditions led to complacency and risky behavior of the population and even medical staff, leading to the spread of SARS to Hong Kong, Southeast Asia, and North America.

Ineffectual coordination

Inter-agency and inter-regional coordination was ineffectual. Li Liming, the head of the national CDC, admitted at a domestic press conference that China's "medical departments and the mass media" lacked proper coordination.[23] The valuable lessons for containing SARS which Guangdong had learned through the deaths of medical staff were not passed on soon enough to other provinces badly hit by SARS, including Beijing.

The SARS management leadership small group headed by the Ministry of Health apparently lacked the authority to coordinate anti-epidemic work among ministries and bureaus which were at the same or higher bureaucratic rank. Moreover, in Beijing the military apparently did not report the full SARS statistics soon enough to the Ministry of Health.[24] Moreover, government and the health authority in mainland China and Guangdong failed to share the up-to-date and reliable SARS conditions and effective treatment with their counterparts in Hong Kong. This caused the rapid and costly spread of SARS in Hong Kong.[25]

Gaps in the law

The Law of Prevention and Treatment of Epidemics contained gaps. It only mandated the immediate upward reports of four epidemics, namely, plague, cholera, AIDS, and anthrax by medical units and personnel or by CDCs to the local and national health departments (Article 21). SARS, a new but highly contagious and deadly epidemic, was not listed. At the press conference on the SARS epidemic in Guangdong on February 11, 2003, the Director of the GDBH explained that the bureau did not publicize the SARS epidemic quickly despite the fact that Heyuan reported to it on the disease on January 2, because the Epidemic Law of 1989 did not stipulate it as a disease that should be publicized immediately.[26]

Epidemic management after April 2003

In response to the ineffectual SARS management in early 2003, the Chinese government moved to overhaul epidemic management. The existing laws and regulations have been amended and new regulations have been introduced in order to fix the loopholes in these documents. In particular, two developments seem of special importance. First, on August 28, 2004 the Epidemic Law of 1989 was amended. Second, on February 26, 2006 the Preparatory National Plan for Emergency Responses during Sudden Public Health Events (the Epidemic Crisis Plan for short) was announced by the State Council. The latter signified that epidemic management institutions at the national level were being formally established. In the following paragraphs, the epidemic management institutions will be outlined. This section analyzes the main aspects of the nationwide epidemic management institutions after April 2003. While the plan and the Epidemic Law supply the most comprehensive rules regarding epidemic management, actual practice will also be examined.

Laws, regulations, and policy documents

The main policy and legal documents governing China's epidemic management include the following: the Epidemic Crisis Plan, the Epidemic Law amended in August 2004; the Law on Health and Quarantine within the

National Boundary promulgated in May 1987; Regulations on Emergency Responses During Sudden Public Health Events (the Health Crisis Regulations for short) promulgated in May 2003; and Regulations on Health and Quarantine Related to Domestic Transport promulgated in March 1999. The Epidemic Crisis Plan classifies major categories of epidemic crises, outlines the national and provincial epidemic management agencies, defines the management responsibilities, and stipulates norms for epidemic reporting and management.[27]

Classification of health crises and epidemics

Four levels of health crises are classified in the epidemic crisis plan: (I) grave (*tebie zhongda*); (II) major (*zhongda*); (III) big (*jiaoda*); and (IV) ordinary (*yiban*). Class I is clearly defined in the plan to include the spread of plague or anthrax in and beyond a large or medium-sized city, or in more than two provinces; spread of SARS or human-infected bird flu; spread of any unexplained epidemic in more than two provinces; appearance and spread of a new epidemic or a once-extinct epidemic; loss of samples of highly contagious pathogen or viruses; imports of highly contagious epidemics from countries or areas in communications with China; and any other grave epidemic identified by the Ministry of Health. In the amended Epidemic Law, Class A epidemics still include only plague and cholera, while SARS, humanly contagious bird flu, and snail fever (schistosomiasis) were newly added to the list of Class B. Now the grave epidemic crises are defined more broadly than they were in the 1989 Epidemic Law, allowing the national government to play a more active role in management of severe, unknown, or new epidemics.

Epidemic management agencies and funding

According to the Epidemic Crisis Plan, the administration remains the key governmental branch directly in charge of coordinating epidemic management, and the health department the key agency in charge of daily epidemic management. At the national level, in cases of need the Ministry of Health can propose to set up Headquarters for Emergency Responses during Sudden National Public Health Events (*quanguo tufa gonggong weisheng shijian yingji zhihuibu*). According to the Health Crisis Regulations, the Headquarters consist of representatives of relevant ministries, bureaus, and offices under the State Council as well as departments of the military, and the Premier would automatically become the General Commander. According to the Epidemic Crisis Plan, the people's government (the administrative branch) of provinces, cities (prefectures), and counties, as well as the military and the armed police should set up their health crisis command centers and expert committees equivalent to the national ones (see below for their descriptions). According to the Health Crisis Regulations, in cases of need the local governments can form headquarters for health crises, which are led by the head of the government (i.e., governor, mayor, or magistrate).

The Office for Health Emergency Responses (*weisheng yingji bangongshi*) is also the Command Center for Emergency Responses during Sudden Public Health Events (*tufa gonggong weisheng shijian yingji zhihui zhongxin*). This office was installed at the Ministry of Health as a bureau-level agency back in April 2004, two years before the national epidemic management institutions were established. It is in charge of managing daily health crises at the national level. The office is assisted by the Expert Consultative Committee (*zhuangjia zixun weiyuanhui*), as well as medical agencies, CDCs, health supervisory agencies, and customs health inspection and quarantine agencies.

Like the epidemic management institutions prior to April 2003, the health department is responsible for organizing medical agencies, CDCs, and health supervisory agencies to investigate and manage health crises, for organizing the expert consultative committee, for declaring the class of the health crisis, and for inspecting and supervising the health crisis management. It is required to build a medical team to respond during epidemics. The health department is also in charge of enforcing health laws and regulations.

The medical units are responsible for receiving, transporting, and treating patients, managing and treating medical wastes and summarizing clinical analyses of epidemics. The CDC plays a key role in the prevention and control of epidemics, for testing and monitoring epidemics, and for direct responses to epidemics. The customs inspection and quarantine agency is responsible for epidemic management at the border checkpoints. The government has budgetary funds to subsidize the professional and technical agencies for managing health crises.

The epidemic management institutions at the national level are replicated at the local levels. For example, back in December 2004, the same year when the Office for Health Emergency Responses Office of the Ministry of Health was installed, the Office for Health Emergency Response at the GDBH (OHERGD) was in operation in Guangdong. In addition, the OHERGD was assisted by a large expert committee comprising 123 experts and by eleven medical expert groups from across the province.[28] Later, in May 2007 the Office for Emergency Responses at the Guangdong Provincial People's Government (the administration) (OERGD) was established. In December of that year, Guangdong promulgated its Preparatory Plan for Emergency Responses during Sudden Public Health Events (the Guangdong Epidemic Crisis Plan for short). Similar to the national plan it classified health crises into four levels, placed the main responsibility for epidemic management on the shoulders of the provincial administration, and suggested principles and measures for epidemic management that were clearly patterned after those in the national plan. The OERGD and the OHERGD have remained the key coordinating bodies for managing crises in general and health crises including epidemics in particular.[29]

It goes without saying that the Party Committee and the Party Secretary at each level remain the ultimate power center behind epidemic management. Therefore, they can also intervene by issuing policy guidelines or instructions.

After April 2003, having learned a bitter lesson from SARS, the trend seems to be that they have paid closer and earlier attention to any emerging epidemic.

It is also worth noting that from April 2003 onward, great efforts have been made to enforce official responsibility on epidemic management. For example, when the nation or a locality is switched to a mode to prevent and contain a spreading epidemic, officials (especially administrative and health) will be held responsible for epidemic management in their jurisdiction. During the SARS campaign, from April to June 2003 thousands of officials lost their posts due to their ineffectual performance or negligent acts in containing SARS.

Prevention stage (planning for epidemic crises)

Ministries, Bureaus, and Offices under the State Council and local people's government at or above the county level are required by the Epidemic Crisis Plan to formulate epidemic crisis preparatory plans in light of their own conditions, the national plan, and the Health Crisis Regulations. The amended Epidemic Law requires the local governments to file their plan to the next higher level (Article 20). According to the Health Crisis Regulations (Article 11), the plan should include the following:

1   the membership and responsibilities of crisis management headquarters;
2   surveillance and early warning of crises;
3   the collection, analyses, reports, and announcement of crises;
4   agencies with expertise for crisis management and monitoring and their tasks;
5   classification of crises and plans for their management;
6   prevention and on-the-spot management of crises; emergency facilities, equipment, medicine, and instruments, as well as reservation and allocation of other materials and technologies;
7   building and training of the crisis management team.

As stated, in December, Guangdong promulgated the Guangdong Epidemic Crisis Plan, detailing agencies in charge, categories of epidemics, and basic measures for epidemic management. The provincial authority formulated 110 public health crisis plans to cope with a great variety of health contingencies, including epidemics.[30]

Moreover, the local governments are required by the Health Crisis Regulations to make efforts to prevent epidemics, educate the public about epidemic management, set up their monitoring and early warning system, and ensure the supplies of equipment and materials for epidemics, and conduct regular drills of epidemic management. The cities with districts are required to establish a special epidemic hospital or designate a capable medical agency to take charge of treating epidemics. It is clear that in the wake of SARS the Chinese authority has paid much greater attention to the prevention of epidemics. As a result, in anticipation of any known epidemics more efforts have been made at this stage than before.

The Chinese national and local governments have stepped up investment in building the CDCs nationwide. By 2004, 6.8 billion yuan had been invested for that purpose. Out of this sum, 634 million yuan was arranged by the National Development and Reform Commission for the first-stage construction project of the National CDC. The construction was inaugurated in 2004, and aimed for 76,000 square meters of floor area.[31] Beefing up the epidemic diagnosis, detection, and monitoring capacity helps China to stem the rise and spread of epidemics.

From 2003 to 2006 the State Council pushed for the building of medical emergency centers nationwide. In centrally administered municipalities, provincial capitals, and prefecture-level cities an existing hospital was selected for upgrade and expansion and to be turned into a designated hospital for treating epidemic patients. In each county a county-level hospital was slated to build an epidemic department or ward. These hospitals nationwide will be the main medical network for directly handling epidemic patients in order to minimize infection. National and local governments each contributed to half of an 11.4 billion yuan fund for helping central and western regions to build up the epidemic medical treatment system. Reportedly, by 2003, epidemic hospitals at the prefecture level were already in operation.[32]

In managing epidemics after April 2003 both the Party and administration have swung into action much earlier than they did for SARS. China's prevention of influenza H1N1 serves as a good example of the operation of the post-SARS overhauled epidemic management institutions. Influenza H1N1 originated in Mexico in early April 2009. By late April the epidemic had attracted international attention. On May 10, China noticed the first imported H1N1 case. The Chinese authority acted more decisively and much earlier at the prevention stage in order to stem the emergence and spread of this infectious epidemic. On April 28 and May 11, President Hu instructed the nation to guard against the flu. On April 30 the Politburo Standing Committee met to discuss the containment of the flu. The State Council meeting on April 30 announced the following measures to prevent H1N1 viruses: (a) cooperation would be initiated with Hong Kong, Macao, and the international community; (b) the Ministries of Health and Agriculture and General Administration of Quality Supervision would collaborate to prevent the epidemic; (c) strict health inspection was to be imposed at the border checkpoints, especially people from the affected regions, and the Law on Health and Quarantine within the National Boundary was to be activated; (d) travel health advisory notices would be issued; (e) cases and unexplained pneumonia and influenza should be monitored closely, cases should be promptly discovered and reported directly and early, and diagnoses, quarantine, and treatment of patients should be provided; (f) live pigs and pork products should be inspected closely; (g) the stock of anti-epidemic equipment, drugs, and medical instruments should be built up; (h) the knowledge on prevention and control of influenza should be popularized.[33]

In addition, the government has invested heavily in vaccination in order to stem the spread of the epidemic among the population. The government allocated over 1 billion yuan of special funds for research and development in vaccination for influenza A. In June 2009 the Ministry of Health received the H1N1 viruses from the WHO. By early September the vaccination for influenza A H1N1 was approved after clinical tests and started to be manufactured in China, the first nation in the world to do so. By January 2010, 59 million Chinese had received the vaccination, whereas the chance for cases of severe side-effects was merely 1.2 out of one million, comparable to the world level.[34]

Some of China's forceful measures in controlling influenza A were questioned by Mexico officials and the U.S. press. The Mexican government accused China of discriminating against Mexican nationals without symptoms, including those who did not go to Mexico for months. For this reason it chartered a plane in May to fly some of its citizens back home. It was reported by the *Washington Post* that international travellers with slight fever or in a flight where a passenger had a fever were quarantined and tested for influenza A.[35]

Monitoring of epidemics

The Health Crisis Regulations contain the following specific requirement for upward reporting of epidemics. Most of these stipulated timelines for epidemic reporting are much more stringent than those in the Implementing Measures of the Epidemic Law. The Measures mandated reports in the cities of any outbreak of Class A epidemics, AIDS, and anthrax within six hours, Class B epidemics within 12 hours, and Class C epidemics within 24 hours (Article 35). It also required provincial health bureaus to report any outbreak of Class A epidemics or mass epidemics to the Ministry of Health within six hours.

1   (Article 19) Provinces are required to report within one hour to the Ministry of Health in the case of an outbreak or a likely outbreak of an epidemic, an unexplained disease affecting a group of people, and mass poisoning, as well as a loss of an epidemic virus sample or a poisonous agent.
2   (Article 20) Epidemic monitoring agencies, medical units, and other work units are required to report within two hours to the health department of the local county government any instance described in Article 19, and the recipient health department should report within two hours to the local government, the health department of the next higher level, and the Ministry of Health.
3   (Article 23) The health department of the province where the epidemic crisis occurs should report promptly to its counterpart of the neighboring province. When necessary, the recipient health department should report promptly to medical agencies in the province.

4   (Article 24) The government publicizes telephone numbers for individuals to report risks for public health, as well as negligence of governmental agencies or officials in responding to epidemics.
5   (Article 25) The Ministry of Health is responsible for publicizing information on health crises and can authorize provinces to publicize health crises in the areas under their jurisdiction. The information should be timely, correct, and balanced.

Furthermore, the amended Epidemic Law (Article 30) specifically requires the medical agencies in the military to report outbreaks of epidemics to the Ministry of Health. This stipulation removes the loophole in the 1989 Epidemic Law.

Again, influenza H1N1 (influenza A) serves as a useful example. Not only were greater efforts made from the start to beef up the monitoring system, but also the disclosure and inter-regional sharing of epidemic information was more forthcoming. From mid-April, the Ministry of Health had started to monitor the epidemic and activate the health crisis management institutions. The Ministry of Finance had also allocated 301 million yuan to support the monitoring system of influenza A. The national budgetary support helped expand the number of laboratories in the system from 63 to 411 and that of designated hospitals from 197 to 556. The Ministry of Health also received budgetary allocation of 63 million yuan for detecting the viruses and providing diagnoses of the influenza. The Ministry of Agriculture also received 31 million yuan for monitoring the epidemic among the animal population and developing vaccination.[36]

In addition, epidemic disclosure had become much more efficient and transparent. On the morning of May 10, 2009, an influenza patient, a student who studied in the United States and visited his family in Sichuan, was found to be weakly positive in the two H1N1 virus tests. The medical experts in Sichuan met to discuss the case and agreed that he constituted a suspect influenza H1N1 patient. On the afternoon of the same day of this medical conclusion, the Health Bureau of Sichuan Province reported the case to the Ministry of Health and the case became the first case of influenza H1N1 in China. On the evening of the same day, the ministry announced the case to the nation.[37]

Chengdu Municipality immediately held a press conference at 3 a.m. on May 11 in order to head-off public panic, setting a rare precedent in press conferences in the early morning in China. Furthermore, inter-regional sharing of epidemic information was much improved. For example, the Bureau of Health in Beijing Municipality learned a great deal about the influenza through the nationwide epidemic reporting system which had information on China's first case of influenza A in Chengdu.[38]

Containment stage (crisis management measures)

The national government and the Ministry of Health are responsible for managing grave epidemics, and epidemics below that level fall on the shoulders of local governments. For a typical health crisis, the Health Crisis Plan (Article 4.2) clearly prescribes the following measures for local governments:

1 Organize relevant departments to join the crisis management.
2 Mobilize personnel, materials, transporting vehicles, and relevant facilities and equipment.
3 Define an area for disease control. When a Class A or Class B epidemic takes place, a local government at the county level or above can declare the epidemic area. Provinces can blockade areas infected by a Class A epidemic under their jurisdiction. However, decisions on blockading large or medium-sized cities, epidemic areas across provinces, major transport routes, or national borders have to be made by the State Council.
4 Adopt dramatic measures to contain epidemics, including restrictions on or closure of fairs, assemblies, cinema shows, factories, business, and schools; restrictions or a halt of massed gathering activities; temporary requisition of houses and transport vehicles; closure of contaminated drinking sources.
5 Manage the migrant population. Introduce epidemic prevention and control of migrants, and quarantine and treat patients.
6 Introduce health inspection at transport hubs and border checkpoints.
7 Promptly release correct and balanced information.
8 Lower-level governments to collect information and dissipate and quarantine relevant people.
9 Ensure supplies of commodities, suppress rumors, and crack down on price gauging and swindling.

Again the case of influenza A can be informative. It was spreading around the world from April 2009 onward. The first imported case of the influenza into China was reported on May 10. Premier Wen held three executive meetings of the State Council to arrange for the prevention of the disease, on April 28, May 5, and May 11, respectively. Many of the aforementioned measures prescribed in the meeting on April 28 remained in place.[39] On April 29, 2009, the Ministry of Health issued a draft technical guide on controlling the swine flu. The next day it renamed the swine flu influenza A H1N1 and put it under Class B epidemics. On May 12, 2009 it promulgated the medical treatment program for the flu.[40]

Upon discovering the first suspected case of influenza H1N1 on May 10, 2009, the Health Bureau of the Chengdu Municipality immediately switched the focus from prevention to containment of the epidemic. It announced four measures at a press conference on May 11:

1 Stepping up cooperation with the customs inspection and quarantine agencies and preventing additional "imported" cases of the influenza;
2 Monitoring potential subsequent cases from the known case and minimizing the spread of the epidemic;

3   Notifying the designated hospitals and fever clinics in the province to promptly report and check the cases of unknown pneumonia and influenza;
4   Publicizing the epidemic and needed measures.[41]

In the following months, Sichuan Province adopted a number of major measures to contain influenza A. They included vaccination of 1.29 million people, especially those who were vulnerable or were likely to be exposed to infection in their posts, arranging different work shifts for employees of governmental agencies and public institutions to reduce congestion and infections, banning of mass assemblies at the schools in Chengdu, and daily reports of the epidemic conditions by the schools and universities during the weekdays to the Chengdu Municipal Government.[42] With these measures in place the majority of residents in Chengdu surveyed were confident that the government would be able to contain the epidemic.[43]

Animal-related epidemic management

The aim of this chapter is to examine human epidemics. Nevertheless, it is also worthwhile to briefly outline the animal epidemic management, as certain animal epidemics can be humanly contagious, such as influenza H1N1 and bird flu.

On February 27, 2006 the State Council promulgated the Preparatory Plan for Managing Major National Animal Epidemics (Animal Epidemic Crisis Plan for short). Like the epidemic crisis plan, the animal epidemic crisis plan classified four levels of animal epidemic crises. It also specified agencies and headquarters managing animal epidemics, as well as monitoring and early warning, and reporting of and principles for managing animal epidemics. In addition to the plan, a number of laws and regulations help define the animal epidemic management institutions: the Law on Prevention of Animal Disease; the Law on Health Inspection of Imported and Exported Animals; and the Regulations on Emergency Responses during Major Animal Epidemics.

The Ministry of Agriculture is the primary national agency in charge of major national animal epidemics. In cases of need during major epidemics, national headquarters can be formed, and the director of the General Office of the State Council and the Minister of Agriculture serve as their head and deputy head, respectively. Major provincial animal epidemics should be managed by headquarters headed by the governor, assisted by local veterinary administrative departments. Local veterinary administrative departments (usually the Bureau of Agriculture) are responsible for local animal epidemics. Animal epidemic prevention agencies and customs health inspection agencies are professional health agencies responsible for surveillance, detection, quarantine, and other medical procedures for containing animal epidemics.[44]

Concluding remarks on epidemic management

This chapter uses epidemic management as a major case study to illustrate the strengthening of crisis management in China in the recent two decades, especially after 2003. Since 1991 China's epidemic institutions have included a legal framework and have involved the administration, the health department, CDCs, hospitals, and clinics. The law and relevant regulations also categorized epidemics and stipulated prevention, monitoring and reporting, and containment procedures. However, prior to April 2003, China's epidemic management was undermined by several institutional weaknesses: Party and administrative leaders' preoccupation with economic growth and social stability, lack of a preparatory plan and a practical guide for epidemic management, weak early warning and detection, inadequate financial input in the medical and anti-epidemic agencies, weak inter-regional and inter-agency coordination, slow disclosure of epidemic information to the public, and loopholes in the Epidemic Law and regulations. As a result, when the first SARS cases caught the attention of the local health department in Guangdong in early 2003, governmental and official responses to the epidemic were secretive, belated, and uncoordinated. As a result, SARS rampaged in Guangdong and northern China, China's economy was temporarily damaged, and its international image was tarnished.

In mid-April 2003, the Hu–Wen leadership acted decisively to manage SARS. It has overhauled epidemic management institutions since then. Information about epidemic conditions became transparent, inter-regional and inter-agency coordination was much improved, official accountability for epidemic management was enforced, and regulations on epidemic management were quickly promulgated.

In the subsequent months, the Epidemic Law was amended and several noticeable loopholes were remedied; a national epidemic management plan was announced, and local epidemic plan was mandated. As a result, epidemic management institutions at the national level have been established. A number of components of epidemic management are similar to those prior to April 2003. They included the agencies involved, their respective roles, and most of the measures prescribed in response to the epidemics stipulated in the previous anti-epidemic institutions or documents. Nevertheless, many significant improvements have been made. The Party and the administration have viewed proactive measures as beneficial instead of detrimental to effective epidemic management and economic growth. Timely and transparent information on epidemics, especially during the monitoring stage, is instituted and the stipulation is largely followed. Institutional preparedness and coordination, as well as financial inputs, have been rightly recognized.

Influenza H1N1 (also known as swine flu) provided a glimpse of the operation of the newly established national epidemic management institutions. Overall, China reacted swiftly and decisively to the epidemic and has been able to minimize the health damage of the virus. Some of its heavy-handed measures, however, were criticized by countries like Mexico or the United States for excessively restricting patients' or suspected patients' rights. These restrictions on people's rights are deemed questionable in countries (such as the United States and the United Kingdom) where personal freedom is extolled. But in China (and probably East Asian countries) with a collective culture and which has been long exposed to the devastation of pandemics, the public apparently cherishes a strong state's swift response to epidemics and quick success of controlling epidemic rampage. The Chinese public seemed to believe that these measures were justified given China's past painful experience with epidemics and its densely populated coastal and central regions. In contrast, the lax measures practiced in North America (and even Europe) seem to lead to a faster spread of the epidemic and a higher toll.

As a result of China's aggressive anti-epidemic efforts, the casualties of influenza A in China have remained relatively low. By January 10, 2010, there were 123,196 confirmed H1N1 cases in China, 113,994 of which were successfully cured.[45] The ratio of cases to the population was about one out of 10,000 and the death to population ratio was roughly one out of 1.8 million. In contrast, according to the estimates by the CDC in the United States, influenza A was estimated to have infected about 60 million people in the United States, about 15 percent of the population and over 480 times higher than that of China.[46] Not surprisingly, it was reported that as high as 85 percent of the Chinese surveyed were satisfied with the government's efforts to control influenza A. Management of influenza A thus became the government's medical effort with the highest public approval in 2009. The WHO also praised China's efforts to contain H1N1 viruses as highly effective, a marked departure from the outright criticism which this body levelled at China in early 2003 for its mismanagement of SARS.[47]

China's swift and aggressive response to the pandemic of influenza A suggests that once China activates its epidemic management institutions at national and local level it can effectively contain viruses and prevent the epidemic from claiming many lives, even though its forceful anti-epidemic efforts entail considerable costs for the freedom of suspected patients and people in possible contact with them.

One critical reason for the quick improvement in China is that once the Chinese state recognizes the importance of effective epidemic management, it can overhaul the flawed institutions. It is also capable of mobilizing its bureaucracy, medical units, and even the population to fight epidemics.

In some ways it is true that the non-democratic nature of the regime may undermine epidemic management, especially when the leaders do not recognize its importance and are preoccupied with other tasks and when epidemic information is held secret. However, once the Chinese authority values the usefulness of swift epidemic management its leaders can act promptly to address the outstanding flaws in the epidemic management institutions, and can discipline the bureaucracy and build the medical system. As a result, they can be transformed into effective fighters against epidemics.

Institution building for managing other major crises

Similar to epidemic management, institutions for managing many other crises have been overhauled or built since 2003. In particular, as stated, in early 2006 nationwide, comprehensive, and multi-level institutions for crisis management were set up in China. This was a landmark development in governance and institution building in China, as the institutions closed a loophole where crises might slip through the gaps of the existing institutions and go unattended.

The crisis management institutions established in 2006 contain the following major elements.[48]

1   Categorization of crises. As stated four types such as public health crises were identified. In addition, like health crises, four levels of crises are classified, including (I) grave (*tebie zhongda*); (II) major (*zhongda*); (III) big (*jiaoda*); and (IV) ordinary (*yiban*).
2   Preparatory plans within the crisis management system. Six types of plans were identified, including comprehensive preparatory plans, specific preparatory plans, departmental preparatory plans (such as those formulated by the Ministry of Public Health), local preparatory plans, preparatory plans by enterprises or public institutions, and preparatory plans by sponsors of large-scale exhibits, cultural, and sports events.
3   Organizations in charge of crisis management. The State Council is the highest organization entrusted with crisis management, which is assisted by the Office for Emergency Responses and Management (*guowuyuan yingji guanli bangongshi*). Ministries and bureaus under the State Council are responsible for crisis management at the national level under their jurisdiction. Local People's Government is responsible for crises in localities under their jurisdiction. Government at all levels can be assisted by a team of experts.
4   Operational procedures, covering forecast and early warning, responses to crises, post-crisis recovery and reconstruction, and information dissemination.
5   Logistics and support.
6   Supervision and monitoring.

Preparatory plans at the national and local levels are drawn up to cover the aforementioned four types of crises, namely, natural disasters, accidents, public health crises especially pandemics and epidemics and public security incidents such as protests.[49] In January 2006 the State Council promulgated a range of preparatory plans covering natural disasters, floods, droughts, earthquakes, geological disasters, forest fires, train accidents, urban subway accidents, aircraft accidents, sea rescues, large-scale power outages, nuclear accidents, work accidents, environmental accidents, and communication disasters. It also issued regulations on fireworks safety and on preventing and treating AIDS, and convened a work meeting on containing bird flu. In addition, it set up an inter-ministerial joint work meeting on closing and overhauling coal mines. In November 2007 the Law on Responding to Emergencies went into effect. The law entrusted the administrative branch of the state (the State Council at the national level and the People's Government at the local levels) with the power to manage crises, and required the administration to adopt necessary measures to prevent and manage crises, including drafting preparatory plans, making arrangements, acquiring needed equipment, and building needed infrastructure and facilities. It also mandated the administration at and above the county-level to train personnel, build emergency-response teams, conduct drills, and spread knowledge to the public regarding crisis prevention and responses.[50] Efforts to overhaul crisis management were also undertaken by local governments. For example, in 2005 the government of Wenzhou City, Zhejiang Province in coastal China issued an overall preparatory plan on responding to emergencies. Similar action was taken by the government of Bazhong City, in the eastern part of Sichuan Province in western China in June 2007. Both preparatory plans were modelled after that of the State Council and took into account certain frequent crises (especially natural disasters) of the locality.[51]

Arguably, crises that pose an immediate challenge to the Party state are public protests. These protests are coined "sudden collective incidents" (*quntixing tufa shijian*). Even in this area the state has made much headway in improving its crisis management capacity. In a handbook on crisis management targeted at officials and firm managers at various levels public protests were categorized by their causes and their scale. Their common causes were identified, and nine principles for managing public protests were summarized. The authors of the handbook emphasized the setup of ten types of mechanisms for detecting, preventing, and handling public protests. These mechanisms included early warning such as frequent visits by officials to the grass-roots levels, mechanisms for releasing tensions and grievances, mechanisms for clearly handling protests including designating a cordoned area, separating protesters from other people, controlling the key buildings and facilities in the area, and employing the police when protests escalated.[52] These prescribed institutions and methods showed the increasing sophistication in the Chinese state in managing public protests. It also reflected the institutional progress it has achieved in overhauling its crisis management.

Conclusions and analyses of the two recent mega-accidents

During 2003–2007 the Party state had made unprecedented progress in overhauling and improving its crisis management institutions. Prior to 2003, China's crisis management institutions were fragmented and concentrated in a few sectors that were most prone to crises. China had no comprehensive national multi-level crisis management system. This vulnerability of such a lack of crisis management institutions was exposed in the SARS epidemic. In the early months of the SARS outbreak the epidemic management was secretive, fragmented and poorly executed. The mismanagement of SARS undermined the reputation of the state outside and within China.

Between 2003 and 2007, alarmed by the ineffective management of the SARS epidemic due to inadequate crisis management institutions, the Chinese leadership, especially President Hu and Premier Wen, spearheaded the efforts to overhaul and build China's crisis management institutions. Using the promulgation of preparatory plans for crises as an indicator, by early 2006 a comprehensive crisis management institution was set up at the national level, and by around 2007 the basic structure of a multi-layer nationwide crisis management institution was formed. In 2007 the law on crisis management was also passed. As stated, crisis management institutions covered a wide range of common and most deadly crises in today's China. Judging by the easy access of books on the topic at bookstores in major cities in China, officials and firm managers were widely exposed to the idea of crisis prevention and the good practice in crisis management. Arguably, building crisis management institutions was one of the most important political achievements of the Hu–Wen leadership in their tenure of 2003–2013. With the basic crisis management institutions in place the Party state is no longer highly vulnerable to any possible crisis (such as the SARS). As reflected in its management of epidemics the regime's management of crises has considerably improved since early 2003. If we accept Dickson's proclamation that "the ultimate test of a state's ability to survive comes from crises," then the Party state has vastly improved its ability to survive and is apparently not in a fatal danger. This transformation is surprisingly swift and relatively successful.

In conclusion it is helpful to review two unprecedented disasters associated with safety in business operation that have taken place in China in 2015. On the night of June 1, 2015 a cruise ship Oriental Star travelling from Nanjing to Chongqing suffered from adverse weather conditions (a likely tornado). It capsized and sank in the Yangtze near Jianli, Hubei. Out of the 454 people on board, only 12 survived. The state reacted swiftly to the incident. Rescuers were quickly dispatched and the operation reached full scale in less than 12 hours. At the height of the rescue and recovery operation thousands of people and over 90 ships and boats were involved. On the next morning after the sinking, Premier Li arrived in Jianli to coordinate the rescue operation. In order to help with the operation in the water he even ordered the Three Gorge Dam in the Yangtze upstream to reduce water flowing through its turbine and to cut its power generation.

It was reported that the body of the ill-fated ship had been extended in order to take in more passengers and generate more revenue. This might have changed the center of gravity of the ship and made it unstable and prone to capsize. In addition, the fact that in highly stormy weather the captain of the ship continued the journey instead of finding a safe place to dock has raised questions about the practice of the sailors and the shipping company.

The other accident took place in Tianjin two months later. Late on the night of August 12, 2015 two explosions from the container storage site of

Ruihai Logistics, a firm handling hazardous materials in the Port of Tianjin in the Binhai New District of Tianjin, ripped through the storage site and devastated multiple nearby buildings and structures. The scores of firefighters who were on the scene fighting the initial fire prior to the explosions were instantly killed. As of August 16, the authorities revealed that 112 were confirmed dead and over 700 were injured. Many of them were harmed by shattered glass and structures in the wake of the massive shock waves from the second explosion. That explosion was recorded at 2.9 on the Richter scale by China Earthquake Network Center. It sent fireballs hundreds of meters into the air, torching thousands of new cars nearby, shattering glass and knocking over and hurting people as far as 10 kilometers away.

The authorities' responses to the accident were swift, yet the firefighting methods in the first hours of the accident were questioned. Soon after the fire in a warehouse at the storage site was reported at 22:50 on August 12, the fire fighters arrived and tried to put out the fire. There was a multitude of chemicals around the site, yet the authorities might not have known for sure due to the inaccurate information reported by the firm or the complexity of the hundreds or even thousands of containers at the site. In addition, the firefighters who arrived the earliest at the site might have lacked the best training and firefighting equipment as the fire was fast spreading. This might have resulted in their use of water to put out the fire, which some analysts argued might trigger violent reactions from chemicals such as sodium cyanide or calcium carbide stored at the site. The morning after the blasts military personnel arrived to assist with help and rescue. Importantly, 200 nuclear and biochemical experts, including a team from the International Atomic Energy Agency, were among them. They helped assess the presence and nature of chemicals at the site, providing valuable information for coping with the continuing fires and subsequent rescue. This swift response from the PLA was in sharp contrast to its belated and hesitant involvement after the Wenchuan Earthquake in 2008 and marked a major improvement in the military-civilian coordination in crisis management under the Xi–Li leadership. This may be attributed to Xi's quick assumption of the CMC Chairmanship and his quick decision-making after the blasts. In the days following the blasts thousands of firefighters from Tianjin and nearby provinces arrived. The fires within the blast zone were largely contained three days after the blasts. The government established a dozen monitor stations near the blast site to assess air quality. It closed off a nearby drainage outlet to prevent harmful substances from leaking into the water. Meanwhile, the state cracked down on rumors spread over social media while allowing its media to provide quicker and closer coverage of the blast sites after the accident.

The national and local leaders also acted quickly. On the early morning of August 13, Huang Xingguo, the Mayor and the acting Party Secretary of Tianjin arrived at the scene to lead the rescue operation. On August 13, President Xi and Premier Li dispatched Minister of Public Security and State Councilor Guo Shengkun to Tianjin to coordinate the management of the crisis. On

August 16, Premier Li arrived in Tianjin to inspect the blast scene and crisis management.

In the wake of the accident news media and social media revealed that hazardous chemicals stored at the site greatly surpassed the legal limit. For example, when applying for business registration Ruihai Logistics was allowed to store 10 tons of sodium cyanide, yet there were probably 700 tons at the site when the blasts went off. Similarly, calcium carbide might have been stored in quantities well over the approved limits. More seriously, upon arrival at the fire scene prior to the blasts the first group of firefighters could not find informed personnel from Ruihai Logistics who could tell them what chemicals and how much of them were stored at the site. This might have resulted in their use of water that might have triggered an explosion when the chemicals reacted.[53]

The fact that the blasts took place in the Binhai New District (BND), an equivalent of the Shenzhen Special Economic Zone near Beijing, is ironic. The BND has become the primary engine of growth in Tianjin and has been viewed as a rare and shining example of local economic dynamism in often economically conservative and backward Northern China in the 21st century. A key pillar of the growth in the BND has been the petrochemical industry and the BND hosts some of the largest petrochemical facilities in the nation. However, as the blasts expose brutally, underneath this rushed push for high growth has been an alarming neglect of codes of safety and laws at least by some of the big firms. The available news sources suggest that in the key firm involved in the blasts apparently safety practice and codes that should have been the essential protocols in its daily business with hazardous chemicals have not been closely observed. The causes of the blasts thus point us back to the central argument about the downsides of pro-growth authoritarianism in Chapter 3. If high growth is achieved at the expense of rules, health, and the environment, it will be unstable and will entail high social costs.

Both accidents have revealed an uneven track record of development in crisis management and crisis prevention. As far as crisis management is concerned, the state has immensely improved its capacity and has by and large swiftly and effectively responded to crises and major accidents after their occurrence. It has also overcome problems of military-civilian coordination which it witnessed and which hamstrung the early rescue operation in the wake of the Wenchuan earthquake in 2008. However, much improvement is needed in crisis prevention. In particular, the two firms involved in the two aforementioned accidents have apparently had problematic practices in following safety standards and proper operational procedures, sowing the seeds for deadly accidents. In addition, the ability and capacity of the local authorities in supervising the corporate observation of safety rules is in question as well. Thus, as far as crises are concerned, the most apparent risk in China is not crisis management where the state has improved significantly since 2003, but crisis prevention. Neglect of rules and laws by local officials, national or local firms, groups, and individuals can generate a high frequency of accidents and man-made disasters. This would place a high demand on the newly expanded crisis management capacity of the state authorities.

Notes

* An earlier version of this chapter was published as "Managing Pandemic/Epidemic Crises: Institutional Setup and Overhaul," in Jae Ho Chung, ed., *China's Crisis Management* (London and New York: Routledge, 2012), 87–107. Reprint by permission. The first two sections and final two sections have been revised.
1 See the endorsement page of Jae Ho Chung, ed., *China's Crisis Management* (London and New York: Routledge, 2012).
2 For literature on SARS in China, refer to John Wong and Zheng Yongnian, eds, *SARS Epidemic: Challenges to China's Crisis Management* (Singapore: World Scientific, 2004); Arthur Kleinman and James Watson, eds, *SARS in China: Prelude to Pandemic?* (Stanford, CA: Stanford University, 2006); Tommy Koh, Aileen Plant, and Eng Hin Lee, eds, *The New Global Threat: Severe Acute Respiratory Syndrome and its Impact* (Singapore: World Scientific, 2003). For a critical analysis of SARS management in Guangdong, refer to Lai Hongyi, "Local Management of SARS in China," in Wong and Zheng, eds, *SARS Epidemic*, 77–98.
3 Zhongguo fazhi chubanshe, ed., *Yingji guanli gongzuo shouce* (*Handbook for Emergency Management*) (Beijing: Zhongguo fazhi chubanshe, 2006), 1–2.
4 Yingdui Tufa Shijian Keti Yanjiuzu (Research Project Group on Emergency Responses), ed., *Geji Lingdaozhe Yingdui he Chuzhi Tufa Shijian Bibei Shouce* (*An Essential Handbook for Leaders at All Levels on Responding to and Handling Emergencies*) (Beijing: Zhongguo Shangye Chubanshe, 2012), 138.
5 Ibid., 138–9.
6 Yingdui Tufa Shijian Keti Yanjiuzu, *Geji Lingdaozhe Yingdui he Chuzhi Tufa Shijian Bibei Shouce*, 138–9.
7 Zou Keyuan, "SARS and the Rule of Law in China," in Wong and Zheng, eds, *SARS Epidemic*, 101–102.
8 For a text of the Epidemic Law of 1989, refer to Xue Lan, Zhang Qiang, and Zhong Kaibin, *Weiji guanli* (*Crisis Management in China*) (Beijing: Qinghua daxue chubanshe, 2003), 348–354.
9 Wang Ke'an, "Zhongguo mianyi shiye de chengjiu yu zhanwang (Achievements and Prospects of the Immunisation Project in China)," *Zhongguo liuxingbingxue zazhi* (*Chinese Journal of Epidemiology*), Vol. 20, No. 6, 1999, posted at: www.yufa ngz.com/xgfg/ylun/200605/214.htm, accessed on July 24, 2010.
10 "Aiguo weisheng yundong (Patriotic Sanitary Campaign)," posted at: http://baike. baidu.com/view/192267.htm, accessed on July 24, 2010.
11 Zou Keyuan, "SARS and the Rule of Law in China," 101–2.
12 Xu Nantie, *Fei dian de dianxing baogao* (*A Typical Report on "Atypical Pneumonia"*) (Nanhai: Guangdong renmin chubanshe, 2003), 4–30.
13 John Pomfret, "China's Slow Reaction to Fast-Moving Illness," *Washington Post*, April 3, 2003, A18.
14 Xu Nantie, *Fei dian de dianxing baogao*, 49–50.
15 Ibid., 54–62.
16 Ibid., 71–4.
17 Ibid., 78.
18 Ibid., 87–90; Yang Chunnan, Xu Qingyang, and Xiao Wenfeng, "Zujizhan: linwei buluan, chenzhe yingzhan (Blocking Action: In the Hours of Danger, Avoid Confusion and Meet the Attack Calmly)," *Xinhua*, April 22, 2003, posted at: http:// news.xinhuanet.com/focus, accessed on April 22, 2003. See Caijing zaizhi bianjibu (Editorial Department of Finance and Economics Magazine), *SARS diaocha tekan*

(*Special Edition of SARS Investigation*) (Beijing: Zhongguo shehui kexue chubanshe, 2003), 156–9.

19 John Pomfret, "China's Slow Reaction to Fast-Moving Illness: Fearing Loss of Control, Beijing Stonewalled," *Washington Post*, April 3, 2003. For a detailed analysis of Guangdong's management of SARS, refer to Tony Saich, "Is SARS China's Chernobyl or Much Ado About Nothing," in Kleinman and Watson, eds, *SARS in China*, 74–8; Joan Kaufman, "SARS and China's Health-Care Response: Better to be Both Red and Expert," in Kleinman and Watson, eds, *SARS in China*, 55–6.

20 For literature on SARS in China, refer to Note 2.

21 For the negative effect of this political concern on detection and treatment of SARS in the national CDD, see Cao Cong, "Chinese Scientists Were Defeated by SARS," in Wong and Zheng, eds, *SARS Epidemic*, 157–80.

22 This point was made in Tony Saich, "Is SARS China's Chernobyl or Much Ado About Nothing," 73.

23 Ibid., 80.

24 According to Saich, Premier Wen, on his visit to the national CDC, criticized the military for not reporting its SARS cases to the Ministry of Health (ibid., 81).

25 For an analysis of fragmented bureaucracy during the initial SARS management, see Lai Hongyi, "Local Management of SARS in China," 87–90.

26 Xu, *Fei dianxing de dianxing baogao*, 78–81.

27 These documents are collected in Zhongguo fazhi chubanshe, ed., *Yingji guanli gongzuo shouce* (*Handbook for Emergency Management*) (Beijing: Zhongguo fazhi chubanshe, 2006), 11–73.

28 "Guangdongsheng weishengting yingjiban jianbao (Briefings of the Office of Emergency Response of the Bureau of Health of Guangdong Province)," No. 1 and No. 4, 2004, posted at: www.gdwst.gov.cn/a/wsjb, accessed on July 25, 2010.

29 "Guangdongsheng tufa gonggong weisheng shijian yingji yu'an (Preparatory Plan of Guangdong Province for Emergency Responses during Sudden Public Health Events)," announced by the Office for Emergency Responses at the People's Government of Guangdong Province, December 2, 2007, posted at: www.gdemo.gov.cn/yasz/yjya/zxya/ggwslya/200712/t20071202_36148.htm, accessed on July 25, 2010.

30 "Guangdongsheng weishengting yingjiban jianbao."

31 "Jianquan tufa gonggong weisheng shijian yingji jizhi gongzuo de baogao (Report on the Work of Improving the Mechanism to Cope with Public Health Incidents)," *Zhongguo rendaxinwen* (*National People's Congress of People's Republic of China Newspaper*), April 15, 2004, posted at: http://health.sohu.com/2004/04/15/22/article219842254.shtml, accessed on July 25, 2010.

32 Ibid.

33 "Wen Jiabao zhuchi Guowuyuan huiyi, bushu zhuliugan fangkong gongzuo (Wen Jiabao Chaired a State Council Meeting and Arranged Prevention and Control of Swine Flu)," *Xinhua*, April 28, 2009, posted at: http://news.qq.com/a/20090428/001205.htm, accessed on April 21, 2010.

34 "Zhongguo chao bacheng gongzong manyi zhengfu fangkong jialiu jucuo (Over Eighty Percent of the Public in China Satisfied with Governmental Measures for Preventing and Controlling Influenza A)," *Guangming Daily*, January 15, 2010, posted at: www.39world.com/healthnews/0123T94O2010849479.html, accessed on April 21, 2010.

35 Ariana Eunjung Cha, "Caught in China's Aggressive Swine Flu Net: Quarantine Measures Keep Cases Down But Virtually Imprison Healthy Travellers," *Washington Post*, May 29, 2009.

36 "Duikang jialiu: woguo zhangfu caiqu de cuoshi (Countering Influenza A: Measures Taken by the Government in Our Country)," posted at: http://13058757.blog.hexun.com/40077804_d.html on November 10, 2009, accessed on April 21, 2010.

37 "Woguo neidi faxian shouli jiaxing H1N1 liugan yisi bingli (The First Suspect Case of Influenza H1N1 Is Found in Mainland of Our Country)," posted: at http://bbs.xxrb.com.cn/thread-99665-1-1.html, accessed on July 29, 2010.

38 "Duikang jialiu: woguo zhangfu caiqu de cuoshi."

39 "Wen Jiabao zhuchi Guowuyuan huiyi, bushu zhuliugan fangkong gongzuo."

40 "Duikang jialiu."

41 "Fasheng shuruxing bingli, wosheng you 'fang' zhuan 'kong' (As an Imported Case of Disease Occurred, Our Province Has Switched from 'Prevention' to 'Control')," announced at Chengdu Municipal People's Government Press Conference, May 12, 2009, posted at: www.chengdu.gov.cn/newsrelease/list.jsp?id=256092, accessed on July 29, 2010.

42 "Fang jialiu kuoshan, jiguan shiye danwei cuoshi shangban (In Order to Prevent the Spread of Influenza A Agencies and Institutions Introduce Different Shifts)," *Huaxi dushi bao* (*West China City News*), September 12, 2009, posted at: www.wccdaily.com.cn/epaper/hxdsb/html/2009-09/12/content_92530.htm, accessed on July 29, 2010; "Shengweishengting zuori zhaokai fabuhui, 129 wan ren jiezhong jialiu yimiao (Provincial Bureau of Health Convened Press Conference Yesterday and 1290 Thousands of People Received Influenza A Vaccination)," December 30, 2009, posted at: http://cd.goodcar.cn/09/1230/000074339.shtml, accessed on July 29, 2010; "Chengdu fangkong jialiu, shixing 'ri baogao zhidu' (In order to Prevent and Control Influenza A, Chengdu Introduces 'Daily Report' Institutions)," September 8, 2009, posted at: www.sina.com.cn, accessed on July 29, 2010.

43 Han Li, "Shiming 'Fangkong jialiu' xinxing zhishu gaoda 94.8% (Confidence Index of City Residents in 'Preventing and Controlling Influenza A' Reached High 94.8%)," *Chengdu shangbao* (*Chengdu Business Times*), November 19, 2009, posted at: www.chengdu.gov.cn/glamor_chengdu/detail.jsp?id=291789, accessed on July 29, 2010.

44 See "Guojia tufa zhongda dongwu yiqing yingji yu'an (The Preparatory Plan for Managing Major National Animal Epidemics)," in Zhongguo fazhi chubanshe, ed., *Yingji guanli gongzuo shouce*, 169–84.

45 "Zhongguo chao bacheng gongzong manyi zhengfu fangkong jialiu jucuo."

46 Data for influenza A in the United States by March 13, 2010 came from the following source: Centers for Disease Control and Prevention (of the United States), "CDC Estimates of 2009 H1N1 Influenza Cases, Hospitalizations and Deaths in the United States, April 2009–March 13, 2010," a document of Centers for Disease Control and Prevention, April 19, 2010, posted at: www.cdc.gov/H1N1flu/pdf/H1N1_Estimates_Apr19.pdf, accessed on April 24, 2010. Earlier data come from the following source: "ECDC Daily Update: Pandemic (H1N1) 2009, January 18, 2010," a document of the European Centre for Disease Prevention and Control, January 18, 2010, posted at: http://ecdc.europa.eu/en/healthtopics/Documents/100118_Influenza_AH1N1_Situation_Report_0900hrs.pdf, accessed on April 23, 2010.

47 "Zhongguo chao bacheng gongzong manyi zhengfu fangkong jialiu jucuo."

48 Zhongguo fazhi chubanshe, ed., *Yingji guanli gongzuo shouce* (*Handbook for Emergency Management*) (Beijing: Zhongguo fazhi chubanshe, 2006), 1–10.

49 Zhongguo fazhi chubanshe, ed., *Yingji guanli gongzuo shouce* (*Handbook for Emergency Management*) (Beijing: Zhongguo fazhi chubanshe, 2006), 1–2.

50 Shan Chunchang, Xue Lan, Zhang Xiulan, and Ding Hui, eds, *Zhongguo Yingji Guanli Dashiji (2003–2007)* (*A Chronology of Management of Emergencies in China, 2003–7*) (Beijing: Shehui Kexue Wenxian Chubanshe, 2012), 311–30, 479–80.

51 Information from http://www.baidu.com on the preparatory plans announced by the government of Wenzhou and Bazhong, accessed 19 August 2014.

52 Yingdui Tufa Shijian Keti Yanjiuzu (Research Project Group on Emergency Responses), ed., *Geji Lingdaozhe Yingdui he Chuzhi Tufa Shijian Bibei Shouce*, 94–129.

53 Sources of information on both accidents came from multiple sources on the internet. They are too numerous to be listed in full.

7   Smoothening leadership succession

In the past 66 years the People's Republic of China has witnessed the most dramatic events closely associated with leadership succession. The most dramatic events in Mao's China included the tragic deaths of Mao's two successors within a less-than-two-year period during the turbulent Cultural Revolution, namely, that of President Liu Shaoqi in November 1969 and then that of Marshal Lin Biao in September 1971. In the reform era the dramatic events associated with leadership succession included the purges of Deng's two successors within less than two and half years—Hu Yaobang's loss of status as Deng's successor in January 1987 and that of Zhao Ziyang in late May 1989 during the Tiananmen protests.

For this reason, the focus of this chapter is to review institutional changes in Chinese leadership succession and their noticeable implications for political stability and progress in China. I will highlight the significance of leadership succession and of its improvement in the first section. I will then review the failures of leadership succession prior to 1992 and the progress in promotion of young leaders in the reform era will be reviewed in the second section. This is followed by an analysis of progress in political succession since 1992 and the emerging norms in the third section. The fourth section is an analysis of the factional politics in reform-era China, especially after 1992. Finally, the successes and limits in leadership succession in China will be assessed.

The theme in this chapter is as follows. Since 1992 the CCP has made considerable progress in institutionalizing leadership succession through arrangements such as age and term limits and three key posts held by the core leader. Despite various limits the CCP has managed to avoid the severe and open splits within the leadership and between the incumbent and the successors as it witnessed during the Cultural Revolution and during 1986–89.

Political preeminence of leadership succession

As in an authoritarian regime the highest political power in China since 1949 has been concentrated in the hands of top leaders. Under a democratic regime, voters play the critical role in deciding the top leader. Under an authoritarian regime political succession is far more tricky and difficult. First, it is the incumbent top leaders and, to some extent, the veteran leaders who have the final say in the selection of the successor to the top leader. Second, succession to the top leadership implies change of leaders with new policy outlooks and a different governance style. It may result in major changes in domestic and external policies.[1]

Third and most importantly, leadership succession in authoritarian regimes (including the communist countries and those regimes in the developing world) has been regarded as one of the major weaknesses of the regimes compared to monarchies or constitutional democracies.[2] Back in 1962 Myron Rush even stated vividly: "In any personal dictatorship or tyranny, one thing is certain: some day there will be a succession crisis."[3]

Prior to 1992 the experience of the CCP fit this description neatly. Between the late 1950s and 1989, leadership succession in China was unsuccessful, ending with purges and even deaths of the successors. During 1989 and early 1992 the tension between the paramount leader and his successor escalated into a showdown. These setbacks will be detailed in the following section.

More importantly, the most serious crises and politically the most destructive events the CCP has experienced since 1949 were intertwined and to various extents originated from the tension between the top leader and his chosen successor. In Mao's China the Cultural Revolution (CR) of 1966–76 was the most destructive for the CCP. The leaders and major institutions of the Party at the national and local levels were attacked, except for those who clustered around Mao. It is no exaggeration to say that during 1966–68 the Party was uprooted by the rebellious masses. As a result of the CR the Party was discredited and undermined. This devastating blow to the Party, nevertheless, was closely inter-twined with the conflict between Mao and his two successors. In the first period of the Cultural Revolution Mao, who orchestrated the event, mobilized the Red Guards and the masses to attack Liu Shaoqi and cadres who embraced Liu's pragmatic economic policies. These national and local leaders were stripped of power. At the second period of the CR, Mao grew suspicious toward Lin Biao who (with his followers) tightly controlled the military. Mao and Lin entered a fierce power struggle, ending with the tragic death of Lin.[4]

In the reform era the single event when the leadership of the CCP seemed to be at risk was the Tiananmen movement in 1989. For months protests broke out and persisted in hundreds of cities including the largest cities throughout the nation. Protestors exposed serious corruption within the Party and called for democratization. In the end the military was called into Beijing to forcefully suppress the popular movement, resulting in a severe blow to the political legitimacy of the Party and the People's Liberation Army that prided them-selves as representing the people. Again, the conflict between Deng and his successor Zhao Ziyang intensified as the movement progressed and it peaked when Deng decided to call in the military to terminate the movement in late May.

Even though leadership succession has become smoother after 1992, upon important junctures when top Chinese leaders are selected rumors about tensions and conflict between the outgoing and the incoming top leaders have continued to resurface and become even commonplace in news reports and analyses on China. Leadership succession thus constitutes the most intriguing yet the most important component of the Chinese politics.[5]

Limited progress and failed succession prior to 1991

Between 1949 and 1991 leadership succession in China had been a failure. Mao could not tolerate the policies and/or power of his first two heirs apparent, initially President Liu Shaoqi and then Marshal Lin Biao. Both of his successors died tragically. Liu died in political desperation and isolation and severe physical pain related to his illness in 1969. Two years later, Lin Biao died in a plane crash on his flight from China to the Soviet Union as he ran for his life. Mao finally settled for his third successor, that is, Hua Guofeng. Hua, a former Party Secretary of Mao's home province, who lacked rich military and administrative experience and an extensive power base, was submissive to Mao and designated by Mao to be his successor. However, slightly over two years after Mao's death in 1976, Hua was outmaneuvered by Deng Xiaoping and was forced to surrender his status as the top post-Mao leader to Deng.

During 1986–1991 Deng's relations with his first two chosen successors seemed to resemble those of Mao. Deng deserted his first two successors after he had a severe clash with them over political reform. Hu Yaobang was replaced by Zhao Ziyang as the General Secretary of the Party in early 1987. Zhao was replaced by Jiang Zemin around May 1989.

The first most important cause of tension between the top leader and his successor has been largely over policies. Mao viewed Liu Shaoqi's pragmatic economic policies as a betrayal of communism. After the CCP came to power in 1949 Liu encouraged the capitalists to continue to manage and expand urban enterprises. He also tolerated an emerging wealth gap among peasants in the wake of the land reform of 1950–2. After Mao's Great Leap Forward (GLF) of 1958–61 ended with the largest famine in Chinese history Liu supported household farming and the abandonment of collective farming.

While Deng agreed with Hu's and Zhao's agendas for profound economic reforms he viewed the political openness of the latter two as their fatal weakness that could undermine the CCP. After Jiang replaced the ousted Zhao in the summer of 1989 Deng abhorred Jiang's economic conservatism during 1989–91. I will detail Deng's relations with each of his three successors below.

Hu Yaobang, the General Secretary of the CCP, was chosen as Deng's successor. During May–November 1978, as the Director of the Organizational Department of the CCP, Hu led an intense ideological debate in China. Formally it was about the criterion for judging truth or the right policies, but in reality the debate was about whether the Party should formally support the policies and ideology of late Mao, which Hua insisted the Party should. Hua was eventually defeated. Hu thus helped Deng to assume the status of the paramount post-Mao leader in late 1978. However, from the mid-1980s onwards, Deng and Hu started to show their differences over two major issues. One was how to respond to calls by intellectuals, college students and liberally-minded Chinese over political reform and democratic initiatives. Hu supported a moderate and restrained response, whereas Deng supported a harsh crackdown by ousting the liberal from the Party and punishing the leaders of the democratic campaign. Their differences intensified during the student protests in several major cities in China in late 1986 and early 1987. The other issue was about the retirement of veteran leaders including Deng through Hu's call for abolition of life tenures. His call during 1985–86 angered Deng. In early 1987 veteran leaders led by Deng, Chen Yun and Bo Yibo forced Hu to resign from his post of the General Secretary of the CCP.

Zhao Ziyang, the then premier, was chosen by Deng as his successor and to take over the post of the General Secretary of the Party. Zhao downplayed the issue of political liberalism that Deng was much concerned with and focused on marketization. During the Tiananmen movement of 1989 Zhao supported a moderate approach toward students' call for democracy. Deng, after seeing Zhao fail to defuse protests from students by mid-May, lost patience and opted for a forceful takeover of the capital from the protestors. When Zhao refused to support the martial law, he was stripped of his post and was placed under house arrest until his death in 2005.

Jiang Zemin, then Party Secretary of Shanghai, was tipped by Deng to be the General Party Secretary for Jiang's ability to subdue massive student protests without resorting to force. Reluctantly assuming the post, Jiang was aware of his precarious position. Upon seeing that economic and even political conservatism was gaining an upper hand in the wake of the Tiananmen crackdown Jiang closely toed the line spelled out by leading conservatives such as Chen Yun and Deng Liqun, and repeatedly ignored Deng's call for re-starting economic reform. For example, in the spring of 1991, *Jiefang ribao* (*Liberation Daily*), the Party newspaper in Shanghai, published an editorial under the pseudonymous author Huang Fuping, calling for a fresh round of economic reforms. This editorial was authorized by Deng Xiaping. However, the main newspapers and journals controlled by the national Party, such as *Qiushi* and *Guangming Daily*, attacked this editorial. Frustrated by Jiang's refusal to rekindle economic reforms, Deng decided to tour southern China in early 1992 in order to campaign in person for marketization. Deng's southern tour was in effect a political showdown with Jiang. Should Jiang have continued to reject marketization he would have been replaced by Deng.[6]

The second cause is the perceived political threat from the successor to the top leader due to the rapidly increasing power or disloyalty of the former. Mao could not sit still to watch Liu overshadow himself after Mao's disastrous policies during the Great Leap Forward of 1958–61. At the Central Enlarged Work Conference in 1962 which was attended by 7,000 national and local elite cadres of the Party, Mao attempted to defuse criticisms. Liu broke out of the silence Mao tried to enforce upon the cadres who attended the meeting. Liu gave an overall negative assessment of the GLF and attributed it to human errors, implicitly criticizing Mao. Many cadres spontaneously echoed Liu's remarks. Mao lost much of his authority among the cadres and had to rally support from the generals, especially Lin Biao.[7]

However, as soon as Lin helped Mao to oust Liu from the Party in 1969, Mao started to become suspicious toward Lin. Lin's four generals controlled four major departments/services of the military and served as respectively the head of the general staff, the navy, the air force and logistical department of the military. In October 1969, without consulting Mao, Lin, as the First Vice Chairman of the Central Military Commission (CMC), issued an order to the military and placed the military in the state of emergency combat readiness in the name of preparing for a possible attack from the Soviet Union. Mao, the Chairman of the CMC, was much displeased.[8] He saw Lin's free exercise of his control of the military as a grave threat to him. Mao could not watch quietly Lin's full-fledged control of major arms and departments of the military. Hence he plotted to undermine Lin's control of the military, triggering a showdown between them that ended in Lin's tragic death and collateral damage to Mao's personal cult and authority in China.

Deng was very unhappy upon learning of Hu Yaobang's call in 1986 for the retirement of veteran leaders, including Deng himself. Likewise, Deng viewed Zhao's revelation in meeting Gorbachev who visited Beijing during the protests in May 1989 that Deng was the ultimate decision maker in China as shifting the protesting students' criticisms away from Zhao and other leaders toward Deng himself.[9]

Grooming of young leaders and partial retirement of veterans

During 1978–92 despite a failure to institutionalize the succession of the core leader, there was a new and encouraging development in promotion of leaders into the Politburo and provincial level.[10] When the succession of the core leader and the top leaders became institutionalized to a limited extent, the role of these young, well-educated and technocratic leaders in the political economy of post-Mao and post-Deng China became noticeable.

Under Deng, young, well-educated, and experienced technocratic leaders were promoted to key national and provincial positions. A study of members of the Politburo, the top echelon of front line leaders of 1977–92 by Lai suggested the following. Maoists and conservatives steadily exited the most powerful political organ in China whereas reformists gradually dominated the Politburo.

A growing percentage of them had work experience in the government (and to a lesser extent the Party) at both national and local levels, were familiar with economic, social, and local affairs, and had graduated from colleges. An overwhelming percentage of young leaders worked in the coastal region and hence might have inevitably favored coastal development. The North consistently appeared to have produced more national leaders than the rest of the nation, yet in 1992 it was surpassed by the East. Specifically, prior to 1992, Beijing, Guangdong, and Sichuan produced more powerful national leaders than the other provinces. In 1992, these provinces were replaced by Shanghai. Therefore, national patrons might have helped the faster development in Guangdong and Beijing in the 1980s and Shanghai after the early 1990s.[11]

Xiaowei Zang identified two career paths among the cadres, namely, Party cadres and governmental officials. He argued that each of these two paths had a different career and credential.[12]

The profiles of the core leader and the premier since 1989 (namely, Jiang Zemin, Zhu Rongji, Hu Jintao, Wen Jiabao, Xi Jinping, and Li Keqiang) suggested that these two top posts tend to be filled by leaders who have had considerable experience of serving at local and national Party or governmental agencies. This mixture of local and national experiences would provide these leaders a unique understanding of the complexity of governance in such a vast and populous nation as China.

Lai also argued that these technocratic young leaders (especially those who were supportive of marketization) helped manage and sustain economic reforms in the reform era. Despite the reservations of conservative leaders over economic liberalization during 1980–1992, reformist young leaders, such as Hu Yaobang, Zhao Ziyang, Wan Li, Qiao Shi, Li Ruanhuan, Zhu Rongji, and members of the Central Committee of the CCP Ren Zhongyi (former Party Secretary of Guangdong) and Ye Xuanping (former Governor of Guangdong), successively helped Deng to design and implement economic reforms. In 1992, young technocratic leaders, such as Qiao Shi, Li Ruihuan, and Zhong Rongji, helped Deng to secure the Party's acceptance of marketization. Since then, they have been sustaining economic reform.[13] Some of these young technocratic leaders, such as Jiang Zemin, Hu Jintao, and Xi Jinping, became the core leader successively. A number of them, such as Zhu Rongji, Li Peng, Li Ruihuan, Wu Bangguo, and Wen Jiabao, emerged as top leaders and were members of the Politburo Standing Committee after Deng.

Since 1978 the CCP has also started to institutionalize the retirement of veteran officials. Research based on extensive interviews revealed that during the retirement process cadres at the middle or lower levels tended to bargain for a good retirement payment or the arrangement of jobs for their children. During 1980–8 4.75 million cadres were retired nationwide. Nevertheless, there was a major exception on the national and provincial levels. Veteran officials were semi-retired, surrendered their frontline posts, and took up advisory and honorary positions at the middle or higher levels (such as the provincial and national levels).[14] At the national level the Central Advisory Commission of the CCP was created in 1982 at the Twelfth Party Congress to accommodate these influential veteran leaders. Deng served as the Chairman during 1982–7 (and also held the CMC Chairmanship until 1989), succeeded by Chen Yun (who served during 1987–92). The presence of veteran leaders led to tensions with the frontline leaders such as Hu Yaobang and Zhao Ziyang.

Emerging norms in succession since 1992

Nevertheless, leadership succession in China has undergone substantial though partial institutionalization. In the post-Deng China, top leaders include all the members at the Politburo Standing Committee (PSC) of the CCP. The number of the PSC members was five during most of the period of 1977–92, and increased to seven during 1992–2002 and during 2013–15. It was nine during 2003–12. Two of the most influential and resourceful leaders include the President (the head of the state), the General Secretary of the CCP, and the Chairman of the Central Military Commission of the State and the Party (all three posts have been held by the same person since 1994) and the Premier (the head of the administration). Other posts include the head of the Party's Central Disciplinary Inspection Commission in charge of investigating the corruption and wrong-doing of party members and leaders, the head of legislature (the Chairman of the Standing Committee of the National People's Congress (NPC)), the head of the Party's united front platform incorporating non-CCP parties, religions, ethnic minorities, business elites, and intellectuals (the Chairman of the National Committee of the Chinese People's Political Consultative Conference, or CPPCC), the Vice President, and the Executive Vice Premier.

Gradually, several norms for selecting top leaders have been accepted by the ruling elites in China. They are age limit, term limit, the right profiles, and the right factional base. Initially, they originated from Deng's efforts back in the early 1980s to promote younger leaders with experience and ability to administer the Party state amidst reform and transformation. Over the decades these norms, especially the first two, were gradually accepted and increasingly clearly specified.

The first norm is age limit. Age limits for top leaders were set largely by exemplary precedents. Back in 1997, before the 15th Congress of the CCP, after debates and a compromise, the then legislative chief Qiao Shi, aged 70, retired. He set an example himself, following a consensus on two following norms that was believed to have been reached within the Party. First, 70 would be the age limit and second, there should be two term limits for top leaders.[15] In 1997 only Jiang Zemin, aged 71, was allowed to serve for another term, as he was the core leader and had become the de facto core leader for only three years. At the 16th Congress in 2002, Li Ruihuan, the Chairman of the National Committee of the CPPCC retired at the age of 68, a precedent apparently was set to lower the age limit to 67. In Chinese this rule was coined "7 up and 8 down" (*qi shang ba xia*). In October 2007, Zeng Qinghong, the Vice President and a member of the PSC, retired as he officially reached the age of 68. Thus he also followed the age-limit precedent set by Li Ruihuan.

The second norm is two term limits for top leaders, who include the PSC members, the President, the Premier, the Chairman of the Standing Committee of the NPC, and the Chairman of the National Committee of the CPPCC. This rule, however, does not apply to their heirs apparent when they are usually appointed as the member of the Politburo prior to their formal assumption of the top posts. These heirs apparent are usually given at least a term at the PSC to familiarize with the routine of these key posts.[16]

The earliest binding rule on two term limits on the president, the legislative chief (the Chairman of the Standing Committee of the National People's Congress), and the premier was written into the Constitution of the People's Republic of China (PRC) in 1982. Article 79 stated as follows: "The term of office of the President and Vice-President of the People's Republic of China is the same as that of the National People's Congress, and they shall serve no more than two consecutive terms." Article 66 of the Constitution stipulated: "The Chairman and Vice-Chairmen of the Standing Committee (of the National People's Congress) shall serve no more than two consecutive terms." Article 87 also prescribed the following: "The term of office of the State Council is the same as that of the National People's Congress. The Premier, Vice-Premiers and State Councillors shall serve no more than two consecutive terms." In addition, Articles 124 and 130 imposed two consecutive term limits on the President of the Supreme People's Court and on the Procurator-General of the Supreme People's Procuratorate, respectively. Article 93 mentioned the terms of the Chairman, Vice Chairmen, and members of the CMC, but did not impose any term limit. The relevant lines of this article stated as follows: "The term of office of the Central Military Commission is the same as that of the National People's Congress."

Table 7.1 contains a list of leaders in the following prominent positions: the CMC chairman, the President, the Party General Secretary, the Premier, the legislative chief, and the head of the Party's united front platform the CPPCC. As Table 7.1 indicates, prior to 1993 all but one leader had served in the same post for over ten years. Li Peng served as the acting premier during 1987–8, as Zhao Ziyang was tipped by Deng Xiaoping to replace Hu Yaobang who was dismissed unexpectedly in early 1987. Li Peng then served as the Premier for two terms during 1988–98. Gradually, the President, the Premier, the legislative chief and the chief of the CPPCC served for two full terms. The exact starting years for the two consecutive terms of these posts are as follows: Presidency, 1993; the chief of the CPPCC, 1993; the Premier, 2003; the legislative chief, 2003. Among these key posts, Jiang Zemin served as the CMC Chairmanship for the longest period, that is, 14 years 10 months from November 1989 to September 2004. Another key rule that evolved gradually after 1989, and which been consolidated for most of the years since 1993, was that the core leader holds three most important posts as the head of the Party, of the nation and of the military.[17] This rule emerged after November 1989 when Deng handed over the CMC Chairmanship to Jiang Zemin, the then General Secretary of the Party. This was Deng's design to boost the authority of the core leader (Jiang at that time). This rule was broken since then only during November 2002 and September 2004, when Jiang Zemin served as the CMC Chairman after he

Table 7.1 Leaders in major posts in the reform era (1978–present)

CMC Chairman	President	General Secretary of the Party	Premier	Chairman of the Standing Committee of the NPC	Chairman of the National Committee of the CPPCC
Hua Guofeng (1976–81)			Hua Guofeng (1976–80)	Ye Jianying (1978–83)	Deng Xiaoping (1978–83)
Deng Xiaoping (1981–89)			Zhao Ziyang (1980–7)	Peng Zhen (1983–8)	Deng Yingchao (1983–8)
	Li Xiannian (1983–8)	Hu Yaobang (1980–7)		Wan Li (1988–93)	Li Xiannian (1988–93)
	Yang Shangkun (1988–93)	Zhao Ziyang (1987–9)	Li Peng (1988–98) [1987–8: Acting Premier]	Qiao Shi (1993–8)	
Jiang Zemin (Nov 1989–2004)	Jiang Zemin (1993–2003)	Jiang Zemin (1989–2002)	Zhu Rongji (1998–2003)	Li Peng (1998–2003)	Li Ruihuan (1993–2003)
Hu Jintao (Sept 2004–2012)	Hu Jintao (2003–2013)	Hu Jintao (2002–12)	Wen Jiabao (2003–13)	Wu Bangguo (2003–13)	Jia Qinglin (2003–13)
Xi Jinping (2012–present)	Xi Jinping (2013–present)	Xi Jinping (2012–present)	Li Keqiang (2013–present)	Zhang Dejiang (2013–present)	Yu Zhengsheng (2013–present)

Source: Multiple lists on these posts at: www.baidu.com, accessed on March 14, 2015.

passed his post of the Party General Secretary to Hu Jintao in November 2002. From 1993 onwards, the General Secretary of the Party also holds the post of President, in addition to the CMC Chairmanship. When Deng handed over the CMC Chairmanship to Jiang in 1989, this was not possible, as the Presidency was taken by Deng's arguably most important ally and manager Yang Shangkun. Only when Yang completed his first term in 1993 could Jiang assume this post. From then on the rule of three top posts held by the core leader has been in place. The core leader would represent the nation in major international forums given China's growing international importance and frequent interaction with major powers such as the U.S., the European Union, Russia, Japan, and India. As the President, the core leader has the power to nominate the Premier and declare war and peace (which he will do competently when he holds the CMC Chairmanship).

The Constitution in 1982, which was formulated and passed under Ye Jianying and especially Peng Zhen, the chief and deputy chief of the legislature, had set into motion the two term limits. The 1982 constitution, however, did not impose any term limit on the CMC Chairman. This was reflected in the afore-mentioned Article 93. It was quite likely that Deng Xiaoping who had been holding that post since 1981 did not want himself to be subject to the two terms limit so that he could maintain his status of the paramount leader in Chinese politics beyond 1991. In addition, the Constitution of the CCP did not impose two term limits on the major posts, especially the General Secretary.

However, under the Party's General Secretary Hu Jintao the General Office of the CCCCP promulgated a document in 2006 entitled "Provisional Rules on the Term of Office of Leading Party and Governmental Cadres." This document stipulated that each term of these cadres lasted five years, that after a leading cadre had served in the same post for over two terms, s/he would not be nominated or appointed for that post again, that after a leading cadre had served at the same level for 15 years, s/he would not be nominated or appointed for any post at that level again. It also stipulated that these rules applied to the head (not the deputies) of the Party, the government, the leg-islature, the CPPCC and their agencies at the national, provincial, and city levels and to the head of the Party, the government, the legislature, the People's Court, and the People's Procuratorate at the county level and above.[18] In effect, this document imposed a tenure limit of maximum 15 years on all national and local leaders unless they were promoted to a higher level. It is worth noting that Jiang Zemin surrendered his CMC Chairmanship to Hu in September 2004, slightly ahead of the deadline of November 2004, when his tenure reached fifteen years.

Managing the handover of the three top posts to the core leaders

The core issue of leadership succession is undoubtedly the succession to the core leader. As stated, the core leader has usually been the head of the Party and the CMC Chairman, which had been the case for Mao during 1949–76. If the succession process is complete, the new core leader holds both posts (and if possible, the Presidency). However, the succession process could also be phased, when the new core leader takes up one or two out of the three posts first, before assuming all three posts at the end. Under Mao, his successor Liu Shaoqi was the President during 1959–66, while Mao remained the Chairman of the Party and of the CMC. As will be discussed immediately below, succession to Deng and Jiang was phased.

Phased succession for Jiang and Hu

Citing an insider of top-level Chinese politics, Zheng suggested the following. Having suffered from Mao's dictatorial rule Deng refrained from installing a core leader among the generation of leaders succeeding him in the early years of economic reform. After the Tiananmen Movement in 1989 Deng realized that a core leader like himself could help the Party weather unexpected changes in the Party leadership. Thus in 1989 Deng declared Jiang Zemin the core of the leadership.[19] As stated, Deng's third successor Jiang took over the Party General Secretary and the CMC Chairman in May and November 1989, respectively.

However, as stated earlier, Jiang's ties with Deng deteriorated in 1990 and especially 1991, when Jiang refused to support the pro-reform editorial published in the Shanghai-based *Liberation Daily*. When Deng launched the southern tour in early 1992, he actually was in a showdown with Jiang, giving Jiang the final warning to embrace Deng's marketization agenda. Should Jiang continue to oppose marketization and ally with the conservative camp, Deng would replace Jiang with another leader. Qiao Shi and Li Ruihuan were believed to be the possible and viable candidates. Jiang quickly pledged his support for Deng, thereby keeping his status as the post-Deng core leader. As stated, Jiang did not assume the Presidency until March 1993. Moreover, Jiang did not formally become the core leader until 1994 and the de facto core leader until 1997. In 1992 Jiang managed to persuade Deng to remove Yang Shangkun from the Vice Chairmanship of the CMC and Yang Baibing as Secretary General of the CMC; Deng still appointed his trusted supporter Liu Huaqing and Zhang Zhen as the CMC Vice Chairmen who ran the daily affairs of the CMC until 1997. Only in 1997 was Jiang able to retire both Liu and Zhang and installed Zhang Wannian and Chi Haotian as Vice Chairmen who were loyal to him. Nevertheless, from 1994 Deng rarely intervened in politics partly due to his deteriorating health and partly due to his determination not to intervene in order to allow Jiang to consolidate his status as the post-Deng core leader. In short, Jiang became the virtual core leader in 1994 and started to control the CMC in 1997. Thus Jiang's succession to Deng was gradual.

Jiang's successor Hu Jintao was selected by Deng, not by Jiang. At the age of 49 Hu was chosen by Deng to be the youngest member of the PSC at the Fourth Congress of the CCP in 1992. It is likely that Deng did so for two reasons. One is that as widely believed Deng feared that the successor picked by Jiang would not be able to sustain the orthodox reformism Deng endorsed. Orthodox reformism refers to Deng's insistence on sustaining market-oriented economic reform while maintaining the single-party rule of the CCP. The other reason might be that Deng did not think Jiang would have the authority and resources which Deng had to appoint his own successor and help his successor to consolidate power.

Hu waited for one decade before finally taking over the post of the General Secretary of the CCP from Jiang in late 2002 and the post of Presidency in early 2003. However, Jiang still held on to the most powerful post, namely, the CMC Chairmanship, until September 2004. Therefore, Hu became the nominal core leader in March 2003 and the de facto core leader in September 2004. Even so, it was believed that Hu was much constrained by Jiang's lingering influence even after September 2004 out of several reasons. First, most of the members of the PSC were Jiang's followers. During 2002–7 five to six out of the nine PSC members were close to Jiang. They included Wu Bangguo, the former Shanghai Party Secretary and then the legislative chief, Jia Qinglin, the head of the CPPCC, Zeng Qinghong, the Vice President, Li Changchun, the propaganda chief, Huang Ju, the Executive Vice Premier, and to some extent, Wu Guangzheng, the Director of the Central Disciplinary and Inspection Commission. Second, the Vice Chairmen of the CMC were followers of Jiang. Since September 2004, despite Jiang's retirement from the CMC Chairmanship, Guo Boxiong and Xu Caihou were Vice Chairmen of the CMC and both held the posts until November 2012 when the 18th Party Congress convened. Xu was in charge of personnel appointment. In 2015 senior military officers revealed that Xu accepted bribes for promoting senior officers and generals, robbing Hu of one of the most important instruments Hu had in commanding the military, that is, personnel appointment.[20] Third, reportedly in an acceptance speech upon assuming his post of the head of the Party Hu promised to consult Jiang on major issues, following the example of an internal Party resolution on consulting Deng in 1987.[21]

Having lived with Jiang's lingering influence in politics, Hu had been seeking opportunities to change this unhealthy state. In 2006, as stated earlier, he arranged for the promulgation of the rules on the tenures of leading cadres, thereby limiting the maximum term of a leader at the same level to 15 years and that of the same post for 10 years. Nevertheless, this rule does not do anything about a retired leader who tried to exercise his influence from behind the scene, like Jiang from 2004–12.

Xi's one-stroke succession of Hu

Hu's chance finally arrived at the 18th Congress of the CCP in late 2012 and the annual session of the NPC in early 2013. At the 18th Party Congress Hu handed over his post of the General Secretary of the Party and more importantly the CMC Chairmanship to Xi Jinping despite Xi's suggestion for Hu to continue. Hu's move was widely viewed as his determination to fully retire. In early 2013 Hu passed the Presidency to Xi. At the 18th Party Congress Hu had two points accepted at an internal Party meeting—first, leaders should not interfere in politics after retirement no matter how high their previous posts were and second, no exception should be made on delaying the handover of posts including the CMC Chairmanship. In addition, Hu abolished the Office of Jiang Zemin at Zhongnanhai, the office compound of the national Party and governmental leaders in Beijing. Hu's full retirement earned him wide praise including from Xi Jinping and possibly many other retired leaders such as Zhu Rongji, Qiao Shi, Li Peng, and Song Ping, as well as applause from cadres in the Party and overseas observers. These veteran leaders appeared in the occasions of the handover of power from the incumbent to the new leaders at the 18th Party Congress, while Jiang was absent.[22] In response to Hu's call, He Guoqiang, the head of the Party's Central Disciplinary Inspection Commission (CDIC), immediately moved out of his office in Zhongnanhai right after the last meeting of the commission. He also stated publicly that he would not interfere in the future operation of the commission. Hu also voluntarily asked that the appearance of his name in official news be listed after the incumbent Politburo members, in a sharp contrast to the past practice of placing Jiang right after the incumbent PSC members and well ahead of the incumbent Politburo members.

Thus in 2013, for the first time since 1978, succession to the core leader was completed in one stroke. Xi has been eager to form an alliance with Hu and his followers, who served in the Communist Youth League in their earlier career. Jiang's influence within the Party has dwindled. Hu apparently still had lingering influence which seemingly was used to help Xi to consolidate his power and to counter Jiang's undue influence. Hu's move allowed Xi to become the core leader since 1976 who could quickly assert his own authority and political ideas. As stated, Wang Qishang's predecessor He Guoqiang had pledged not to meddle in the affairs of the CDIC. The quick completion of leadership succession during 2012–13 paved the way for an unprecedented anti-corruption campaign since 1949 that Xi engineered and Wang Qishan executed.

Mode of politics and factions

One issue that has been investigated extensively by the existing literature is the role of formal institutions, political groups such as factions, and personal connections such as *guanxi* in China from 1949 to the present. Given the abundance of the studies on the topic and given that the focus of this chapter is on the institutionalization and improvement of succession to top leaders (at the PSC level), it suffices here to briefly discuss the actual operation of politics in three roughly divided periods, namely, late Mao (1965–76), the first period of reform (1978–89), and the later decades of the reform era (1989 to the present). The main issues to be covered are the role of formal rules and institutions, norms accepted by the elites, personal ties, and factions. I will draw on some of the available studies and on the personal observations of the author.

Simply put, in late Mao's China (1965–76) Mao's personal authority and political maneuvering was a driving force in political events. While Mao overshadowed Chinese politics during this period, political factions, especially those tolerated by Mao, did interact with each other in order to secure first their political and institutional survival and then maximization of political resources and status. Ideology was far more important than institutions in defending oneself from attacks or in justifying attacks on any leaders. Mao himself was the setter of political rules and the ultimate arbitrator of conflict among major factions. Factions often tried to upstage each other in interpreting and implementing Mao's verdicts and instruction. Importantly, there had been a noticeable lack of institutionalization of tenures and succession. Leaders exited politics due to death and purges, not due to the end of the institutionalized tenures.[23] There were not clear requirements about prior experience for top leaders, nor clear prescriptions about the post they should hold. The winning faction attempted to take all the key posts and grab all the resources.[24]

In the early period of the reform era (1978–89), the dictatorship of a supreme leader gradually gave way to a collective leadership coordinated and orchestrated by a paramount leader (Deng himself). The most important decisions were often sanctioned by the eight elders (including Deng Xiaoping, Chen Yun, Li Xiannian, Peng Zhen, Yang Shangkun, Bo Yibo, Wang Zhen, and Song Renqiong). These decisions were then accepted and implemented by the front-line leaders who included Hu Yaobang, Zhao Ziyang, Wan Li, Li Peng, Jiang Zemin, Zhu Rongji, and Qiao Shi until 1995. Ideology was no longer primary political vocabulary. Rather, the extent of marketization, the actual results of policies and the issue of one-party dominance of the CCP were the main issues in policy debates.

In this period, factions operated on the basis of policy preferences (especially over marketization and political reform), institutions, and power and political resources. The main factions among national leaders included conservatives headed by Chen Yun, orthodox reformists headed by Deng, and moderate reformists led initially by Hu Yaobang and then Zhao Ziyang. Their main differences were over whether China should embrace a market economy (which conservatives opposed and the two reformist factions supported), and over whether China should accept political reform and a degree of political liberalism to improve the highly authoritarian regime (which only the moderate reformists supported). Thus the main basis for these factions was policy preferences. Within each of these grand factions existed factions usually centered around individual powerful leaders and their institutions. Some of these factions, such as the Communist Youth League and the Shanghai Gang, became influential in the post-Deng era. Hu Yaobang was believed to be the founding father of the Communist Youth League faction due to his long association with the League. Zhao Ziyang's faction included many national and local administrators, such as Zhao himself, Zhao's deputy Tian Jiyun at the State Council, Zhao's secretary Bao Tong, and Liang Xiang, the leader of Hainan Province.

During the period from 1978–89 tentative attempts to institutionalize leadership succession were made, yet veteran leaders remained influential and personal ties could significantly improve one's chances of promotion or winning political support. Efforts to institutionalize succession politics were reflected in the two term constitutional limit on the president, the premier, and the head of the legislature. Considerable efforts were also made to cultivate and promote young and better-educated leaders (including Jiang, Zhu, and especially Hu Jintao and Xi Jinping). Some efforts were made to gradually retire veteran leaders.

However, there were apparent limits, as the eight elders remained influential in politics despite their lack of prominent political positions (other than Deng's CMC Chairmanship until 1989) until 1992. In 1992 even without any official post Deng was able to rally support from the military and the Party for his marketization program. Furthermore, personal ties remained highly relevant in official promotion. There were numerous stories on the internet about Jiang courting Deng Xiaoping, Chen Yun, and Li Xiannian through personal favors in order to win promotion into national leadership and to win political support. This period was thus characterized by the co-existence of personal and institutional authority and rules.[25]

In the post-Tiananmen period of the reform era progress has been made in institutionalizing the succession process. As stated, age limits, two-term limits, and fifteen year caps on national and local leaders were gradually installed. The norm that the core leader holds three posts seems to have been established initially in 1993 and especially by Hu's one-stroke hand-over of these three posts to Xi Jinping during late 2012 and early 2013. There have also been established requirements of prior local and national services for future leaders. In addition, prior to the final assumption of their top national posts successors-in-waiting (including the successors to the core leader and the premiership) would serve as the PSC member for one full term to cultivate their skills in this highest level of the decision-making body.

In this period the importance of policy-based groups may decline to some extent, whereas the institutionally-originated factions have gained prominence. These factions tended to originate from a location (such as Shanghai) or a political, governmental-economic, or educational institution where the members worked, studied, and met (such as the Communist Youth League or Qinghua University). Later the common background served as a base for their career mobility and promotion. These factions included the Youth League faction (*tuan pai*), the Shanghai Gang (*Shanghai bang*) led by Jiang Zemin, the Princelings (*taizi dang*) such as Zeng Qinghong and later Xi Jinping, the Secretary faction (*mishu bang*) such as Wen Jiabao who had worked at the General Office or the Secretariat of the CCCCP (or secretaries of prominent leaders), and the petroleum gang (*shiyou bang*) headed by Zeng Qinghong and later Zhou Yongkang who had worked in the powerful petrochemical SOEs or related ministry. In addition, two prominent universities, namely, Qinghua and Beijing (referred to briefly as *Beida*), also serve as a basis for identifying leaders from a similar background.

As seen in Table 7.2, other than the Shanghai Gang or the League Faction, membership of factions can be fluid and overlapping. For example, Jiang can be regarded as the sole leader of the Shanghai Gang as well as a leader of the princelings, Zeng Qinghong is both a leader of the princelings during 1999–2007 and a key member of the Shanghai Gang, Hu Jintao is a leader of both the Youth League faction and the Qinghua clique, Xi is a leader of the princelings and of the Qinghua Clique after 2012, and Li Yuanchao is a member of the League faction, princelings, and Beida clique.

The overlapping membership renders the clear association of a leader to only one specific faction and to the leader of the faction difficult. Therefore, factional association in Chinese politics is helpful but far from a determinant factor in analyzing and predicting the relationship between and conflict among leaders. Xi Jinping put Bo Xilai, another princeling member, into jail, though many observers and the people from their generation like to put both in the same category due to their highly similar age, background, experience, and career. Xi did not get along well with Jiang either, nor did Jiang get along well with Li Peng, even though they were all princelings. Likewise, Wen Jiabao was obviously not an ally of Ling Jihua who served as the secretary of President Hu. Ling allied himself closely with Zhong Yongkang, thereby resulting in his political fall when Hu and Xi decided to go after Zhou and Bo. Among these factions, the coherence and unity in the ranked order is arguably the Shanghai Gang, the League Faction, the Petroleum Gang, the Qinghua clique, the Beida clique, the princelings, and the Secretary Gang.

It is equally difficult to pinpoint the policy preferences of all these factions. Cheng Li believed that the Shanghai Gang was elitist, as it tended to embrace the interests of the coast and the segments of society that are highly internationalized and developed. He suggested that the League faction tended to

Table 7.2 Main factions in post-Tiananmen China

	Leaders (most notable members or MNM)	Notable members	Peak of Power
The League Faction (Tuan pai)	Hu Yaobang (1982–87); Hu Jintao (1992–2012)	Hu Qili; Wang Zhaoguo; Li Keqiang; Li Yuan-chao; Han Zheng; Hu Chunhua	2002–12
Shanghai Gang	Jiang Zemin (1985–present)	Wu Guanzheng; Huang Ju; Zeng Qinghong; Chen Liangyu	1997–2012
Princelings	MNM: Li Peng (1987–97); Jiang Zemin (1997–2012); Zeng Qinghong (2002–7); and Xi Jinping (2012–present)	Li Peng; Bo Xilai; Wang Qishan; Yu Zhengsheng; Li Yuanchao; Liu Yan-dong; Li Xiaopeng	Since 2013
Secretary Clique	MNM: Yang Shangkun (1988–92); Wen Jiabao (2002–12)	Yao Yilin; Wang Zhaoguo; Zeng Qinghong; Ling Jihua	1988–92; 2002–12
Petroleum Gang	Zeng Qinghong (1999–2007); Zhou Yongkang (2002–12)	He Guoqiang; Wu Yi; Jiang Jiemin	2002–12
Qinghua Clique	Zhu Rongji (1992–2002); Hu Jintao (2002–12); Xi Jinping (2012–present)	Wu Bangguo; Wu Guanzheng; Huang Ju	1997–present
Beida Clique	Li Keqiang (2007–present)	Li Yuanchao; Hu Chunhua; Bo Xilai; Li Zhaoxing; Cai Wu	2012–present

Sources: Cheng Li, *China's Leaders: The New Generation* (Oxford and New York: Roman & Littlefield, 2001); Cheng Li and Lynn White, "The Sixteenth Central Committee of the Chinese Communist Party: Emerging Patterns of Power Sharing," in Lowell Dittmer and Guoli Liu, eds, *China's Deep Reform* (Lanham, MD: Rowman & Littlefield, 2006), 108–14.

be populist in that it paid closer attention to the inland regions and segments of the Chinese society that have not done marvelously well in marketization in the past decades.[26] On the other hand, it is hard to discern the political view of the other factions.

My own observations of factions are the following. First, the politically most powerful members of the princelings at present who are represented by Xi and Wang Qishan want to uphold the CCP's one-party leadership by cleansing corruption, extolling Mao's preaching of plain life among cadres, and improving the material life of the public. Ironically, even Bo Xilai, prior to his fall from power, seemed to share this view. Second, the view of the Secretary Gang may be too diverse to describe. Third, students from Qinghua University tended to be less critical about the Party's past and policies and more realistic in providing an immediate solution of the problems, while those from Beijing University tended to be more independent in their thinking, be more critical of the existing policies and more liberal in their outlook. However, alumni from both universities had been trained and socialized by the Party and the bureaucratic apparatus and might have already embraced many values extolled by the Party.

At present a mixture of power interests, policy preferences, factional associations, and emerging institutionalization jointly shape the behavior and preferences of leaders in China.[27] For example, despite condemning Bo Xilai to a jail term for his life, Xi seems to have played up some of the acts Bo practiced in Chongqing, such as reciting Mao's moral commandments to cadres to avoid extravagance and take criticism, and forcefully investigating official corruption. In addition, Xi seems to be going after the corruption scandals of Zeng Qinghong, though they were the most prominent princelings and believed in safeguarding the political course of their fathers. The main underlying reason may be that Bo, Zhou and Zeng were alleged to plan to undermine Xi's status as the core leader after Hu, which clearly violated the Party's norm. This brings us to one of the last topics in the chapter, that is, politics in China since 2013 when Xi was installed as the core leader.

Elite politics since 2013: Xi's swift power consolidation

Xi apparently forged a political coalition with Hu at the 18th Party Congress when Hu handed over his posts of the General Secretary of the CCP and the CMC Chairmanship. For Xi Hu's help was indispensable for his effective ruling as the core leader since late 2012 and for countering the remaining threats from potential rivals, including Bo Xilai, Zhou Yongkang, Zeng Qinghong, as well as the lingering influence of Jiang himself. For Hu, his handover of the key posts helped establish a solid precedent of timely succession and helped subdue Jiang's intended control of China's politics. In addition, a coalition with Xi also helped to ensure that prominent members of the League faction, such as Premier Li Keqiang, Vice Premier Wang Yang, Vice President Li Yuanchao, as well as Politburo member and prominent provincial leader Hu Chanhua, would fare well in the coming years and sustain the relevance of the faction in Chinese politics.

In contrast, the influence of Jiang swiftly decreased. Jiang was forced to pledge his acceptance of Xi's status as the new core leader. Reportedly soon after the 18th Party Congress Jiang wrote to the Party to ask for his ranking in official news reports to be lowered. In addition, according to reports outside China he told Xi in 2013 that Xi only needed to heed the correct elements of Jiang's remarks once Jiang reached 88 (i.e., after August 2014 given Jiang's birthday in August 1926) and that Xi needed not pay attention to Jiang's remarks once Jiang was aged 90 and over (i.e., after August 2016).[28] In July 2013, when meeting Henry Kissinger, Jiang declared that China needed a strong leader and that Xi was very competent and able and had acted decisively in the wake of riots in Xinjiang.[29]

Xi has apparently also swiftly consolidated his power and has even formally established his leadership over his peers at the PSC. In November 2013, at the conclusion of the Third Plenum of the 18th Central Committee, Xi became the head of two new and powerful organizations, the National Security Commission and the Central Leading Group for Comprehensively Deepening Reforms. In January 2015 the head of the Party Groups of the State Council, the NPC, the CPPCC, the People's Court, and the People's Procuratorate, reported successively the work of their organization to Xi, the Party chief. Presumably, these heads were the Premier, the legislative chief, as well as the heads of the CPPCC, and the People's Court, and the People's Procuratorate. They were thus procedurally subject to the scrutiny of Xi. The official media coined this an important political rule. This was the first time when the head of these organizations reported their work to the Party in the reform era. Through exercising his prerogative Xi established his prominence over his colleagues at the PSC.[30]

Successes and limits in leadership succession

As stated, leadership succession, coupled with domestic political conflict, has dealt the CCP the gravest damages since 1949. The reasons can be straightforward. The successor, once trusted by the incumbent core leader, would develop a considerable power base and a sizable following within and outside the Party and would have a fair degree of legitimacy. When the successor clashes with the core leader, it will not only result in inevitable political damages and purges, but also will undermine the authority and popularity of the core leader and may even invite public skepticism of the CCP regime as a whole. At the end of the Cultural Revolution, especially as a direct consequence of the meteoric rise and fall of Lin Biao, many Chinese became disillusioned with Mao's radical ideology and even the Party itself. Similarly, Deng resorted to military suppression in order to put down the persistent student protests in spring of 1989 and to crush potential internal dissent especially from Zhao. The crackdown on the perceived "people's movement" caused unprecedented losses of legitimacy of the Party and the PLA as representatives of the people which the official propaganda had long portrayed.

Nevertheless, to the great surprise of many overseas China analysts and scholars, since 1989 noticeable and significant progress has been made in institutionalizing and better managing leadership succession in China. To be accurate, some of the progress dated back to the early 1980s, when the Constitution mandated two-term limits on the Presidency, the Premiership, the legislative chief, and the head of the court and the procuratorate, and when Deng started to groom young and well-trained leaders and gradually retired veteran leaders except for a selected few including himself.

However, leadership succession was still threatened by the uneasy and fundamentally complex relationship between the core leader and his heir apparent.[31] Two factors could still cause tensions and a rift in their relationship. First, if the core leader sees that his successor would betray his political line and legacy, it is inevitable that he would clash with the successor and even try to find a replacement. This has been the cause for conflict between Mao and Liu, between Deng and his first two successors (i.e., Hu and Zhao), and between Deng and Jiang between 1990 and early 1992. After 1992 Deng and his successors have succeeded in preventing tensions of this type from exploding openly. In the reform era and through purging liberally-minded leaders such as Hu and Zhao, Deng firmly established what I call orthodox reformism among the young generations of Chinese leaders whom he helped to groom. The young leaders include Hu Jintao and Xi Jinping who was groomed as a promising local leader in the 1980s and the 1990s. They embraced Deng's ideas of supporting pro-market economic reforms while firmly defending the one-party rule of the CCP. Moreover, Deng compelled Jiang to accept his pro-market economic reform agenda and had this agenda written into the Party's constitution at the Fourteenth Party Congress in late 1992. Likewise, Jiang managed to install his ideological formulation, that is, "Three Represents" into the Party Constitution at the Sixteenth Party Congress in 2002, which proclaimed that the Party represented the most advanced productive forces and culture and the fundamental interests of the overwhelming majority of the Chinese people. Hu also had his own political ideas coined "the scientific concept of development" ratified into the Party's constitution at the Seventeenth Party Congress in October 2007. Together with Deng's and Jiang's political ideas it constituted the theory on socialism with Chinese characteristics.

Second, if the core leader refuses to relinquish his posts in time, the tension between them will emerge. This has been the case in Deng–Hu relations during 1985–87 and the Deng–Zhao relationship in 1989. To help his heir apparent to establish authority, Deng surrendered his CMC Chairmanship to Jiang in November 1989 and allowed Jiang to take up Presidency from Yang Shangkun when the latter's first term expired in 1993. From then on, the aforementioned "the core leader holds three top posts" norm was largely observed in the following years. Between November 2002 and September 2004 Jiang continued to serve as the CMC Chairmanship in the name of helping Hu Jintao to consolidate his power and giving him time to establish his control over the military. In September 2004 Jiang finally allowed Hu to assume the post and hold three top posts (the General Secretary of the Party, Presidency, and the CMC Chairman) at the same time, thereby becoming the core leader. At the Eighteenth Party Congress Hu even went a step further by handing over both the posts of the General Secretary of the Party and the CMC Chairmanship to Xi, enabling the latter to become both the de facto and de jure core leader immediately.

Importantly, age limits (initially 71 or 70 and later 67) and two term limits on the top leaders who have assumed their designated post have been firmly enforced since 1997. These top leaders are the PSC members and the heads of the nation-state, the Party, the military, the State Council, the legislature, the CPPCC, the CDIC, the propaganda-culture-education-science cluster, as well as the No. 1 deputy head of the State Council. As stated, in 2006 the Party has further consolidated a two term limit on the same post for national and local leaders and a fifteen-year maximum tenure on the post at the same level. These rules institutionalize the exits of the national and local leaders and help to avoid tensions between the incumbent leaders and their successors.

It is worth noting that a number of these norms came about when Chinese leaders set an exemplary precedent, thereby enabling the acceptance of a new rule on retirement within the Party. For example, in 1997 Qiao Shi retired from his post as the legislative chief, thereby resulting in a norm of retirement from top Party and state posts at the age of 70. A couple of years later Li Ruihuan and Zeng Qinghong retired, setting and consolidating the rule for retirement at the age of 68. In 2002 Hu Jintao handed over all three posts to Xi Jinping, setting an important rule that retired leaders should retire all at once and should refrain from obstructing the governance of their successors. This string of exemplary precedents, whether made out of personal virtues or political necessities, has helped the Party to progress and forge ahead with much-needed institutionalization.

In addition, there seem also to be emerging norms on grooming a pool of talents and preparing them to be the top leaders (or the PSC members). Potential candidates will be appointed in key provincial and then national leadership posts and will become Politburo members prior to becoming the PSC members.

Thanks to these intricate institutional rules the CCP has avoided major, open and damaging rifts among the top leaders regarding leadership succession. Since 1992 there has never been open disagreement among the top leaders regarding the choice of the successor to the core leader. The status of Jiang as the successor to Deng, Hu's status as the successor to Jiang, and Xi's status as the successor to Hu have never been disputed by the top Party leaders, at least not by more than one PSC member. Even though Zhou Yongkang was said to have colluded with Bo Xilai to replace Xi who he thought was too weak. Up to the present Zhou has been the only PSC member who was known to have been involved in this plot. Other much more senior PSC members, such as Hu and Wen, sternly opposed the plot.[32] In addition, no other PSC members apparently joined Zhou in conspiring to replace Xi as Hu's successor. Therefore, no deadly conflict like the Cultural Revolution or the Tiananmen Movement has ever taken place after 1992 due to leadership succession. In this regard the CCP has managed to avoid the largest minefield that many analysts associate with authoritarian regimes.

Nevertheless, there are limits to leadership succession in China. First, conflict still breaks out in the course of power consolidation of the new core leader. Since 1992 each of the new core leaders has purged at least one Politburo member for the sake of establishing his authority within the Party. Jiang purged Chen Xitong, Beijing Party Secretary in 1995. Hu purged Chen Liangyu, Shanghai Party Secretary in 2006. Xi and Hu purged Bo Xilai, Chongqing Party Secretary in 2012 and Zhou Yongkang, a PSC member and former tsar of police and public security in 2014. Second, a retired core leader may continue to meddle in politics after his formal surrender of top posts. This is best illustrated by the case of Jiang during 2002–12. He staffed the PSC with members of his faction and the CMC with Vice Chairmen (initially Zhang Wannian and Guo Boxiong and then Guo Boxiong and Xu Caihou) loyal to himself, undercutting the authority of Hu to a considerable degree. Third, a number of these rules are hidden and are not clearly stated. In addition, it is unclear whether all aspects of leadership succession are institutionalized. For example, how the heir-apparent to the core leader or the other top leaders are selected is not totally transparent. This process could still be subject to political manipulation and bargaining among factions.

However, even over the aforementioned second point, progress has been made. In late 2012, Hu, despite and against Xi's urging, handed over his posts as the head of the Party and the military, and established a new internal Party rule against interference of retired top leaders in politics. Hu's efforts have apparently helped to marginalize Jiang's political influence in China.

The fact that the CCP has escaped traumatic political events and has forged a set of rules governing succession politics suggests that even in the most explosive and potentially damaging area the Party has been able to make surprising progress. This indeed demonstrates the agility, pragmatism, and flexibility of the CCP regime.

Notes

1 Valarie Bunce argued that new leaders in the communist countries might institute new policies in order to appeal to the public and sustain their power. See Valarie Bunce, "Elite Succession, Petrification, and Policy Innovation in Communist Systems: An Empirical Assessment," *Comparative Political Studies*, Vol. 9, April 1976, 3–42.
2 See, for example, Dankwart A. Rustow, "Succession in the Twentieth Century," *Journal of International Affairs*, Vol. 18, 1964, 104–13.
3 Myron Rush, "The Khrushchev Succession Problem," *World Politics*, Vol. 14, No. 2, January 1962, 259–82.
4 For an analysis of the power, legitimacy, and interaction between Mao and other leaders, refer to Frederick C. Teiwes, *Leadership, Legitimacy and Conflict in China* (Armonk, NY: M.E. Sharpe, 1984).
5 For a recent analysis of the significance and some of the development in leadership succession, refer to Yongnian Zheng, *The Chinese Communist Party as Organizational*

Emperor (Abingdon and New York: Routledge, 2010), 45–70 (Chapter 3). For a discussion of leadership succession and changes up to the early 2000s, refer to John Wong and Zheng Yongnian, eds, *China's Post-Jiang Leadership Succession: Problems and Perspectives* (Singapore: Singapore University Press and the World Scientific, 2002).

6 For an analysis of the politics of succession to Deng, see Gao Xin, *Jiang Zemin de Quanli Zhi Lu* (*Jiang Zemin's Road to Power*) (Hong Kong: Mirrors Books, 1997), 169–98.

7 For accounts of the conflict between Liu and Mao, refer to "Chongxin jiedu Liu Shaoqi yu Mao Zedong de hezuo yu douzheng (2)" (Re-interpret Cooperation and Conflict Between Liu Shaoqi and Mao Zedong), posted at: http://blog.dwnews. com/?p=40228, accessed on July 23, 2008; "Liu Shao de 'turan xiji', Mao xiahuai, Lin Biao jiujia" (A Surprise Attack from Liu Shaoqi Startled Mao Who Was Rescued by Lin Biao), posted at: http://forum.dwnews.com/threadshow.php?tid= 872592&extra=page%3D1, accessed on October 28, 2011.

8 "Shi Hai: Mao Zedong yu Lin Biao de jiuci chongtu – qinmi dao juelie" (The Sea of History: Nine Clashes Between Mao Zedong and Lin Bao as Their Close Ties Broke), posted at: http://news.wenxuecity.com/messages/200903/news-gb2312-811567.html on March 10, 2009.

9 For a brief overview of leadership conflict during the reform era, refer to Hongyi Lai, *Reform and the Non-State Economy in China: The Political Economy of Liberalization Strategies* (London and Basingstoke: Palgrave Macmillan, 2006), Chapter 3. Information on Deng's tensions with Hu and Zhao came from numerous reports online.

10 In this chapter the core leader (the paramount leader during 1978–94) refers to the most powerful leader. He was Deng during 1978–94, Jiang Zemin during 1994–2004, Hu Jintao during 2004–13, and Xi Jinping from 2013 to the present. Top leaders referred to about a dozen to two dozen of the most influential leaders in China. During 1978–95 they included the members of the Standing Committee of the Politburo (front line leaders) as well as eight to a dozen powerful veteran leaders including Chen Yun, Li Xiannian, Peng Zhen, Yang Shangkun, and Bo Yibo. For a discussion of the leadership core, refer to Zheng, *The Chinese Communist Party as Organizational Emperor*, 76–83.

11 Lai, *Reform and the Non-State Economy in China*, 108.

12 See Xiaowei Zang, *Elite Dualism and Leadership Selection in China* (Abingdon and New York: Routledge, 2003).

13 Lai, *Reform and the Non-State Economy in China*, 108.

14 For an in-depth study of retirement of officials, refer to Melanie Manion, *Retirement of Revolutionaries in China: Public Policies, Social Norms, Private Interests* (Princeton, NJ: Princeton University Press, 1993). She conducted personal interviews of 36 cadres. Only two of them were at the ministerial levels, and 15 of them at the bureau level. She distributed questionnaires among 245 cadres, none of them at the ministerial level, 6 at the bureau level, and 204 at the section level and below. All these cadres were in Beijing. Thus her field research targeted mainly middle-level cadres.

15 Frederick C. Teiwes, "Normal Politics with Chinese Characteristics," in Jonathan Unger, ed., *The Nature of Chinese Politics: From Mao to Jiang* (Armonk, NY and London: M.E. Sharpe, 2002), 249.

16 For a discussion of age and term limits, refer to Gang Lin, "Leadership Succession, Intra-Party Democracy, and Institutional Building in China," in Weixing Chen and Yang Zhong, eds, *Leadership in a Changing China* (New York and Basginstoke: Palgrave Macmillan, 2005), 38–40.

17 See John Wong and Hongyi Lai, "The Hu–Wen New Deal," in Wong and Lai, eds, *China into the Hu-Wen Era: Policy Initiatives and Challenges* (Hackensack, NJ, London, and Singapore: The World Scientific, 2006), 5–6.

18 For a brief explanation of this document, refer to a posting at: http://zhidao.baidu. com/link?url=Z34Hge9xz1okQRxePzoJ67zQUoIWFYBmWtszrpQuE-3aa6EnrwF lZuEjTNaX2s90vxNqaXp_sFtIAa7Wr4V7p, accessed on March 14, 2015.

19 See Zheng, *The Chinese Communist Party as Organizational Emperor*, 76–7.

20 "Shaojiang zhi Xu Caihou jiakong Hu Jintao, bufen beishan" (Lieutenant Generals Accused Xu Caihou of Undermining Hu Jintao's Power and Parts of Their Remarks Were Deleted), posted at: http://china.dwnews.com/news/2015-03-09/ 59639972.html, accessed on March 10, 2015; "President's Predecessor 'Isolated' by Deputies Who Acted as Proxies for Jiang Zemin: Sources," *South China Morning Post*, Wednesday, March 11, 2015, posted at: www.scmp.com/news/china/a rticle/1734663/hu-jintaos-weak-grip-chinas-army-inspired-president-xi-jinpings-mili tary, accessed on March 14, 2015.

21 For a discussion of these points, refer to Yongnian Zheng, "The 16th National Congress of the Chinese Communist Party: Institutionalization of Succession Politics," in Weixing Chen and Yang Zhong, eds, *Leadership in a Changing China* (New York and Basingstoke: Palgrave Macmillan, 2005), 18. For Hu's pledge to seek Jiang's view, refer to Erick Eckholm, "China's New Leader Promises Not to Sever Tether to Jiang," *The New York Times*, November 21, 2002.

22 "Xi Jinping zan Hu Jintao gaofeng liangjie, Jiang Zemin quexi" (Xi Jinping Praised Hu Jintao for His Exemplary Conduct and Nobility of Character and Jiang Zemin Was Absent), posted at: http://18.dwnews.com/news/2012-11-15/589 62370.html, accessed on 15 March 2015. Also see "Hu's Full Retirement is Aimed at Limiting Legacy of Jiang," *Asahi*, November 14, 2012, posted at: http://ajw.asahi.com/a rticle/asia/china/AJ201211140055, accessed on March 15, 2015.

23 For an indepth analysis, see Frederick C. Teiwes, *Leadership, Legitimacy and Conflict in China* (Armonk, NY: M.E. Sharpe, 1984). Also see Jonathan Unger, ed., *The Nature of Chinese Politics: From Mao to Jiang* (Armonk, NY and London: M.E. Sharpe, 2002), especially Lowell Dittmer, "Modernizing Chinese Informal Politics," 3–37.

24 See Tang Tsou, "Chinese Politics at the Top: Factionalism on Informal Politics? Balance-of-Power Politics or a Game to Win All?" Jonathan Unger, ed., *The Nature of Chinese Politics*, 98–160.

25 See Jonathan Unger, ed., *The Nature of Chinese Politics*; Lowell Dittmer, Haruhiro Fukui and Peter N.S. Lee, eds, *Informal Politics in East Asia* (Cambridge: Cambridge University Press, 2000).

26 Cheng Li, "Deciphering Hu's Leadership and Defining New Elite Politics," in Wong and Lai, eds, *China into the Hu-Wen Era*, 82–7.

27 Dittmer argued that policy groups with an informal structure and taking "coherent positions on policy issues of interest to its constituency" is the dominant operational type of group politics in China. See Lowell Dittmer, "Informal Politics Among the Chinese Communist Party Elites," in Dittmer, Fukui and Lee, eds, *Informal Politics in East Asia*, 137.

28 See "Huidao zhongjie laoren ganzheng? Xi Jinping jinwo sanzhang huangpai" (Xi Jinping Holds Three Trump Cards in His Fight to Sever the Interference from the Elders), posted at: http://china.dwnews.com/news/2015-02-04/59633995.html, accessed on February 4, 2015.

29 See "Jiang Zemin jie yanqing Jinxinge quanjia hanjian lumian, yizai mingque biao-tai ting Xi Jinping" (Jiang Zemin's Rare Appearance at Entertaining the Family of Kissinger with a Dinner Aims to Show Explicit Support for Xi Jinping), posted at: www.backchina.com/news/2013/07/22/253683.html#ixzz3UXnDW22D, accessed on March 16, 2015.

30 "Gei changwei ding guiju, Xi Jinping chonggou Zhonggong gaoceng quanli gejiu" (Setting a Rule for the PSC Members, Xi Jinping Re-configures Power at the High

Level of the CCP), posted at: www.wenxuecity.com/news/2015/01/20/3964554.html, accessed on January 20, 2015.
31 For an insightful analysis of this relationship, refer to Shiping Zheng, "Crossing the Political Minefields of Succession: From Jiang Zemin to Hu Jintao," in Wong and Zheng, eds, *China's Post-Jiang Leadership Succession*, 59–86.
32 See "Diaocha 12: Bo Xilai Shijian Wanzheng Diaocha" (Investigation Volume 12: A Complete Investigation of the Bo Xilai Incident), posted at: https://books.google. co.uk/books?id=NvEhBAAAQBAJ&pg=PT142&dq=周永康否认阴谋&hl=en&sa =X&ei=W6gKVZHKAczoUqOkgPAN&ved=0CBsQ6AEwAQ#v=onepage&q= 周永康否认阴谋&f=false, accessed on March 19, 2015.

8 Intra-Party and grass-roots democracy

How far has it gone?[*]

It is agreed by many China experts outside China that lack of democracy constitutes one of the main defects in China's political system. Over 16 years after the tragic ending of the Tiananmen movement in 1989, few signs are suggesting that the Chinese Communist Party (CCP, or the Party) is ready and willing to embark upon the path of democratization. Attempts to organize any opposition movements were usually cracked down on forcefully, and media freedom or free election still seem a remote possibility.

Surprisingly, despite this limit, there have been multiple schemes to introduce democracy at the grass-roots level and within the CCP in the reform era. Village elections may well be the best-known scheme to promote grass-roots democracy in China, and they still take place. In addition, China observers have also taken note of experiments whereby citizens are consulted over local policies in certain localities as well as initiatives aiming at promoting transparency and democracy within the Party in recent decades. The most prominent examples included regularized and empowered Party Congress in some localities as well as elections of the Party secretaries in townships in Sichuan and Zhejiang. This movement has been termed intra-Party democracy (*dangnei minzhu*) in China.[1]

However, at the time of writing some of these schemes have persisted whereas some have been halted. It is thus necessary to survey the main types of initiatives that aim to bring in democracy and allow for a greater degree of political participation in China. It is also helpful to explore why some of these schemes would surface and persist under the authoritarian Party state and why others have been called off.

This chapter aims to give an overview of intra-Party and grass-roots democracy in China, especially since the 1980s. In the next section I will discuss initiatives regarding intra-Party democracy from 1988 to the present, analyze the causes of these initiatives and assess their limits. I suggest that intra-Party democracy has been a primary approach that the CCP has favored in overcoming political problems associated with the authoritarian regime. In the following section I will examine semi-competitive selection of leaders, which is made a topic parallel to intra-Party democracy, despite the fact that it relates to the latter to some extent. In the ensuing section I will briefly discuss two grass-roots elections, that is, the much-discussed and much-studied village elections and the urban neighborhood elections. In the following section I will examine initiatives aiming at promoting public deliberation and supervision mainly at the local levels and will discuss some of the notable experiments. In the final section I will briefly discuss the progress and limits of these democratic experiments in China.

I argue in this chapter that these democratic schemes and experiments revealed enthusiasm toward the introduction of democratic elements in the governance of the administration and the Party in a number of localities and that tentative results suggested democracy helped to ease public discontents. However, I suggest that due to the fear of color revolution and internal concerns with losses of the power of the Party and of the central government, grass-roots democratic schemes such as village elections have not been allowed to take place at a higher level (such as township) and intra-Party democratic attempts have been largely halted in recent years. Xi even appears to guard closely against Western democracy and liberal ideology.

Intra-Party democracy

As we will see, intra-Party democracy aims to overcome the over-concentration of power in the hands of a few individuals at local levels, especially the Party secretary.[2] It also aims at introducing better institutions for the selection and promotion of local officials, as well as advancing limited (but hopefully effective) transparency and accountability in local governance. The success of such reform efforts has been mixed, and intra-party democracy is probably best understood as the first step in China's long march toward democratic selection of local leaders, officials, and legislators (most of whom are Party members) instead of just their appointment usually and virtually by the Party secretary; supervision of national or local Party leaders by lower-level bodies, such as the Party committee, the Party congress, and Party members. Some scholars even include the selection of candidates for Party leaders via elections or ballots by a group of selectors as intra-Party democracy. Nevertheless, should the selectors include non-Party members this type of initiative cannot be strictly viewed as intra-Party democracy.

In the following section I will focus mainly on the permanent representation of the Party Congress and the decision of the Party committee by ballots. The semi-competitive selection of leaders will be examined in a section that immediately follows, though the Party tends to view it as part of intra-Party democracy. This point may be reflected in some of the Party documents I will cite in this section on intra-Party democracy. The section on intra-Party democracy comprises of the following components: a review of history on the evolution of intra-Party democracy, followed by a discussion of the permanent representation of the Party congress and of decision of the Party committee by ballots.

Evolution of intra-Party democracy

Early experiments with intra-Party democracy in the 1980s

On the 13th Party Congress in 1987, under the push from General Party Secretary Zhao Ziyang and with support from Deng Xiaoping, the Party accepted a program for political reform that would separate the Party from the administrative branch (termed the people's government in China) and separate the administrative branch from enterprises. In 1988 the Department of Organization (DOO) of the CCCCP also implemented experiments with permanent representation of the Party congress in a few localities, including Taizhou City, Zhejiang Province.[3] In March 1988, the DOO of the CCCCP promulgated "Provisional Methods regarding Multi-Candidate Elections of the Provincial, City and County Congress." While favoring multi-candidate elections and increasing competitiveness of elections, the document failed to provide highly operational procedures regarding many aspects of elections.[4] It thus failed to generate substantial competition in the election of delegates for local Party congress.

In the wake of the Tiananmen movement and crackdown in the middle of 1989, the reform program was largely abandoned. No genuine attempt was made to clearly separate the Party from the government, and limited attempts were made to withdraw the government from management of enterprises. Experiments with permanent representation of the Party congress were stopped in most places except for one district in Taizhou of Zhejiang.[5]

Development in intra-Party democracy: 1990–2002

In the 1990s the national Party authority initiated few efforts to promote intra-Party democracy. Nevertheless, at the grass-roots levels innovative and bold attempts to introduce elements of democracy in the Party surfaced in several localities in the nation. A more restrictive innovation was the elections of cadres by officials at the same level or locality, instead of appointment by the Party committee and leaders by the next higher level. In this regard, the national Party authority facilitated and actively promoted the practice nationwide. Some local Party branches introduced an institution of allowing the local Party committee or the standing members of the committee to decide appointment of cadres through secret ballots. This institution was coined the "ballot-decision" system *(biaojue* in Chinese). In 1995, the CCCCP promulgated "Provisional Rules regarding Selection and Appointment of Party and Governmental Leading Cadres." It called for the open, fair, competitive, and merit-based selection of Party cadres and governmental officials. In the following years experiments with new methods of appointing cadres accelerated in the nation. In June 1996 Daxing'anling Prefectural Party Committee in Heilongjiang Province, a Party committee at a higher level than the county, started to decide on cadre appointment through ballots by standing members of the Party committee. In 1998, the experiment was also conducted at lower levels such as townships. In 1998 Shenzhen City adopted the "ballot-decision" system in cadre appointments at a court in Longgang District, Buji Township, and Pingshan Township. In 2001 this institution was adopted by Hainan Provincial Party Committee which carried out an experiment whereby the city and county Party secretary, mayors, and county governmental chiefs were appointed through secret ballots by the provincial Party committee. By July 2002 76 percent of localities in Sichuan, including 83 cities and districts in 15 prefectures, had conducted trial implementation of allowing standing Party committee members to appoint over 10,000 cadres through secret ballots.[6]

In July 2002, the CCCCP promulgated "Rules regarding Selection and Appointment of Party and Governmental Leading Cadres." The document sanctioned the "ballot decision" system that was experimented with in the aforementioned localities. Article 33 stipulated that a member of the leadership team of the Party Committee and Government at the prefectural and county levels should be nominated by the Party committee at the next higher level, then be reviewed at a meeting attended by all members of the Party committee at the prefectural or county level, and be voted upon by these members through secret ballots. It also stipulated that when the Party committee was adjourned the members of the Party standing committee should consult the members of the Party committee before reaching a decision.[7]

Intra-Party democracy under Hu Jintao and Xi Jinping

Many China observers outside China saw the formal inauguration of Hu Jintao-led Chinese leadership around 2002 as a fresh start for China's endeavor toward democracy.[8] There were indeed several noticeable signs of interest in intra-Party democracy from the report of the 16th Party Congress in late 2002. The report, drafted under the close supervision of Hu, indicated that the leadership paid greater attention to democracy than its predecessor at the previous two Party Congresses that were convened in 1997 and 1992, respectively. More importantly, the report apparently referred to intra-Party democracy as a viable path for taking the nation down toward political openness. It declared: "Intra-Party democracy is the life of the Party and has important demonstration and stimulating effects on people's democracy."[9]

At the 4th Plenum of the 16th Central Committee of the CCP in 2005 "A Resolution regarding Strengthening the Building of the Party's Governing Capacity" was passed. The resolution proclaimed that development of intra-Party democracy was a key component of political reform and building of political civilization. The resolution also approved two policies in reforming the Party's election system. The first was to improve the methods by which nominees for Party posts were produced by increasing the number of candidates nominated for elections in relation to that of the available posts (that is, increasing the competition through the multi-candidate election). The other was to gradually expand the number of grass-roots Party leaders that were produced through direct elections. It called to establish and perfect "systems by which the standing committee of the Party is accountable to the Party committee, reports its work to the latter and is supervised by the latter." It also called to set up an institution by which the Party congress could propose motions, and delegates of the congress could exercise their influence, monitor the outcome of their motions, communicate with their constituencies, and pass on their opinions to the Party organizations.[10]

Since Hu Jintao became the Party's General Secretary in November 2002 and the State President in March 2003, he has publicized a series of measures that resulted in a moderately greater degree of democracy in the CCP at the national and local levels. These innovative measures for intra-Party democracy are discussed below.

In October 2007 the CCP held the Seventeenth Party Congress. In his report delivered to the Congress, Hu Jintao devoted part of a section (three paragraphs) to intra-Party democracy. He pledged to expand intra-Party democracy in the following areas, most of which have been discussed above.

1   The rights of Party members, including democratic discussion would be respected and transparency in Party affairs be enhanced;
2   The Party Congress would adopt a tenure system for Party delegates and would implement permanent representation of Party Congress on a trial basis in selected counties, cities and districts.
3   Voting would be introduced when local Party committees discussed and decided on major issues and when they appointed cadres to key posts.
4   An institution would be established, whereby the Politburo regularly reported its work to plenary sessions of the Central Committee and accepted their oversights, and the standing committee of local Party committees at all levels would do the same to plenary sessions of local Party committees.
5   Candidates for leading posts in grass-root Party organizations would be recommended both by Party members and the public in an open manner and by the Party organization at the next higher level. Explorations would be made to extend direct election of leading members in grass-root Party organizations in more localities.[11]

Xi Jiping succeeded Hu as the General Secretary of the CCP at the Eighteenth Party Congress in November 2012. As to be explained below, two progresses in intra-Party democracy since 2012 apparently took place mainly at that congress, namely a slight enhancement of competition in selection of delegates to the congress and the authorization of delegates to propose motions. The resolution of the Third Plenum of the Eighteenth Central Committee of the CCP in 2013 has been hailed as the most important document outlining the governance program of the leadership of President Xi Jinping and Premier Li Keqiang. However, the resolution only made one mention of intra-Party democracy by promising to promote it but without any concrete measure. Xi's apparently conservative stance over democratic initiatives will be discussed later in the chapter.

The following section is devoted to the empowering of the congress and decisions by the Party committee via ballots, two primary mechanisms for promoting intra-Party democracy and progress regarding these mechanisms. Information on the former mechanism is much more readily available than the second mechanism. The discussion on the first mechanism will thus be more detailed than that on the second one.

Empowering the Party congress

Starting from 1988, with the approval of the DOO, twelve cities, counties, and urban districts in the Zhejiang, Heilongjiang, Shanxi, Hebei, and Hunan Provinces had conducted experiments with permanent representation of Party congress. In Zhejiang, Zhaojiang District of Taizhou (later Zhaojiang City) and Shaoxing City undertook measures to regularize the Party congress and enhance its power. These two localities reduced the number of delegates of the Party congress and reduced the size of the constituency of each delegate in order to help delegates to familiarize themselves with their constituency and to be their effective representatives. Delegates were also given rights and responsibilities when the congress was adjourned. They were organized into a delegation, would convene delegation meetings, and could still exercise their power. In the smaller Zhaojiang District, the congress met once a year, instead of once every five years as the norm; in the larger Shaoxing City, the Party congress met twice or thrice every five years. The congress became the highest decision making and supervisory agency of the local Party, especially in Zhaojiang. In the two cities especially Zhaojiang, the Party committee and its agencies were altered. In Zhaojiang the standing committee of the local Party was abolished, and the Party congress and the Party committee became the top organs of the local Party. Major decisions were approved by the annual meeting of the congress. Instead of meeting only once and at most twice a year the Party committee became the daily leading organ of the local Party. It was responsible for implementing decisions made by the Party congress. The number of members of the Party committee was reduced and no alternate members were elected. The experiment with a regular Party congress won overwhelming approval by Party delegates and helped to improve political participation of delegates and their supervision of the Party committee. A survey of the delegates of the Party congress in Zhaojiang and Shaoxing suggested that over 73 percent of the respondents approved of the aforementioned major changes in the selection of delegates and operation of the Party congress. In addition, Zheng argued that this reform resulted in the following positive changes. The quality of delegates was improved and their participation in Party affairs enhanced; delegates communicated more frequently with Party members and made themselves heard better when the congress was adjourned; and the local Party was more cohesive as participation was opened up.[12]

Nevertheless, experiments with the regularized Party congress in other localities encountered grave difficulties. In addition, these experiments failed to divide the power of the Party committee and alter the way power was exercised within the local Party. By the mid-1990s most of the experiments of this kind had been abandoned or terminated.[13]

It was proposed in the Work Report of the 16th Party Congress that the experiments with the permanent representation of the Party congress at the city and county levels should be extended and that the role of the Party committee in Party affairs should be enhanced. This aimed to address the predominance of the Party secretary or the standing committee members and their possible power abuse. Experiments were conducted in Guangdong (such as the Bao'an District in Shenzhen), Zhejiang, Hubei, Sichuan, and Shandong (such as Rushan) with a special focus on dividing power within the Party and encouraging democracy. In addition, experiments were undertaken to abolish the standing committee, grant daily decision-making power to a full Party committee elected by the Party congress, and directly elect the Party secretary and Party delegates.[14]

In Luotian County of Hubei Province in late 2003, the standing committee of the county Party committee, which comprised the Party secretary, five deputies, and five standing committee members, was replaced with a Party committee of fifteen members who were directly elected by the Party congress. The county Party congress was convened once a year. When it was adjourned, members of the Party committee decided the political, economic, cultural, and social policies, appointments, dismissals, and supervision of cadres through secret ballots.[15]

In September 2004 a direct election of delegates for the Party congress was held in the Yucheng District and Yingjing County of Ya'an County in Sichuan Province, the first election of this kind at the county level in the nation.[16] Delegates were empowered to supervise the work of the Party committee and even dismiss and appoint cadres. The Party congress met once a year and held two organized activities. They were also granted two additional powers, electing and dismissing additional members and alternate members of the Party committee and electing additional members of the Party disciplinary and inspection committee, and initiating motions.[17]

In July 2004, Beijing Party Committee promulgated the municipality's trial version of "Rules for Internal Supervision of the Chinese Communist Party." The document stipulated that the office meeting of the municipality Party secretary was not the highest-level decision-making body and that it could not determine major issues. This was the first time that a formal and authoritative document of the municipality's Party made such a stipulation. It helped to limit the power of the Party secretary.

At the national level, the Party Congress was not permanently represented. Nevertheless, the CCCCP reports major Party affairs to the delegates of the Party Congress when it was adjourned. An office for liaison with delegates of the provincial Party congress has been established in 20 provinces. Some localities, such as the Bao'an District of Shenzhen City, followed the former practice. However, many other localities that were not slated for experiments with permanent representation of the Party congress did not follow the practice. Ye Duchu, a professor at the Central Party School, argued that localities could have adopted the former practice as long as conditions permitted.[18]

For the aim of allowing the Party congress to play a greater role, a degree of competition has also been introduced in the selection of delegates of the national and local Party congresses. In March 1988 the DOO issued a document regarding multi-candidate elections of the delegates of provincial, city and county delegates. In the selection of the delegates for the Fourteenth, Fifteenth, and Sixteenth National Party Congresses that were held in 1992, 1997 and 2002, respectively, 10 percent candidates more than the number of the delegates were nominated. This gap increased to 15 percent for the Seventeenth and Eighteenth National Party Congresses that were held in 2007 and 2012, respectively.[19] In addition, at the local level direct elections were held to select delegates to the Party congress in Yucheng District and Yingjing County in Ya'an City, Sichuan in 2002.[20]

Another initiative to enhance the role of the Party Congress has been to allow delegates of the Congress to propose motions. In 2008 a policy document of the CCP permitted delegates of the national and local Party Congress to jointly sponsor motions. In the following years several provinces undertook experiments. For example, in 2011 at the Tenth Party Congress of Hunan Province 229 motions sponsored by delegates were received, and 181 of them were accepted by the Party Congress. The DOO of the Hunan Party Committee required relevant agencies to respond in writing to the motions within deadlines or to offer an explanation if they failed to do so. By the end of June 2012 70 percent of the proposed motions had been concluded. In November 2012 the report delivered by Hu to the Eighteenth National Party Congress stipulated that delegates of the congress could propose motions to the Congress to be considered by the relevant agencies of the Party.[21] It is likely that the earliest chance for the delegates to exercise their newly-gained privilege is the Nineteenth Party Congress in 2017. Some critics or scholars, however, question the effectiveness and significance of this initiative by arguing that the national and local Party congresses are often carefully orchestrated by the national or local Party leaders and that in this context delegates cannot make significant changes in the agenda of the congress.[22]

Decisions by the Party committee via ballots

The traditional convention within the CCP is that the Party secretary holds the most power in deciding on policies and personnel appointment. This practice could result in abuse of power, corruption, wrong policies, and the appointment of corrupt or incompetent officials. When members or standing members of the Party committee decide on these matters by casting secret ballots, it could reduce the centralization of power in the hands of the Party Secretary as well as the aforementioned shortfalls.

The earliest experiment was conducted in Jiaojiang of Taizhou in Zhejiang in 1988 and in Hejiang in Sichuan in 1989. During 1996–2001 the Party committee or the Standing Committee in Daxing'anling Prefecture in Heilongjiang Province, Shenzhen City in Guangdong, and Hainan Province used secret ballots in appointing local officials. The most dramatic experiments were in two provinces. The first was Hainan, where in 2001 the provincial Party committee adopted this institution in deciding on the appointment of Party and government leaders in the cities and counties. The second was Sichuan, where by 2002 reportedly 76 percent of the localities in the province had adopted the institution. In 2002 the Guangdong Provincial Party Committee (GPPC) decided on the choice of three prefecture-level cadres via ballots. It decided by ballots on the appointment of 58 cadres of the provincial government in 2003. In 2002 the CCCCP issued rules on appointment of Party and government leaders of cities and counties and sanctioned decision by secret ballots by local Party committees.[23] This institution has thus gained the approval of the national Party.

Semi-competitive selection of leaders

In addition to intra-Party democracy such as an empowered Party Congress and Party committee decision-making through ballots, various schemes of semi-competitive selection of leaders have aimed to reduce the concentration of power in the hands of the Party Secretary and ease the likelihood of appointment of corrupt, incompetent, or abusive officials at various ranks. In this section I will start with semi-competitive appointments of officials at the grass-roots levels (namely, the villages), and then talk about those at a higher level. The term semi-competitive implies a degree of political competition that may not be as free as that in elections in Western liberal democracy. One caveat is that the discussion here purposefully leaves out the election of village chiefs and members of the village committees. This topic will be covered in a separate section on grass-roots elections.

In order to address the aforementioned issues of over-concentration of power and of appointment of the wrong cadres, the national Party authority issued a set of Party documents related to elections of Party posts. In June 1990 the Central Committee of the CCP (CCCCP) promulgated "Provisional Rules regarding Election Work in Grass-root Organizations of the Chinese Communist Party." In January 1994, it finalized the regulations and promulgated "Rules regarding Election Work in Grass-root Organizations of the Chinese Communist Party." These rules spelled out detailed procedures for elections for the Party at the grass-roots level.[24]

These documents tried to institutionalize elections for Party posts and improve the Party's legitimacy. Nevertheless, it is far from clear that these documents are well observed. Growing popular complaints and disillusion with the corruption of Party members and officials appeared to suggest that these documents have not achieved their original intents of improving the quality and conduct of Party officials.

Semi-competitive elections of local legislators[25]

The conventional practice in legislative elections in China has been that the Party state involves itself extensively in each major stage of the process, from nomination of the candidates, campaigns (very scant campaign activities except for formalistic official publications of the name and profile of the candidates), voting, and vote counting.

In a number of areas in China, independent candidates emerged, aiming to be spokesmen of public concerns and to exercise legislative oversight of the administration. In 1998 Yao Lifa, a self-nominated candidate, was elected as a legislator in Qianjiang City of Hubei Province in 1998. In 2003 a dozen independent candidates (ICs) in Shenzhen, 32 ICs in Qianjiang, and over 20 ICs in Beijing ran for local legislative elections, and two in Shenzhen and three in Beijing were elected as district legislators. During 2006–7 candidates nominated by voters were elected as county and township legislators in Wenzhou of Zhejiang Province, in Haian County of Qinghai Province, in Liaoyang City of Liaoning Province, in Kunmin City of Yunnan Province, and in Shandong Province.[26] These were the earliest cases of independent legislators in China.

Semi-competitive elections of village Party leaders

As stated earlier, in 1990 and 1994 the CCCCP tried to overcome the problems with the central and hierarchical appointment of officials through promulgating new rules. However, these new rules were not closely observed nationwide. At the grass-root level Party members and officials in some localities had a strong spirit of innovation and demanded more dramatic changes in order to cope with serious problems of corruption and autocratic rule of local leaders. Three innovative institutions have earned wide attention.

One of these three institutions was coined "two-ballots system," which related to Item 2D in Table 8.1. The system originated from the peasants' initiatives to remove a mis-behaving village Party secretary. In January 1991 peasants in a village in Zhenguan Township, Hequ County of Shanxi Province went to the Township Government, listed 23 mistakes committed by the village Party secretary, and demanded the replacement of the Party secretary with an elected one. An investigation by the township confirmed the villagers' claim about the errors by the Party secretary. According to the rule, the township Party committee could dismiss the village Party secretary, nominated new candidates and let village Party members select a new Party secretary. Nevertheless, the villagers wanted to have a say in the election of the new Party secretary and refused to accept nominees by the township without their consent.

Table 8.1 Categories and initiatives of democratic experiments, 1990s–present

Category	Significance	Selected Initiatives (Time, Location, and Scope)
1. Intra-Party Democracy		
1A. Empowering of the Congress	Congress delegates could have the oversight over policies and cadre appointments by Party Committees or Secretary	National experiment in 12 cities, counties, and urban districts in 1988, including Jiaojiang and Shaoxing in Taizhou, Zhejiang. Experiment in Luotian County in Hubei and in Ya'an City in Sichuan during 2003–4. In 2012 the CCP permitted the delegates of the National Party Congress to propose motions. In selecting the delegates to the National Party Congress during 1992–2012 10%–15% more candidates than the delegates were nominated to increase competition.
1B. The Party Committee Balloted on Appointment or Policies (decision by ballots)	Reduce the centralization of power in the hands of the Party Secretary or those of the few top local Party leaders.	Experiments in Zhejiang and Sichuan during 1988–9. Experiments in Shanxi, Heilongjiang and Guangdong (Shenzhen) during 1996–8. Experiments in Hainan and Sichuan were boldest. In 2002 the CCCCP issued rules on appointment of leading cadres and sanctioned decision by ballots.
2. Semi-Competitive Selections of Leaders		
2A. Semi-competitive selection of national leaders	Reduce the centralized control of designation of successors of top leaders by incumbent top leaders.	In 2007 and 2012 members of the CCCCP and veteran leaders balloted for the candidates for the PSC.
2B. Semi-competitive selection (SCS) of county or bureau-level officials	Reduce the centralized appointment power of Party Secretary at the prefecture level	SCS of 11 county-level cadres (CLCs) in 1996 and of 20 CLCs in 2003 in Henan Province. SCS of two county magistrates in Jiangsu Province in 2003. SCS of 22 bureau-level officials in Shenzhen in 2010. SCS of over 10 deputy bureau-level officials in three national ministries in 2010.
2C. Semi-competitive selection (SCS) of township leaders	Rectify the single-handed appointment of township head or deputies by the county Party secretary (PS). Allowed far more applicants to be considered.	Qualified applicants applied and conducted low-level campaigns. 100 or more township cadres or elites chose the final candidate for the county Party Secretary to approve. 1. Start of the experiment in Sichuan: SCS of deputy township chiefs (TCs) in 10 townships in Bazhong during 1995–6. SCS of 5000 township chiefs (TCs) and deputies in Sichuan during 2001–2. 2. 2001–2: SCS of 12 township chiefs in Hubei Province, and of a TC each in Guangxi, Guizhou and Jilin. 3. 2003–5: SCS of 39 TCs in Jiangsu, of 17 TCs in Yunnan, of 2 TCs in Chongqing and of 1 TC in Zhejiang.

Category	Significance	Selected Initiatives (Time, Location, and Scope)
2D. Semi-competitive elections of village party leaders	Ensure that the village Party secretary (VPS) would have popular support.	In 1991 in a village in Shanxi Province each peasant household could cast a ballot for the candidates for the VPS and Party members made the final choice. The Department of Organization (DOO) of the Party Committee in Shanxi popularized the "two-ballots" mechanism in the province.
2E. Semi-competitive elections of local legislators	Ensure local legislators exercise oversight of local officials and voice public concerns	In 1998 an independent candidate (IC) was elected as a legislator in Qianjiang of Hubei Province in 1998. In 2003 ICs emerged in local legislative elections in Shenzhen, Qianjiang, and Beijing. During 2006–7 ICs were elected as county and township legislators in Zhejiang Province, Qinghai, Liaoning, Yunnan, and Shandong.

3. Grass-roots Elections (of Administrative Posts)

Category	Significance	Selected Initiatives (Time, Location, and Scope)
3A. Village Elections	Allow rural residents to openly and democratically select the chief and administrative committee members of their villages	The earliest village elections were held in Guangxi in 1980. This innovation was promoted by the state in 1981. During 1981–7 indirect elections were held to elect the village committees. Village elections were held in over half of provinces during 1988–90 and in all but one province during 1991–4.
3B. Urban Neighborhood Elections	Allow urban residents to openly and democratically select the chief and administrative committee members of their urban residential neighborhoods	Initial elections emerged in some areas in the mid-1980s and spread to many provinces in the 2000s.

4. Public Deliberation and Supervision

Category	Significance	Selected Initiatives (Time, Location, and Scope)
4A. Openness in Village and Township Accounts and Affairs	Allow residents to supervise the use of public funds and village cadres.	Accounts and affairs of villages were publicized in many villages nationwide. Since 2000 the state pushed for transparency in public affairs of townships. By now the government claimed this transparency has been implemented in over 93% of townships.
4B. Village Assemblies and Village Representative Assemblies (VRA)	Enable representatives of rural residents to participate in daily decisions of their villages and supervise their leaders	In 1990 the Ministry of Civil Affairs affirmed the local creation of VRA. By 1997 half of the villages had set up VRA. These bodies now exist and function to varying extents in many villages in China.

Category	Significance	Selected Initiatives (Time, Location, and Scope)
4C. Public Hearings and Deliberation over Governmental Policies and Budget	Allow citizens to participate in the deliberation of major local policies and of use of budget for public projects.	In December 1997 the NPC approved the Law on Price and Article 23 mandated public hearings when prices of goods were decided. During 1999–2000 open hearings on public policy were first held and then spread in Wenling in Taizhou (prefecture-level city) of Zhejiang Province. In 2005 local governmental budget was subject to the comments from hundreds of selected local representatives.

Sources: Lai Hairong, *Zhongguo nongcun zhengzhi tizhi gaige* (*Reform of the Political System in Rural China*) (Beijing: Zhongyang bianyi chubanshe, 2009); Hongyi Lai, "Intra-Party Democracy in China," in Zhengxu Wang and Colin Durkop, eds, *East Asian Democracy and Political Development in China* (Singapore: Konrad Adenauer Stiftung, 2008), 207–24; Hongyi Lai, *Hu Wen quan toushi* (*Hu–Wen under Full Scrutiny*) (Hong Kong: Wenhua yishu chubanshe, 2005), 97–104; Joseph Fewsmith, *The Logic and Limits of Political Reform in China* (Cambridge and New York: Cambridge University Press, 2012); Shi Weimin *et al.*, *Zhongguo cunmin weiyuanhui xuanju lishi fazhan yu bijiao yanjiu* (*Historical Evolution and Comparative Studies of Elections of Village Committees in China*) (Beijing: Zhongguo shehui kexue chubanshe, 2009), Vol. 1, 1–97.

At the end the township agreed to the compromise solution whereby each peasant household sent one voter to elect candidates for the post and Party members in the village elected among the candidates the village Party secretary. The newly elected village Party secretary calmed the discontent of the villagers. In March 1992, the Organizational Department of the Huqu Party committee coined this practice "two-ballots system" and expanded it to other townships in the county. The Organizational Department of the Shanxi Provincial Party Committee popularized it within the province.[27] Reportedly, the DOO of the CCCCP has accepted the two-ballots system and has renamed it as two nominations and one election (*liang tui yi xuan*). This institution was adopted in Inner Mongolia, Shaanxi, and Anhui Provinces. This institution allowed villagers to nominate final candidates for the village Party secretary and allowed village Party members to choose among them the village Party secretary.[28] At both stages the selectors (first villagers and then Party members at the village) choose their preferred candidates through votes, but as there are no opposition parties and no reported competitive open campaigns in the process, these elections can thus be seen as semi-competitive ones.[29]

Semi-competitive selection (SCS) of township leaders

Another institutional innovation was "direct or public selection of township officials." Its aim was to rectify the single-handed appointment of township head or deputies by the county Party secretary (PS) and to allow more applicants to be considered for these township posts. Once the vacant posts (usually the township chiefs (TCs) or their deputies) were announced, qualified applicants were allowed to apply and conduct low-key and non-ostentatious campaigns. In contrast to the aforementioned semi-competitive elections, the final candidates for these official posts were chosen by scores to hundreds of local elites and representatives, instead of all the qualified adults in the localities.

The earliest effort in introducing this institution was the SCS of deputy TCs in 10 townships in Bazhong City, Sichuan Province during 1995–6. This was followed by SCS of 300 township Party Secretaries, chiefs, and deputy chiefs in the province during 1998–9. I will detail below the SCS of TCs in Sichuan in 1998.

In 1998 the public selection of township chiefs was pioneered in Shizhong District, Suining City in Sichuan Province. This was in direct contrast to the secretive appointment by the district Party committee dominated by the district Party secretary. The district was one administrative level above the township. The district selected six candidates through exams out of 68 officials. Then 100 selectors comprising of officials, villager representatives, and delegates to the people's congress in the township conducted an oral interview of the candidates and chose two finalists. The people's congress of the township selected out of the finalists the township chief.[30]

The experiments in Shizhong District in Suining City were the boldest as they involved direct elections. In November 1998 the authority in Shizhong District even held a direct election of the township chief of Buyuan Township, and a direct election of the Party secretary of Dongchan Township, first elections of the kind in the nation.[31] In the election in Buyan Township, the candidates were allowed by the local state to engage in the following forms of campaign activities: (1) mobilization of votes via family or kinship ties or via social networks such as friends and colleagues; (2) publication of candidates on media such as on TV or radio and via posters; (3) campaigns via a procession of motorcycles and speeches at villages or elementary schools; (4) a promotion of campaign slogans; (5) debates among candidates. Nevertheless, the absence of clear opposition parties and intense and open debates on the mass media rendered the campaigns only semi-competitive.[32]

In the following years this initiative was trialed in other localities in Sichuan and beyond. From 2001 to 2002 SCS was applied in the appointments of 5000 township chiefs (TCs) and deputies in Sichuan, 12 township chiefs in Xianning and a township PS in Hubei Province, and a TC each in Guangxi, Guizhou and Jilin. During 2003–5 this institution was adopted in the appointments of 39 TCs in Jiangsu Province, of 17 TCs in Honghe City of Yunnan Province, of two TCs in Chongqing and of one TC in Zhejiang Province.[33]

In several localities township Party secretaries were elected directly by Party members or Party congress and township chiefs by people's congress. In 2003, a direct election of a township Party secretary by Party members was held in Lingshan Township, Pingchang County of Sichuan Province. In September 2004, Party members also directly elected the Party secretary in Longrao Township, Changshan County of Zhejiang Province.[34] In February 2003, the authority in Xian'an District of Xianning City in Hubei Province adopted the two-ballots system and allowed the Party congress to directly elect a township Party secretary and delegates of the people's congress of township to directly elect the township director.[35]

Semi-competitive selection (SCS) of county or bureau-level officials

Around the same time efforts were introduced in the localities to make the selection of officials above the township level more competitive in order to reduce the centralized appointment power of the Party Secretary at the prefecture level and to select more able and more honest officials who were more suitable to the local constituents. Instead of merely allowing the standing Party committee (especially the Party secretary at the related level and the Party committee at the next higher level) to play a dominant role in appointing officials, these liberally-minded localities wanted other leaders, members of the local political elites, and even representatives of residents in the locality to have a say in the process. The new selectors included the members of the Party committee, selected heads of governmental departments, some of the legislators, and representatives of residents. Nevertheless, as not all the selectors of cadres are residents, Party members, and legislators within the locality, these experiments are termed competitive and open selection of cadres, rather than direct elections of them as characterized by some Chinese sources.

The recorded cases included SCS of 11 county-level cadres (CLCs) in 1996 and of 20 CLCs in Xuchang City, Henan Province in 2003; SCS of the magistrate of Pei County in Xuzhou City and that of Jintan County in Changzhou City in Jiangsu Province in 2003; SCS of 22 bureau-level officials (BLOs) in Shenzhen City in Guangdong in 2010; and SCS of over 10 deputy bureau-level officials in three national ministries in 2010.[36]

After the 16th Party Congress of 2002 this practice has been adopted more frequently nationwide. Hunan openly recruited 73 financial and taxation officials; Ningxia recruited section (*chu*) -level officials; Wuhan Municipality of Hubei Province openly selected 68 leading cadres, 22 of whom were at the bureau level; and Anhui Province openly recruited department-level leading cadres.

One of the best-known cases was the first open selection of township and county chiefs in Jiangsu Province under the leadership of Li Yuanchao in 2003. As the provincial leaders called for a reform of cadre management systems, furthering of democracy, and more competition among cadres, the experiments of open recommendation and selection of officials were unfolded in June 2003. In late June, the authority in Suyu County in Jiangsu started the earliest open recommendation and selection of township Party and governmental chiefs. A total of 33 candidates competed for the posts of eleven township directors. I shall describe in detail the experiments in Jiangsu.

In August, the post of the magistrate of Feixian County of Xuzhou City was vacated. Jiangsu provincial leaders intended to fill the post through open selection. The first stage of the process was "public recommendation." On October 21 and 22, over 70 cadres in Xuzhou City applied for the post. They all had a

college and above diploma, were under 45 in age, had served as a leader or a
deputy in the city, county, and district governmental agencies or enterprises and
institutions under the leadership of the city Party committee for over two years.
A delegation of 754 selectors at the deputy-section level and above was chosen,
comprising members of the Party, government, legislative, and political consultative conference in the city, departments of the city Party committee and
city government, as well as companies and institutions directly led by the city.
Each of these selectors chose six candidates out of the 70 by filling out a
"democratic recommendation form." The twelve candidates with the highest
votes went on to the next round. Then about 30 top leaders of the city, all of
whom were at the deputy-city level and above, selected six out of the twelve
candidates.

The six remaining candidates entered the "public selection" stage. Candidates
were required to write an investigation report, and give a speech and answer
questions from selectors comprising 7–8 "judges" and 123 "representatives of
public opinions" ("representatives" in short). Afterwards, a survey of the opinions
of the selectors would be conducted in order to determine the final winner.
"Judges" were leaders of the Department of the Organization of the Jiangsu Party
Committee and the Planning Commission of the Jiangsu People's Government,
the "first hands" of a county and a city other than Xuzhou and Feixian, a
leader of the Feixian County, and two to three leaders of Xuzhou City. As far
as members of the "representatives" were concerned, 30 percent of them were
leaders, legislators, and members of the political consultative conference of the
localities in Feixian County, 30 percent leaders of counties and districts of
Xuzhou City, and 40 percent leaders, legislators, and members of the political
consultative conference of institutions and units directly under the leadership
of the city.

In order to reduce scores based on personal ties and ensure fairness in the
process, a number of measures were taken. The profile of the selectors and
questions were kept secret until the last minutes. The six candidates were
stripped of all phones and pagers and were prohibited from making external
communication. The hand-written investigation reports were also typed into
computers before being given to the judges. Candidates addressed three
required questions raised by the judges and two questions from the participants. Candidates did so in the order determined by a lottery. "Judges" and
the "representatives" recorded and graded the performance of the candidates
and even applauded their outstanding answers. The written and oral exams were
primarily case analyses, which were designed to test the candidates' empirical
knowledge. For each candidate their investigation report, speech plus questions and answers, and marks by "representatives" contributed 30 percent, 30
percent, and 40 percent, respectively, of their final score.

The Department of Organization (DOO) of the province scrutinized the
top three scorers and nominated two of them as the candidates for the
post. The city Party committee voted on the two candidates. The top scorer
became the final candidate for the county magistrate and was reported to the

provincial DOO for approval. He was the deputy secretary general of Xuzhou City Government and aged 39.[37]

Semi-competitive selection of national leaders

Understandably SCS of national leaders would have far greater implications for development of China as a nation. In this regard two unprecedented and potentially significant changes have been introduced in recent decades. These changes would have the effects of breaking the tight centralized control of the appointment of hundreds of national leaders by top leaders and the centralized appointment of their successors by incumbent top leaders.

Consultative selection of the Central Committee (CC) and the Central Disciplinary Inspection Committee (CDIC) for the Eighteenth Party Congress

In choosing the candidates for these two committees 59 survey teams were dispatched to 31 provinces and 130 national agencies and enterprises from July 2011 to June 2012. Meanwhile, nine survey teams were sent to the military and the armed police. A total of 42,800 cadres were slated as candidates for the two committees likely as a result of recommendation by the DOO at various levels. The 67 survey teams selected and talked with 27,000 of these candidates. The PSC held 11 meetings to listen to the reports of these survey teams and decided on the list of recommended candidates for the two committees. At the Eighteenth Party Congress 9.3 percent more candidates than the seats of the CC and 8.5 percent more candidates than the members of the CDC were submitted to the delegates of the Congress who voted to decide the results. This gap was slightly larger than the 8.3 percent gap adopted in the election of the CC and the CDIC at the Seventeenth Party Congress in 2007.[38]

Selection of members of the Politburo by veteran leaders via ballots

In 2007 and 2012 incumbent and retired national leaders, presumably including the members of the CCCCP and veteran leaders such as Jiang Zemin, Li Peng, Qiao Shi, and Zhu Rongji, were given a ballot containing the list of over 200 potential candidates for the Politburo. Each of them cast one ballot for the candidates. The Party produced a list of candidates for the Politburo on the number of votes received by each candidate and submitted the list to the CCCCP of the Seventeenth Party Congress. Xi Jinping and Li Keqiang emerged as the front-runners and became the successor to the President and the Premier, respectively. They were elected as the two new members of the Politburo Standing Committee. In 2012 Hu again presided over the balloting for the five candidates for the Politburo Standing Committee. This was arguably the boldest and most far-reaching measure to further intra-Party democracy in China.[39]

The aforementioned forms of semi-competitive selection of cadres do represent a break from the past practice whereby officials are appointed solely by their superiors often at the disregard of the opinions of their colleagues and the citizens in the locality. If these measures are genuinely implemented, able, competent and honest officials are more likely to be appointed.

Nevertheless, as most of these measures involved semi-competitive selections of officials, the organizers of the selection tended to be the government or the Party, and most of the selectors were political elites especially officials at similar levels of appointment. There was very limited extent of transparency that rendered supervision of the process difficult. This would give rise to possible manipulation of the process by the leaders or agencies in charge. Thus, it was possible though probably unusual that candidates favored by the leaders could gain privileged information about the process and even some of the possible questions in interviews or exams.[40]

Furthermore, despite all these measures only officials at the lowest level are subject to elections by local residents or Party members. That is to say, village Party secretaries and local legislators in several townships, counties, or urban districts were elected by secret ballots, and voters were more or less free to cast their votes. In other cases the citizens had little say in the process. Thus, these political reform initiatives fell well short of the concept of democracy which is understood throughout the world and which is associated with free and competitive elections.

Grass-roots elections (of administrative posts)

The third set of measures for democratic advancement in China were elections at the villages and urban residential neighborhoods. Village elections have been much studied. I will thus provide a brief overview of the elections. Elections in the urban residential neighborhoods are an under-studied recent development, and there is little information available. For these reasons while I will try to provide as many details as possible, my analysis of urban neighborhood elections will also be brief.

Village elections

The earliest village elections were held in Yishan and then Luocheng Counties, Guangxi in 1980. Economic reform in China that started in late 1978 resulted in the abolition of the people's communes in the countryside. As a result, no administrative bodies took care of village affairs. In order to fill this administrative vacuum villagers introduced the elections to form a village committee of five members in a village in Yishan County in Guangxi, a provincial-level ethnic autonomous region, in February 1980. After various reports on the issue during 1981–2, in 1982 Peng Zhen, the Director of the Central Political and Legal Affairs Committee of the CCP and the deputy chairman of the Standing Committee of the National People's Congress (NPC, China's national legislature), publicly voiced his support for the innovation. In August 1982 the CCCCP formally required experiments with the setup of village committees in all localities. During 1983–87 indirect elections were held to elect the village committees. In 1987 the Standing Committee of the NPC adopted the Organic Law of Village Committee (draft). During 1988–90 village elections were held in over half of provinces. During 1991–4 village elections took place in all but one province.[41] Tianjian Shi, one of the best scholars on village elections, offered the political-leadership explanation for the spread of village elections in China after 1987. He suggested that middle-level open-minded officials at the Ministry of Civil Affairs in China utilized the implementation process of the Organic Law to overcome the strong opposition.[42]

A study based on a random survey of 520 villages throughout China during the second half of 2005 to the first half of 2006 revealed the following picture of village elections in China. Among the coastal, central, and western regions most villages (ranging from 54 percent to 65 percent of them) had had 5–8 village elections. Only 33 percent to 42 percent of the villages had had four elections or less. Apparently, migrants into a village and the wages of the village cadres could significantly and positively increase the numbers of elections at a village.

Regarding the emergence of the preliminary candidates, 57 percent of the tentative candidates surfaced in open nomination, 23 percent were nominated by the local Party committee and the local government, and 20 percent of them were nominated by villagers or candidates themselves. Two ways, namely, ballots by villagers' representatives (48.5 percent of the cases), followed by consultation and preliminary section (43.8 percent), were apparently widely used in finalising the candidates on the ballot. Candidates for village committees were publicized to the voters in two methods, namely, posters in a public place (50 percent–52 percent) and the village assemblies (40 percent–42 percent).

It was found that the higher the wages of village cadres, the more likely it was that tentative candidates emerged through open nomination (*hai xuan*) and to a lesser extent nomination by villages and the candidates, and the less likely it was that they were nominated by the Party and the government. Thus higher salaries for cadres induced competition in the elections.

Village elections obviously changed the way politics operated in the village. In 71 percent of the surveyed villages village assemblies, the most representative meetings, were convened and chaired by the director of the village committee (or the village chiefs). This suggested a fair degree of democracy in operation. In only 25 percent of the surveyed villages the assemblies were chaired by the village Party secretaries who were regarded as the most powerful leader in the villages but who were not elected. The latter villages did not seem to enjoy a high degree of democracy.

Village budget is one of the most significant economic resources for villages. The village budget was approved by the director of the village committee (DVC) who was not the village Party secretary in 43 percent of the villages in the western region and 35 percent of those in the central region, but only 20 percent of those in the coastal region. The budget was approved by the village Party secretary who was also the DVC in 1/3 of the villages in the coastal provinces, 28 percent of the villages in the central region, and only 13 percent of the villages in the western region. The budget was jointly approved by the village Party secretary and the DVC in 22 percent to 24 percent of the villages across these three regions. In villages with low cadre wages (less than 300 yuan a month) the DVC tended to approve the budget and keep the village stamp. In general, in villages with higher cadre wages (over 600 yuan a month) the village Party secretary who was also the DVC tended to approve the budget and the village secretary or the village accountant tended to keep the village stamp.[43] These villages thus experienced the concentration of power into one person (the Party secretary who was also the DVC), higher governance efficiency, as well as division of labor among village leaders as the stamp was kept by the village secretary, not by the DVC.

As seen in 71 percent of the villages village assemblies were convened and chaired by the DVCs and as to be elaborated, village elections have done much in furthering representatives and official accountabilities of the village committees as well as public participation in public affairs. Nevertheless, there have been several frequently voiced concerns with village elections in recent years. These concerns include vote buying by the candidates including rural entrepreneurs, the strong role of clans or kinships in electoral results, coerced voting by local tyrants, and the dominance of strong men in village elections and politics.[44]

Elections in urban residential communities

Villages are the lowest level of administration in rural China. In urban China the lowest level of administration is a residential community that is administered by a residents committee (RC) (*jumin weiyuanhui*, or *juweihui* in short). The earliest election of residents committees took place in the mid-1980s. By 2006 each of the 31 provinces in China had held two to seven elections of RCs.

In 1990 the Organic Law of Urban Residents Committees took effect. The law required the setup of a residents committee for every 100 to 700 urban households via elections. It also stipulated that a residents committee comprised of five to seven members including the director and a deputy director. The law entrusted the residents committees to enforce laws and policies of the state; implement the public health, social relief, family planning, and youth policies of the state; maintain public security, arbitrate disputes; attend to the public interests of the residents; and pass the opinions of the residents to the government. The law also stipulated that the residents committees should be formed via votes by individual residents, resident households, or representatives of groups of residents.[45]

In a study on the composition of the membership of residents committees across the provinces four indicators were examined, namely, age, gender, education, and the CCP membership. It was concluded that the composition varied widely across provinces. In particular in Beijing, Tianjin and Shanghai members of the residents committees tended to age over 41 and were female and they tended to have college or above education and include a below average share of Party members. In Hebei, Zhejiang, Fujian and Guangdong, members of the residents committees tended to be female, enjoyed an above average share of Party membership and college or above education, and were aged under 40.[46]

Elections of residents committees have been hindered by the lack of direct elections in many localities and pervasive state or bureaucratic intervention in the elections. In 1998 the earliest experiments with direct elections of residents committees were undertaken in Qingdao. In the experiment, candidates were nominated directly by ten or more residents. They delivered campaign speeches at the meeting of representatives of residents who then voted to choose the final candidates. All qualified residents would then cast votes on these candidates to choose the members of the residents committees. In 2002 Guangxi became the first province to implement direct elections of residents committees. By July 2003 experiments with direct elections took place in ten provinces and major cities, including Beijing, Shenzhen, Wuhan, Nanjing, and Ningbo.[47] By 2008 the MCA revealed that only 22 percent of the residents committees were formed via ballots from residents and hence through direct elections. The remaining 78 percent of residents committees were formed through indirect elections, namely, ballots by representatives of resident households and by resident groups. The state proposed to implement direct elections in half of the urban communities by 2010. The MCA also planned to push up the percentage to 80 percent by 2015.[48] However, it is unclear whether these targets are being met. Furthermore, in some localities the residents committees or sub-district offices of the city government nominated the candidates for the residents committees.

In addition, a study on a residential community in Beijing in 2007 revealed that residents committees devoted only a small portion of their time to the political autonomy of residents. For example, these committees shouldered 253 tasks, 64 percent of which related to assisting the government and its sub-district offices with administrative works concerning public health, public security, social relief and welfare, and youth education. Out of the remaining 36 percent of tasks, some regarded the building of the Party in the grass-roots level and the others related to the self-rule of the residents. Thus, even though resident committees are primarily designed to organize the self-rule of the residents, they were too pre-occupied with the grass-roots services for the government and the Party and had little time and energy to promote the self-rule of residents.[49]

Public deliberation and supervision

The fourth and last set of measures for furthering democracy in China aims to encourage public participation in deliberation of public affairs and in supervision of officials at the local levels. Three measures fall under this category. The first two relate to and serve to consolidate village elections and rural democracy that have just been discussed. The third measure supposedly covers both rural and urban areas in localities undergoing the experiments, though this measure is more pertinent and useful for urban residents there. All these measures, especially the first two, have been covered extensively by the existing literature. The following account will thus be brief and aim to provide a quick overview.

Openness in village and township accounts and affairs

A Chinese scholar proposed that three institutions, namely, village elections, democratic decision-making, and democratic management were critical to rural democracy. He argued that transparency in village accounts and affairs would enable rural residents to exercise their rights to supervise village officials and ensure proper use of public funds.[50] Likewise, transparency of the public affairs of townships would enable residents in the townships to supervise local officials and official use of local funds.

From the mid-1980s to the early 1990s experiments with transparency in public affairs in villages were conducted in a number of provinces, in a likely response to the embezzlement of public funds and corruption of village cadres amidst opaqueness of village affairs. One of the earliest efforts to promote transparency of public affairs (TPA) at villages was made in Gaocheng County of Hebei Province in May 1989. In December 1990 the CCCCP required villages in the country to set up procedures for furthering TPA at the villages in order to enable villagers to supervise the village committees. Four years later the MCA promoted TPA as one of the objectives of then on-going demonstration work on furthering the self-rule of villages. TPA was eventually included in the Organic Law of Village Committees promulgated in 1998, and was later also included in many provincial and local laws and regulations on the self-rule of villages. These laws and regulations mandated openness regarding elections, major decisions, and public budget of villages.[51]

A nationwide representative survey of 2005–6 suggested that by and large TPA was observed at most villages, that the village budget was publicized monthly in 21 percent of the respondent villages, quarterly in 40 percent of the village, and twice a year in 24 percent of the villages. Only 2 percent of the villages failed to publicize their budget. In addition, a supervision team for TPA was set up in 82 percent of the villages in the central region, 84 percent of these villages in the western region, and 91 percent of the villages in the coastal region. The aforementioned study on the basis of this survey also concluded that higher cadre wages, a higher level of average income of villagers, and the popularity of telephones and computers at the village seemed to contribute to the existence of a supervision team for TPA. In addition, a higher level of villagers' income, a wider use of telephones, and a larger number of migrants into a village seemed to contribute to more frequent publicizing of the village budget.[52]

The national authority (which refers to the CCCCP and the national government) also promoted TPA at the townships as early as December 2000. In that month it promulgated a "Notice regarding Comprehensive Implementation of the Institution of Transparency of Public Affairs in Agencies of Political Powers of Townships Throughout the Nation," announcing the move toward TPA of townships. By the official requirements the budget, personnel appointment and judicial affairs of townships were made public. By the mid-2000s 93 percent of townships in China claimed to have achieved TPA.[53]

TPA has helped to reduce public grievances and increase the self-restraint of township officials. TPA enabled the public to form a better understanding of public affairs in their locality on the basis of facts instead of rumors and reduced public discontent due to misunderstanding of the conduct of local officials. It was reported that in the first year of TPA the number of public petitions to a higher authority and bypassing the usual bureaucratic layers in Hubei Province declined sharply by 68 percent and the number of registered cases of tension between cadres and the masses dropped by an even larger 76 percent. Moreover, officials realized that TPA could reveal certain seriously illegal activities that they might engage in and might trigger public outrage. They thus tried to avoid these activities.[54]

Limits to TPA at townships are apparent. At the township level TPA can be viewed as a healthy formality instead of a critical institution ensuring public supervision. Officials could choose not to reveal sensitive public matters such as certain personnel appointments and detailed contents of the budget. Furthermore, many of the decisions that are publicized have been decided and the public has slim chances of reversing the decisions. Therefore, TPA may not result in effective supervision of officials by the public.[55]

Village assemblies and Village Representative Assemblies (VRAs)

Village committees of 5–7 members are elected to run the villages. Nevertheless, villagers could better ensure that their opinions were heard and that the village committee conducted themselves properly if policies and decisions were discussed by villagers at village assemblies or by villagers' representatives at the village representative assemblies. In 1990 the Ministry of Civil Affairs affirmed the role of VRAs. By 1997 half of the villages in China had set up VRAs. These bodies now exist and function to varying extents in many villages in China.

According to the aforementioned study based on the 2005–6 rural survey, in 83 percent of the surveyed villages the village committee (VC) delivered a report to the village assembly in the last three years; in 12 percent of the surveyed villages the VC did so in one or two of each of the last three years; in 4 percent of the surveyed villages the VC failed to do so.[56]

Taken together with aforementioned findings from this survey, village assemblies and village representative assemblies have been set up widely throughout China. Their presence and operation have served to enhance public participation in decision-making and public supervision of village affairs and village cadres.

Public hearings and deliberation over governmental policies and budget

Since the late 1990s national laws mandated public hearings on certain judicial matters and changes in prices of goods. Public hearings have indeed taken place especially over prices. Specifically, an article in the national law on administrative punishment in 1996 required a public hearing before any punishment was given out. In December 1997 the NPC passed the Law on Price and Article 23 of the law mandated public hearings prior to decisions on prices of goods. The Law on Legislature passed in 2000 stipulated that public hearings should take place in the process of making of laws or regulations.[57]

Inspired partly by national public hearings leaders in certain localities introduced public hearings in other matters, such as governmental policies that could have vast implications on local residents, such as mergers of schools and public projects. They even held hearings over official performance and governmental budgets. These efforts aimed at encouraging citizens to participate in the deliberation of major local policies and of use of budget and in supervision of officials.

The most noticeable local experiment on public hearings took place in Wenling (county-level city), Taizhou (prefecture-level city), Zhejiang Province.[58] In 1999 the Party committee of Wenling designated Songmen Township as a key location to trial an educational campaign on modernization of agriculture and the countryside; it also worked with the Songmen Party committee to create a forum on the topic. Due to the unexpectedly warm public reception the forum was held four times, attracting 600 attendants. At the forum the organizers received 110 inquiries from the public. Officials responded on the site to 84 of them and promised to follow up with the remaining 26 cases. The Party committee of Wenling City coined these open dialogues and open hearings on public policies as democratic consultations. In 2000 it expanded the experiments to the administrative departments of the city government, all urban districts, urban residential communities, townships, villages, public organizations, and non-state enterprises in Wenling. Democratic consultations of the departments of the city government covered the new policies, changes in the existing administrative system or procedures, and new items for fees or services. Issues discussed at democratic consultations of urban districts, townships and villages included major policies or major projects that could affect significantly a large number of local residents. An item could be placed on the agenda of democratic consultations when it won the support of over one-fifth of the local legislators or representatives of local regions.

Participants usually included local legislators, relevant social groups, and citizens who had stakes in the issues to be discussed. Under the principle of equality participants at the talks would speak freely and could make harsh comments on officials. Officials at the talks usually passed on the opinions of the attendants to local leaders in charge. The chair of the talks would explain later the decisions of the local leaders on the issues and the underlying rationale. Usually when a policy or project arouses strong objections from the citizens, local leaders would abandon or significantly mend the original policies or the project design by taking into account their opinions.[59]

In 2004 Wenqiao Town of Wenling convened a democratic consultation on a project on water diversion from Jidunkeng Reservoir and consequential expansion in the budgetary items on basic construction. In the next year Songmen Town invited legislators and representatives of citizens to participate in the discussion and formulation of local governmental budget. In the same year Zeguo Town invited 300 randomly selected local citizens out of the local population of 120,000 to discuss and select projects for urban construction funded by the governmental budget. The 300 citizens filled out a questionnaire indicating their preferences for these projects and their opinion served as a reference point for decisions on these projects by local leaders.[60] Democratic consultations have earned endorsement from higher-level leaders. In the 2010s Zhejiang Party Secretary Zhao Hongzhu stated that the Wenling-type democratic consultation meetings could be implemented throughout the province.[61]

Similar attempts to invite public oversight on governmental budget surfaced in a few cities in China. In 1998 Jiaozuo City in Henan Province suffered from severe fiscal shortages and problems. In 2008 the Party committee and the government of Jiaozuo set up public hearings on local governmental budget in order to avoid a repeat of the fiscal disaster in 1998. In 2009 the legislature of Minhang District in Shanghai also organized public hearings on fiscal budget.[62]

Obviously, when public hearings are done faithfully in order to solicit public opinions on public policies, governmental budget, and public projects, decision makers would have a far more reliable sense of public sentiments toward the major policies. Sometimes public opinions on these significant policies or projects could be very different from what policymakers expected. Such public feedback will thus be critical for decision makers to avoid public grievance and to maintain their political legitimacy.

Nevertheless, there are several grave limits to democratic consultation meetings. First, as a study suggested, the experiments in Wenling have degenerated in the recent years. In Songmen and Wenqiao Towns the democratic consultation meetings have become irregular and have been subject to manipulation by the local government. The new local leaders held that the binding nature of democratic consultation meetings unnecessarily impeded government's effectiveness and had the potential to cause troubles.[63] Few-smith also confirmed that the experiment with participatory budget process in Xinhe Town of Wenlin was reversed when the Party secretary was promoted and when his successor arrived.[64] Second, only a small number of cities in China have adopted public hearings systemically. Third, while public hearings are arguably most commonly held on prices of major goods, such as water, there have been skepticisms that many of the public hearings are merely staged shows and are formalities short of substance.

Conclusion

In the reform era there have been multiple drives and initiatives to push forth democracy and to reduce the over-concentration of power in the CCP and the hands of the Party secretary at all levels, and to reduce corruption, incompetence and abuse of power by officials. These initiatives have helped reduce abuse of power and have helped defuse the criticisms about lack of democratic progress in China to a limited extent. Furthermore, these initiatives have inspired hopes from observers for democratic breakthrough in China.

The earliest experiments were village elections that were initiated by villagers in Guangxi in 1980 and later embraced by the leaders of the national legislature and then the CCP. By 1994 village elections were held in all but one province. Apparently, as stated above, village elections have brought many far-reaching positive changes in the governance in villages. In the urban communities and sub-districts experimental elections of residents committees emerged much later, mostly in the mid-1980s. Elections of residents committees had been popularized throughout China by the mid-2000s. Nevertheless, the positive effects of the RC elections are likely very limited, because only 22 percent of these elections were indirect in 2008 and because the government or grass-roots organizations with governmental ties intervened in elections extensively.

Furthermore, other than village committees (administrative leaders of villages), village Party secretaries, and to some extent resident committees (administrative leaders of urban communities), as well as legislators and delegates of the Party Congress at various levels tend to be filled by non-competitive and formalistic elections. The only improvement seems to be the growing adoption of public recommendation and public selection of officials (which I coin semi-competitive selection of officials) by many local governments as well as national ministries. Even this measure does not involve elections and only involves political elites as selectors of the final candidates for the official posts. Furthermore, even the bolder experiments with semi-competitive selection of officials at the township level seem quite limited considering that it took place in less than 5 percent of the 44,821 towns and townships in China around 2004.[65]

Considering that the multiple layers of the political power structure in China stretch from village (or urban communities in the cities), townships (towns), through counties (or urban districts), prefectures, provinces, to the national level, elections have only managed to cover the lowest level, namely, villages or urban communities. The limits of electoral democracy in China are thus apparent. Keep in mind that there are over 10,000 counties, 300 prefectural-level cities, and 31 provinces at local levels in mainland China. None of these administrative layers have experienced genuine and competitive elections throughout its jurisdiction.[66] Very few localities have also systemically institutionalized public hearings and democratic consultation meetings in formulating policies developmental plans and local governmental budget. Therefore, there are still clear obstacles against citizens' political participation.

Furthermore, little political progress has been brought about by some of the aforementioned measures of political reform. For example, permanent representation of the Party congress has faithfully been implemented in very few localities. Moreover, the so-called decisions of the Party committee by secret ballots do not prevent the centralization and even abuse of power in the hand of the Party secretary. The rampant abuse of power and transgression of due process in the campaign of fighting the mafia in Chongqing under the Party secretary Bo Xilai provides a vivid example.

As stated, one of the most impressive measures in intra-Party democracy is that in selecting the new President and the new Premier Hu consulted with hundreds of current and past top power holders in China and even invited them to vote. It remains to be seen whether Xi Jinping will honor this innovation.

Furthermore, progresses and experiments with intra-Party democracy have apparently been halted in the recent years.[67] There was evidence of reluctance of the Party leaders in supporting further liberal political reforms. For example, in August 2006 the CCP official journal *Qiushi* (*Seeking Truth*) published an article criticizing direct elections of township leaders. This was widely interpreted by many as the opposition of the Party against the liberal measure.[68]

Finally, the telltale signs about the political stance of the current leadership offer no ominous evidence about progress in democratization in China in the foreseeable future. The Carter Center, a think tank in which the former U.S. president Jimmy Carter was closely involved, has been monitoring, studying, and promoting village elections in China since the 1990s, and has been studying government transparency in later years. In December 2012, shortly after he succeeded Hu as the General Secretary of the CCP and the Chairman of the CMC, Mr. Xi proposed to Mr. Carter that the Carter Center should refocus on U.S.–China relations. In addition, an order from the authorities in Yuncheng, a city in central China, revealed that a thorough nationwide investigation into the activities of foreign nongovernment organizations in China was conducted from May through July 2014 and that every village and every department was told to protect the safety of the nation's political system and social stability.[69]

For these and other reasons, the aforementioned political reform measures are a long way from achieving full democracy within the ruling party and throughout

China. To borrow Mao's famous saying, these democratic initiatives are merely "the first step in a long march."

Notes

* Much of this chapter is newly written. Part of the sections on intra-Party democracy and competitive selection of officials were published as "Intra-Party Democracy in China: The First Step in a Long March," in Zhengxu Wang and Colin Durkop, eds, *East Asian Democracy and Political Development in China* (Singapore: Konrad Adenauer Stiftung, 2008), 207–24. Reprint by permission. These published segments have been revised and much extended.

1 In this chapter intra-Party democracy refers to democratic institutions within the CCP and democratic activities practiced by CCP leaders, officials, and members, as well as elite members who are likely to be Party members. It includes (1) permanent representation of Party congress and (2) decisions by the Party Committee via ballots. Selection of officials by local Party committee members or by a group of selectors such as local Party and administrative leaders and local representatives, which is coined semi-competitive election by some analysts, may relate to intra-Party democracy. Nevertheless, it is treated separately from intra-Party democracy due to the possible involvement in official selection by citizens who are not Party members.

2 Excessive power in the hands of the local Party secretary has given rise to serious problems. In a number of high-profile corruption cases, a significant number of key leaders in localities were found to be implicated in scandals and tried to protect each other. No officials could question their conduct and prevent their abuse of power. For example, when serving as the Party Secretary of Hebei Province in the 1990s, Cheng Weigao allowed his secretary and a former secretary to be involved in business scandals and act autocratically. He even detained illegally a local cadre, who wanted to expose the power abuse of his secretaries, and sent him to labor reform for two years. See "Nanfang Zhoumo: Weile zhengyi ta yu Cheng Weigao jiaoliang banian" (Southern Weekend: He Contended with Cheng Weigao for Eight Years for Justice), posted at: http://Inews.sina.com.cnlc/2003-08-14/I534566525s. shtml, accessed on February 18, 2008.

3 Zheng Changzhong, *Zhongguo Gongchandang Dangnei Minzhu Zhidu Chuangxin* (*Innovation in Intra-Party Democratic Institutions within the Chinese Communist Party*) (Tianjin: Tianjin Renmin Chubanshe, 2005), 224–25, 230.

4 Ibid., 260.

5 Ibid., 225–26, 231–32.

6 Ibid., 292–93.

7 See the CCCCP, "Rules Regarding Selection and Appointment of Party and Governmental Leading Cadres", July 9, 2002, posted at: www.xinhuanet.org; Zheng, *Zhonggo Gongchandang Dangnei Minzhu Zhidu Chuangxin*, 291–94.

8 For an overview of lively discussion on intra-Party democracy by senior official analysts in China during 2000–2002 right before Hu came to power, refer to Zheng, *Zhongguo Gongchandang Dangnei Minzhu Zhidu Chuangxin*, 3–21.

9 Zheng, *Zhongguo Gongchandang Dangnei Minzhu Zhidu Chuangxin*, 436–40.

10 Zheng, *Zhongguo Gongchandang Dangnei Minzhi Zhidu Chuangxin*, 436.

11 Hu Jintao, "Hold High the Great Banner of Socialism with Chinese Characteristics and Strive for New Victories in Building a Moderately Prosperous Society in all Respects: Report to the Seventeenth National Congress of the Communist Party of China on Oct. 15, 2007," *China Daily*, October 25, 2007.

12 Zheng, *Zhongguo Gongchandang Dangnei Minzhu Zhidu Chuangxin*, 301–3.

13 "The CCP Attempts to Change the Current Situation of Over-Concentration of Power," posted at: www.chinesenewsnet.com on July 2, 2004; Zheng Changzhong, *Zhongguo Gongchandang Dangnei Minzhu Zhidu Chuangxin*, 303.

14 "The CCP Attempts to Change the Current Situation of Over-Concentration of Power"; Zheng, *Zhongguo Gongchandang Dangnei Minzhu Zhidu Chuangxin*, 302–4.

15 "Directly Elect Delegates for the Party Congress," *Xinwen Zhoukan* (*Newsweek*), posted at: www.sina.com.cn on October 1, 2004.

16 Zheng Changzhong, *Zhongguo Gongchandang Dangnei Minzhu Zhidu Chuangxin*, 290.

17 "Directly Elect Delegates for the Party Congress," *Xinwen Zhoukan* (*Newsweek*), posted at: www.sina.com.cn on October 1, 2004.

18 "Expert Suggests that There Are Still Misunderstandings About Stipulations in the Rules regarding Supervision within the Party in Localities," posted at: www.china news.com.cn on July 5, 2004.

19 "Dangnei minzhu: gaige de qierudian?" (Intra-Party Democracy: A Point of Breakthrough for Reform?), posted at: http://cn.nytimes.com/china/20120924/cc24qia ngang6/print/ on September 24, 2015, accessed on April 19, 2015.

20 Zheng, *Zhongguo Gongchandang Dangnei Minzhu Zhidu Chuangxin*, p. 291.

21 "Dang daihui daibiao ti'an zhi" (The Institution of Motions by Delegates of the Party Congress), posted at: http://baike.baidu.com/view/9583420.htm, accessed on April 19, 2015.

22 "Dang daihui daibiao ti'an zhidu de kunjing ji chulu" (The Dilemma of the Institution of Motions by Delegates of the Party Congress and Remedies), posted at: http://114.247.135.140/llyj/xswtyj/zzdyj/201310/t20131008_295009.htm#, accessed on April 19, 2015.

23 Zheng, *Zhongguo Gongchandang Dangnei Minzhu Zhidu Chuangxin*, 292–5, 299.

24 Ibid., 257–62.

25 Semi-competitive elections in this book refer to the fact that there are no opposition parties and no reported competitive open campaigns in the process.

26 Lai, *Zhongguo nongcun zhengzhi tizhi gaige*, 196–200.

27 Ibid., 276.

28 "Self Rule of Villagers, Relations Between the Two Committees and China's Political Transformation," posted at: www.ccrs.org.cn on October 5, 2005; Zheng, *Zhongguo Gongchanciang Dangnei Minzhu Zhidu Chuangxin*, 276.

29 Lai Hairong defined and used this concept in his insightful study of elections of township and village posts in rural China. See Lai Hairong, *Zhongguo nongcun zhengzhi tizhi gaige*, 1.

30 Zheng, *Zhongguo Gongchanciang Dangnei Minzhu Zhidu Chuangxin*, 277–9, 289–90.

31 Ibid.

32 Lai, *Zhongguo nongcun zhengzhi tizhi gaige*, pp. 63–6.

33 Lai, *Zhongguo nongcun zhengzhi tizhi gaige*, pp. 71–2.

34 "Zhejiang Elected Township Party Secretary by Ballots," *Ming Pao*, September 10, 2004.

35 Wu Ming, "Reform in Xian'an Township of Hubei Province," cited in Zheng, *Zhongguo Gongchandang Dangnei Minzhu Zhidu Chuangxin*, p. 281.

36 This is based on the author's collection of various news reports published in China.

37 "Jiangsu Experiments with Personnel Reform and First County Director is Chosen Through 'Open Recommendation and Open Selection'," Source: *Dongfang Zao Bao* (*Oriental Morning Post*), posted at: http://nevws.xinhuanet.com on December 8, 2003. For a detailed analysis of intra-Party democracy in China, refer to Lai Hongyi, *Hu Wen quan toushi: Hu Wen shizheng neimu quan jiedu ji Zhongguo weilai zhanwang* (*Hu–Wen under Full Scrutiny: A Comprehensive Inside Story of Governance under Hu and Wen and Prospects for Future China*) (Hong Kong: Wenhua yishu. chubanshe, 2005).

262 Intra-Party and grass-roots democracy

38 "Zhonggong 18 da shixing le dangnei minzhu? Xuezhe yaotou huo diantou" (Was Intra-Party Democracy Implemented at the Eighteenth Congress of the CCP? Some Scholars Shook Heads Whereas Others Nodded), posted at: www.voachinese.com/content/china-20121116/1547791.html, accessed on April 19, 2015.

39 "Zhou Ruijin: Cong lishi shijiao kan shibada" (Zhou Ruijin: The Eighteenth Party Congress from a Historical Perspective), posted at: www.boxun.com/news/gb/china/2013/01/201301031425.shtml#.VTQJeDn7VhA on January 3, 2013, accessed on April 19, 2015.

40 Conversations with scholars and officials in China regarding public selection of officials, 2005.

41 Shi Weimin *et al.*, *Zhongguo cunmin weiyuanhui xuanju lishi fazhan yu bijiao yanjiu*, Vol. 1, 1–97.

42 Tianjian Shi, "Village Committee Elections in China: Institutional Tactics for Democracy," *World Politics*, April 1999, 385–412.

43 Xiao Tangbiao and Shi Haiyan, "Zhongguo nongcun chunmin zizhi yunxing de qiuyu tezheng yu jingji beijing" (Regional Characteristics and Economic Context of the Operation of Self Rule by Villagers in China's Countryside), in Tang Jin, ed., *Da Guoqe: Jicheng Minzhu* (*Major National Policies: Grass-roots Democracy*) (Beijing: Renmin ribao chubanshe, 2009), 83–96.

44 Tang Jin, ed., *Da Guoqe: Jicheng Minzhu* (*Major National Policies: Grass-roots Democracy*) (Beijing: Renmin ribao chubanshe, 2009), 1.

45 "Zhonghua renmin gongheguo chengshi jumin weiyuanhui zhuzhifa" (The Organic Law of the Urban Residents Committees of the People's Republic of China), posted at: http://baike.baidu.com/link?url=3cVSVPXCMi_mJsTQTUE17V6phRU0tMnsccLgU1KlclqlXYlukQ5aWYxDT2riOI67OCxT5kqGAXN0pdU7uWtuZ_, accessed on April 23, 2015.

46 Shi Weimin, *Zhongguo shequ juminhui xuanju yanjiu* (*A Study of Elections of Community Residents Committees in China*) (Beijing: Zhongguo shehui kexue chubanshe, 2009).

47 Chen Wenxin, "Zhongguo chengshi shequ juweihui zhijie xuanju: Fazhan lichen yu xianshi kunjing" (Direct Elections of Residents Committees in Urban Communities in China: The Course of Development and Actual Dilemma), *Gansu Lilun Xuekan*, No. 2, 2008.

48 "Minzheng bu guanyuan biaoshi chengshi shequ zhixuan 2010 nian da 50%" (MCA Officials Revealed that 50% of Urban Districts Would Hold Direct Elections by 2010), *Renmin ribao* (*People's Daily*) (overseas edition), August 4, 2008, 5; Zheng Quan, "Shequ juweihui xuanju huodong de xianzhuan, wenti ji duice" (The Current Situation, Problems and Remedies in Elections of Residents Committees in Residential Communities), posted at: http://doc.qkzz.net/article/5c55a5a8-6904-4874-8628-d95afffb0f55.htm, accessed on April 12, 2015.

49 "Woguo chengshi jumin zizhi fenxi" (An Analysis of Self-rule of Urban Residents in Our Country), posted at: www.cssn.cn/zzx/zgzz_zzx/201405/t20140515_1163710.shtml on May 15, 2014, accessed on April 23, 2015.

50 Liu Youtian, *Cunmin zizhi* (*Self-rule by Villagers*) (Beijing: Renmin chubanshe, 2010), 167–76.

51 Ma Baocheng, "Cunji zhili yu xiangcun zhengzhi wending" (Village Governance and Political Stability in the Countryside), in Ying Donghua, ed., *Cong Guanli Dao Zhili: Zhongguo Difang Zhili Xianzhuang* (*From Management to Governance: The Current Situation of Local Governance in China*) (Beijing: Zhongyang bianyi chubanshe, 2006), 91–101.

52 Xiao and Shi, "Zhongguo nongcun chunmin zizhi yunxing de qiuyu tezheng yu jingji beijing," 83–96.

53 Peng Zongchao and Zhong Kaipin, "Zhengwu gongkai yu xiangzhen zhili" (Transparency of Public Affairs and Township Governance), in Ying Donghua, ed., *Cong Guanli Dao Zhili*, 76–90.
54 Ibid.
55 Ibid.
56 Xiao Tangbiao and Shi Haiyan, "Zhongguo nongcun chunmin zizhi yunxing de qiuyu tezheng yu jingji beijing."
57 Baogang He, "Participatory and Deliberative Institutions in China," in Ethan Leib and Baogang He, eds, *The Search for Deliberative Democracy in China* (New York and Basingstoke: Palgrave Macmillan, 2006), 180.
58 For a detailed account of the experiment, see Fewsmith, *The Logic and Limits of Political Reform in China*, 142–69.
59 Chen Yimin, "Minzhu kentan: Wenlingshi jiceng minzhu de chuangxin he shijian" (Democratic Talks in Sincerity: Innovation and Practice in Grass-roots Democracy in Wenling City), in Li Fan, ed. *Zhongguo jiceng minzhu fazhan baogao 2004 (A Report on the Development of Grass-roots Democracy in China)* (Beijing: Shijie zhishi chubanshe, 2005), 144–69.
60 Ibid.
61 Fewsmith, *The Logic and Limits of Political Reform in China*, 167.
62 Li Fan, ed., *Zhongguo jiceng minzhu fazhan baogao 2009 (A Report on the Development of Grass-roots Democracy in China)* (Beijing: Huawen chubanshe, 2009), 223–58, 259–71.
63 Dragan Pavlicevic, *State Building, Public Participation and Democratization in China: Non-Electoral Participatory Mechanisms in Zhejiang*, PhD Thesis (Nottingham: University of Nottingham, July 2014), Chapter 5.
64 Fewsmith, *The Logic and Limits of Political Reform in China*, 155.
65 I compute the percentage using data in Lai Hairong, *Zhongguo nongcun zhengzhi tizhi gaige*, 22
66 Lai, *Zhongguo nongcun zhengzhi tizhi gaige*, 22.
67 Conversations with scholars on Chinese politics from China, 2010.
68 Lai Hairong, *Zhongguo nongcun zhengzhi tizhi gaige*, 131.
69 "Beijing Aims to Blunt Western Influence in China: Carter Center Think Tank Sees Shift in How it is Received by China Authorities," *Wall Street Journal*, November 11, 2014, posted at: www.wsj.com/articles/beijing-aims-to-blunt-western-influence-in-china-1415756626, accessed on February 9, 2015.

Part 4

Conclusion

9 Durability of the Party state

The life span of unified regimes in China[*]

Introduction

This chapter consists of two major parts. The first part is an overview of the main historical periods in China and an analysis of the pattern of the life span of unified regimes in China. In the twenty-two periods of the past four thousand years, China disintegrated into contending kingdoms in eight of these periods, and united during the other fourteen periods. The thirteen periods of unity prior to 1949, including twelve dynasties and one republic, varied widely in length from about five hundred to under twenty years. Scholars have long noticed dynastic interchange between unity and chaos. However, few have seriously asked: What accounts for the different longevities of the already-ended thirteen periods of national unity? Is there any pattern in the life spans of the periods? The first part of this chapter is devoted to addressing these questions.

In the first part of the chapter I identify and explain a pattern of Chinese historical regimes. The longevity of a unified regime is negatively correlated with the length of preceding disorder. This is so for two possible reasons. First, the longer the previous disorder, the more difficult it would be for the rulers of a newly-unified regime to neutralize powerful centrifugal forces and external threats and to provide services for the population. Second, the longer the previous disorder, the more likely these new rulers would be deluded by their own historical achievement of unifying the long-divided nation and so commit political mistakes. Their mistakes allowed the forces for division to surface and disintegrate the nation. This chapter aims to invite scholars to discuss and debate Chinese historical patterns, rather than to construct a thorough treatise. Meanwhile, it is also natural that an original view on China's history will invite criticisms as well as agreement and that only through debates can we re-examine and expand our knowledge and falsify hypotheses.

In the second part of the chapter I will draw lessons from the historical studies and examine factors that favor or hinder the longevity of the Party state. On the basis of a historical study I argue that the Party state enjoys a set of factors that seem to bode well for its durability, including the absence of formidable and immediate foreign invaders and of organised and armed domestic opposition. The historically-implied longevity of the current regime, however, is constrained by the growing significance of ideational powers of individual rights, the rule of law, transparency, supervision of power holders, and democracy. It is also constrained by the growing impact of technology, especially information and transport technology, that in turn serve to improve the public understanding of the deficiencies of the Chinese system against the aforementioned ideational powers.

Arguments on dynastic cycles

In his brilliant work, Mark Elvin suggested that organizational, economic, and military advantages helped the Chinese Empire to survive external conquests. He proposed that a high-level equilibrium prevented technological innovation and industrial revolution in China. Yet his discourse did not touch the length of unified periods.[1] Scholars also commented on individual dynasties. Derk Bodde, for example, argued that the Qin overextended its resources in expanding from a state into an empire.[2] Nevertheless, his argument may not hold because decades prior to the unification the area of the Qin already exceeded that of the six states combined. Thus conquering the remaining six states was no longer a mission impossible.[3]

On the other hand, Jin Guangtao and Liu Qingfeng advanced the following argument. Unified dynasties that emerged after division, such as the Qin, the Western Jin, and the Sui, tended to be short-lived; in contrast, those that were built after peasant uprisings, including the Former Han, the Later Han, the Tang, the Ming, and the Qing, tended to last longer. Jin and Liu suggested that the former preserved anti-unification forces, such as rich families and senior officials of previous kingdoms, and that the latter were relatively free of these forces, because violent peasant uprisings had wiped them out.[4] Their argument offers a hint at varying life spans of the dynasties. In a similar vein, Chen Jiarong remarked that unity of China under the Qin, the Sui, and the Republic of China (ROC) lasted only briefly. He reasoned that all three regimes bore too heavy historical burdens.[5] Whereas Jin and Liu failed to treat the Yuan and the ROC as short-lived unified regimes, Chen failed to put the Western Jin and the Yuan in the same category. Finally, they did not propose any general connection between the length of a unified dynasty and its preceding period.

Aside from Jin and Liu's and Chen's discussion, the remaining relevant literature appears to be about the dynastic cycle of Chinese history. They explain the rise and fall of dynasties, rather than dynastic life spans, in terms of personalities of leaders, political legitimacy, official and the ruling class corruption, and the land tax system. The earliest proponent of the dynastic cycles in China was probably Sima Qian, the founder of historiography in China. According to Sima, "a dynasty begins in virtue and ends in vice ... Virtue is based here on the behaviour of the ruler and involves, among other things, proper reverence for spirits. Virtue, Sima Qian argues, overrides even bad portents sent from the spirits. And vice, so to speak, involves improper reverence."[6] Modern scholars of Chinese history have stripped off the superstitious element in Sima Qian's theory of dynastic cycles and reinterpret virtue and vice in rational and Confucian terms. They argue that a dynasty-founder seized the Mandate of Heaven (*Tian Ming*) not only through heeding the need of the people, but also by virtue of his upright, strong, and self-disciplined personality and his tight control of official corruption. However, their successors could inherit the power by birth. Thus they tended to indulge in leisure and entertain women, wine, arts, or extravagant hobbies. As members of the imperial family, eunuchs, and senior officials tried to usurp power, these groups often clashed with one another, and the regime failed to take care of the population. Then the dynasty lost their Mandate of Heaven. Meritorious leaders would assemble political backing to topple the decadent regime, and set off another cycle of dynasties.[7] A variant of this argument traced dynastic decline to the elites' extravagance, greed, and insensitivity to the needs of the populace, instead of those of merely the ruler.[8]

The second school points to the importance of tax and revenue. The military, bureaucracy, and public services of the regime depended heavily on revenue, especially land tax in imperial China. After years of war, at the beginning of each dynasty large land-possession was destroyed, and land left wild. The state usually redistributed land to peasants, and the state could tax them with ease. Over time, people who had power or wealth, or political connections gradually increased their land-holdings and exempted themselves from taxes. As land tax declined, so did the state's revenue, as well as its military power and social services. Weak national defence invited external invaders. Failure to provide basic social services, such as channelling rivers, led to human tragedies, such as disastrous floods. In addition, some of the peasants who lost their land turned into bandits and rebels. At the end, external threats and domestic protests brought down the regime.[9]

Although these two accounts emphasize the significance of distinct political factors as stated above, they both point to the devastating effects of corruption of the ruling class on the regime. These accounts, however, have been criticized for their lack or neglect of rigorous empirical evidence. Limited space prevents me from elaborating on the criticisms.[10] Suffice to say, these arguments on the Chinese dynastic cycle have yet to answer the question "Why were some Chinese periods of unity shorter than the others?" Before an answer to the question is proposed, an examination of the length of the unified regimes and their preceding periods will be helpful.

A pattern of the Chinese unified regimes

As stated, among the twenty-two periods of Chinese history, unity was achieved in fourteen periods, whereas national division marked the other eight periods (Table 9.1). For now I will focus on the twenty-one already-ended periods prior to the PRC.

Table 9.1 Chinese historical periods (regimes) from the Shang Dynasty to present

Category	National Unity	National Division
Numbers	14	8
Name	Shang, Western Zhou, Qin, Former Han, Later Han, Western Jin, Sui, Tang, Northern Song, Yuan, Ming, Qing, Republic of China (ROC), and People's Republic of China (PRC)	Spring and Autumn, Warring States, Three Kingdoms, Eastern Jin and the Sixteen Kingdoms, Southern and Northern Dynasties, Five Dynasties and Ten Kingdoms, Southern Song and Jin, and late Qing and Northern Warlords (Republic)

In this chapter the length of unity or a unified regime is that period when the government controlled a unified country.[11] To be specific, unity satisfies the two following criteria. First, the government had direct or indirect jurisdiction over much of the country. If the government lost pivotal areas of China (such as the lower Yellow River valley or the Yangtze valley), or when the regime lost its ability to control and suppress armed rivals in the pivotal areas, disorder thus fell upon the regime. Second, the regime enjoyed sovereign integrity and respect for its authority. Localities and other nations recognized the central government as the legitimate authority for the whole country. If a regime suffered from major and repetitive defeats or invasions by foreign powers and allowed foreign powers to intrude extensively into its foreign and domestic affairs, this period is considered disorder. This was exactly the case of the late Qing Dynasty. The length of division, by default, is the number of the years when the country was still not unified.

Several points need to be clarified here. First, history books record longer lengths of some dynasties than those given here. The reasons are as follows. First, I consider that a unified dynasty started from the year its founder controlled the country. In contrast, some historians take the year the founders pronounced the birth of their dynasties yet were still fighting their armed rivals. Second, some dynasties lost their authority over the country before the ceremonial demise date. Indicators of an end of a regime's authority over the country include losing one of the pivotal areas (the lower Yellow River valley or the mid- and lower Yangtze valleys) to a rival regime, losing its abilities to suppress growing rebels or foreign invasion, or having their capitals sacked and emperors captured. Examples of a regime losing its abilities to suppress expanding rivals include the Qin after its main force was defeated by Xiang Yu in Julu in 207 B.C., as well as the Yuan's loss of its main force in a battle against the Red Turbans in 1354. Most of these marking events come directly from respectable textbooks and manuals on China's history and are thus credible. In Tables 9.2A and 9.2B, I take pains to record the starting and ending years of unified regimes, and record the events that mark the start and end of these regimes. In addition, I record the start and end of periods of disorder and describe them in detail.

Table 9.2A Life span and details of the unified regimes

Dynasty/ republic	Span (years)	Starting Year	Ending Year	Starting Event	Ending Event
Shang	554	1600 B.C.	1046 B.C.	Tang, the leader of the tribe Shang, defeated Jie, the exploitative and tyrannical king of the Xia and established the Shang Dynasty.	Zhou, the last Shang king, was defeated by Zhou's King Wuwang, the founder of the Zhou in 1046 BC.
Western Zhou	271	1041 B.C.	770 B.C.	The Shang King Zhouwang aroused public anger for protracted warfare, exploitation, and tyranny. He was defeated by the Zhou's King Wuwang. The Shang was interned in 1046 BC. I counted the length of the war as one year. The founding King of Zhou Wuwang died two years afterwards (roughly 1044 BC). Wuwang's brother, Duke of Zhou, or known as Zhougong, spent three years in quelling the rebellion by his brothers and Zhouwang's son Wugeng (completed around 1041 BC), much expanded Zhou's territory and consolidated Zhou's rule over the formerly Shang's territory. Thus the period prior to the consolidated Zhou lasted for five years.	Shenghou, the father of the queen of Western Zhou's last King Youwang, united nomadic troops, defeated Zhou, and killed Youwang in Lishan. King Pingwang was forced to move the capital from Feng and Gao to Luoyang in 770 B.C.
Qin	14	221 B.C.	207 B.C.	Ying Zheng, the king of the Qin state, led a ten-year campaign and conquered six other states. He unified China in 221 B.C. and founded the Qin Dynasty.	Chen Sheng and Wu Guang rebelled in 209 B.C., triggering nationwide uprisings against the Qin. In 207 B.C., Xiang Yu, a rebel leader, crushed the Qin's main forces in Julu. In 206 B.C. the Qin's Emperor Ziying surrendered to Liu Bang, another rebel leader.
Former Han	207	202 B.C.	5 A.D.	In 202 B.C., Liu Bang defeated Xiang Yu. Xiang committed suicide. Liu established the Han in a unified China.	Wang Mang established 2-year-old Liu Ying as the Han's emperor, and himself as a de facto emperor.
Later Han	154	36	190	By 36 A.D., Liu Xiu, the founder of the Later Han, had crushed the peasant rebellions and defeated other forces. After decades of rebellions and warfare at the end of the Former Han he unified China.	In 190, one year after he abolished Emperor Shaodi and established puppet Emperor Xiandi, Dong Zhuo moved the capital. Warlords and rebellions disintegrated the Later Han's rule.

Dynasty/ republic	Span (years)	Starting Year	Ending Year	Starting Event	Ending Event
Western Jin	36	280	316	Sima Yan, the founder of Western Jin, seized power from Cao Huan of the Wei in 265. He defeated the other two kingdoms (the Shu and the Wu) and united China in 280.	Liu Yao, a Xiongnu leader, seized Chang'an, the Jin's capital, captured Jin's Emperor Mindi.
Sui	27	589	616	Yang Jian, who proclaimed the Sui Dynasty in 581, defeated the Chen in 589, the remaining kingdom in China. Hence China was united.	Three major rebel groups (Hebei, Wagang, and Jianghuai) dis-integrated the Sui's rule in 616, forcing the Sui's Yangdi to retreat to the south. He died in a coup two years later.
Tang	279	628	907	After 11 years of warfare, Li Yuan, the founder of the Tang, defeated other troops that rebelled against the Sui in 628. China was united under the Tang.	In 907, Governor Zhu Chuanzhong abolished Aidi of the Tang and established the Liao Dynasty.
Northern Song	148	979	1127	After 19 years of warfare, the Northern Song defeated other military forces and kingdoms, and unified China in 979.	Jin troops seized the Song's capital Kaifeng, and captured two emperors (Huizong and Qinzong) as hostages.
Yuan	78	1276	1354	In 1276 the Mongolian troops under the Yuan entered Lin'an, the capital of the Southern Song, and captured the Song emperor.	In 1354, the main force of the Yuan under its prime minister disintegrated in a confrontation against Red Turban rebels. From then on, the Yuan was unable to crush various growing rebel forces.
Ming	273	1368	1641	By 1368, Zhu Yuanzhang's troops had defeated his rival rebels, seized the Yuan's capital, and advanced through central to southern China. China was united.	In 1641, nationwide rebellions reached their peak, the Qing army defeated the Ming troops in Liaoning, and the Ming was on the defensive thereafter. Three years later it was overthrown.

Dynasty/republic	Span (years)	Starting Year	Ending Year	Starting Event	Ending Event
Qing	189	1664	1853	Qing's troops conquered southern China (including Guangdong, Yunnan, and Sichuan), and defeated remaining resistant troops in the mainland in 1664.	Taiping Rebels captured Wuchang and Nanjing in early 1853. In 1860, British-Franco troops invaded Beijing, the capital, and plundered and destroyed the imperial Yuanming Garden. In the period the Qing suffered from repetitive foreign invasions and degenerated into spheres of influences of major powers, or a semi-colony. From 1858 till 1928 China's customs and its foreign trade tariffs were managed by Westerners, especially the British who served the interests of Western powers and Japan. China lost its economic sovereignty and its manufactured goods suffered from unregulated foreign competition and astoundingly high tariffs in the western markets.[12]
Republic of China	*12*	*1930*	*1949*	After the successful Northern Expedition, Jiang defeated the coalition troops of warlords in the Zhongyuan (Central China) Battle in 1930 and established his control over a united China.	1) Intermission war of 1938–1945. Japan's invasion and occupation of eastern and central regions of China. 2) *The end of unified ROC in 1949.* The nationalist troops lost three key military campaigns and lost northern China (including Beijing and Tianjin) to the communists.

Notes: Italics stand for estimates. The starting and ending years of the Xia and the Shang Dynasties and the starting year of the Western Zhou are still preliminary and subject to confirmation of further historical research.
Sources: Zang Yunpu, Wang Yundu, Zhu Chongye, He Zhendong, and Ye Qing, *Zhongguo shi dashi jinian* (*A Chronology of Major Events on the Chinese History*) (Ji'nan: Shangdong jiaoyu chubanshe, 1984); Wang Fuchang and Guo Wenliang, *Zhongguo jinxiandai fazhan shi lun* (*A Treatise on China's Modern Development History*) (Guangzhou: Zhongshan daxue chubanshe, 1997); Tian Changwu and An Zuozhang, *Qin Han shi* (*A History of the Qin and Han*) (Beijing: Renmin chubanshe, 1993); Fang Xuanling, Chu Suiliang, and Xu Jingzong, *Jin shu* (*Books on the Jin*) (Beijing: Zhonghua shuju, 1974), Vol. 1; Lü Simian, *Sui Tang Wudai shi* (*A History on the Sui, the Tang, and the Five Dynasties*) (Shanghai: Shanghai guji chubanshe, 1984); Chi-ch'ing Hsiao, *Meng Yuan shi xin yan* (*Recent Studies on the Mongolian and the Yuan's History*) (Taipei: Yunchen wenhua shiye gufen youxian gongsi, 1994); Fu Yiling, Yang Guozhen, and Chen Zhiping, *Mingshi xinbian* (*A New Compilation on the History of the Ming*) (Beijing: Renmin chubanshe, 1993); Zheng Tianting, *Qing shi* (*A History on the Qing*) (Taipei: Yunlong chubanshe, 1998); entries on the Xia, Shang, Western Zhou dynasties and on their founding leaders posted at: www.baidu.com and on Wikipedia and google, accessed on August 8–9, 2014.

Table 9.2B Details on disorder preceding the unified regimes

Unified Dynasty/ Republic	Years of Preceding Disorder	Starting Year of Disorder	Ending Year of Disorder	Start and End of Disorder and Length
Shang	*1*	1600 B.C.	1600 B.C.	Jie, Xia's tyrannical king, fought against Tang of the Shang and was defeated and overthrown. (Since historical records suggest the war was brief, I take its length as one year.)
Western Zhou	*5*	1046 B.C.	1041 B.C.	Zhou's king Wuwang fought against and defeated Zhouwang, the tyrannical Shang king, and overthrew the Shang around 1046 BC. I counted the length of the war as one year. Soon after the founding of the Zhou and upon the death of the founding king of Zhou Wuwang around 1044 BC, the Duke of Zhou Zhougong spent three years in quelling the rebellion by Zhou's son Wugeng around 1041 BC. Thus war between the Shang and Zhou lasted for five years.
Qin	549	770 B.C.	221 B.C.	In the period of Autumn and Spring (770 B.C.–403 B.C.), China was divided into kingdoms. This period was followed by another divisive period Warring State (403 B.C.–221 B.C.). These two periods lasted 549 years. In 221 B.C. the Qin defeated the six kingdoms and united China.
Former (Western) Han	*5*	*207* B.C.	202 B.C.	Start: Xiang Yu defeated the Qin's main army in Julu. End: Liu Bang defeated his rival Xiang Yu.
Later (Eastern) Han	13	23 A.D.	36 A.D.	Start: In Kunyang in 23 A.D. rebels defeated the main forces of Wang Mang, a impulsive ruler of the Former Han. Wang was overthrown the next year. End: Liu Xiu, the founder of the Later Han, quelled the armed forces across the country and united China.
Western Jin	90	190	280	In 190, one year after he established puppet Emperor Xiandi, Dong Zhuo moved the Later Han's capital. The Later Han's rule hence degenerated into warlords and contending kingdoms. Between 190 and 280, China was divided into three kingdoms. The Western Jin united China in 280.

Unified Dynasty/ Republic	Years of Preceding Disorder	Starting Year of Disorder	Ending Year of Disorder	Start and End of Disorder and Length
Sui	273	316	589	Start: Nomadic captures of the Western Jin's capital and emperor put an end to the Jin in 316; through the Eastern Jin, Northern and Southern Dynasties (including 16 kingdoms in Northern Dynasties). End: Emperor Wendi of the Sui conquered the Chen of southern China, and Lingnan surrendered to the Sui. The Sui united China in 589.
Tang	12	616	628	Start: Following a rebellion in the Changbai Mountain in 611, by 616, three major rebellious groups disintegrated the Sui's rule. (Sui's emperor Yangdi was killed two years later.) End: Li Yuan, the founder of the Tang Dynasty, succeeded in defeating or recruiting contending military rivals.
Northern Song	72	907	979	Start: With Zhu Wen's abolition of the Tang in 907, China entered North-South division. Five Dynasties succeeded consecutively in the north (plus one kingdom near Shanxi in the north), and nine kingdoms in the south. End: In 979, the Song's Emperor Taizong conquered the last kingdom and unified China.
Yuan	149	1127	1276	Start: The Jin's capture of the Northern Song's capital and emperors. Through: Liao, Jin, and Mongol empires. End: In 1276, the Yuan (Mongolian) army captured the Southern Song's capital, and the Southern Song's emperor surrendered.
Ming	14	1354	1368	Start: Red Turban rebels defeated the main force of the Yuan in Gaoyou in 1354. End: Zhu Yuanzhang's general Xu Dai seized Yuan's capital in 1368.
Qing	23	1641	1664	Start: By 1641, nationwide rebellions reached their peak, and the Ming was on the defensive thereafter and was overthrown three years later. End: In 1664, the Qing defeated 13 resisting armies.

Unified Dynasty/ Republic	Years of Preceding Disorder	Starting Year of Disorder	Ending Year of Disorder	Start and End of Disorder and Length
Republic of China	77	1853	1930	Start: Taiping rebels seized Nanjing, and sent a shockwave to the Qing. Through: The Taiping Rebellion of 1851–64 and the Nian Rebellion of 1855–68, Boxer Uprising of 1899–1900; numerous foreign intrusions and unequal treaties degrading China into spheres of influences of major powers and a "semi-colony," including the British and French seizure of Beijing (the capital), defeat by Japan between 1894 and 1895, and 8-country invasion of Beijing in 1900; uprisings between 1906 and 1908, 1911 revolution overthrowing the Qing Dynasty, independence of 17 of the 24 provinces afterwards, Warlord Governments, and the Northern Expedition between 1926 and 1928. End: In 1930, Jiang Jieshi (Chiang Kai-shek) defeated or recruited the main warlords and unified China.

Notes: Italics stand for estimates. The starting and ending years of the Xia and the Shang Dynasties and the starting year of the Western Zhou are still preliminary and subject to confirmation of further historical research.

Sources: Zang Yunpu, Wang Yundu, Zhu Chongye, He Zhendong, and Ye Qing, *Zhongguo shi dashi jinian* (*A Chronology of Major Events on the Chinese History*) (Ji'nan: Shangdong jiaoyu chubanshe, 1984); Wang Fuchang and Guo Wenliang, *Zhongguo jinxiandai fazhan shi lun* (*A Treatise on China's Modern Development History*) (Guangzhou: Zhongshan daxue chubanshe, 1997); Tian Changwu and An Zuozhang, *Qin Han shi* (*A History of the Qin and Han*) (Beijing: Renmin chubanshe, 1993); Fang Xuanling, Chu Suiliang, and Xu Jingzong, *Jin shu* (*Books on the Jin*) (Beijing: Zhonghua shuju, 1974), Vol. 1; Lü Simian, *Sui Tang Wudai shi* (*A History on the Sui, the Tang, and the Five Dynasties*) (Shanghai: Shanghai guji chubanshe, 1984); Ch'i-ch'ing Hsiao, *Meng Yuan shi xin yan* (*Recent Studies on the Mongolian and the Yuan's History*) (Taipei: Yunchen wenhua shiye gufen youxian gongsi, 1994); Fu Yiling, Yang Guozhen, and Chen Zhiping, *Mingshi xinbian* (*A New Compilation on the History of the Ming*) (Beijing: Renmin chubanshe, 1993); Zheng Tianting, *Qing shi* (*A History on the Qing*) (Taipei: Yunlong chubanshe, 1998); entries on the Xia, Shang, Western Zhou dynasties and on their founding leaders posted at: www.baidu.com and on Wikipedia and google, accessed on August 8–9, 2014.

On the other hand, the Southern Song is treated as a period of division, because it controlled only the southern part of mainland China, and it lost the north to the Jin. This treatment is in line with my above definition of a unified regime.

Third, the ROC of the mainland (or the ROC of 1930–1949) and the PRC since 1949 are regarded as unified regimes, but not the ROC since 1950. During most of the time of 1930–1937 and 1945–1949, the ROC controlled most of China proper.[13] In contrast, the effective control of the ROC since 1950 has been restricted to Taiwan and several small islands, and cannot be regarded as a unified regime of China. Second, even though the PRC has yet to extend its jurisdiction to Taiwan, or form a larger China including Taiwan, Beijing controls all of China proper (including the Yellow River and the Yangtze valleys) and most of the Chinese territory from the preceding ROC. In this sense, it is more appropriate to treat it as a unified regime, rather than a regime of disorder.

Tables 9.2A and 9.2B provide more information on the Chinese historical periods. The life span of the thirteen regimes of national unity prior to 1949 ranged between 12 and 554 years and averaged 172 years. Excluding the Shang and the Western Zhou, the range was 12 and 279 years, and the average 129 years. Similarly, the length of disorder preceding these unified regimes varied widely (Table 9.2B), from 549 years preceding the Qin to one year preceding the Shang, averaging 99 years (or 116 years for the regimes since the Qin). If only unified regimes since the Qin are considered, the periods of division prior to these regimes averaged 116 years. These periods of divisions ranged from 5 years prior to the Former Han to 549 years prior to the Qin.[14]

Figures 9.1 and 9.2 scatterplot the data on the length of preceding disorder and that of the ensuing unified regimes, as well as the trend line that depicts the relationship between the two lengths. Figure 9.1 includes all unified regimes since the Shang. Figure 9.2, on the other hand, incorporates only the unified regimes since the Qin, because these regimes were all centralized polities governed by a bureaucracy and were thus comparable. Both figures display a clearly inverse relation between the length of disorder and that of the ensuing unified regime. In other words, the longer the preceding disorder, the more short-lived the subsequent unified regimes.

In addition, unified periods that immediately followed a unified period tended to be long-lived (Tables 9.2A and 9.2B). After replacing the unified Xia Dynasty, the unified Shang Dynasty prospered for hundreds of years. So did the Western Zhou that followed the Shang Dynasty, the Former Han that inherited a unified China from the short-lived Qin, and the Later Han that succeeded the Former Han. The Tang built its longer life span in a country unified by the preceding Sui, so did the Ming that followed the unified Yuan and the Qing that inherited a unified China from the Ming. All these inheriting regimes lasted at least 154 years.[15]

A statistical test on the length of preceding disorder and that of unified regimes supplies convincing evidence. In the test, the natural log of the life span of the unified regime is regressed on the natural log of the length of preceding disorder. Only the eleven unified regimes since the Qin Dynasty are included in the analysis because these dynasties are centralized regimes and comparable. The regression result is as follows (the t score of the coefficients is in parentheses below them).

$$\ln \text{ (regime length)} = -0.650 \ln \text{ (disorder length)} + 6.894$$
$$\quad\quad\quad\quad\quad\quad\quad (-4.19) \quad\quad\quad\quad\quad\quad\quad\quad (10.8)$$

(Equation 1)

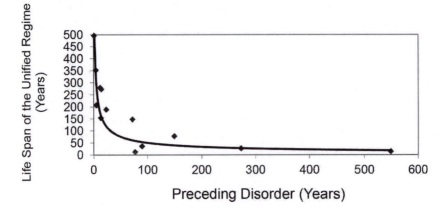

Figure 9.1 Preceding disorder and duration of unified regimes (since the sixteenth century B.C.)

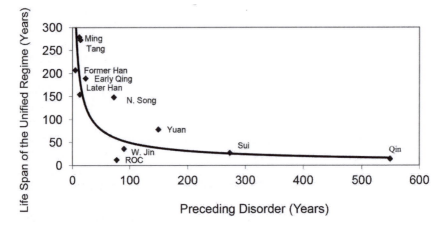

Figure 9.2 Preceding disorder and duration of unified regimes (since 770 B.C.)

Adjusted R square = 0.623, F score of the equation = 17.53, significance level of F = 0.0024. Equation 1 can be also written as Equation 2:

$$Regime\ length = \frac{986}{DisorderLength^{0.650}}$$

(Equation 2)

The test results confirm that the life span of the unified regimes is negatively correlated with the length of the previous disorder and that this inverse correlation is statistically highly significant. This correlation begs for an explanation.

Perils of lengthy division

It thus seems that rulers following longer division would have greater difficulties in sustaining their regimes. Although these new rulers might not face the same set of challenges and risks, most of their gravest challenges and risks were associated with and aggravated by long periods of division. Let us ponder on challenges and risks that most frequently confronted unified regimes after prolonged division.

First, the challenges. Under the surface of national unity lurked both old and new disintegrating forces.

1 After prolonged division and civil war, newly defeated warlords might still have broad political and social bases, and foreign nations might have grown into potentially more dangerous rivals. A study revealed that among the 278 top officials under Wendi who founded the Sui, 56.5 percent were officials of the Northern Zhou, a kingdom during the preceding division, and 81.6 percent were from previously wealthy families. Both groups had considerable influence on their own.[16] Li Yuan, who seized the Sui's capital and founded the Tang Dynasty, was a grandson of a key general of the Northern Zhou state preceding the Sui.[17]

2 Factions or members of the victorious elite might be more easily lured by political spoils from their unification feat and clash against each other. The founder of the new regime needed to act wisely to get these hostile or conflicting forces under control. After Khubilai, the Yuan Empire followed the Mongol tradition of selecting a new ruler by consensus at an assembly of the princes and noble. The elites were often divided over candidates supported by imperial bureaucracy and those by powerful field army in the steppe. They fought chronically among themselves.[18]

3 As the state declined during the period of disorder, local elites might have increased their landholdings at the fiscal expense of the state. Since the late Later Han, local landlords and gentry had been expanding their land holdings and controlling peasant households. Partly for this reason, the households on the state's registry declined sharply from 9.93 million in 145 A.D. under the Later Han, to 2.46 million in 280 A.D. when the Jin unified China.[19] The state's fiscal base was thus dramatically scaled back.

4 Last but not least, the unifier of the country also needed to select an able and reliable successor who could well manage various challenges. Three of the five short-lived unified regimes disintegrated under an ill-fit successor. Emperor Shihuang of the Qin banished his honest and upright eldest son Fusu to the border for his advice against burdening the people with military service, and allowed Eunuch Zhao Gao with a capital criminal record and brutal yet incapable son Huhai to accompany him. This

gave Zhao and Huhai a chance to disobey Shihuang's order to establish Fusu as the emperor. They usurped power and mismanaged the empire. After much hesitation Emperor Wudi of the Jin also allowed his idiotic son Sima Zhong to be his successor. After Wudi's death, Zhong's wife usurped power and ignited a 16-year struggle among the dukes, weakening the empire. Three hundred and thirty-three years later, deceived by his second son Yang Guang's rumours and pretentious virtue and out of his excessive suspicion, Wendi of the Sui allowed Guang to replace his level-headed successor and eldest son Yang Yong. While Yong had advised his father to give the people time to recover from long disorder, Guang engaged in wasteful and over-ambitious undertakings, bringing down the empire.[20]

In addition, prolonged civil war during the division might have devastated more severely the economy and basic infrastructures, such as irrigation. Political and administrative agencies could be more defunct, and justice might have been administered even further below acceptable standards. The population would demand from the new regime basic services, such as programs for economic recovery, channelling of rivers, repairs of irrigation systems, redistribution of land to landless peasants, and administering of justice. These services were vital for the welfare of the population and for the new dynasty to earn political legitimacy. About the time when he unified a long divided country, Wendi of the Sui embarked on rehabilitation of the nation. He introduced the examination system to select the talents to fill the office.[21] He also restricted the peasants' corvee to twenty days each year, reduced taxes and corvee for three years within the nine years after the unification, and channelled the waterway in Shandong to reduce floods.[22] These measures improved the lives of people.

Second, the risks. Political mistakes had graver consequences after lengthier disunity than in other historical periods. Three risks stand out. The first risk was more powerful foes for the new regime after long disunion. Potential rivals were more ready to challenge the regime, and the elite more anxious to demand power or wealth from the new rulers. Political forces that emerged in previous disunion did serve as effective leaders of protests against the regimes after long disorder. Xiang Liang and Xiang Yu, the generals who led the rebellious troops to crush the Qin's army, were respectively the son and nephew of a known general of the Chu state which was defeated by the Qin.[23] The Nationalists of the ROC were defeated by their former foes and friends during disorder in the warlord era. Nationalists, together with the Chinese Communist Party (CCP), led the Northern Expedition to defeat warlords and laid the foundation for the ROC. Jiang Jieshi's alliance with old warlords helped him to fight their communist rivals, yet prevented him from carrying out thorough reforms to meet popular demands. That allowed the CCP to upstage the KMT (National-ists).[24] Even religious elements from previous disunion might challenge the unified regime. Han Shantong, along with his apostle Liu Futong, helped arrange the rebellion of Red Turbans through religious preaching, which led to the final demise of the Yuan. Han was a grandson of a follower of the White Lotus religion that was founded in the Southern Song Dynasty when China was divided.[25]

The second risk is a less patient populace. After prolonged division, the population would be more eager for welfare improvement, less tolerant of new tyranny, and more permissive of brief violence for a better government. If the new regime failed to deliver, they would rather go through renewed conflict again in order to bring forth a responsible government. The Qin's unification indeed ended enormous sufferings inflicted on the population in the past 549 years during the Autumn and Spring and the Warring States. It was estimated that during the Warring States soldiers accounted for as much as one-quarter of the population, the number of wars exceeded 300, and soldiers killed surpassed 2 million.[26] However, the Qin's brutal exploitation brought little relief to the people. It was estimated that 70 percent of the labor force was compelled to work for the Qin on military and construction projects without pay, an average peasant had to perform three months of labor services each year, and after paying for taxes and rents an average family of five might be left with 50 shi of grain, well short of the 90 shi that was needed to feed itself.[27] Twelve years after the unification, Chen Sheng led an armed rebellion. Two years later, determined rebels uprooted the Qin.[28]

The third risk is that new rulers after lengthier separation were even more tempted to commit errors because of wrong choices or a failure to identify the challenges. After their historical achievement of unifying a long-divided and war-inflicted country, new rulers might become self-contented or arrogant, might misjudge how much exploitation the population would endure, and might do little or too much to consolidate his government. They might thus find extravagant court life, such as magnificent palaces and mausoleums as well as massive parades justified rewards for his efforts. In other cases, they might develop a wrong sense of invincibility or impatience, and might embrace ambitious projects of nation building, causing popular resentment and triggering rebellions. In the first four years of his reign, Emperor Yangdi of the Sui Dynasty commanded at least seven huge undertakings: building a giant new capital in Luoyang with a perimeter of 50 li, digging the Grand Canal, erecting forty palaces, digging 3,300 large grain cellars, repairing the Great Wall, cruising with thousands of vessels to Jiangdu, and campaigning against Koguryo.[29] His three campaigns against Koguryo were driven "by his conception of the majesty and cosmic centrality of the empire" and "by his image of himself as destined to great victories against all who resisted the benevolent transforming influence of the Central Kingdom."[30]

At such a difficult beginning of a regime after a long division, the ruler needed both prudence and skills to handle these tasks well. He needed to make no serious blunders in meeting the major challenges, such as neutralizing potential rivals, building infrastructures as well as suppression and defence systems, improving the populace's material well-being, and restraining self-indulgence. He also needed to undertake the selected projects without over-burdening the population. Finally, he needed to make con-cessions to the rivals and the elite without compromising the fate of his government.

Causes of falls of short-lived regimes

The five short-lived regimes fell because they failed to meet daunting challenges and grave risks described above. In addition, distinctive precarious circumstances and erroneous policies played a role. Due to limited space I can only briefly review the causes summarized in Table 9.3. [31]

Emperor Shihuang of the Qin ended a 549-year division of China through his iron fist. He placed himself in the ranks of China's legendary rulers and deities and hence assumed the title Huangdi. However, he provided scant peace for the populace. Within a decade after the unity, he undertook 20 huge enterprises that required corvee of millions. Among them, a southern expedi-tion involved 700,000, building the Great Wall, army posts and barricades 500,000, and constructing the Afang Palace 1.5 million. Seventy percent of the nation's labor force might have been engaged in the state's corvee; much of the land was left untilled; two-thirds of peasants' harvest might go into taxes and rents. In addition, Shihuang relocated the population ten times, involving probably one-fifth of the population.[32] Shihuang burned invaluable books and buried 1,160 learned scholars alive in order to silence dissenters, alienating the regime from the educated.[33] The Qin's draconian penal code produced over a million criminals out of a population of 20 million.[34] Ironically, it was Chen Sheng and his followers, facing the death penalty for failing to meet the deadline for military service due to delays by rain, who first rebelled and triggered nationwide uprisings. Shihuang, as described above, also failed to select an able successor. His son Huhai and Eunuch Zhao Gao murdered Fusu and able offi-cials, including Li Si, and ruthlessly exploited the people. They failed to adjust policies to ease the people's anger and suppress rebellions.[35] Three years after Shihuang's death the mighty Qin crumbled.

After unifying the country in 280, Emperor Wudi of the Western Jin redistributed land to peasants, relocated migrants, encouraged people to cultivate unused land, built irrigation, and raised taxes. He helped economic recovery and strengthened the state. However, Wudi indulged in leisure with thousands of concubines, and made disastrous arrangements for succession, as described. Perceiving the future threat from his shrewd daughter-in-law Jia against his idiotic son Sima Zhong, Wudi allowed members of his family to head 27 large dukedoms and over 500 fiefdoms and control over half of the registered households. After Wudi's death, Jia usurped power. Although the dukes removed Jia, they fought among themselves and invited ethnic minorities to fight on their side. The 16-year power struggle undermined the Jin.[36]

An important social change, namely, growing discontent and presence of minorities in Northern China, also destabilized the regime. With the decline of the central government after the Yellow Turban rebellion in the Later

Table 9.3 Short-lived regimes of national unity and causes of their collapse

Period	Duration of Unity	Duration of Preceding Division	Causes of the Fall of the Regime
Qin	14 years; 221–207 B.C.	549 years; 770–221 B.C.	Excessive slave labor and exploitation for building palaces and the Great Wall created human tolls and impoverished the population. Burning books alienated the intellectuals. Elements of the elites from warring states survived government's suppression. Draconian law created large numbers of criminals and discontented people, and caused a group of army recruits to rebel in 209 B.C. Emperor Shihuang failed to arrange in time for an able and prudent successor. Malevolent Emperor Huhai and Eunuch Zhao Gao murdered able officials and mishandled the rebellions, allowing them to grow and succeed.
Western Jin	36 years; 280–316 A.D.	90 years; 190–280 A.D.	Emperor Wudi's enfeoffment created powerful dukes potentially independent of the center. Wudi failed to replace his idiotic successor with able kin. Powerful gentry drew peasants away from the state's tax roll, reducing the state's revenue. Usurpation of power by an empress and fighting among the dukes weakened the empire. Migration of ethnic minorities, Han's suppression of minorities, and migration of the Han to the south due to nomadic murder and warfare weakened the ethnic base of the state. Liu Yuan, a leader of the Hun Tribe, was able to seize the Jin's capital in 316 A.D.
Sui	27 years; 589–616 A.D.	273 years; 316–589 A.D.	Wendi failed to select a prudent successor. Yangdi's over-ambitious and ruinous undertakings, including construction of the Grand Canal and luxurious and magnificent palaces, extravagant imperial cruises, and three failed invasions of Korea, caused massive suffering and outrage. Elites of conquered kingdoms were still powerful. Yangdi fled the capital to the south amidst widespread rebellions in 616 A.D.
Yuan	78 years; 1276–1354 A.D.	149 years; 1127–1276 A.D.	Infighting among the elite over the choice of khaghans and numerous disasters weakened the empire. The court's over-spending, hyperinflation, heavy exploitation, and racial discrimination alienated much of the Han population. Uprisings by laborers in a river-channelling project in 1351 led to a string of rebellions. The khaghan's suspicion of his prime minister and infighting among the elite prevented the Yuan from destroying the main rebel force. Rebels eventually overthrew the Yuan.

Period	Duration of Unity	Duration of Preceding Division	Causes of the Fall of the Regime
Republic of China	12 years; 1930–38, 1945–49	77 years; 1853–1930	Japanese invasion further weakened the Nationalists and allowed communists to grow. Failure to implement land reform and improve peasants' life stripped Nationalists of a rural base and rural support. Corruption and hyperinflation weakened the Nationalist power base in the cities. Suppression alienated intellectuals. With disciplines, ideological appeals and peasants' support for land reform, communists took over power in 1949.

Sources: Zang Yunpu, Wang Yundu, Zhu Chongye, He Zhendong, and Ye Qing, *Zhongguo shi dashi jinian* (*A Chronology of Major Events on the Chinese History*) (Ji'nan: Shangdong jiaoyu chubanshe, 1984); Wang Fuchang and Guo Wenliang, *Zhongguo jinxiandai fazhan shi lun* (*A Treatise on China's Modern Development History*) (Guangzhou: Zhongshan daxue chubanshe, 1997); Tian Changwu and An Zuozhang, *Qin Han shi* (*A History of the Qin and Han*) (Beijing: Renmin chubanshe, 1993); Fang Xuanling, Chu Suiliang, and Xu Jingzong, *Jin shu* (*Books on the Jin*) (Beijing: Zhonghua shuju, 1974), Vol. 1; Lü Simian, *Sui Tang Wudai shi* (*A History on the Sui, the Tang, and the Five Dynasties*) (Shanghai: Shanghai guji chubanshe, 1984); Ch'i-ch'ing Hsiao, *Meng Yuan shi xin yan* (*Recent Studies on the Mongolian and the Yuan's History*) (Taipei: Yunchen wenhua shiye gufen youxian gongsi, 1994); Fu Yiling, Yang Guozhen, and Chen Zhiping, *Mingshi xinbian* (*A New Compilation on the History of the Ming*) (Beijing: Renmin chubanshe, 1993); Zheng Tianting, *Qing shi* (*A History on the Qing*) (Taipei: Yunlong chubanshe, 1998); entries on the Xia, Shang, Western Zhou dynasties and on their founding leaders posted at: www.baidu.com and on Wikipedia and google, accessed on August 8–9, 2014.

Han, ethnic minorities that used to be nomads, including the Hun, Jie, Xianbei (Sienpi), Qiang, and Di, moved eastward into the lower Yellow River valley. Warlords and the Wei also recruited minorities to fight on their behalf. A high estimate placed the population of minorities in the north at 8.7 million. In contrast, after decades of warfare, the Han population in the north either died, or migrated to the south. Minorities thus accounted for over half of the population in the north.[37] Many of them were exploited by the Han, and some were ambitious and able fighters. As the Jin was weakened by the infighting, Liu Yuan, a leader of the Hun tribe, seized the Jin's capital and captured the emperor in 316 A.D.

Wendi of the Sui erred fatally in choosing narcissist and over-ambitious Yang Guang as his successor.[38] Yangdi, as stated, inflicted tremendous sufferings and material losses on the population through his numerous huge undertakings. For example, he ordered two million laborers to build Dongdu (the Eastern Capital) on corvee, one million men and women to dig the Grand Canal, and one million laborers to repair the Great Wall. Yangdi set tight deadlines for the projects, causing many deaths and much land untilled. When Yangdi cruised to Jiangdu, his fleet spread 200 li (1 li = 531 meters), and people within 500 li had to offer food free.[39]

Yangdi's three campaigns against Koguryo during 612–614 finally sealed the fall of the Sui. He mobilized over a million to serve as soldiers, and two million as logistics suppliers. Ship builders for the army were forced to work days and nights in the water, and many had their lower bodies filled with maggots. Thousands died. As a result of wars, food prices went up and many families were driven into poverty. Yangdi's excessive control left little discretion to generals at the front line. As a result, his expeditions ended in heavy casualties and no strategic breakthrough.[40] By 616, nationwide uprisings forced Yangdi to retreat to the south. Among over 100 rebel forces, former senior officials of the Sui, namely, Li Mi and Li Yuan, led two of the four major forces.[41] Li Yuan eventually replaced the Sui with the Tang.

The Yuan leadership succeeded in co-opting the Han elite and other ethnic groups, and to some extent, borrowing Chinese institutions. It oversaw regionally uneven recovery of the economy and population.[42] However, the empire was undercut by succession conflict as well as political, fiscal, and natural stresses. First, recurrent succession conflict destabilized the regime. "During these 39 years [of the Mid Yuan], nine khaghans ascended the throne, reigning on average for only 4.3 years. Six of these nine became khaghan only after heated disputes or even armed struggles. Two of the nine were killed, and another was reported missing after being overthrown."[43] The result was short reigns, frequent change in senior officials, and volatile policies.[44] Second, noble inheritance under the Yuan was rigid and costly. The regime allowed the offspring of princes to maintain their parents' rank, instead of down-grading it as under the Tang. This sizable group of powerful elites increased the difficulties of choosing a khaghan. The khaghan had to spend a large sum to appease the group.[45] Third, infighting among the rulers deprived them of the chance to crush the rebels. During his able chancellor Toghtō's siege of the chief rebel force, the khaghan Toghōn Temür dismissed him out of suspicion, costing the Yuan "political and military initiative" and allowing "the successor dynasty, the Ming" to emerge.[46] Similarly, when the Red Turbans were distraught with infighting after 1359, Toghōn Temür often watched women dancing overnight, and his generals were clashing among themselves.[47] Fourth, the khaghans' excessive spending on buying off the princes and on religious activities, the government's over-printing of money, and bureaucrats' extortion increased the fiscal burden on the populace. Finally, repetitive natural disasters also wracked the regime. In the 14th century, 36 severe winters, unprecedentedly frequent floods, serious epidemics, and numerous famines had consumed a vast amount of resources, impoverished millions, and prepared a social hotbed for rebellions.[48]

Similarly, the ROC, the most recent short-lived regime, suffered from external and inherent disadvantages. First, the ROC, which inherited a weak country from the late Qing, was hamstrung by Japanese invasion. In 1933 and 1934 Nationalists dealt a devastating defeat to the Red Army. Communists had a weak force and a small base in the north in 1937.[49] The Japanese invasion in 1937, however, forced Nationalists to halt their attack on communists, and provided communists much needed breathing space. Another serious problem was failure of land reform. Jiang Jieshi (Chiang Kai-shek) tried to build bureaucratic control in the countryside and appease local gentry and the warlords.[50] He thus put off serious land reform and failed to address the grievances of landless and poor peasants. In contrast, the CCP established its control in the countryside by cleaning up corruption and exploitation and redistributing wealth and land. It also encouraged peasants to form organizations, join its army, and defend their new gains.[51] The third problem is unrestrained corruption. Nationalists used money and interests to lubricate their political machine. Their representatives misused public funds, imposed fiscal burdens on the people, failed to administer justice, and endangered people's interests. Finally, the government's failure to solve economic problems, including unemployment, poverty, and especially hyperinflation, cost itself public support, especially in the cities.[52] Nationalists' failure was due to their eagerness to wage the civil war against the CCP and their reluctance to impose temporary control of the economy out of the fear of offending the speculative business community.

To sum up, rulers of the five unified regimes after prolonged civil wars had to meet a number of challenges. They included containing internal or external rivals, providing basic social services and justice, improving the welfare of the population, living a plain life, and making prudent decisions. Nevertheless, these rulers tended to mishandle these tasks, inviting powerful disintegrating forces to inundate the fledgling regime.

With limited space, I can only briefly discuss the six long dynasties, especially those after the Qin. The causes for the falls of the six long unified dynasties are outlined in Table 9.4. Early rulers of these five dynasties had several advantages. First, the Former Han, the Tang, and the Ming followed a short-lived unified regime, and their rulers learned a bitter and useful lesson from the quick downfall of their predecessors. Lu Jia pointed out to Gaozu of the Former Han that the Qin fell quickly because of its heavy corvee on the population and harsh legal punishment. The earlier emperors of the Former Han, including Gaozu, Wendi, and Jingdi, heeded his admonition. They reduced taxes and corvee, encouraged tillage, and promoted agriculture. Similarly, Taizong of the Tang asked scholars to compile histories on the Jin and the Sui in order to learn from and avoid their quick falls. Taizong was also open-minded enough to accept his officials' honest advice and even outright disapproval.[53]

Second, most of the early emperors of the five long regimes adopted several far-sighted policies that encouraged an honest government and an improvement in people's livelihood. These policies included seeking talents, promoting well-performing officials, rebuilding the government and the legal system, streamlining bureaucracy, redistributing land to peasants, cutting taxes and corvee, freeing serfs, and building irrigation. Most of the rulers until the middle of these six regimes were able and attentive to state affairs and oversaw a rising country. They included Gaozu, Wendi, Jingdi, and Wudi (in his late years) of the Former Han, Guangwudi, Mingdi, Zhangdi, and Hedi of the Later Han, Taizong, Empress Wu, and early Xuanzong of the Tang, the first six emperors of the Northern Song, Taizu, Renzong, and Xuanzong

Table 9.4 Long dynasties of unity

Period of Unity	Years	Causes of the Downfall	Preceding Period	Length (Years)
Xia	470; 2070 B.C. – 1600 B.C.	Corrupt, tyrannical, exploitative, and decadent king. He was defeated by Tang, the head of a fief under Xia in the battle of Mingtiao.	The period of five legendary rulers, the last one being Shun the Great.	?
Shang	554; 1600 B.C. –1046 B.C.	Prolonged war against the neighboring Yi; tyrannical, suppressive, and decadent king Di Xin. Rebellion led by Zhou, a powerful vassal kingdom.	Xia	470
Western Zhou	271; 1041 B.C. –770 B.C.	Exhaustion by prolonged war against neighboring tribes; decadent and tyrannical king; mistreatment of powerful dukes and queen.	Shang	554
Former Han	207; 202 B.C. –5 A.D.	Numerous military adventures, insufficient revenue, land seizure by corrupt officials, and extravagant and decadent emperors.	Qin	14
Later Han	154; 36–190.	Bloody struggles among officials-scholars, royal family, and eunuchs, insufficient revenue, seizure of land from peasants by imperial members, eunuchs, and officials, decadent emperors, and powerful warlords.	Former Han	207
Tang	279; 628–907	Empowered governors in the wake of rebellions led by nomadic generals recruited by the Tang, decadent emperors and abuse of power by imperial family members, loss of government's fiscal base, and increasing tax burdens on the people.	Sui	27
Northern Song	148; 979–1127	Jurchen Troops from a nomadic state Jin seized the Song's capital Kaifeng, and captured two emperors (the retired Huizong and Qinzong) as hostages. Prior to this the Song court was weakened by rivalling factions supporting and opposing reforms, and the Song army was weakened by the excessive restrictions imposed by the court.	Five Dynasties and Ten Kingdoms	72
Ming	273; 1368–1641	Decadent emperors and abuse of power by eunuchs, land seizure by the powerful, reduced state tax base, increases in tax burdens and the numbers of landless peasants and rebellions, and external threats posed by the Manchu that attracted the elite troops of the Ming.	Yuan	78

Period of Unity	Years	Causes of the Downfall	Preceding Period	Length (Years)
Qing	189; 1664–1853	The empire was undermined by the following sets of factors or events— (1) repetitive defeats by imperial powers, losses of tariff autonomy, and unprotected domestic industry encroached upon by foreign competition; (2) domestic rebellions, especially the Taiping Rebellion; (3) the rise of assertive regions and provinces and influential generals especially Yuan Shikai; (4) the refusal of the Qing court to adopt pragmatic and decisive modernization.	Yuan	78

Notes: The starting and ending years of the Xia and the Shang Dynasties and the starting year of the Western Zhou are still preliminary.
Sources: See Tables 9.2A and 9.2B.

of the Ming, and Kangxi, Yongzheng, and Qianlong of the Qing. Many of them were ranked among the most successful rulers in the Chinese history.[54]

Third, these unified regimes would not be overthrown during or right after the reign of the rulers who made these mistakes. Their decline was gradual.[55] For example, the earlier rulers of Former Han, the Ming, and the Qing allowed the princes or generals to head vassal states or kingdoms. Later these states rebelled. However, rebellions ended quickly, and the country remained united. In 154 B.C., seven kingdoms of the kin of Liu Bang rebelled against the Former Han's Jingdi, and occupied half of the country's territory. However, after just three months, the rebellion was crushed, and these kingdoms were fatally weakened. Under the Ming, Emperor Jianwendi weakened seven vassal states led by the imperial kin. In 1399, Zhu Di of the Yan state rebelled and defeated Jianwendi three years later. Upon coming to the throne, however, Zhu Di continued to undermine the vassal states and strengthened the center's power. In 1673, Wu Sangui led three vassal states to rebel. Kangxi of the Qing skilfully led a counter-offensive, put the rebels under control in 1676, and defeated them in 1681.

These regimes' resilient unity benefited from the following key factors. First, the empire was free of long-existing disintegrating forces that harassed regimes after prolonged division. Second, in the earlier years of the regime the rulers pursued sound policies of improving the economy and people's livelihood, and as a result, the empire had sufficient resources and popular support to weather the rebellion.[56]

The life span of the communist regime

An interesting and relevant question remains: what do the findings imply for the life span of the People's Republic of China (PRC)? In the remaining limited space, I can point out several implications. In addition, I will

Table 9.5 Predictions on the life span of the CCP regime

Prediction	Years of preceding division (or the basis for the estimate)	Predicted life span	Likelihood of predicted life span	Start of division	End of division	Predicted ending year of the CCP regime
1	1	986	Unlikely	January 1949. By then the PLA had taken over the Northeast (October 1948), areas between Beijing and Nanjing (November 1948), Beijing and Tianjin (January 1949).	Late December 1949. By then the PLA had conquered the Northeast (October 1948), areas north of Nanjing (January 1949), Nanjing (April), Shanghai (May), Xinjiang (September), Guangdong (October), Chongqing (November), Chengdu, and Yunnan (December)	2935
2	3.5	437	Unlikely	June 1946 when the Chinese civil war broke out.	See above	2386
3	11	207	Possible	1938 when Japanese troops started full-scale invasion of coastal and central China, forcing the Nationalist government to retreat to Chongqing.	See above	2156
4	Based on the shortest unified regime that followed a unified regime (the Later Han)	154	Probable			2103

Prediction	Years of preceding division (or the basis for the estimate)	Predicted life span	Likelihood of predicted life span	Start of division	End of division	Predicted ending year of the CCP regime
5	Based on the long-lived unified regime since the Qin with the shortest longevity due to 72 years of division preceding the dynasty (Northern Song)	148	Probable			2097
6	Based on the longest unified regime since the Qin (the Tang)	279	Possible			2228
7	Based on the longest record of a one-party regime in the world (the Soviet Communist Party, in power from 1917 to 1991)	74	Possible, though unlikely			2023

provide estimates of the possible life span of the PRC. As stated above, we have good reasons to treat the ROC in the Mainland and the PRC as unified regimes. The aforementioned findings suggest that the length of disorder preceding the PRC has important implications for the life span of the CCP regime. The following paragraphs are thus devoted to a close examination of the length of division preceding the PRC and the possible life span of the CCP regime.

Table 9.5 outlines seven predictions of the life span of the CCP regimes. The first six predictions are based on the aforementioned findings, and the last prediction is based on the international experience. Each of these predictions will be discussed briefly. The fourth and the fifth predictions seem probable, the third, sixth and seventh predictions seem possible but not so likely, and the first and the second predictions seem implausible.

It is appropriate to date the start of the CCP's effective control of the country in 1949, when the PLA took over mainland China, except Tibet.[57] An important question is: When should the start of disorder preceding the PRC be placed? Among all the unified regimes, the ROC and the PRC are atypical, because their founders had cooperated with and fought against each other for years prior to the start of both republics, and experienced some years of disorder together.

There are three ways of counting the disorder prior to the PRC.

1　The gap between the end of the ROC and the beginning of the PRC can be taken as the disorder. Then the pre-PRC disorder lasted for only about a year (from January 1949 to late 1949). This is obviously too short. With only one year of division, Equation 2 yields 986 years of predicted life span of the CCP regime, which is impossibly long (for the reasons to be discussed). Almost no dynasty in verified Chinese history had lasted this long.

2　From the outbreak of the Chinese civil war in June 1946 when the CCP controlled a quarter of China's population, till late December 1949 when most of mainland China except Tibet fell into the hands of the Chinese Communists, the civil war lasted about 3.5 years. With this length of division Equation 2 will yield regime longevity of 437 years. Both predicted life spans are unlikely and can be rejected outright. No unified regimes in the Chinese history have ever surpassed 554 years (the Shang's record), and no unified regimes since the Qin have ever existed over 279 years (the Tang's record).

3　The third way is to place the start of the division prior to the PRC in 1938. In that year Japanese troops started full-scale invasion of coastal and central China, forcing the Nationalist government to retreat to Chongqing. The Japanese full invasion of China (1938–1945), along with the civil war (1946–1949), can be taken as disorder. During 1945–1948 the Nationalist government did control much of the population and territory of China. However, in 1945 when the Japanese troops surrendered as a result of their defeat in World War II over 120 million people and nearly one million kilometres of area were controlled by the CCP. In other words, a quarter of the population and about one-tenth of the Chinese territories (or 14 percent of the Chinese territories excluding Tibet and Xinjiang) were controlled by the CCP. This interpretation will give the disorder 11 years. Using Equation 2 we would then predict that the PRC might last for 207 years, or until 2156. A life span of 207 years is possible, but seems incredibly long.

In addition, we can draw insights from the life spans of the dynasties and republic in the Chinese history and project the possible longevity of the current Party state regime.

1   The CCP regime may well be able to match the life span of the shortest unified regime that followed a unified regime (the Later Han) and lived for 154 years. Both the PRC and the Later Han were similar as they were unified regimes founded after a unified regime. The PRC replaced a short-lived unified regime the ROC, and the Later Han succeeded the almighty Former Han that established the political and ideological institutions and shaped the boundary of the forthcoming Chinese empires. Should this be true the CCP regime will live until 2103. This predicted life span is probable, even though it may be longer than many analysts would believe.

2   One may also draw inspiration from the shortest life span of the long unified regime in the Chinese history since the Qin. This record was held by the Northern Song, which lasted for 148 years. If the longevity of the CCP regime was only lucky enough to match that of the Northern Song, its ending year will be 2097. Again, this predicted longevity of the PRC is probable, though impressively long for many analysts.

3   If the longevity of the CCP regime was only lucky enough to match that of the Tang, the longest unified regime in the Chinese history since the Qin, it can then be expected to last 279 years. Its ending year will be 2228, and this will be a truly eye-opening record of an authoritarian regime in the contemporary world. This predicted longevity is possible though highly unlikely.

Finally, we can apply the insights from the life span of one-party regimes in the world to our analysis of the longevity of the CCP regime.

1   The CCP is a single-party regime. In the world the longest one-party regime that has ever existed was probably the Communist Party of the Soviet Union (CPSU). It seized power from Tsarist Russia in 1917 and lost power in 1991, spanning over 74 years. The other long-enduring one-party regime was the Institutional Revolutionary Party (PRI) that ruled Mexico from 1929 to 2000, with a life span of 71 years. The PRI lost the presidential election to the opposition, namely, the conservative National

Action Party (PAN) in 2000, thereby ending the PRI's long reign of the country. If the CCP is only able to match the CPSU's record, its ending year will be 2022, only years away. Should this materialize, it would take place under the current President Xi Jinping should he be healthy and politically resilient enough to serve out his two terms of the Presidency ending in 2023. Given his revealed commitment to keep the CCP in power, it seems that 2022 will become a year when the CCP reaches a new world record of the longest-reigning single-party regime in the world, instead of a year of its doom as the ruling party.

Thus the possible life span of the current CCP regime ranges from 74 years on the low end, to 279 years on the high end. Given that the CCP has not confronted either deadly external threat or any persistent and organized domestic opposition or rebels (with a brief exception of 1989), its life span may be blessed toward the high end. Personally, I think the life span of the CCP regime may be able to match that of the Northern Song or that of the Later Han and prolong its rule till 2097 or 2103.[58] It is also possible that the CCP regime may live long enough to approach the amazing record of the Ming of 273 years and may last around the year of 2,222. Both the CCP regime and the Ming, as Mao was aware of back in 1944, share a good number of similarities. Another possible and less likely scenario is that the regime may last well beyond the 74 years record set by the CPSU but fail to match the life span of the Northern Song or the Later Han period.

The causes of the falls of the unified regimes in Chinese history can be enlightening for our analysis of the political fortune of the CCP regime. Among the eleven unified regimes since the Qin six of them (55 percent) were terminated by domestic forces such as rebellions by peasants, elites and troops and usurpation of power by generals or ministers. These regimes included the Qin, the Former Han, the Later Han, the Sui, the Tang, and the Yuan. One regime, or 9 percent of these regimes, that is, the Northern Song, was ended by foreign invaders. Four regimes (36 percent of these regimes) were ended by the deadly combination of external invaders and domestic rebellions or usurpation of power. They were the Western Jin, the Ming, the Qing, and the ROC. It is worth noting that the last three unified regimes prior to the PRC fell under the third category and ended only after decades of lethal devastations of external invaders, domestic rebellions, or power usurpers. It is thus logical to believe that only a formidable cocktail of domestic opposition (especially rebellions and external invasion) would be fatal enough to put an end to the PRC.

Similar to other unified regimes after unified ones, the PRC has several advantages. First, it is free of any lasting organized resistance and opposition. In contrast, the ROC in the Mainland had to fight militarily against the armed communists and politically against liberal parties and intellectuals. Second, until now the PRC has been free from external invasion. In contrast, the Qing suffered from constant assaults of foreign invasions, and the ROC in the Mainland was invaded by Japan. These two advantages should bode well for the PRC. For the foreseeable future the PRC is not under any imminent threat from foreign invasion. As long as the CCP leaders are cunning enough (which they have been up to the present) to avoid a major military conflict with the much better equipped U.S. army and to a lesser extent, the Japanese forces, the PRC would be free of major foreign invading forces for the foreseeable future. Even a major war with the U.S. or Japan would not automatically result in China being invaded should the PLA perform poorly in the warfare, though the CCP would lose much popular support due to military setbacks. Nor do the prospects of an armed or well-organized opposition seem likely in the horizon. As analyzed in an earlier chapter the CCP continues to keep close eyes on any potential group with considerable organizational power and has banned any organized opposition. It is thus unlikely that any formidable organized group will emerge in the PRC in the foreseeable future when the CCP leadership refuses to accept the democratization program.

In addition, the PRC, especially since 1992, has done relatively well in avoiding choosing feeble and incapable leaders. Unlike the short-lived regimes such as the Qin, the Western Jin, and the Sui, since 1992 the Party state has selected a more or less capable top leader, who has undertaken significant tasks in helping the Party state to cope with one of the imminent headaches and to prolong its life span. Jiang Zemin, who succeeded Deng Xiaoling (the architect of China's historical reform and remarkable revival) in 1997 and led China until 2003, consolidated the course of economic reform, and guided China to smoothly enter the World Trade Organisation in 2001, thereby enabling China to enjoy a decade of economic growth above 10 percent per annum. Hu Jinto, who succeeded Jiang formally in 2003 and substantially in 2004 and stayed in power until 2013, launched a series of policies to ease the fiscal and economic burdens of peasants and improve the well-being of the population with the lowest income in China. He also started to introduce policies to address environmental problems in China. Upon assuming the top leadership in 2013 Xi Jinping wasted no time in consolidating his power. Soon he orchestrated the much-watched trial of Bo Xilai, a Politburo member, one of the two dozen top incumbents in China, and the former Party Secretary of Chongqing. Together with the Party discipline chief, Wang Qishan, Xi unleashed investigations of an unprecedented number of officials and big corporations for corruption. Their anti-graft campaign culminated in the purge and investigation of the former public security tsar Zhou Yongkang, a former member of the Politburo Standing Committee and one of the top nine leaders of China. Xi-Wang's cleansing of official and business corruption aimed to ease public anger and prolong the CCP's rule. The relative success of the Party state in leadership succession and selection has to do with the institutionalization of leadership succession discussed in Chapter 8.

Michael Mann suggested that imperial China was a major example of an authoritarian state with high capacity in two powers, infrastructural power and despotic power.[59] In a similar vein the PRC has high infrastructural and despotic power. Through employing modern institutions and technology, the

Party state has exercised abundant power through the society and has systemically penetrated the Chinese society. It has increased adult literacy, uses its propaganda machinery, censors commercialized media, and monitors the internet and mobile phone calls. Using up-to-date technology and equipment the Party state has built nationwide high-speed rail and automobile transport, television, internet, and mobile phone systems, enabling its political commands and official announcements and personnel to swiftly reach people and social groups throughout the vast country. Through controlling and censoring the media, mobile phone messages, and the internet it succeeds to a large extent in projecting a positive image of the Party state leaders and fending off calls for democratization. In addition, it reserves massive despotic power through controlling all major official appointments and the vast military and security forces. It also obstructs the organization of protests and stamps out potential protests through its tight monitoring of the media, the internet, and mobile phone text messages. As long as the CCP continues to wield infrastructural and despotic power, the regime can be strong enough to maintain its monopoly of political power for a long time to come.

Caveats do apply to the above estimates. First, the length of disorder preceding the PRC is difficult to gauge, as discussed. Second, while China's past historical forces discussed above may continue to operate, the following factors also play a role.

1   The rate of decline in the regime, exemplified, say, in the decline of its fiscal administration or state capacity.[60]
2   The strength of forces challenging the regime, revealed in outbreaks of nationwide rebellions (such as the 1989 protests) and their timing in terms of the age of the regime.
3   Internal pressure for regime change in order to control corruption and regain popular support, or due to enlightened leadership.
4   External pressure and forces, such as democratization, Western pressure, globalization, and the need to regain Taiwan through democratization.
5   Technology linking the Chinese with the outside world. The Chinese with access to the internet can have political information different from that which is censored by the government, and are likely to think and act independently.

Among these points, the role of new ideas and new technology from the West merits a brief discussion. Only from the late Qing onwards have a growing number of the people (starting from the most educated ones) in China become aware of the better political and economic institutions in the West and Japan. Pressures from new political ideas and new technologies may shorten its long life span as forecast in Equation 2 and other aforementioned predictions. This situation is vastly different from the previous unified regimes. As discussed in Chapter 3, in the reform era Chinese consciousness about their individual rights (especially social rights and property rights) has grown considerably. Many Chinese have accepted the rule of law and transparency as good practice in politics. In addition, a growing percentage (albeit probably still a minority) of Chinese believe in the need to install genuine democratic institutions and checks and balances in China. New information and transport technologies also play a significant role in shaping the political mind-set of the Chinese. Millions of Chinese tourists travel outside China with the aid of modern aviation technologies. Those who travel to developed economies such as the U.S., Western Europe, Australia, Japan, and South Korea would come to appreciate the best practice associated with the resilient institutions there, such as the rule of law, democracy, respect for human rights, press freedom, and freedom of speech. In a similar vein, new informational technologies, especially the internet and mobile phones, enable the Chinese to expand their knowledge about the best practice in politics in the world. These technologies also help the Chinese to express their opinion in the chat-rooms and blogs. Over the years, with the increasing level of personal income and an easier access to new technologies, the Chinese consciousness of their economic and social rights will heighten, and their interests in the rule of law, political transparency and incrementally political participation will grow.

As a result, although the CCP enjoys the advantages of no imminent foreign invaders and no credible organized opposition and despite the fact that it closely monitors political information in the media and communications on the new technological platforms, it may feel the need to heed in some way public opinion, especially the Chinese consciousness about their economic and social rights and their gradually increased interest in politics. In the long run the regime may have to gradually open up the political system. Some of these changes may not result in the immediate end of the CCP regime, but can help remedy the conventional lack of responsiveness to popular concerns.

Predicting the longevity of the PRC is a tricky and risk-fraught business. Nevertheless, the future of the current regime may well be a mixture of historical forces elaborated in this chapter and the five factors described above. While internal and external pressures and advancing technology will compel the regime to democratize, historical forces, especially the absence of internal and domestic threatening forces, enable the regime to prolong itself. The result may be gradual political changes over a prolonged period.

Notes

* An earlier version of this chapter was published as "The Life Span of Unified Regimes in China," *China Review*, Vol. 2, No. 2, Fall 2002, 93–124. Reprint by permission from the Chinese University Press. The first two sections and especially the final section have been revised.

1 Mark Elvin, *The Pattern of the Chinese Past: A Social and Economic Interpretation* (Stanford, CA: Stanford University Press, 1973), 17–23.

2 Derk Bodde, "The State and Empire of Ch'in," in *The Cambridge History of China (CHOC)*, Vol. 1, edited by Denis Twitchett and Michael Loewe (London and New York: Cambridge University Press, 1986), 89.

3 Zhang Quanxi, Zhang Yiqing, Wang Yuanchao, Wang Chaozhong, and Zhang Renzhong, eds, *Jianming zhongguo gudai shi (A Concise History of Ancient China)* (Beijing: Beijing daxue chubanshe, 1999), 105. This succinctly written textbook incorporated historical and archaeological findings in China.

4 Jin Guangtao and Liu Qingfeng, *Xingsheng yu weiji (The Cycle of Growth and Decline)* (Hong Kong: The Chinese University Press, 1992), 372–5.

5 Chen Jiarong, *Zhongguo lidai zi xingzhi, shengshuai, luanwang (The Rise, Rule, Prosperity, Chaos, and Downfall of the Chinese Dynasties)* (Kowloon, Hong Kong: Xuejin shudian, 1989), 546.

6 Michael J. Puett, *To Become a God: Cosmology, Sacrifice, and Self-divinization in Early China* (Cambridge, MA: The Harvard-Yenching Institute, 2002), 301.

7 John K. Fairbank, *China: A New History* (Cambridge, MA: Belknap Press, 1992), 48; J. K. Fairbank, *The United States and China*, 4th edn (Cambridge, MA: Harvard University Press, 1983), 103.

8 See Fairbank, 1992, 48; Jin and Liu, pp. 63–80.

9 See Fairbank, 1992, 48–49; Fairbank, 1983; Jin and Liu, 81–104; Bodo Wiethoff, *Introduction to Chinese History from Ancient Times to 1912* (Boulder, CO: Westview Press, 1975); Wang Weihai, "Household Registry and the Cyclic Change of Chinese Feudal Dynasties," *Zhongguo yanjiu (China Studies)*, Vol. 2, No. 12, 1997.

10 For discussion and criticisms on dynastic cycles due to the morals of the rules, refer to Hans Bielenstein, "Wang Mang, the Restoration of the Han Dynasty, and Later Han," in Denis Twitchett and Michael Loewe, eds, *CHOC* (Cambridge: Cambridge University Press, 1986), Vol. 1, 259–62, and Mansvelt Beck, "The Fall of Han," in *CHOC*, Vol. 1, 357–76. For further discussion and an empirical critique of the land-tax argument, refer to Ray Huang, *Taxation and Governmental Finance in Sixteenth-Century Ming China* (Cambridge: Cambridge University Press, 1974), 308–9.

11 From the Qin Dynasty onward, China composed largely China proper (south to the Great Wall), and the area varied over historical periods. Tibet, Xinjiang, Qinghai, Yunnan, and the areas north to the Great Wall were less important for the integrity of the Chinese empire than the middle and lower reaches of the Yellow, Huai, and Yangtze Rivers. See historical notes on provinces in *Zuixin shiyong Zhongguo dituce (Updated Practical China Maps)* (Beijing: Zhongguo ditu chubanshe, 1992).

12 See a description of the general customs and tariffs on imports in modern China in Zheng Xuemeng, *Jianming Zhongguo Jingji Tongshi (A Concise General History of China's Economy)* (Beijing: Remin Chubanshe, 2005), 636–39.

13 Since the Qin, China's key regions include the middle and lower Yellow River and the Yangtze valleys.

14 The civil war between the Shang troops and the troops from the Zhou state lasted briefly. Due to the lack of precise data, I treat the length of the war as one year.

15 Even the Xia, the first recorded period was preceded by a period of unity. According to the Chinese legends, preceding the Xia was a unified period under Chief Shun.

16 Tang Qinfu, "A Quantitative Study of the Basis of the Governance of the Wen Di of the Sui," *Shangyao shizhuan xuebao (Shangyao Normal College Journal)*, 1987. Cf. Jin and Liu, 372–3.

17 Howard J. Wechsler, "The Founding of the T'ang Dynasty: Kao-tsu," in Denis Twitchett and John K. Fairbank, eds, *CHOC* (Cambridge: Cambridge University Press, 1979), Vol. 3, 150.

18 Han Yulin, Chen Dezhi, Qiu Shusen, Ding Guofan, and Shi Yikui, *Yuanchao shi* (*A History on the Yuan Dynasty*) (Beijing: Renmin chubanshe, 1986), 7–8.

19 Wang Zhongying, *Wei Jin Nanbeichao Suichu Tang shi* (*A History on the Wei, Jin, North-South Dynasties, Early Sui, and Tang*) (Shanghai: Shanghai renmin chubanshe, 1961), pp. 67–82, 103, and 136.

20 Han Sheng, *Sui Wendi zhuan* (*A Biography of Wendi of the Sui*) (Beijing: Renmin chubanshe, 1998), 449–67.

21 Han, *Sui Wendi zhuan*, 356–9 and 369–76.

22 Ibid., 244–52.

23 Michael Loewe, "The Former Han Dynasty," in Denis Twitchett and Micahel Loewe, eds, *CHOC* (Cambridge: Cambridge University Press, 1986), Vol. 1, 113; Zhang *et al.*, 142–3.

24 Pepper discussed arguments on Jiang's alliance with the warlords espoused by Ch'ien Tuan-sheng, Ch'i His-sheng, Wu Ch'i-yuan, and Ch'u An-p'ing. See Suzanne Pepper, "The KMT-CCP Conflict 1945–1949," in John K. Fairbank and Albert Feuerwerker, eds, *CHOC* (Cambridge: Cambridge University Press, 1986), Vol. 13, Part 2, 749.

25 Zhang *et al.*, *Jianming zhongguo gudai shi*, 560–4.

26 Xu Liaoran, *Ren yu shen: ershi shiji renmen yanzhong de Qin Shihuang* (*Man and God: Shihuang of the Qin in the Eyes of People in the Twentieth Century*) (Beijing: Zhongguo guoji guangbo chubanshe, 1995), 2–10. Analyses in his book built on a large body of historical and archeological studies on the Qin.

27 Xu, *Ren yu shen*, 198–201.

28 Zhang *et al.*, *Jianming zhongguo gudai shi*, 141–3.

29 Wei Zheng and Linggu Defen, *Sui shu* (*Books on the Sui*) (Beijing: Zhonghua shuju, 1973), 60–96; Wang Yi, *Sui Tang yu Housanhan guanxi ji Riben qian Sui shi qian Tang shi yundong* (*The Sui's and Tang's Relations with Three Later Koreas and Japan's Movements of Sending Envoys to the Sui and Tang*) (Taipei: Taiwan Chung Hwa Book Company, Ltd. 1972), 33–8; Zang Yunpu, Wang Yundu, Zhu Chongye, He Zhendong, and Ye Qing, *Zhongguo shi dashi jinian* (*A Chronology of Major Events on the Chinese History*) (Ji'nan: Shangdong jiaoyu chubanshe, 1984), 143–4; Zhang *et al.*, 360–8.

30 Arthur Wright, "The Sui Dynasty," in Denis Twitchett and John K. Fairbank, eds, *CHOC* (Cambridge: Cambridge University Press, 1979), Vol. 3, 146.

31 In this chapter I focus on the political factors so that I can present my argument coherently within limited space. I have no intention of ruling out other relevant and non-political factors. For example, population pressure, discussed by P'ing-ti Ho, Jones and Kuhn, and Huang, and the high-level equilibrium trap, discussed by Elvin, did play a role in China's slow march toward modernization from the Ming to the Qing. See P'ing-Ti Ho, *Studies on the Population of China, 1368–1953* (Cambridge, MA: Harvard University Press, 1959), 257–300; Susan Mann Jones and Philip Kuhn, "Dynastic Decline and the Roots of Rebellion," in Denis Twitchett and John K. Fairbank, eds, *CHOC* (Cambridge: Cambridge University Press, 1978), Vol. 10, 107–163; Elvin, *The Pattern of the Chinese Past*. The population pressure has persisted from the Ming to the PRC. This pressure subjects the state to limited revenue, a constant political headache regarding high food price and poverty, crises due to natural disasters, intense economic conflict among groups, and difficulties to maintain peace.

32 Xu, *Ren yu shen*, 118, 198–201 and 129.

33 Jian Bozan, *Qin Han shi* (*A History of the Qin and Han*) (Beijing: Beijing daxue chubanshe, 1983), 60–1.

34 Tian Changwu and An Zuozhang, *Qin Han shi* (*A History of the Qin and Han*) (Beijing: Renmin chubanshe, 1993), 67.

35 Wang Juchang, *Qin shi* (*A History of the Qin*) (Shanghai: Shanghai guji chubanshe, 2000), 44–55; Xu, *Ren yu shen*, 240–9. Wang's book was based on compiled extensive ancient historical records on the Qin.

36 Fang Xuanling, Chu Suiliang, and Xu Jingzong, *Jin shu* (*Books on the Jin*) (Beijing: Zhonghua shuju, 1974), Vol. 1, 72–82; Wang, *Wei Jin Nanbeichao Suichu Tang shi*, 138–41.

37 Wang, *Wei Jin Nanbeichao Suichu Tang shi*, 111–31.

38 Han, *Sui Wendi zhuan*, 449–67; Cen Zhongmian, *Sui Tang shi* (*A History of the Sui and the Tang*) (Beijing: Gaodeng jiaoyu chubanshe, 1957), 36–7.

39 Lü Simian, *Sui Tang Wudai shi* (*A History on the Sui, the Tang, and the Five Dynasties*) (Shanghai: Shanghai guji chubanshe, 1984), 28–32; Zhang *et al.*, *Jianming zhongguo gudai shi*, 366.

40 Lü, *Sui Tang Wudai shi*, 37; Wang, *Sui Tang yu Huosanhan guanxi ji Riben qian Sui shi qian Tang shi yundong*, 38; Zhang *et al.*, *Jianming zhongguo gudai shi*, 360–8.

41 Cen, *Sui Tang shi*, 73–84; Zhang *et al.*, *Jianming zhongguo gudai shi*, pp. 368–70.

42 Han *et al.*, *Yuanchao shi*, pp. 254–389; Ch'i-ch'ing Hsiao, *Meng Yuan shi xin yan* (*Recent Studies on the Mongolian and the Yuan's History*) (Taipei: Yunchen wenhua shiye gufen youxian gongsi, 1994), 413–28 and 460–500.

43 Ch'i-ch'ing Hsiao "Mid-Yüan politics," in Herbert Franke and Denis Twitchett, eds, *CHOC* (New York: Cambridge University Press, 1994), Vol. 6, 558.

44 Hsiao, "Mid-Yüan Politics," 558; Huang Shijian, *Yuanchao shi hua* (*Remarks on the History of the Yuan*) (Beijing: Beijing chubanshe, 1985), 210–13; Zhang *et al.*, *Jianming zhongguo gudai shi*, 557.

45 Li Zhi'an, *Yuandai fenfeng zhidu yanjiu* (*A Study of the Yuan's Enfeoffment System*) (Tianjin: Tianjin guji chubanshe, 1992), 247–318 and 334–6; Zhang *et al.*, *Jianming zhongguo gudai shi*, 558.

46 John Dardess, "Shun-ti and the End of Yüan Rule in China," in Herbert Franke and Denis Twitchett, eds, *CHOC* (New York: Cambridge University Press, 1994), Vol. 6, 578. For a discussion on the Yuan's daunting task of balancing contending political forces, see John Dardess, *Conquerors and Confucians: Aspects of Political Change in Late Yuan China* (New York and London: Columbia University Press, 1973).

47 Huang, *Yuanchao shi hua*, 227–30.

48 Darddes, *Conquerors and Confucians*, 585–6.

49 Zhang Yufa, *Zhonghua Mingguo shigao* (*A Manuscript on the History of the Republic of China*) (Taipei: Lianjing chuban shiye gongsi, 1998), 239–46 and 289–306.

50 Lucien Bianco, "Peasant Movements," in John K. Fairbank and Albert Feuerwerker, eds, *CHOC* (Cambridge: Cambridge University Press, 1986), Vol. 13, Part 2, 270–328; Philip A. Kuhn, "The Development of Local Government," in *CHOC*, Vol. 13, Part 2, 345–52 and 358–60.

51 Suzanne Pepper, *Civil War in China: The Political Struggle, 1945–1949* (Berkeley, CA: UC Press, 1978), Chapter 7; Pepper, "The KMT-CCP Conflict 1945–1949," 751–8; Prasenjit Duara, *Culture, Power, and the State: Rural North China, 1900–1942* (Stanford, CA: Stanford University Press, 1988); Lih Tung-Fang, *Chung-kuo Minkuo shi* (*The First Seventy-Eight Years of the Republic of China: 1912–1988*) (Taipei: You-shi Cultural Enterprise Limited, 1990).

52 Pepper, *Civil War in China*, Chapter 4.

53 See Tian and An, *Qin Han shi*, 105–215; Cen, *Sui Tang shi*, 108–9; Fang *et al.*, *Jin shu* (*Publisher's Explanation*), 2–3; Wei and Linggu, *Sui shu* (*Publisher's Explanation*), 1–5.

54 For a discussion on early and successful emperors of the Former and Later Han, see Tian and An, *Qin Han shi*, 105–68, 189–214, 280–325, and 361. For studies on

early and able emperors of the Tang, see Song Changbin, Zeng Beibei, and Wang Xiaoping, *Sheng Tang fengcai: Tangchao xingshuai qishilu* (*Graceful Bearing of the Flourishing Tang: Apocalypse of the Rise and Fall of the Tang Dynasty*) (Taipei: Nianlun wenhua shiye youxian gongsi, 1998), 123–212; Howard J. Wechsler, "T'ai-tsung the Consolidator," in Denis Twitchett and John K. Fairbank, eds, *CHOC* (Cambridge: Cambridge University Press), Vol. 3, Part I, 188–241; Denis Twitchett and Howard J. Wechsler, "Kao-tsung and the Empress Wu," in *CHOC*, Vol. 3, Part I, 242–89; Richard W. L. Guisso, "The Reign of the Empress Wu, Chung-tsung and Jui-tsung," in *CHOC*, Vol. 3, Part I, 290–332; Denis Twitchett, "Hsüan-tsung," in *CHOC*, Vol. 3, Part I, 332–463. For analyses on early and effective rulers of the Ming, refer to Fu Yiling, Yang Guozhen, and Chen Zhiping, *Mingshi xinbian* (*A New Compilation on the History of the Ming*) (Beijing: Renmin chubanshe, 1993), 27–47 and 78–141. For an examination of the early emperors of the Qing, see Zheng Tianting, *Qing shi* (*A History on the Qing*) (Taipei: Yunlong chubanshe, 1998), 295–324, 369–410 and 411–56.

55 For historical accounts of the regimes, refer to Denis Twitchett and John K. Fairbank, eds, *The Cambridge History of China* (Cambridge: Cambridge University Press, 1978–98); Zhang *et al.*, *Jianming zhongguo gudai shi*.

56 See Tian and An (note 34, this chapter, 295), 141–146 and 152–155; Fu *et al.* (note 54, this chapter, 295–296), 59–65; Zheng (note 54, this chapter, 295–296), 276–289; Zhang *et al.* (note 4, this chapter, 292), 151–153, 158–160, 162, 592–593 and 654–656.

57 He Li, Gao Huamin, Xiao Donglian, Deng Yun, and Qi Biao, *Zhonghua Renmin Gongheguo shi* (*A History of the People's Republic of China*) (Beijing: Zhongguo dang'an chubanshe, 1995), 12.

58 I thank Professor Baogang He for bringing to my attention of the life span of one-party regimes in the world in our discussion of the longevity of the CCP regime in the summer of 2013.

59 Michael Mann, "The Autonomous Power of the State: Its Origins, Mechanisms, and Results," *Archives européenes de sociologie*, Vol. 25, 1984, 185–213.

60 Shaoguang Wang, "The Rise of the Regions: Fiscal Reform and the Decline of Central State Capacity in China," in Andrew Walder, ed., *The Waning of the Communist State* (Berkeley, CA: University of California Press, 1995), 87–113. For a historical study of the fiscal situation of a dynasty, refer to D.C. Twitchett, *Financial Administration under the Tang Dynasty* (London and New York: Cambridge University Press, 1963).

10 The future of governance in China
Toward authoritarian flexibility and durability

Where the Party state in China is heading and how well it can fare are questions that have captivated growing attention from analysts and decision makers. They would like to know whether the regime is undergoing incremental democratization that would lead to a fundamental opening of the authoritarian regime in the foreseeable future. Likewise, they would like to come to grips with the likelihood of the immediate demise of the regime and nationwide upheavals and instability should the regime resist democratization in the coming decade. Having traversed the vast terrain of political development in China in the reform era, we are now in a good position to address these issues and gain a useful glimpse of the future of the Chinese state.

In this concluding chapter I will first review the findings from the preceding chapters regarding the possible direction and fate of the Party state. I will then examine the recent development of politics under the current leadership of President Xi Jinping. In light of several major policies introduced by him I will address a much-discussed claim about the inevitable collapse of the Party state under these policies. Finally, I will return to the flexibility and durability of the Party state, issues that have been central to the analysis of this book.

Authoritarian flexibility in managing crises in governance

Since 1978 the Party state in China has met a number of daunting and even potentially fatal challenges. In seeking and hammering out the solution the Party state has displayed resilience, flexibility, and pragmatism without comprising its authoritarian nature. Eventually and to the surprise of many observers and scholars the Party state has handled the most pressing tasks in governance relatively well. I will briefly review these tasks one by one below.

The first challenge was a low living standard and a backward economy. When the economic reform started in 1978, China's economy was saddled with numerous inefficient SOEs that dominated industry and urban commerce, and the population faced chronic food shortage and could only consume barely enough grain and little meat to support their subsistence. The nation also had one of the lowest levels of per capita GDP in the world and had scant economic exchanges with the outside world in the forms of investment and trade. Against this context and as stated in Chapter 3, the Party state has successfully introduced pro-growth authoritarianism since 1978, resulting in high economic growth for over three and half decades that is unprecedented in human history. After suppressing with brute force the popular calls for democracy in 1989 and having thrashed once-dominant conservatives who sternly opposed marketization in 1992, Deng firmly installed pro-growth authoritarianism in China.

The core of pro-growth authoritarianism is orthodox reformism, which emphasizes economic reforms that value (if not worship) the contribution from market forces on the one hand and embraces the Party's leadership on the other.[1] One of the climaxes of marketization in China was the determined push by President Jiang Zemin and Premier Zhu Rongji to enter the WTO in 2001 and bring the bureaucracy, SOEs and other domestic firms in line with the rules and codes for a market economy honored by the organization with over 100 member-states/economies.

In the wake of pro-growth authoritarianism China improved its worldwide rank of per capita gross national income (GNI) from the 175th out of 188 economies in 1978 to the 112th out of 213 in 2012. Within 34 years China moved upward from one of the poorest nations in the world to a middle-income country with a near average global rank of per capita GNI. This is a feat that few observers in 1978 would have believed that the Party state could accomplish, especially given that China is the most populous nation with about one-fifth of the world's population. As a result of the economic miracle the Party state has regained the legitimacy that was nearly destroyed by Mao's destructive campaigns, especially the Cultural Revolution of 1966–76 and the Great Leap Forward of 1958–61.

In the recent two decades the side effects of pro-growth authoritarianism have become increasingly apparent. In response, the Party state has endeavored to rectify these problems by attempting to address environmental issues, crack down on rising official corruption and ease abuse of power in officials' pursuit of high growth. These efforts are still ongoing and are expected to continue in the years to come.

A second and daunting challenge for the Party state, as detailed in Chapter 4, was widespread discontent from rural residents in inland China and from laid-off workers throughout urban China in the 1990s. In the 1990s popular discontent in the countryside was so high that rural residents blatantly expressed their desire for leaders of armed rebellions in their talk with national top leaders.[2] Moreover, escalating urban unemployment in the wake of drastic restructuring of SOEs resulted in frequent and mass protests by laid-off workers in the cities, especially provincial capitals and major cities in the northeast. Even Beijing was flooded with hundreds of protesters and petitioners on a regular basis. It seems that the hinterland of China had degraded into social upheavals and instability and that the national capital and the Party state were besieged by a disgruntled and deprived populace. Few could expect the Party state to have a quick and easy escape from this quandary of governance.

In the 2000s the Party state, especially under President Hu and Premier Wen, made the improvement of the living standard of rural residents a top priority of their governance agenda. They introduced a series of policies to ease the fiscal burdens on the peasants, introduce welfare programs in the country-side, and improve agricultural productivity and accelerate rural transformation. These policies had by and large removed the burdens on peasants that were imposed by the state, and had helped the income of rural residents to grow at a decent rate in the 2000s. In addition, the state has helped rebuild rural cooperative health care and is introducing arguably for the first time ever in Chinese history pension schemes in the countryside. Rural residents thus held a high regard for the Hu–Wen leadership.

Meanwhile, in order to address the economic hardship of the urban unem-ployed Premier Zhu and his successor spent a vast amount of budgetary funds on building the minimum living allowances for the urban unemployed. They also rebuilt and expanded health insurance and pensions coverage in the cities. These measures help moderate the economic uncertainties inflicted on residents and employees in the cities. As a result, protests and petitions by the urban unemployed in the cities were no longer the most severe concern for the Party state toward the end of the first term of the Hu–Wen leadership around 2008.

The third challenge, as suggested in Chapter 5, was the reviving society and the possible loss of the control of the Party state over large social organiza-tions with a strong mobilization capacity. The latter is significant as the Party state views its dominance over other organizations and social groups as one of the core components of its one-party rule. Since 1978 hundreds of millions of Chinese have increasingly sought faith and spiritual fulfillment in religions, and a variety of religious organizations and groups have mushroomed in China. According to a survey conducted by the Center on Religion and Chinese Society (CRCS) of Purdue University and by the Horizon survey firm and on the analysis of scholars at the CRCS in 2007, the self-identified followers of major religions totaled 253 million, about 19.2 percent of the population, nearly doubling from the number (136 million) of followers of the five major religions in 1999. Moreover, the number of social groups and organizations, including the formally registered ones, have been growing exponentially. The rapidly expanding social activities prompted a number of scholars to claim in the 1990s that China's civil society, as a state-societal intermediate, was rising.[3] Meanwhile, the deteriorating ability of the state to manage the society was noted.[4] Against ongoing popular conversion to religions instead of communist or official ideology many observers naturally wonder how the Party state could have sustained its power and relevance without antagonizing the population.

Surprisingly and as documented in Chapter 5, the Party state has adopted a sophisticated and calculated strategy in managing the society and especially religions. On the one hand, it has shown a greater tolerance for non-political and non-organized social activities. It has re-defined the forbidden zone (activ-ities banned by the state) more narrowly to cover mainly organized social activities opposing either the state or its fundamental principles in regulating the society. It has thus relied on the coopted organizations of five officially-recognized religions to manage the majority of the believers of these religions. As far as faiths outside these five religions, such as folk religions and super-stitions, are concerned, the state allows considerable space for their existence and operation. Since around 2008 and in the second term of the Hu–Wen administration the government also allowed religious groups to play a greater role in undertaking charitable work and in promoting the morality of the people.

On the other hand, the Party state has maintained its ban against the underground Catholic church. Since the late 1990s it has outlawed so-called evil cults and has targeted large and well organized religious groups that operate outside the official organizations of five major religions. The best examples have been the outlawing of Falun Gong, Zhong Gong, and Xiang Gong after the mass protests by Falun Gong in Beijing in 1999. Through adopting this dual strategy the state has maintained its monopoly of key organizational instruments while leaving scope for spontaneous religious activities to take place.

The fourth challenge, as detailed in Chapter 6, was improper management of crises, especially epidemics. In practicing pro-growth authoritarianism officials laid a heavy emphasis on GDP growth at the expense of the well-being of the population, including public health. Little attention and funds were channeled into public health, resulting in inadequate institutions and funding for epidemic prevention. In the early weeks of the outbreak of the SARS epidemic management was undermined by officials' obsession with high economic growth and with concerns with social instability. Officials covered up epidemic conditions, under-stated the risks of SARS, and tried to manage the epidemic secretively. This secretive approach to epidemic management resulted in public ignorance of the pandemic risks and of the best practice in epidemic control such as the quarantine of suspected or infected patients. This eventually led to a rampant spread of the disease. The Hu–Wen leader-ship back-pedaled to contain the damages that the pandemic had inflicted on the economy and on the image of the Party state at home and abroad. Through mass mobilization and a nationwide campaign the Party state brought SARS under control within months. In the following years it also endeavored to overcome the shortfalls of pro-growth authoritarianism by building a nation-wide and multi-layer crisis management system and by devoting a larger amount of funds to epidemic prevention. In the following years the epidemic management institution had withstood the tests from the outbreaks of swine flu and H1N1 bird flu. China apparently responded to these potentially deadly epidemics swiftly and effectively.

The fifth challenge, discussed in Chapter 7, was potential and devastating blows to the Party due to improper management of leadership succession. This challenge has been near fatal for the CCP, as some of the gravest devastations the CCP suffered, including the Cultural Revolution and the 1989 Tiananmen Movement, were tied with failed leadership succession. The crux of the problem was a lack of institutionalization of leadership succession. In the reform era a set of rules and norms have been progressively introduced and tightened in order to provide for orderly leadership succession at the national and local levels. Age limits and term limits have been introduced and closely observed. After 1989 a norm has emerged to allow the paramount leader to assume three key posts, namely, the Presidency, the General Secretary of the CCP, and the CMC Chairmanship. Hu's decision to hand over all these three posts to Xi in late 2012 represented a genuine and historical step toward instant and complete power transfer from the incumbent paramount leader to the leader-in-waiting. Largely as a result of these institutional arrangements the Party state has escaped the devastations due to failed leadership succession since 1989.

The aforementioned cases of the Party state's management of governance crises reveal the strong ability of the regime to adjust, adapt, and respond to new and unforeseen challenges. First, it is able to identify the most pressing challenge and problem. In the late 1970s the leaders recognized the gross inefficiency of Mao's economic policies and then embarked on economic reform in 1978. They embraced pro-growth authoritarianism. Since the 2000s the Chinese leaders became aware of the defects of pro-growth authoritarianism. They introduced policies and invested a huge sum in order to improve the material well-being and social security of rural and urban residents. It also mended the loopholes in epidemic management, and has started to address environmental degradation. The Party state also recognizes the populace's desire for religious faiths and activities and has adopted a calculated and partial relaxation of its control of religious activities reforming its religious policies.

Second, the Party state has been flexible in its ideological formulation, institutional development and renewal, and policy responses. Take pro-growth authoritarianism, for example. In his tour to southern China in 1992 Deng promoted liberal economic reforms. He even negated the core dictum of communism that condemned private ownership, private firms, and the market. He justified his action by proclaiming that the ultimate criterion for deciding whether or not to adopt an economic institution or policy was to see whether it could generate economic growth. In 2001 the CCP even allowed domestic capitalists to become its members. This was the exact opposite of what Marx and Engels set out to achieve in creating communists in their *Communist Manifesto*, i.e., to bury capitalism. Take another example. In managing the boom in religious activities the Party state adopts a calculated strategy by differentiating between the potential threats from various religious groups and activities to its own monopoly of power. It was bold and sensible in leaving considerable space for spontaneous religious activities alone. However, it is highly vigilant in guarding against and restricting organized and large religious groups outside the co-opted organizations for the five religions that it endorses. The final example is leadership succession. In overcoming the fatal clashes between the incumbent leaders and their successor that had persisted for four decades, an elaborate set of rules has been introduced in the reform era that mandates timely retirement and minimizes deadly conflicts between the incumbent leader and their heir-apparent.

Third, the Party state would take swift and drastic measures to remedy grave problems without comprising its monopoly of power. This was reflected in its abandonment of Mao's emphasis on political campaigns and its launch of economic reform in 1978. This was also reflected in the dismissals of two ministerial-level officials and the launch of an open and nationwide campaign against SARS in early 2003 in the wake of rapid spread of SARS. During 2012–13 President Hu decisively passed over all his three major posts to his successor Xi, thereby setting an unprecedented example for complete and timely power transfer in the history of the CCP. His move aims to cure once and for all the perennial conflict between the top leader and his successor before and even after the formal power transfer.

This is not to deny that the Party state still confronts several daunting challenges. The most critical one is the lack of political opening, the rule of law, transparency, free and competitive elections, and effective public and media supervision of officials. These inadequacies help to a large extent to account for persistent social instability in China despite its breakneck economic growth for the past 37 years. Nevertheless, the Party state has chosen to meet this challenge through a dual strategy. On the one hand and as documented in Chapter 8, the Party state has embraced certain measures in order to satisfy the public yearning for democracy at the grass-roots level and to reconcile different opinions and interests of major power holders in the national and local Party. It has endorsed and promoted village elections since the 1980s. In the last decade, it has tried to promote direct elections of residents committees in urban communities. It also tolerates schemes to promote public supervision and deliberation in decision making in certain localities, such as democratic consultation meetings in Wenling City of Zhejiang Province. Furthermore, progress has been made toward intra-Party democracy, especially through competitive and semi-competitive selection of leaders at the local and national levels.

On the other hand, the Chinese leaders have rejected Western liberal democracy and have refused to allow elections of township Party and government leaders to be spread throughout the country. Furthermore, they still uphold the Party's leadership, ban open opposition parties, and despise free and competitive elections. In this regard, we can see clearly the flexibility of the Party state in tolerating and even undertaking certain democratic initiatives, as these initiatives can ease the desire of the population toward democracy, reduce popular discontent over abusive, incompetent or corrupt officials, and allow the regime to select qualified, honest, and competent leaders at the national and local levels. More importantly, we can see the bottom line of the Party state, namely, to protect one-party rule in China. It is within this context that I argue that the regime has demonstrated authoritarian flexibility. That is to say, the regime can be flexible and adaptable in resolving pressing crises and challenges, yet in doing so it always wants to sustain instead of undermining the one-party regime. This is the ultimate objective when it displays a remarkable degree of pragmatism and flexibility in addressing the aforementioned challenges.

Governance program of Xi Jinping: decisive orthodox reformism

As President Xi Jinping and Premier Li Keqiang assumed their posts in early 2013 and as they are expected to stay in power until early 2023, it is necessary and helpful for me to review several major policies of the Xi–Li leadership. The governance agenda of Xi can be briefly summed up as "two reforms and two antis": forging of economic reform and institutional reform; anti-corruption and anti-political liberalism. Overall, Xi still stays on the path of orthodox reformism that I explained earlier. Let me explain each of the four features of Xi's governance program.

Economic reform: ambitious agenda, difficult implementation, and intervention impulses

On the Third Plenum of the Eighteenth Central Committee of the CCP in November 2013 a "Decision of the Chinese Communist Party Central Committee on Several Major Questions About Deepening Reform" was passed. This policy document outlined the key reform agenda of Xi up to 2020. As will be outlined below, this document contained a wide range of encompassing economic and administrative reforms. The most critical objective was to give market forces a "decisive" role in allocating resources, to withdraw the government from resource allocation, and to establish a transparent, fair, open, orderly, and competitive market system.[5] The proclaimed bold reforms include the following ones.

1 The government will focus on macroeconomic management, market regulation, public service delivery, supervision of society, and environmental protection.
2 The state will protect private property as it does public property.
3 The government's (administration's) approvals of investment projects will be reduced significantly. The government will heed the environment, production capacity, residents' income, jobs, social protection, and public health in economic growth.
4 Governmental budgets will be made transparent.
5 Sales taxes will be converted into value-added tax (VAT) in order to free businesses and consumers from double taxation.
6 The market entry will be made uniform and various corporations can enter the market of various sectors as long as the sector is not on the list of no entry.
7 SOEs will be sustained but be made efficient.

8   Pricing of water, oil and gas, power, and telecom services will take into account in a greater degree supply and demand.
9   A fair market for land use will be promoted.
10 Financial market reforms will be pursued.
11 Intellectual property rights will be protected via a special court.

Earlier, in September 2013 the State Council approved the Shanghai Free Trade Zone (FTZ) with 29 square kilometers. The FTZ would enjoy simplified administrative approvals for new firms and low or even no tariffs. It would also have expedient mechanisms regarding dispute resolution, currency exchange, corporate establishment, and the flow of foreign investment into a number of sectors. In December 2014 three additional FTZs were mapped out by the NPC, including Guangdong FTZ of 116 square kilometers covering Nansha (Guangzhou), Shenzhen and Zhuhai, Tianjin FTZ of 120 square kilometers, and Fujian FTZ of 118 square kilometers covering Fuzhou, Xiamen and Pingtan.[6]

Given the number and scope of these proclaimed reforms the reform agenda of Xi is ambitious.[7] These proclaimed reforms are likely to encounter fierce opposition from entrenched interests likely including bureaucrats, SOEs, and corporate circles. It remains to be seen how fast and how far these reform measures can be implemented.

In addition, as the sharp decline in the share prices of the Chinese stock exchanges in 2015 suggested, the Chinese authoritarian state confronts the challenging task of fulfilling its proclaimed reform for further marketization while it is acutely sensitive to the political fallouts of huge fluctuation in the markets. From June 11–29, 2015, the Shanghai Stock Composite Index fell by over 20 percent, resulting in a loss of around 21 trillion yuan. It was estimated that over 100 million Chinese individual investors suffered dearly from this downturn. As the half-year boom of the Chinese stock exchanges was abruptly ended, massive complaints and panics from Chinese shareholders became visible. In response, Premier Li Keqing, rumored to be acting under pressure from President Xi, brushed aside the moderate and incremental remedy suggested by the top banking and financial securities chiefs, and opted in early July for a forceful rescue of the stock markets. For this purpose the state mobilized 1.7 trillion yuan through stabilizing funds and through funds from large and especially state-controlled traders and investors. Such a move clearly deviated from the decades-old state policy of not blatantly interfering with the operation of the stock markets and prompted skepticism from external analysts toward the effectiveness of such interventions and toward the pro-market agenda of the Xi–Li leadership. However, in light of the central theme of this book, that is, pragmatic authoritarianism, this move is logical given the state's preoccupation with political support and legitimacy and its utilitarian resorts to tools that it deems effective for this purpose. So the state may push for marketization that it recognizes can generate economic growth. It may also revert to intervention into the markets when it sees that sharp downturns or apparent downsides of the markets are undermining its popular support.

Institutional reform: centralization of power and judicial reform

In order to push ahead with these ambitious and challenging reforms and with his sweeping anti-corruption drive and overcome stubborn opposition, Xi centralized power swiftly and has assumed a much larger political role compared to his predecessors Jiang and especially Hu. For these aims he has created two new agencies and has obtained more political power. It was announced at the Third Plenum of Eighteenth CCCCP in November 2013 that Xi headed two powerful and new agencies. The first one was "the Leading Small Group for Overall Reform" that oversees the implementation of the aforementioned reform measures. Premier Li Keqiang, Li Yunshan, the Director of the Department of Propaganda of the CCCCP, and Executive Vice Premier Zhang Gaoli serve as the deputy heads. The other was the National Security Commission, for which Premier Li and Zhang Dejiang, the Chairman of the Standing Committee of the NPC, serve as deputy heads.[8] Furthermore, as mentioned in Chapter 7, in January 2015, Xi, as the General Secretary of the CCP, listened to Premier Li's report on the Party Group of the State Council which Li heads, Zhang Dejiang's report on the Party Group of the NPC which Zhang leads, Yu Zhengsheng's report on the Party Group of the Chinese People's Political Consultative Conference that Yu heads. The official news media coins this practice an important institution,[9] indicating Xi's determination to institutionalize this practice and place himself well above the Politburo Standing Committee members in hierarchy.

Xi has also forged ahead with bold reform of the judicial system in order to ensure that laws are well respected and closely observed. So far three moves have been noticeable. First, a number of celebrities and notable entrepreneurs and firms have been punished for illegal acts. Several nationally known entertainment stars were detained and then received a penalty for using illegal drugs. They included the son of movie superstar Jack Chan and Wang Xuebing, a well-known actor. Foreign multi-national corporations in China, such as Microsoft and Toyota, have been investigated and then fined for monopoly practice. Second, upon coming to power he abolished the labor and reform institution whereby transgressors of the law, including dissidents were detained and sent to labor camps. This institution subjected the detained to extra-legal punishment and had been abused in its actual application. Third, the aforementioned resolution passed at the Third Plenum of the Eighteenth CCCCP outlined judicial reform measures, including legal review of major policies to ensure their compliance with the existing laws, simplified and unified law enforcement, and setting up centralized procuratorate and court systems that would enable them to be free from interference from provincial and local Party and governmental leaders.

Anti-political-liberalism

The numerous reform initiatives that have been outlined above suggest that Xi aims to unleash the boldest round of economic and institutional reforms since China's WTO accession in 2001 and next to liberal economic reforms promoted by Deng. Nevertheless, Xi's stance over political reform has been surprisingly conservative so far. He has remained firm over the Party's monopoly of power and unswayed by the trend toward democratization in the developing world in recent decades. The following cases illustrate his commitment to one-party rule in China.

As stated in Chapter 8, around December 2012, shortly after the Eighteenth Party Congress, Mr. Xi proposed to the former U.S. president Jimmy Carter that the Carter Center should shift its focus away from village elections and governmental transparency and toward U.S.–China relations. Around August 2013 shortly after Xi assumed the post of President, an internal policy document coded as "Document No. 9" was circulated among cadres in China. The document contained a list of seven topics under the category "don't-mentions" (*qi bu jiang*), i.e., topics banned from public discussion. The "seven don't-mentions" included "constitutional democracy, universal values, civil society, market liberalism, media independence, criticizing errors in the history of the Party, and questioning the policy of opening up and reforms and the socialist nature of the regime." Most of these taboo topics related to political liberalism.[10] In mid-April 2015 Gao Yu, a Chinese female journalist, was sentenced to seven years in jail for leaking the internal "Document No. 9" outside China and for revealing state secrets. In June 2014, the head of a team dispatched by the CDIC even claimed that numerous scholars from the Chinese Academy of Social Sciences (CASS) were penetrated by Western forces and propagated questionable views harmful to the Party state.[11] Many intellectuals in China may feel the pressure against their making politically liberal comments or discussing meaningful political reforms. Some even sense a return to Mao's era as far as official restrictions on discussion on democracy are concerned.

Anti-corruption

One of the most-watched of Xi's governance measures is the anti-corruption campaign, which is executed by Wang Qishan, the chief of the CDIC of the CCCCP. One former PSC member (Zhou Yongkang) and three former Politburo members (Bo Xilai, Xu Caihou, and Guo Boxiong) were among the most senior leaders implicated in the campaign. The Politburo is the top political agency in China with two dozen of the most powerful leaders. According to one report, during 2014–15 alone 12 officials at the minister level and above and 65 officials at the deputy minister level were implicated in corruption probes.[12] The level and the number of national leaders and senior officials being implicated in this campaign have thus been unprecedented since 1949 (see Table 10.1). This anti-corruption campaign has been hailed by many as the most sweeping in the 65 years history of the PRC.

Bo Xilai, a former Politburo member and the former Chongqing Party Secretary, was the first tiger to fall under the anti-graft axe wielded ostensibly by Xi and Wang. He was sentenced to a life term in jail in October 2013. His two alleged crimes included (1) accepting bribes of over 20 million yuan ($3.3 million), including a villa in southern France and five million yuan in embezzled state funds, and (2) dismissing Wang Lijun as the policy chief in Chongqing in order to cover up his wife's murder of a British business partner, Neil Heywood.[13] He vigorously defended himself at the court and appealed against the sentence, albeit to no avail.

The next set of tigers revealed by the Chinese state was top generals. Xu Caihou, a former Politburo member and Vice CMC Chairman, was investigated for corruption in March 2014. Reportedly, he accepted a large sum of bribes in exchange for the rampant sales of officer posts in the military. The investigators found one ton of cash in Renminbi, Euros, and U.S. bank notes, as well 300 kilograms of precious stones. Among numerous cases of bribery Xu accepted 40 million yuan and four apartments from desperate Gu Jinshan, a Deputy Director of the General Logistics Department of the PLA who was being investigated for taking bribes.[14] In July 2015 Xu's colleague Guo Boxiong, another former Politburo member and the other Vice CMC Chairman, was ousted from the Party and subject to formal criminal investigation for accepting bribes from officers who sought promotions.

In July 2014 Zhou Yongkang became the highest-ranked leader to undergo anti-graft probes in the history of the PRC that was founded in 1949. He was a member of the PSC and a former tsar of the security and policy system. In April 2015 Zhou was charged formally for accepting a huge sum of bribes, abuse of power and intentional disclosure of state secrets.[15] Thanks to the political clout of Zhou, his son Zhou Bin obtained commercial concessions and incurred huge losses of state assets. Zhou Bin amassed wealth of reportedly at least 20 billion yuan.[16] Reportedly Zhou Yongkang also gained sexual favors from female stars via the former deputy head of the CCTV Li Dongsheng. In June 2015 Zhou was sentenced to life in prison and he accepted the sentence without appeal.

Furthermore, two deputy heads of the CPPCC are being investigated. One of them is Ling Jihua, a former director of the General Office of the CCCCP and a former secretary of President Hu. Hu, however, reportedly insisted that he was unaware of Ling's political collusion with Bo and Zhou, as well as his corruption and that Ling was not his close follower. Reportedly, Ling ran "Xishan Society" through his sister-in-law. Ling accepted a large amount of bribes for helping to arrange for a promotion for officials who came from his home province Shanxi. For example, 10 million yuan was the price tag for an official being promoted to be a mayor. This association also became a vehicle for him to increase his influence and power base.[17] In addition, he was said to

Table 10.1 Selected leaders or officials investigated for corruption, 2012–present

Name	Official Post	Time of Fall from Grace	Official Reasons for Investigation	Outcome or Status
Wang Lijun	Former Vice Mayor and Public Security Chief of Chongqing	February 2012	Defection to the U.S. Consulate Office; involvement in a murder	Sentenced to 15-year jail term in Sept 2012
Bo Xilai	Politburo member; Former Chongqing Party Secretary	March 2012	Accepting bribes; abuse of power	Sentenced to life in jail in Sept 2013
Zhou Yongkang	PSC member; Head of Central Political and Legal Affairs Commission	June 2015	He and his son were reported to have accepted hundreds of billion yuan in bribes and to have abused his power	Sentenced to life in prison for bribery, abuse of power, and disclosure of state secrets
Ling Jihua	Second deputy head of the CPPCC; Director of the United Front Department of the CCCCP	December 2014	Accepted bribes; abuse of power; revealing state secrets; formed a political alliance with Bo and Zhou	Ousted from the Party, lost official posts and under criminal investigation in July 2015
Gu Jinshan	Deputy Director of the General Logistics Department of the PLA	May 2012	Accepted huge sums of bribes	Being charged for corruption by the Procuratorate in April 2014
Xu Caihou	Politburo member; Vice CMC Chairman	March 2014	Accepted large sums of bribes in exchange for promoting officers	Died of illness in March 2015
Guo Boxiong	Politburo member; Vice CMC Chairman	July 2015	Accepted large sums of bribes in exchange for promoting officers	Expelled from the Party; under criminal investigation
Yang Dongliang	Director of the State (National) Administration of Work Safety; member of the 18th CCCCP; vice mayor of Tianjin Municipality from 2001 to May 2012.	August 2015	Under investigation of the Central Commission for Disciplinary Inspection (CCDI) for "severe violation of discipline and law" in the wake of the explosions in the Port of Tianjin	Obviously he was relieved of his official post following the official announcement of investigation.

Name	Official Post	Time of Fall from Grace	Official Reasons for Investigation	Outcome or Status
Zhou Benshun	Party Secretary of Hebei Province	July 2015	Violated Party rules and laws; possibly had colluded with Zhou Yongkang and Ling Jihua	Under investigation and lost his post
Jiang Jiemen	Former Chairman of CNPC; Director of State Assets Supervision Administration	September 2013	Accepted bribes and illegally transferred state assets to Zhong Yongkang's son	Pending results of investigation
Bai Enpei	Party Secretary of Yunan Province	August 2014	Accepted bribes alleged of billion yuan; bribed Zhong Yongkang's son	Pending results of investigation
Li Dongsheng	Deputy head of the CCTV and of the Ministry of Public Security	December 2013	Accepted bribes; provided favors to Zhong Yongkang	Pending results of investigation
Su Rong	Deputy head of the CPPCC; former Jiangsu Party Secretary	June 2014	Accepted a huge amount of bribes and sold offices	Pending results of investigation

Note: Names in bold denoted the most senior officials/leaders who were investigated for corruption. Sources: Multiple news reports, including the following posting; "Zhongong shibada yilai de fa fubai gongzuo" (Anti-Corruption Work since the Eighteenth Congress of the CCP), posted at: http://zh.wikipedia.org/wiki/中共十八大以来的反腐败工作, accessed on March 15, 2015.

collude with Zhong Yongkang and Bo Xilai to cultivate political power in order to undermine the leadership of Xi. In July 2015 Ling was ousted from the Party, lost official posts and was under criminal investigation. The other deputy head of the CPPCC who fell from grace was Su Rong. Su served as the Party Secretary of three provinces, namely, Jiangxi, Qinghai, and Gansu. Reportedly he was a follower of Zhou Yongkang and accepted numerous bribes.[18] In July 2015 Zhou Benshun, the Party Secretary of Hebei Province and a former secretary of Zhou Yongkang, was announced to be under investigation for violation of Party rules and laws. He was said to have helped Ling Jinhua to cover up the scandalous crash of a Ferrari in Beijing City that claimed the life of Ling's son and injured two of his lady friends.

In addition to going after the rogue officials, Xi also issued eight rules in early 2013 to compel officials to reduce extravagance in dining, entertainment, and domestic and overseas travel for leisure on official budget. The rules also aim to curtail official spending on business cars and offices. Liberal observers tend to question the effectiveness of these rules.[19]

Nevertheless, available evidence suggests that these rules seem to be fairly rigorously enforced, as the dining business across China fell significantly since the promulgation of these new rules. In addition, multiple officials and scholars from China the author met in the UK informed the author that they had to make their stay outside China very tight and focus primarily on business, leaving almost no single day solely for sightseeing. Of course, no one can say that these rules can totally stamp out official extravagance.

Last but not least, the anti-corruption campaign may have served Xi–Li's endeavor to remedy loopholes in governance in the wake of catastrophes. In August 2015, amidst official efforts to contain damage and pollution and clean up the site after the deadly explosion in the Port of Tianjin, Yang Dongliang, Director of the State Administration of Work Safety of the State Council and a member of the 18th CCCCP, was under investigation of the Central Commission for Disciplinary Inspection (CCDI) for "severe violation of discipline and law." Yang's sudden political trouble may have to do with the explosions in the Port of Tianjin, as he served as vice mayor of Tianjin Municipality from 2001 to May 2012. It has been speculated that the Ruihai Logistics (it was at its storage site the blasts took place) had breached a series of regulations and safety rules and had evaded charges and inspection due to its use of official connections. Understandably, as President Xi ordered that the investigation pursue the question of who was responsible for the blasts, more charges will be brought forth against corporate leaders and governmental officials as the investigation into the causes of the blasts deepens.

Will Xi's policies accelerate the demise of the Party state?

The governance program of Xi has attracted much attention from observers inside and outside China. One of the most noticeable and recent analyses has been a highly critical and pessimistic one by David Shambaugh, a worldrenowned China scholar. According to him, the five following signs indicate the growing vulnerability of the Party state and suggest that Xi's governance will only take the CCP much closer to the point of breakup.

First, among China's economic elites, 64 percent of the richest people (or 393 millionaires and billionaires) polled by Shanghai-based Hurun Research Institute in a recent year were well prepared to flee China as they sense the deep-rooted problems in China and lack confidence in the regime.

Second, after assuming power in 2013, President Xi has stepped up political repression in China, which was intensified by his predecessor back in 2009. The Document No. 9 that opposes the "Western values" such as constitutional democracy and press freedom only indicated the leadership's insecurity.

Third, despite the fact that the Party's propaganda machine drums up Xi's political slogans such as the "China Dream" and the "mass line," many Party loyalists merely paid lip service to them instead of believing in them.

Fourth, due to the one-party system, lack of the rule of law and of economic transparency, as well as the prominence of patron-client relations, corruption has engulfed the Party state, the military, and the society in China. Even Xi's unprecedentedly ferocious anti-corruption campaign cannot eradicate it. This campaign is a selective purge of political clients and allies of the former top leader Jiang Zemin. Xi himself belongs to the party's "princelings" who are "widely reviled" in China.

Finally, China's economy is trapped in systemic problems. State-owned enterprises and local party cadres have blocked the ambitious reform measures that Xi proclaimed in November 2013.

According to Shambaugh, the five aforementioned "increasingly evident cracks in the regime's control can be fixed only through political reform." However, Xi has tightened the political grip. Thus China "will never become an innovative society and a 'knowledge economy'—a main goal of the Third Plenum reforms." In particular, Shambaugh laments Xi's political conservatism in comparison with his more open-minded predecessors and their aides. He stated as follows: "In effect, for a while Mr. Jiang and Mr. Hu sought to manage change, not to resist it. But Mr. Xi wants none of this. Since 2009 (when even the heretofore open-minded Mr. Hu changed course and started to clamp down), an increasingly anxious regime has rolled back every single one of these political reforms (with the exception of the cadre-training system). These reforms were masterminded by Mr. Jiang's political acolyte and former vice president, Zeng Qinghong, who retired in 2008 and is now under suspicion in Mr. Xi's anticorruption campaign—another symbol of Mr. Xi's hostility to the measures that might ease the ills of a crumbling system." Shambaugh is probably aware of the fact that the CCP, which has been in power for over 65 years, is fast approaching the reign of 74 years of the CPSU, the longest by any single-party regime. He thus ends with a very pessimistic note: "We cannot predict when Chinese communism will collapse, but it is hard not to conclude that we are witnessing its final phase. The CCP is the world's second-longest ruling regime (behind only North Korea), and no party can rule forever."[20]

Shambaugh has boldly described the likely scenario of the CCP regime as follows. First, the regime has entered the final phase of its rule and the likelihood for the CCP regime to collapse is quite high. Second, "Communist rule in China is unlikely to end quietly. A single event is unlikely to trigger a peaceful implosion of the regime. Its demise is likely to be protracted, messy and violent." Third and possibly related to the second point, as his sweeping anti-graft campaign has alienated the critical Party, state, military and commercial power holders, Xi may even "be deposed in a power struggle or coup d'état." Gordon Chang echoed Shambaugh's view by pointing to the mounting debts in China. He declared that the Chinese government could well exhaust its huge foreign exchange reserves and "go broke" in 2015 when defending its free-falling renminbi and stocks.[21]

I have deep respect for the scholarship of Shambaugh, and I cited his work frequently in Chapters 1 and 2. However, I find it difficult to agree with his diagnosis of the prospects of the CCP in his commentary. All the five evident cracks in the CCP regime discussed by Shambaugh are not new. Most, if not all, of them existed for certain periods in China's reform era. First, the cold responses from the cadres and the population to the political slogans of the Chinese leaders surfaced as early as the 1970s in late Mao's years. After decades of traumatic political campaigns initiated by Mao many Chinese officials and citizens were no longer interested in the political ideals promoted by the Party and its leaders. In the reform era Jiang's slogans and ideological formulation of "Three Represents" and Hu's "socialist harmonious society" were also received half-heartedly at best in general or even coldly by many cadres. The populace's and officials' lack of enthusiasm in ideology does not necessarily undermine the Party. Party leaders could not impose their slogans and dictate the action of Party members if the latter find these ideological formulations do not suit the reality and operational needs of their agencies. In fact, one could even argue that this allowed cadres to concentrate their energy on critical issues in governance involving their localities or agencies, instead of lofty slogans. The cadres would thus resort to feasible solutions in their daily work and this political pragmatism, rather than unrealistic and blind application of slogans, would better help sustain the Party state.

Second, capital flight is neither new nor the most serious problem in the reform era. An available estimate on capital flight covers the period of 1984–2012. It is true that China's capital flight in absolute terms more than doubled during 2011–12. However, in terms of capital flight to GDP ratio, which is a more accurate barometer of the size of capital flight, it was 5 percent in 2012, significantly below the 7 percent during 2006–7, and far below the range of 8 percent–14 percent in the 1990s and the 2000s. Thus, capital flight out of China was far more serious during the above periods. But China's economy and the CCP regime had not been hampered (at least not solely by capital flight) during this period.[22]

Third, economic slowdown is indeed happening in China, but it does not necessarily drag the Party into demise, at least at its current rate of around 7 percent a year. In the reform era China's economic growth has hit a snag several times. Annual GDP growth was merely 7.5 percent–7.8 percent during 1979–80 and even dropped to 5.2 percent in 1981. During the 1989–90 period GDP annual growth set the lowest records in the reform era, registering 4.1 percent and 3.9 percent, respectively. A decade later the growth decelerated to 7.8 percent in 1998 and 7.6 percent in 1999. During 2012–13 GDP growth rate slowed down significantly for the fourth time, hitting 7.7 percent a year. However, compared to the previous low rates, the GDP growth in 2012–13 was the highest and was at a par with the average annual growth of 1998–9, which was 7.7 percent.[23] The Party state has survived the previous slow economic growth and even lower GDP growth. It would be inconceivable that it cannot survive this time. Nowadays China's economy confronts a series of major internal constraints such as an astonishing extent of pollution and less-than-ideal domestic consumption. China also suffers from a slow external demand for its exports due to the financial crisis. Given these problems and given that China's per capita GDP has grown to about US$7,000, a very decent level and far above that of US$195 in 1981, US$314 in 1990, and US$865 in 1999, the Chinese population is more ready to accept a slower growth rate than in the previous periods of slowdown. In addition, as noted by Shambaugh and as will be discussed in greater detail below, Xi no longer tries to claim legitimacy solely on delivering a high growth rate of GDP. He claims legitimacy also by launching a sweeping anti-graft campaign and by easing popular discontent toward decades-old blatant corruption. Thus economic slowdown could cost him less popular support than could have been the case for his predecessors.

Fourth, political repression may do far less damage to the one-party regime in China than Shambaugh claims. Shambaugh may be right in suggesting that political repression revealed political conservatism of Xi in sharp contrast with Jiang and Zeng and that Xi led China down the path away from the necessary changes to overcome structural flaws in the one-party regime. However, we need to be aware of a highly unpleasant fact—the Party state has resorted to political repression to sustain itself since it has founded the PRC in 1949 and through weeding out dissidents the Party state has effectively (though deplorably in the eyes of many around the world) contained any potential threat toward the regime and has enabled it to continue its monopoly of power. As I stated in Chapter 9, most of the previous unified regimes in China were overthrown by either domestic armed rebellions or by these rebellions coupled with external invasion. Xi's political repression, which is disliked by many in the democratic world, may serve to pre-empt rebellions in China. Therefore, as well analyzed in Chapter 9, the one-party regime in China is still likely to last for a considerable period.

Fifth, the widespread anti-graft campaign could help Xi to garner popular support and could partially reverse the rampant spread of the venomous disease in the Party state. This is true despite the fact that his campaign might not be able to eradicate corruption once and for all. To start with, the Chinese population has witnessed growing and rampant corruption in the reform era and has long longed for a radical cleanup of this institutional ill. At the grass-roots level many Chinese citizens learn about the alarming extents of official corruption through rumors. A few examples suffice to illustrate the degree of corruption and consequential popular outrage and cynicism toward officials. Officials in the poorest counties in China spared no public funds in building luxurious offices. Officials were rumored to have embezzled a large amount of public funds that were allocated to help out victims in the devastating Wenchuan earthquake in 2008 that claimed over 70,000 lives. At the local level as long as one has a connection with an official in charge and is willing to pay a bribe he or she can easily get things done despite this approval going directly against the official rules and having no legal ground.[24] Having worked for decades as a local official, Xi should have known too well the gravity of official corruption in China.

By clamping down on official corruption, Xi realizes that he would gain popular support and has his legitimacy bolstered immediately. This was revealed in multiple public opinion polls in China in 2013. In an opinion poll in 21 provinces in November 2013 by the National Statistical Bureau 79 percent of the respondents thought that cadres they knew had improved their work style since the eight anti-graft rules were announced by the Party, 87 percent of the respondents believed that corruption and improper acts by officials had been lessened, and 77 percent of the respondents agreed that the investigation of officials violating laws and rules and penalties was vigorous and penalties were forceful. The Chinese Academy of Social Sciences polled 7,388 people in 31 provinces and found that 74 percent of the respondents expressed confidence in the anti-graft campaign, up significantly from 2011. Furthermore, a poll of 17,000 Chinese by the China Youth Daily suggested that 90 percent of respondents firmly supported the anti-corruption campaign.[25] The Pew Research Center found in its polls in China that a massive 92 percent of the urban respondents had confidence in Xi to do the right thing.[26]

As I stated in Chapter 9, most of the previous unified regimes in China were overthrown by either domestic armed rebellions or by these rebellions coupled with external invasion. By launching a thorough cleanup of corruption in the military, Xi was intent on checking against highly corrosive practices such as promoting generals and officers who bribe their superiors and falsified results in the military drills.[27] By doing so Xi could help strengthen the military and enable it to better prevent external intruders. Indirectly and in the long run his anti-graft campaign thus serves to deter external invaders and prolong the life of the Party state.

Viewed from historical precedents in the long term, anti-graft campaigns do help significantly prolong the life of unified regimes in China. The Ming Dynasty provides one illustration. It is believed by many observers of Chinese history that Zhu Yuanzhang, the founding emperor of the Ming, masterminded the sternest and harshest anti-corruption campaign in the history of China. He set a rule to execute any official who had accepted a bribe over 60 Chinese Tael (roughly 2,300 grams) of silver (roughly US$1,100 in current price, or roughly 112 percent equivalent of one year of per capita GDP in Ming Dynasty according to online sources). It was estimated that during his reign of the nation for 31 years 100,000 to 150,000 officials lost their lives for corruption and that few local officials survived his anti-graft campaign to serve for a full term. In one case of embezzlement of tax grain, he executed hundreds of officials below the deputy ministers of all the six ministries. In another case his son-in-law was executed. His campaign seemed extremely bloody and excessive. Nor did it completely eradicate the corruption of officials. One key reason was that Zhu and his successors kept salaries of officials at a level that was artificially lower than in the other dynasties.[28] It is worth noting that the current Party state did not blindly follow this implausible practice. In order to survive or live a comfortable life commensurate to their social status, officials in the Ming Dynasty had no choice but to accept bribes. Despite these shortfalls, Zhu Yuanzhang's ruthless anti-corruption campaign did help the empire to deal with one of the perennial and fatal causes of popular discontent in imperial China. Thanks to his popular anti-graft campaign, rebellions during Zhu's entire reign of 31 years were rare, small scale and restricted to remote and border areas. In 1511 A.D., 143 years after the founding of the Ming, Liu Lu and Liu Qi led an armed rebellion that posed a first direct threat to the national capital Beijing.[29] Nevertheless, according to Chen Jiarong, the large-scale and sustained armed rebellions only erupted in 1627 and had spread across the empire since then.[30] The primary cause of rebellions was heavy taxes and officials' merciless exploitation of the peasants. In 1644, 277 years after its founding the Ming was eventually overthrown by peasant rebel Li Zicheng. Nevertheless, thanks to Zhu's harsh rules against corruption and his draconian laws against official exploitation of the population the dynasty seemingly had avoided persistent and massive uprisings of the populace until 1627, 259 years after the founding of the Ming.

Xi's extensive corruption probes have reportedly triggered waves of suicides of officials. According to a report by China Youth Daily, from January 1, 2013 to April 10, 2014, 54 officials died in unusual circumstances in China, and 23 (or 42.6 percent) of them committed suicide. Depression was the largest cause of suicides. The noticeable cases of suicide included Xu Ye'an, Deputy Director of the National Bureau of Letters and Visits and Ba Zhongren, the President of China Railway Corporation.[31] While Xi's anti-graft campaign might be harsh on Chinese officials, it did stem or slow down the rampant spread of corruption within the Chinese bureaucracy and society. As stated, the overwhelming majority of Chinese polled in multiple surveys in 2013 felt the positive effect of the campaign on easing corruption. Thus the campaign apparently has the effect of restraining official waste, controlling corruption, easing popular discontent, and earning legitimacy and support from the public for the regime. It will thus help the regime to prolong its life, even though it fails to change the nature of the regime.

Indeed, no one can predict for sure the eventual life span of the CCP regime. In Chapter 9 I present and explain my analysis of the likelihood of the durability of the Party state and the likely coming scenario of the Party state in China. I argue that despite the possibility of a quick collapse of the CCP regime a more likely scenario is that the Party state can last for a considerable period. As stated above, the major policies introduced by Xi have not altered the fundamental factors in my estimate of the likely endurance of the Party state in the foreseeable future.

Conclusion: toward authoritarian flexibility and durability

In 2014 the International Monetary Fund (IMF) announced that China surpassed the U.S. in GDP in purchasing power parity terms.[32] A reputed journal *The Economist* projects that by 2021 China will overtake the U.S. in nominal GDP.[33] As the world's largest economy the nature and evolution of the political regime in China naturally has vast implications not only for China itself but also for the rest of the world.

China has clearly resisted the well-known global trend toward greater political freedom and democracy. During 1983–2013 the percentage of countries worldwide that were classified as politically "not free" declined from 33 percent to 25 percent.[34] As China's economic miracle unfolds many predict or expect China's political regime to develop toward a more open and liberal one. However, to their bitter disappointment China's leaders have pursued the opposite direction coined by Freedom House as "authoritarian resistance" in the last decade. Specifically, "the Chinese Communist Party leadership has developed a complicated apparatus of controls and punishments designed to maintain rigid one-party rule and prevent the expression of dissent, while at the same time enabling China to become a global economic powerhouse."[35]

At the first glimpse it may seem that the Chinese leaders are pursuing a suicidal course, or a mission impossible, by bucking the trend. However, this view is simplistic. As explained in detail in this book, this authoritarian endeavor is far more elaborate, calculated, and comprehensive than many have expected. In order to resist the global and domestic pressures for them to open up and consolidate the authoritarian regime at home the Chinese leaders are practicing pragmatic authoritarianism. They have modified institutions and have introduced policies in order to provide a pragmatic solution of the most pressing problems in governance. In doing so they also ensure that the Party retains its firm control of political power. Some of these policies or institutions may go against the conventions of the Party, but they are adopted as long as they resolve the problems and do not undermine the Party's rule. Such pragmatism in governance, coupled with its continued control of human and physical capital as well as a wide range of institutional and physical resources, enables the Party to find immediate and effective solutions to the pressing problems in governance. Thus, in embracing pragmatic authoritarianism the Party state has demonstrated authoritarian flexibility. Swift resolution of these problems also enables the Party state to prolong its rule and demonstrates endurance of authoritarianism.

To summarize, in its economic governance the Party state installed and later adjusted pro-growth authoritarianism; it also introduced policies to address the plights of inland peasants and urban unemployed. In social governance, the Party state contains the well-organized groups that challenge its ideology and control, but tolerates social activities not affiliated with these groups. In political governance the Party state imitates a wide range of successful practices and reformulates ideology, sustains its control of key state branches through official appointments and continues to censor the media in order to weed out information and discussion that could damage the image of the Party. More importantly, the Party state has overhauled institutions for crisis management, has introduced norms and rules to institutionalize the process of leadership succession and has avoided open and fatal conflict. Moreover, it has made efforts to increase administrative efficiency and political transparency and to install some degree of official accountability by dismissing officials for their failure to avert crises in governance. It has shown a certain degree of tolerance of grass-roots and intra-Party democratic initiatives. In recent years Xi has launched a sweeping anti-corruption campaign in order to check rampant corruption and to remedy the popular cynicism toward the conduct and honesty of officials.

By adopting pragmatic authoritarianism the Party state has created the most impressive economic miracle in modern history (reflected by the highest growth for 37 years and benefiting the largest number of people). It has also weathered a number of formidable challenges and has resolved many daunting problems. This list of resolved crises is staggeringly long: the sluggish economy and nationwide shortage of foods and other basic items in daily life in late Mao's years, the widespread albeit subtle popular doubts about the Party's legitimacy at the end of the Cultural Revolution, the nationwide protests in 1989, protests by assertive Falun Gong sect with hundreds of cells and tens of millions of followers nationwide in the late 1990s, the SARS epidemic in 2003, failed leadership successions from 1949 until 1991, widespread discontent in rural China and from urban unemployed from the mid-1990s to the mid-2000s, and popular discontent over rampant corruption in the nation in the reform era.

As the Party state has thrived by practicing pragmatic authoritarianism, there is no reason to believe that the CCP will abandon it and toll its own death bell in order to win the cheers of international spectators. Of course, we cannot say with absolute certainty that this scenario will last for decades, as history and reality often evades the predictions of analysts. Nevertheless, as China is poised to be the ultimate economic superpower on the world stage and as we have learned about the resilience of unified regimes founded after another unified one in Chinese history, we need to be prepared to see authoritarian flexibility and endurance in China, regardless of whether we like it or not. This preparedness will help us to avoid unrealistic expectations and unnecessary errors in observing and interacting with China.

Notes

1 For an analysis of orthodox reformism in China, refer to Lai, *Reform and the Non-State Economy in China*, (New York and London: Palgrave Macmillan, 2006), 61–76, 81–88, and 97–99.

2 It was noted that in 1993 a peasant in Renshou County of Sichuan Province made clear this wish to Wan Li, the leader of the NPC. See Thomas Bernstein, "Farmer Discontent and Regime Response," in Merle Goldman and Roderick MacFarquhar, eds, *The Paradox of China's Post-Mao Reforms* (Cambridge, MA: Harvard University Press, 1999), 213. This version was different from the one I learned from a former grass-roots cadre in inland China which I cite in Chapter 4. Nevertheless, the similar content of the story illustrated the alarming extent of peasants' discontent toward the local Party state.

3 See White, "The Dynamics of Civil Society in Post-Mao China," in Brian Hook, ed., *The Individual and the State in China* (Oxford: Clarendon Press, 1996), 196, 198; Brook and Frolic, eds, *Civil Society in China* (Armonk, NY: M.E. Sharpe, 1997), 3.

4 Walder, *The Waning of the Communist State* (Berkeley, CA: University of California Press, 1995).

5 "Zhonggong zhongyang guanyu quanmian shenhua gaige ruogan zhongda wenti de jueding" (Decision of the Central Committee of the Chinese Communist Party on Several Major Questions About Deepening Reform), posted at: http://news.xinhuanet.com/politics/2013-11/15/c_118164235.htm, accessed on April 28, 2015.

6 "China Announces Location of New Free Trade Zones, Expands Shanghai FTZ," posted at: www.china-briefing.com/news/2015/01/06/china-rolls-new-ftzs-expands-current-one.html on January 6, 2015 by China Briefing, accessed on April 28, 2015.

7 For a tentative analysis of Xi's reform agenda, refer to Arthur R. Kroeber, "Xi Jinping's Ambitious Agenda for Economic Reform in China," posted at: www.brookings.edu/research/opinions/2013/11/17-xi-jinping-economic-agenda-kroeber on November 17, 2013, accessed on October 14, 2014.

8 See various news reports posted at: http://news.takungpao.com/mainland/focus/2014-01/, accessed on April 28, 2015.

9 See "Jiquan zhilu" (The Road Toward Power Concentration), posted at: www.wenxuecity.com/news/2015/01/20/3966235.html, accessed on January 21, 2015.

10 "China's Political Spectrum under Xi Jinping," posted at: http://thediplomat.com/2014/08/CHINAS-POLITICAL-SPECTRUM-UNDER-XI-JINPING/, accessed on April 28, 2015.

11 "'Diren henduo!' Zhongjiwei zhi Shekeyuan bei shentou" ('Many Enemies!' The CDIC Suggests CASS Has Been Penetrated), posted at: www.dw.de/, accessed on April 28, 2015.

12 See the list of implicated officials in "Zhongong shibada yilai de fa fubai gongzuo" (Anti-Corruption Work Since the Eighteenth Congress of the CCP), posted at: http://zh.wikipedia.org/wiki/中共十八大以来的反腐败工作, accessed on March 15, 2015.

13 "Bo Xilai Found Guilty, Sentenced to Life in Prison," posted at: www.wsj.com/articles/SB10001424052702303730704579090080547591654, accessed on May 2, 2015.

14 "Fenghuang Zhoukan Zhongbang Dujia: Guozei Xu Caihou Chachao Neimu" (An Exclusive and Explosive Coverage by *Phoenix Weekly*: An Inside Story of the Investigation and Confiscation of National Thief Xu Caihou), posted at http://blog.sina.com.cn/s/blog_4b8bd1450102v516.html, accessed May 2, 2015.

15 "Zhou Yongkang shexian shouhui xielu guojia mimi deng bei tiqi gongsu" (Zhou Yongkang is Indicted for Being Involved in Taking Bribes, Disclosing State Secrets, and Other Suspected Crimes), posted at: http://yn.people.com.cn/news/domestic/n/2015/0403/c228494-24375391.html, accessed on May 2, 2015.

16 "Zhou Yongkang qinxin xiezhu qintun shu baiyi guoyou zichan chutaoshi beizhua" (Zhong Yongkang's Trusted Aide Who Assisted with the Embezzlement of Tens of Billions of Yuan of State Assets Has Been Arrested When Attempted to Flee Abroad), posted at: www.wenxuecity.com/news/2013/08/03/2558092.html, accessed on May 2, 2015.

17 "Ling Jihua saozi chumian maiguan 1 ge shizhang yaojia 1000 wan" (Sister-in-law Sold Offices on Behalf of Ling Jihua and a Mayor Post Was Priced at 10 Million Yuan), posted at: www.wenxuecity.com/news/2014/12/23/3893213.html, accessed on December 24, 2014.

18 "Su Yong xian Zhou Yongkang guanxiwang 'Qinghai 3 ren zu' youyuan zaijian" (Su Rong Was Trapped in the Connections Web with Zhou Yongkang and the Qinghai Trio Met Again Fortunately), posted at http://www.wenxuecity.com/news/2014/06/18/3365975.html, accessed January 14, 2015.

19 "Elite in China Face Austerity Under Xi's Rule," *New York Times*, March 27, 2013, posted at: www.nytimes.com/2013/03/28/world/asia/xi-jinping-imposes-auster ity-measures-on-chinas-elite.html?_r=0, accessed on March 17, 2015.

20 David Shambaugh, "The Coming Chinese Crackup," *Wall Street Journal*, March 6, 2015, posted at: www.wsj.com/articles/the-coming-chinese-crack-up-1425659198, accessed on March 10, 2015.

21 Ibid. Gordon Chang, "2015: The Year China Goes Broke?", *The National Interest*, September 1, 2015, posted at: http://nationalinterest.org/print/feature/2015-the-yea r-china_goes_broke_13749, accessed on January 1, 2016.

22 The ratio was computed by the author using the data on China's GDP in *China Statistical Yearbook 2013* (Beijing: China Statistical Press, 2013) and the estimates on China's capital flight in Tables 2A and 2B in Frank R. Gunter, "China Capital Flight 1984–2012." The latter is posted on the following website: http://cbe.lehigh. edu/sites/cbe.lehigh.edu/files/documents/China%20Capital%20Flight%201984-2012 %2013Aug14%20vr%202.pdf, accessed on May 4, 2015.

23 Data on China posted at: http://data.worldbank.org/, accessed on May 3, 2015.

24 These cases were based on the author's readings of numerous reports online and his conversations with people who have first-hand observations and experience in China in the last two decades.

25 "2013 zhengfeng suji minyi shuqi da muzhi" (Thumbs Up in Polls for Rectifying Work Style and Tightening Rules in 2013), *Renmin ribao* (*People's Daily*), January 3, 2014, posted at: http://pic.cssn.cn/tp/201401/t20140103_934587.shtml, accessed on April 28, 2015.

26 Pew Research Center, "Global Opposition to U.S. Surveillance and Drones, But Limited Harm to America's Image," July 14, 2014, posted at: www.pewglobal.org/ files/2014/07/2014-07-14-Balance-of-Power.pdf, accessed on May 4, 2015.

27 See "'Superman' Soldier Used Steamed Rice to Make Himself 'Invincible'," *South China Morning Post*, January 21, 2015.

28 "Zhu Yuanzhang 'zhongdian fanfu' weihe shiban?" (Why Zhu Yuanzhang's draconian anti-corruption failed?), posted at: http://news.xinmin.cn/rollnews/2011/ 08/11/11695303.html (Guanming Wang) on August 11, 2011, accessed on April 28, 2015. For an insightful analysis of politics in the Ming Dynasty, refer to Huang Renyu, *Wanli shiwu nian* (Beijing: Sanlian shudian, 2000). This is the revised Chinese version of Ray Huang, *1587, A Year of No Significance* (New Haven, CT: Yale University Press, 1981).

29 "Mingchao minbian" (Uprisings in the Ming Dynasty), posted at: http://baike.ba idu.com/item, accessed on May 4, 2015.

30 Chen Jiarong, *Zhongguo lidai zi xingzhi, shengshuai, luanwang*, 448–51.

31 "Yiyu yinjiu fubai, dahu yilai 54 guanyuan fei zhengchang siwang" (Depressing, Drunk and Corrupt, 54 Officials Died Abnormally Since "Tigers" Are Being Hunted), posted at: http://china.dwnews.com/news/2014-04-10/59464112.html on April 10, 2014, accessed on April 11, 2014.

32 "China Economy Surpasses US In Purchasing Power, But Americans Don't Need to Worry," posted at: www.ibtimes.com/china-economy-surpasses-us-purchasing-p ower-americans-dont-need-worry-1701804, accessed on May 5, 2015.

33 "Chinese and American GDP Forecasts: Catching the Eagle," *The Economist*, August 22, 2014, posted at: www.economist.com/node/21590331/print, accessed on May 5, 2015.

34 "The Democratic Leadership Gap," Freedom House, 2014, posted at: https://free domhouse.org/sites/default/files/Overview%20Fact%20Sheet.pdf, accessed on May 5, 2015.

35 Arch Puddington, "Freedom in the World 2014: The Democratic Leadership Gap," posted at: https://freedomhouse.org/report/freedom-world-2014/essay-dem ocratic-leadership-gap#.VUnr1zn7VhD, accessed on May 5, 2015.

Index

Please note that page numbers relating to Figures will be in italics followed by the letter 'f', while numbers indicating Tables will be in the same format but contain the letter 't'. Any references to Notes will contain the letter 'n', followed by the relevant Note number.